THE FIRST OF THE TUDORS
A Study of Henry VII and His Reign

Henry VII

From the portrait in the possession of The Society of Antiquaries
of London (reproduced by permission).

THE FIRST OF THE TUDORS

A Study of Henry VII and His Reign

by

Michael Van Cleave Alexander

ROWMAN AND LITTLEFIELD
Totowa • New Jersey

Copyright © Rowman and Littlefield, 1980

First published in The United States of America by
Rowman and Littlefield, Totowa, New Jersey

Library of Congress Cataloging in Publication Data

Alexander, Michael Van Cleave, 1937-
   The first of the Tudors.

   Bibliography: p.
   Includes index.
   1. Henry VII, King of England, 1457-1509.
2. Great Britain—History—Henry VII, 1485-1509.
3. Great Britain—Kings and rulers—Biography.
I. Title.
DA330.A43   942.05′1′0924 [B]   79-28135
ISBN 0-8476-6259-4

Printed in The United States of America

Contents

Preface

Only rarely does Henry VII of England receive the recognition he deserves. Most historians dispute any claims to greatness on his behalf and give only grudging praise to his most obvious accomplishments: the pacification of the country after the bloody interlude of the Wars of the Roses and the acquisition of greater financial resources than were to be enjoyed by any other ruler in English history. It is curious that most writers have been so reluctant to acknowledge Henry VII's achievements, particularly since his closest French counterpart, Henry IV (1589-1610), is by common consent one of the greatest monarchs in all of French history. Like the later French king, Henry VII captured the throne by force, which he quickly justified by revitalizing the basic institutions of national life after a long period of political turmoil. But whereas the French ruler is universally praised for his work, Henry VII is seldom given more than a fraction of his just due. How does one account for this strange phenomenon?

First, Henry VII has always been overshadowed in the public mind by his more colorful and flamboyant son, Henry VIII. This is amply attested by the publication of a recent biography of Henry VII's wife, Elizabeth of York, with the subtitle "The Mother of Henry VIII."[1] The second Tudor ruler, who was so obviously endowed with what we today call "charisma," is well known to the general public because of his six wives and the problems he encountered in divorcing the first of them, which prompted him to break with Rome and thus to inaugurate the English Reformation. Second, Henry VII differed from his son in being genuinely interested in governmental matters from the time of his accession, which caused him to apply himself diligently to administrative tasks, often of a routine and even prosaic nature. This had the obvious effect of making him seem a bit dull even to his contemporaries, a kind of sixteenth-century "man in the grey flannel suit." Yet because monarchy was still a very personal form of government during his lifetime, much of the efficiency of the central government can be attributed to his efforts alone.

Several other factors help to account for the general lack of interest in Henry VII's era, which has been studied in much less detail, albeit with greater objectivity and less passion, than the relatively brief reigns of his grandchildren Edward VI and Mary I. There is less surviving evidence for the earlier than for the later periods of Tudor history; but of greater significance, perhaps, is the fact that there is a lingering sympathy in some circles for Richard III, the Yorkist king who was overthrown and killed at Bosworth in 1485. Richard III was a capable and, in some ways, a tragic figure; and during the last two centuries a good many writers have been more concerned to rehabilitate him than to analyse the contributions of the founder of the Tudor dynasty. Moreover, once Henry VII mounted the throne, there was a general dearth of colorful personalities at his court, such as predominated during most other reigns of the late medieval and early modern periods. Henry VII always placed a premium on ability and experience; so while his councillors formed an unusually capable and cohesive group, they were almost as cautious and unexciting as the king himself. Who today remembers a Fox, a Lovell, or a Heron in the same way one is still intrigued by the doings of a Wolsey or a Cromwell? In addition, there is still the widely held view, unquestioned in many quarters, that the court of Henry VII was a mean and parsimonious place, devoid of all pageantry and ceremonial. Nothing could be farther from the truth, for Henry VII was well aware of the need to project an aura of magnificence. Indeed he recognized that "the national prestige—as well as the king's own—depended in part upon the splendour of the Court."[2] If the ceremonial of his court became a trifle less grand during his last five years on the throne, that was owing to complex circumstances I hope to explain in the body of this book.

Despite the valuable contributions of S. B. Chrimes, R. L. Storey, J. R. Lander, and other scholars, it is obvious that most students of the period have failed to capture the personality of the first of England's Tudor rulers. Following Polydore Vergil, the Italian humanist who arrived in England only eight years before Henry VII's death, almost all of the king's biographers have pictured him from his overthrow of Richard III as an elderly man and have stressed his financial exactions, his morbid piety, his harsh treatment of the defenseless Catherine of Aragon, and the other less than admirable policies of his last few years on the throne. Furthermore many recent writers, under the influence of G. R. Elton's administrative studies, have interpreted his reign as little more than an extension of the

Middle Ages and have concentrated on governmental matters to the exclusion of almost everything else.

The purpose of this book, which is intended for students and general readers and not for specialists, is to provide a more balanced presentation of Henry and his reign, to give adequate attention to his earlier years on the throne, when most of his policies were uncommonly successful and his considerate treatment of others was both widely recognized and admired, and to assess such non-governmental matters as the cultural and geographical contributions of the period, which were not to be equalled until the time of Elizabeth I. I also hope to demonstrate how the king's growing fears about the future of his House contributed to the alleged breakdown of his character in the years after 1503.

In order to explain the circumstances that brought Henry to the throne—and a few years before Bosworth no Englishman would have wagered that he would ever become king—I have begun my account of the reign with a discussion of the events following Edward IV's unexpected death in April 1483. Without an understanding of the complicated happenings between that time and August 1485, many of Henry's later acts, as well as the periodic attempts to unseat him, would be unintelligible. So I beg the indulgence of the reader if it at first appears that I have given too much space to the events leading up to the fateful encounter on Bosworth Field.

In writing this book I have incurred a number of obligations, which mere words are insufficient to repay. I first wish to acknowledge the many kindnesses of my colleagues in the Department of History at Virginia Polytechnic Institute and State University and of the efficient and cooperative staff of the Carol M. Newman Library. Professor Pierre Jacoebée of the Foreign Languages Department read and criticized the first six chapters with a discerning eye, for which I will always be grateful. As ever my wife Ann, who is a trained historian, has been a willing and understanding helpmate. I am also indebted to the following firms for kind permission to use quotations from books published by them: Harcourt Brace Jovanovich, Inc., for *Before the Armada: The Emergence of the English Nation*, by R. B. Wernham; Princeton University Press for *The Correspondence of Sir Thomas More*, edited by Elizabeth F. Rogers; and Oxford University Press for *English Literature in the Sixteenth Century, Excluding Drama* by C. S. Lewis, and for *An Introduction to Tudor Drama*, by Frederick S. Boas.

Yet my greatest debt is unquestionably owed to all those earlier scholars on whose works I have attempted to build. Too numerous to mention by name, they have provided much of the factual information, as well as a fair number of the ideas, contained in this book. And although I have tried to advance a fresh and convincing interpretation of the period, I could not possibly have done so without the benefit of their monographs, articles, biographies, editions, and collections. To them, therefore, this book is gratefully dedicated.

Blacksburg, Virginia
November 10, 1979

I

Yorkist Prelude

Englishmen who welcomed in the year 1483 saw no reason to doubt that the House of York was in firm possession of the throne. The current monarch, Edward IV, was "a goodly personage . . . of visage lovely, of body mighty, strong and clean made; howbeit . . . somewhat corpulent and burly but nevertheless not uncomely."[1] Edward was in fact a strapping warrior king who stood 6′ 4″ tall and was revered for his physical prowess and moral courage, which in turn made him the sort of commander troops would gladly follow into battle. Even more important, since his overthrow of the hapless Henry VI in 1461, he had given ample proof of his political and administrative talents.

Knowing the realm could not prosper while the Crown was prey to the turbulent baronage of the time, Edward had begun the work—to be completed by Henry VII—of revitalizing the monarchy and restoring the rule of law to a country whose main institutions were on the verge of total collapse. He himself had supervised the work of the courts in an effort to strengthen the jury system and the administration of justice. By increasing the funds handled by the Chamber of the Household, he had reformed the administration of the royal finances, which had thereby recovered from the disastrous slump of the mid-fifteenth century. In addition he had established an important precedent by appointing councillors to rule over the distant northern counties as well as Wales and the Welsh marches in his name. So effective were his policies, even if they were imperfectly implemented, that they were emulated by his successors for well over a century.

Thus as the year 1483 dawned, few Englishmen can have suspected that the Yorkists would soon lose their grip on the organs of power. Edward himself was still in his prime, being only slightly more than forty years old. Should he die or be assassinated, there were two sons as well as five daughters and scores of nieces and nephews waiting to succeed him. But the Yorkists' possession of the throne was more fragile than it appeared. Their court, so peaceful and orderly to outsiders, was riven by bitter hatreds; and once the unifying force of Edward's personality was removed, a fatal divisiveness overcame the House of York. This paved the way for a resumption of the Wars of the Roses and made possible the ultimate triumph of Henry Tudor, the political heir of the last Lancastrian king, Henry VI.

Late in March 1483 Edward IV fell ill, perhaps because he had gorged himself on a Lenten dinner of fruits and vegetables, as the French chronicler Thomas Basin believed. Yet an Italian cleric in England, Dominic Mancini, maintained soon afterwards that the king "allowed the damp cold to strike his vitals, when one day he was taken in a small boat with those whom he had bidden go fishing, and matched their sport too eagerly."[2] Regardless of the origins of his malady, it quickly developed into pneumonia, which in turn was complicated by a massive stroke, and on 9 April he died. A week later he was buried in the great new chapel at Windsor he had built for the Order of the Garter.

On the king's death the throne passed to his elder son, Edward V, whose accession was announced by a proclamation issued on 11 April. The new monarch was but twelve years old, while his brother Richard, Duke of York and Norfolk, had not yet attained his tenth year. Thus control of the new government would have to be vested in a Protector or a group of regents until the new king came of age. On his deathbed Edward IV had realized this; and in a codicil to his will,[3] he empowered his own brother Richard, Duke of Gloucester, to direct the affairs of state, which in effect made it possible for Richard to usurp the throne. Thus the late king must assume much of the responsibility for the tragic events that occurred within a few months of his death.

That Richard of Gloucester was soon in fact plotting to displace his nephew on the throne was owing not only to his official position as Lord Protector of the realm; it was also a consequence of at least three other factors.

First, it must be acknowledged at the outset that Richard of Gloucester was an extraordinarily capable man. Indeed he was probably the most able and experienced leader England had to offer after the death of his elder brother. Born at Fotheringhay in 1452, he was just now entering the prime of life, although his outstanding abilities had long been evident. In 1470–71 he had given invaluable aid to Edward IV during the crisis fomented by the treacherous Warwick the Kingmaker; and during the years since 1471 he had headed the Council that had governed England's northernmost counties in Edward IV's name. In that capacity he had done an excellent job, even persuading the two great families of the region, the Nevilles and the Percys, to live in peace and harmony with one another. He had thereby established a degree of tranquillity that had been absent from the North for many years. Even more significant for his public reputation, Richard was a capable fighting man and an experienced general. Although not as large and burly as Edward IV, there is no reliable evidence that he was of low stature or that he was a hunchback, as Shakespeare portrayed him and legend has always remembered him. Neither is there any reason to believe the slanderous charges spread soon after Bosworth by the disillusioned antiquary John Rous, who maintained that Richard had lain in his mother's womb for two years and that he had been born with both a full set of teeth and a full head of hair. On the contrary, very little is definitely known about Richard's appearance. According to a foreign ambassador who had an audience with him in 1484, he had extremely wiry arms and was of about the same height as most other upper-class Englishmen;[4] except for this and the fact that he had a dark or swarthy complexion, virtually nothing is known about his physical presence. Although Richard was probably not the outstanding physical specimen that Edward IV had been, he was a capable and resourceful military leader, and as recently as 1482 he had won great prestige for himself. During that year he had conducted a successful nine-month siege of Berwick, the great fortress that stood guard over the border between England and Scotland. Berwick had been held by the Scots since its surrender to them twenty years earlier by Margaret of Anjou, the embittered wife of Henry VI; and its retention by one of England's traditional enemies was considered a national humiliation. That Richard succeeded in recovering the fortress in 1482 caused his reputation to soar to ever greater heights; and in April 1483 there was no other Englishman who could rival him as a military and political leader.

A second crucial factor that contributed to Richard's usurpation of the throne was the diplomatic situation that existed during the spring of 1483. Shortly before he died, Edward IV had committed himself to an invasion of France. In effect, Edward had agreed to reopen the Hundred Years' War, with an eye to recovering Gascony and Normandy for the English Crown. A successful assault on France would of course enable the king to win military glory for himself, while it would permit his aristocratic supporters to acquire booty and plunder. During the early months of 1483, a number of English peers and gentlemen began to mobilize their retainers, who were soon to be seen jostling one another in the streets of London. Thus there was a crisis atmosphere at the time, as a major war between England and France seemed about to break out. As a result many people began to question whether this was any time for a boy of twelve to be allowed to mount the throne. Edward V was still a minor, without military experience of any kind. Yet his uncle, the Duke of Gloucester, was England's most respected fighting man, and under the circumstances it might be better to allow him to become king. Considerations such as these help to explain why so many of the English nobles acquiesced in the usurpation of Richard III.

The final factor that enabled Richard to displace his nephew on the throne was the almost total lack of support that existed at the time for the claims of Edward V and his younger brother, the Duke of York and Norfolk. This was a result of the almost universal contempt felt for their mother Elizabeth Woodville and her relations. A beautiful raven-haired woman, Elizabeth Woodville had become the wife of Edward IV in 1464, and almost at once their union proved to be one of the most disastrous marriages in English history, because the Woodvilles were so undistinguished, despite the marriage of Elizabeth's father, Richard, to Jacquetta of Luxembourg. Little more than a minor country family with no perceptible wealth or influence, the Woodvilles had rarely appeared at court before. As a result the older and more powerful aristocratic families regarded them as upstarts and held that Edward IV had demeaned himself by marrying a woman of such lowly station. The disdain of England's greater families for the Woodvilles soon proved to be well-founded, for they were in fact a scheming and avaricious band. They were determined to accumulate as much wealth for themselves as they possibly could and, once Elizabeth became the king's official consort, utilized every possibility at their disposal. They failed in their attempt to secure large grants of crown lands, since Edward IV had already given large tracts to those who had helped him to capture the throne and would do nothing more to lessen the size of the royal demesne. But they did succeed in obtaining several lucrative offices for themselves. Even before Elizabeth's marriage to Edward IV, her father Richard Woodville was created Earl Rivers as well as Lord Treasurer and Lord Constable of England, which so incensed Warwick the Kingmaker that he had him executed in 1469, thereby triggering the crisis of 1470–71. After Edward IV's recovery of the throne in 1471, Elizabeth's brother Anthony was created second Earl Rivers and appointed both a Knight of the Garter and Governor of the Isle of Wight.

Some years later, in 1482, Elizabeth's youngest brother, Lionel Wood-ville, was granted the rich bishopric of Salisbury.

Far more lucrative than these offices conferred on his wife's kinsmen were the marriages that Edward IV helped to arrange between them and wealthy members of the aristocracy. The twenty-year-old John Woodville was betrothed to the Dowager Duchess of Norfolk, believed to be at least a decade older than her actual sixty-five years. Almost as unpopular was the union between Thomas Grey, Marquess of Dorset, the queen's elder son by her first marriage,[5] and Anne Holland, daughter of the exiled Duke of Exeter. Neither were the queen's many sisters neglected. Mary became the wife of Lord Herbert's eldest son, who was created Lord Dunster just for the occasion, while Jacquetta was pawned off on Lord Strange of Knockyn. Eleanor and Anne were espoused to the heirs of the Earls of Kent and Sussex, respectively. But the marriage that most harmed the Woodville cause was the one they arranged between their homely daughter Catherine and the great Henry Stafford, Duke of Buckingham. One of the wealthiest peers in all of England, Buckingham was a direct descendant of Edward III with a claim of his own to the throne. He was extremely proud of his lineage and never forgave the Woodvilles for forcing one of their line on him.

Such arrangements as these caused most Englishmen to conclude that the only aim of the queen and her relatives was to line their own pockets. Richard of Gloucester was known to hold such views, for he often spoke disparagingly of the Woodvilles and maintained that his brother's marriage to Elizabeth had sullied the Crown. Rather than mingle with his sister-in-law and her circle, he had preferred to remain at Middleham Castle, his baronial stronghold in Yorkshire, and had appeared at court only on rare ceremonial occasions. Because of this, the Woodvilles had no illusions about his feelings towards them; and once Edward IV died, they arranged for the new king to be crowned with all possible speed, scheduling his coronation for 4 May. For there was no precedent for a Lord Protector after the formal enthronement of a new ruler: in the past the office of Protector had lapsed as soon as the coronation of a new monarch occurred. Thus, should the Woodvilles outflank him in this way, Richard would find himself cast totally aside. He would be defenseless should the queen-mother seek vengeance for past insults; and in his view he must either demand the authority intended for him by his late brother or be prepared to accept whatever treatment his enemies saw fit to accord him.

Fortunately for Richard, he could count on the support not only of Buckingham, whose hatred of the Woodvilles was notorious, but also of

John, Lord Howard, probably the most powerful man in East Anglia. Lord Howard was convinced that the Woodvilles had withheld a rich inheritance from him, and during the spring of 1483 he was anxious to find a way to even the score with them. Five years earlier Elizabeth Woodville had sought to provide for the future of her youngest son, the Duke of York, who was then but four years old, by arranging for him to marry Anne Mowbray, a child of five. Anne Mowbray was the sole heir of John Mowbray, fourth Duke of Norfolk, who had died in 1476. Thus little Anne Mowbray had inherited the vast estates in eastern England that had formerly belonged to her father, and she was undoubtedly the richest heiress in all of England. Shortly after Prince Richard and Anne Mowbray were betrothed in 1478, the prince was granted the titles that had been held by her father: he was created Duke of Norfolk as well as Earl of Nottingham. Moreover, a parliamentary act passed about the same time stipulated that should Anne Mowbray die without having children of her own, her estates were to become the property of her husband instead of reverting in the normal way to her blood relations. Anne Mowbray did in fact die before she was able to have children. Her death occurred in November 1481, at which time the vast Mowbray inheritance passed into the formal ownership of the youngest son of Elizabeth Woodville. All of this was naturally anathema to Lord Howard, whose mother had been a leading member of the Mowbray family. Lord Howard had every reason to consider himself the rightful heir of the Mowbrays and to feel betrayed by the arrangements made on Prince Richard's behalf. Once the death of Edward IV was announced, he let Richard of Gloucester know that he was prepared to give him unswerving support, provided that Gloucester aided him in the recovery of the Mowbray lands and titles.

With the support—even encouragement—of men like Lord Howard and the Duke of Buckingham, Richard of Gloucester inevitably decided on a bold course designed at first only to ensure his own domination of the new government but which was quickly broadened to involve his assumption of the throne. This is not the place to recount the complicated events that occurred between Edward IV's death on 9 April and the end of the first week of June, by which time Richard's ultimate objective was becoming obvious to most observers. Those events have been skilfully chronicled by S. B. Chrimes, E. F. Jacob, Paul Murray Kendall, Alison Hanham, and other accomplished historians. At this point it is only necessary to observe that by 7 June, Richard was the undisputed master of London with all its resources. He had appointed John Wood, William Catesby, and other able partisans to key positions in the government, thereby creating a machine of sorts that he could easily control from his headquarters at Crosby Hall, in Bishopsgate Street. He had easily convinced the Council to recognize him as Lord Protector, with no safeguards, it should be noted, to prevent an abuse of his power.[6] He had secured several successive postponements of Edward V's coronation, now scheduled for 22 June. And he had lodged the young king in the royal apartments in the Tower, where his movements could be controlled with little or no effort. In effect the son and heir of Edward IV was held under house arrest at the Tower from 19 May until his eventual murder by an unknown assassin.

Richard's actions naturally threw fear into the heart of Elizabeth Woodville and her small circle of adherents. As he made his first moves towards usurping the throne, she attempted to raise an army with which to confront her brother-in-law. But her pleas for assistance were ignored, so she took sanctuary in the Abbey along with her brother Lionel, her sons Prince Richard and the Marquess of Dorset, and all five of her daughters by Edward IV. Thus the Woodville faction proved to be no stronger than a house of cards and was unable to mount a campaign of any kind against its archenemy.

The only individual with any chance of defeating the Protector's plan was William, Lord Hastings, the longtime Chamberlain to the late king, who was regarded, however, with deepest suspicion by the queen-mother. During previous years there had been recurrent ill will between Lord Hastings and the Woodvilles, who held him responsible for Edward IV's debaucheries and his liaison with the notorious Jane Shore. As a result, during the weeks immediately following the late king's death, Hastings had taken Gloucester's side against the queen-mother. Indeed he had rendered Gloucester the invaluable service of keeping him informed of current developments in the capital; and at one point the Chamberlain even threatened to cross the Channel to Calais if the Woodvilles attempted to garrison London with their retainers.[7] Yet, paradoxically, Hastings revered the memory of the late king and wanted no harm to befall his children. By the beginning of June he could see that because Richard intended to claim the throne for himself, the two sons of Edward IV were in great danger, since their continued existence would always pose a dire threat to his position. Therefore, when it was really too late, Hastings made frantic efforts to create a coalition that might be able to stop the Protector in his tracks. He even made overtures to Elizabeth Woodville in the Abbey, who was as distrustful of his motives as ever. Unfortunately for the Chamberlain, his every move was being reported to Gloucester by Catesby, a lawyer who had once been one of Hastings's confidential advisers but was now firmly committed to the Protector's cause.[8]

Because of Casteby's reports, Richard decided that the Chamberlain must be eliminated. His first move was to summon reinforcements from Yorkshire, where he had had a large personal following for many years. On 10 June he sent a message by Sir Richard Ratcliffe, a trusted henchman, urging the mayor of York, John Newton, to hasten to London with as many recruits as he could muster "to aid and assist us against the queen, her bloody adherents and affinity, which . . . intend to murder and utterly destroy us and our cousin the Duke of Buckingham and [all] the royal blood of the realm."[9] After addressing a similar appeal to the relations of his wife Anne Neville, the Protector began to lay his plans for Friday the 13th of June, when the Council was to meet again, one part at Westminster and the other at the Tower. The session at the Tower, which had been called to consider the preparations for Edward V's eventual coronation, began peaceably enough. But after a brief recess Richard reentered the Council chamber and began to hurl accusations at the Chamberlain. When Hastings sought to defend himself, the Protector shouted "Treason! Treason!," whereupon his guardsmen burst into the room. A brief scuffle ensued, during which several men, including Archbishop Rotherham of York and the 63-year-old John Morton, Bishop of Ely, were wounded and afterwards arrested. As for Lord Hastings, he was seized and dragged down to the Tower green, where he was told to confess his sins and prepare to die. Then he was thrown face downward on a log and beheaded.[10]

The summary execution of Lord Hastings on 13 June was Richard of Gloucester's first great mistake. It guaranteed that he would soon be denounced as a tyrant, even by as fervent a Yorkist as the elderly antiquary from Warwickshire, John Rous. This was the case because Lord Hastings was not permitted any sort of trial: he was required to pay the supreme penalty without receiving due process of law, which Englishmen had considered their birthright since at least the time of Magna Carta. On 13 June Richard still did not claim the throne openly for himself. But he was the effective head of the government, and his administration was rapidly becoming the very opposite of the rule of law. One thinly disguised murder would follow another until that respect for government which is the hallmark of an ordered society was altogether destroyed. Then Richard would be swept away by a whirlwind he had done so much to sow.

While the younger son of Edward IV remained in sanctuary, Gloucester knew it would be futile to proceed with his plans, which would collapse of their own weight unless the younger prince could be retrieved from the Abbey. Yet he also knew it would be safe to entrust this delicate task to Lord Howard, who wanted nothing more than to gain possession of the current holder of the Mowbray lands. On 16 June Lord Howard and Thomas Bourchier, Archbishop of Canterbury since 1455, led a delegation to the Abbey to "persuade" Elizabeth Woodville to surrender her youngest son into his uncle's safe-keeping. The queen-mother was at once on her guard and at first seemed inflexibly opposed. But the Abbey was surrounded by troops, and Lord Howard and the archbishop, an elderly man with no understanding of the issues at stake, used two arguments to wear down her resistance. First, they maintained that Edward V was in sore need of his brother's company, since he had no youthful companions in the Tower; and second, they insisted that it would be unseemly for the younger prince to remain in sanctuary, "as though the one brother stood in danger and peril of the other."[11] After much weeping and pleading for guidance, the dowager queen sorrowfully handed over her youngest son, knowing she might never see him alive again. Had she guessed that the patent roll of Edward V would be closed the next day and a new one opened, her fears would have been greater still.

In order to justify the "disinherison" of his two nephews, the Protector needed to find an explanation that would convince the populace of London. An argument of sorts was soon provided by Robert Stillington, Bishop of Bath and Wells, who maintained that Edward IV had been pre-contracted to Lady Eleanor Butler, widow of Sir Thomas Butler and daughter of Gilbert Talbot, Earl of Shrewsbury. According to this story, Edward had obligated himself to marry Lady Eleanor, with the result that his later union with Elizabeth Woodville was bigamous and all their children illegitimate. If such were actually the case, Edward V and his brother were both bastards with no claim whatsoever to the throne and Gloucester was the late king's legal heir. Such a story can be discounted on two grounds, however. First, no proof has ever been adduced to show that a pre-contract between Edward IV and Lady Eleanor was ever concluded; and second, even if one was, it would not have affected the status of Edward IV's two sons, who were both born after the lady in question died.[12]

Because Bishop Stillington's story was such an unconvincing one, the Protector decided to contest the legitimacy of his own two brothers, Edward IV and George, Duke of Clarence, who had been executed for treason in 1478. Observing that he was a head shorter than they had been and that he bore a striking resemblance to their late father Richard of York (ob. 1460), whereas they had not, Gloucester charged that neither of his elder brothers had been a true son of their alleged father. Rather the mother of all three of them, Lady Cecily Neville, Dowager Duchess of York, had committed adultery and given birth to her two eldest sons by an unnamed lover. This slanderous accusation brought forth a vigorous denial from Lady Cecily, who angrily denounced her youngest son for telling such a pernicious lie and never forgave him.[13]

Despite the weakness of such arguments, Richard felt they must be circulated through the capital and directed a popular preacher, Ralph Shaa, to include them in his sermon at Paul's Cross on Sunday the 22nd of June. On that day the friar addressed a large crowd on the text "bastard slips shall never take deep root." He also utilized several complicated arguments to prove that the children of Edward IV "were not the rightful inheritors unto the Crown, and that King Edward was not the legitimate son of the Duke of York as the Lord Protector was." Such remarks were poorly received, however, and the friar never recovered the reputation for truthfulness that he had formerly enjoyed. Indeed the Great Chronicle of London maintains that he became so remorseful for what he had said that he entered a period of decline and died shortly thereafter.[14]

On 24 June Buckingham gave a masterful speech before a carefully selected assembly at the Guildhall and won unanimous support for his demand that Richard be acknowledged as the rightful king. Once the duke's position had been endorsed by Thomas FitzWilliam, Recorder of London, a petition requesting Richard to take the throne was drawn up, and on 25 June it was presented to him at Baynard's Castle by a delegation that included a number of lords, aldermen, and clerics, as well as Buckingham and the Lord Mayor, Edward Shaa. According to an eyewitness, it was there and then that "the whole business was transacted, the oaths of allegiance given, and other indispensable acts duly performed." The next day Richard appeared in Westminster Hall to take the monarch's seat in the Court of King's Bench, which clarified that a new reign had in fact begun.[15]

During the nine days that elapsed before his coronation in the Abbey, Richard dispensed generous rewards to his friends and partisans. Lord Howard was given the great office of Lord Admiral and created Duke of Norfolk, while his son Thomas was granted the Earldom of Surrey. In addition the Howards received the greater part of the vast Mowbray inheritance, which had so long eluded them.[16] William Catesby was entrusted with several offices that had formerly belonged to Lord Hastings. Although the post of Lord Chamberlain was reserved for Viscount Lovell, Catesby was made Chancellor and Chamberlain of the Exchequer, an esquire of the body, and on 30 June his patent as Chancellor of the Earldom of March was confirmed. As for Buckingham, whose support during the past few weeks had been invaluable, he was appointed Great Chamberlain as well as Lord Constable of England. In addition Richard pledged that Buckingham should receive the great Bohun inheritance, worth more than £700 a year, which had once been the property of his ancestor Humphrey, Earl of Hereford and Northampton. While such largesse was being handed out in the capital, a grimmer note was being sounded in Yorkshire, where several members of the Woodville faction had been imprisoned for more than six weeks. During the last week of June Richard's captives were transferred from their respective gaols to Pontefract Castle, where, on the 25th, they were executed without benefit of trial. Among those beheaded at that time were Elizabeth Woodville's brother Anthony, second Earl Rivers; Elizabeth's younger son by her first marriage, Sir Richard Grey; and Sir Thomas Vaughan and Sir Richard Haute.[17]

Immediately after the coronation on 6 July,[18] preparations began for a royal progress towards the West and North. Richard wanted to show himself and his wife Anne to the inhabitants of the outlying sections as a way of currying popular favor. Exactly when the royal train left London is unclear, but by 23 July it had passed through Windsor and arrived at Reading, where Lady Hastings appeared and was assured that her late husband would not be attainted and that all the family's rights and possessions would be respected. As a great authority on the period once observed, "Whatever other evil there was in Richard's character, there was nothing mean and paltry."[19] On his arrival at Oxford, the king received a warm welcome from William Waynflete, Bishop of Winchester and principal benefactor of Magdalen College. After short visits to Gloucester, Tewkesbury, and Worcester, Richard proceeded to Warwick, where he remained an entire week. Then he appeared at Coventry and several other midland towns before arriving at Pontefract, where he was joined by his ten-year-old son Edward, who rode in from Middleham Castle and was created Prince of Wales on 24 August. Within another week the royal train had passed through the portals of York, where the king and his wife were welcomed by the Lord Mayor and granted handsome presents of money and plate.

While Richard was absent on his progress, the situation was taking a dangerous turn for him in the environs of London. During August rumors became widespread that the two sons of Edward IV had been murdered in the Tower and that Richard himself was responsible for the crime. Dominic Mancini believed that the princes were already dead, or would be so shortly, when he departed for the continent several days after the coronation. During the latter part of June the two boys had frequently been seen "shooting and playing in the garden by the Tower"; but then they had been withdrawn "into the inner apartments of the Tower proper, and day by day began to be seen more rarely, till at length they ceased to appear at all."[20] No documents signed by Edward V after 16 June, the day his younger brother joined him in the Tower, have yet been discovered; and a royal warrant issued late in July directed that final payment be made to thirteen men for their services to "Edward bastard, late called King Edward V,"[21] which suggests that he and Prince Richard were both dead by that juncture. If not, it seems improbable that they lived more than a few weeks longer. Certainly they were not alive in October, when Richard returned to London from his progress, for he did nothing to produce them, which was the only way he could answer the dangerous charges being levelled against him not only in his own realm but on the continent. Informed observers therefore had every reason to hold him responsible for the crime; and in January 1484 the Chancellor of France, who had doubtless been in contact with Mancini's patron, Archbishop Cato of Vienne, formally charged Richard with the deed in a speech before the States-General at Tours. When in November 1485 Richard was posthumously attainted by Henry VII's first parliament, it was held that he was guilty of "shedding infants' blood."[22]

The traditional account of the princes' murder is Sir Thomas More's classic *History of King Richard the Third*, which was written thirty years after the events it reported. More was a young boy in 1483 and probably received most of his information from his father, a prominent lawyer in the capital, and from the father of his first wife, John Colt of Netherhall, Essex, whose own father had been Chancellor of the Exchequer to Edward IV. Many historians contend that More's chief source was the table talk of John Morton, Bishop of Ely from 1479 until 1486 and afterwards Archbishop of Canterbury. This seems improbable, however, for More was only briefly a page in Morton's household and at the time was little more than twelve or thirteen years of age. Regardless of the source of More's information, his account was based on a firmly established oral tradition.[23]

Once Richard III reached Warwick on 8 August (according to More's narrative), he sent an order by John Green for the Constable of the Tower, Sir Robert Brackenbury, to have the two princes murdered, but the upright Brackenbury refused to comply (although he later gave his life for Richard at Bosworth). Thereupon Richard called in James Tyrell, one of the Chamberlains of the Exchequer, and directed him to see to the deed. Tyrell went to the Tower, gained possession of the keys, and enlisted the services of Miles Forest, one of the princes' four jailers, who had a long record of previous criminal activity. To assist Forest, Tyrell selected his own horsekeeper, John Dighton, "a big broad strong knave." About midnight one evening, after the princes' other servants had been dismissed, Forest and Dighton stole into their bedchamber "and suddenly lapped them among the bedclothes—so bewrapped and entangled them, that within a while . . . they gave up to God their innocent souls into the joys of heaven." After the princes had been killed in this way, their bodies were buried at the foot of a staircase in the White Tower by a cleric in Brackenbury's employ; and Tyrell then galloped back to Warwick to inform the king, "who gave him great thanks, and, as some say, there made him a knight."[24]

Unhappily there is no documentary evidence to prove or disprove More's story.[25] Even worse, More's *History of King Richard the Third* is filled with numerous errors of fact, while the speeches he attributed to his principal characters were clearly modelled on those of ancient Roman political figures, about whom he had read. For these reasons such writers as Horace Walpole, Sir Clements Markham, and Josephine Tey not only dispute the truthfulness of his account but also maintain that the princes were still alive when Henry Tudor seized the throne in 1485, thereby implying that Richard III's conqueror was the actual perpetrator of the crime. Yet all the leading scholars of the last half century, including A. F. Pollard, J. H. Hexter, and R. S. Sylvester, contend that the outline of More's story is truthful, at least in spirit.[26] Of greater significance, circumstantial evidence strongly suggests that the most important parts of More's account are in fact correct.

During a period of renovation in 1674, two skeletons were unearthed beneath the staircase in the White Tower at the base of which More maintained the princes' bodies had been buried. On orders from Charles II these skeletons were placed in a burial urn in the Abbey, where they remained undisturbed until July 1933, when they were examined by Professor William Wright of the Royal College of Physicians and Dr. George Northcroft, an expert on children's dentistry and a former president of the British Society of Orthodontics. After a prolonged study the two scientists reached the following conclusions: (1) the bones were those of brothers, for they showed clear signs of consanguinity; (2) at least one of the children had suffered a cranial fracture from a sharp blow on the head, which suggests that he died a violent death; (3) the age of the older child was "somewhere between the age of twelve and thirteen" (Edward V was in fact within a few months of his thirteenth birthday at the presumed date of the murder); and (4) the age of the younger child was "about mid-way between nine and eleven" (Prince Richard was only a few days short of his tenth birthday in August 1483). After explaining the techniques used during the course of the examination, Professor Wright wrote in summary:

The evidence that the bones in the urn are those of the Princes is in my judgment as conclusive as could be desired, and definitely more conclusive than could, considering everything, have reasonably been expected. Further, their ages were such that I can say with complete confidence that their death occurred during the reign of their usurping uncle, Richard III.[27]

Most scholars now agree that the bones analyzed by Professor Wright and Dr. Northcroft were those of the princes, who were murdered sometime during the summer of 1483, as More contended. But the question of responsibility continues to bedevil historians, for there is no consensus that Tyrell, acting on orders from the king and in conjunction with Forest and Dighton, was the main perpetrator of the crime. Although G. R. Elton, A. L. Rowse, and other scholars accept More's explanation in entirety, the late Paul Murray Kendall rightly warned that there is not enough evidence to convict anyone of the crime.[28]

An intriguing theory has been advanced of late by Melvin Tucker, the biographer of Thomas Howard, Earl of Surrey and second of the Howard Dukes of Norfolk. With the obvious exception of Richard III, no one profited more from the elimination of the princes than the Howards; and Professor Tucker therefore maintains that John Howard, who received the Dukedom of Norfolk only a few days before Richard's coronation, may well have been responsible for the murder. When Richard and his train set out on their progress towards the West and North, John Howard accompanied them only as far as Windsor and then returned to London to superintend alterations to Crosby Hall, where Richard had resided until his seizure of the throne. Howard remained in the capital until 11 August, when he departed for his own estates in East Anglia. Thus he was in London during the critical period when the princes were probably killed. Furthermore, as Lord Admiral and one of Richard's most prominent supporters, he had easy access to the Tower should he need it. And as Professor Tucker discovered from one of the Howards' account books, Sir John "procured two sacks of lime soon after Edward V was installed in the Tower. Was Howard waiting for the Duke of York to join his brother for the opportunity to use it? Only the death of the Duke of York was essential to Howard, but perhaps he was willing to do away with Edward V for a consideration. The death of both Princes was necessary for Richard III's purposes."[29]

Regardless of whether the main perpetrator of the crime was Lord

Howard, Sir James Tyrell, or the Duke of Buckingham (as Professor Kendall believed),[30] it is indisputable that Richard III bears a heavy responsibility for what happened. In a monarchy like that of late medieval England there was no place for a deposed king, and by his usurpation of the throne he instantly put both princes in mortal danger. Their lives would always be a threat to his; and even if he shrank from giving a direct order for their elimination, he knew that he could count on one of his more zealous supporters to do the deed for him. His more politically-minded subjects realized this and did not require rigorous proof to substantiate their suspicions. Thus there was widespread disenchantment with the king as rumors of the princes' murder spread farther and farther afield during the late summer of 1483. Given these circumstances, it might be possible to overthrow Richard and place someone more upright and law-abiding on the throne. One of the first persons to sense the possibilities was Lady Margaret Beaufort, Dowager Countess of Richmond, who had played a conspicuous role at Richard's coronation, having carried Queen Anne's train.

Born in 1443, Lady Margaret Beaufort was a direct descendant of Edward III by his fourth son, John of Gaunt, Duke of Lancaster and Earl of Richmond. Lady Margaret's father, John Beaufort, third Earl and first Duke of Somerset, died within a year of her birth; but because she was his sole heir, she inherited wide estates that guaranteed her a prominent position. She became a royal ward and, at the age of twelve, was given in marriage to Henry VI's half-brother, Edmund Tudor, who had recently been created Earl of Richmond.[31] Sent to Wales in 1455 to superintend the king's estates there, Edmund Tudor fell ill of the plague and died in November 1456, leaving his young wife seven months' pregnant. At Pembroke Castle on 28 January 1457, the fourteen-year-old Margaret gave birth to a son, Henry of Richmond, who would in due course establish himself on the English throne. Three years after her first husband's death, Lady Margaret married into the Stafford family: her second husband was a grandson of the first Duke of Buckingham. When he died a decade later, Lady Margaret took for her third husband Thomas, second Lord Stanley, with whom her relationship was always platonic in nature. Although Lord Stanley was an important landowner in the northwest midlands, Lady Margaret naturally continued to think of herself primarily as Dowager Countess of Richmond.

Small and frail, Lady Margaret was nevertheless a woman of indomitable spirit, and during the summer of 1483 she began to conspire against Richard III. Through her doctor, a Welshman named Lewis, she made overtures to Elizabeth Woodville, who was still in sanctuary at the Abbey,

and suggested a marriage between her son Henry of Richmond and the
dowager queen's eldest daughter, Elizabeth of York. In this way the
claims of Lancaster, which had devolved on the Tudors twelve years
earlier,[32] could be fused with those of York, and this might encourage
Richard III's subjects to overthrow him and elevate the young couple to
the throne. Of course Lady Margaret might have sought regal power for
herself, since she naturally occupied a more prominent place in the
succession than her son. But she instinctively knew that few men would
fight on behalf of a forty-year-old woman, so she made no effort to
advance her own claim and concentrated on promoting her son's.

There were two weaknesses to Lady Margaret's plan, however. First,
her son's claim to the throne was not a convincing one, for it came to him
through the Beaufort line, which, even as late as the 1480s, had a taint of
illegitimacy about it. Henry's great-grandfather, John Beaufort, first Earl
of Somerset (ob. 1410), had been the eldest son of John of Gaunt by his
third wife, Catherine Swynford, with whom Gaunt lived for some years
before they were legally married. Thus the Beaufort children were born
before their parents were technically man and wife; and even though a
parliamentary act of 1397 had removed the stigma of bastardy from them,
many people still remembered that there was something a bit questionable
about the Beaufort-Tudor claim. In addition many observers were aware
that when Henry IV's first parliament confirmed the act of 1397, a proviso
was added which barred the Beauforts forever from the succession.
Whether that proviso, which had been inserted at Henry IV's insistence,
would have been upheld by a court of law is questionable; but it
nevertheless created serious doubts about the validity of Henry Tudor's
claim.[33] Notwithstanding such considerations, however, the principle of
indefeasible hereditary right had been grievously weakened, if not destroyed, by the repeated deposition of reigning kings since 1399.
Moreover, the fact that Henry's rather shaky claim, the weakest of any
successful pretender since 1066, was eventually accepted should perhaps
be seen as the measure to which Richard III failed to win the hearts and
minds of his subjects.

The second and more serious weakness of Lady Margaret's plan was the
fact that her son was a shadowy and little-known figure to most Englishmen in 1483. He had lived in exile on the continent since 1471, when
for safety's sake he fled abroad with his uncle Jasper Tudor, Earl of
Pembroke. Even Lady Margaret knew remarkably little about her 26-
year-old son, for they had been separated for over twenty years.

After his mother's second marriage in 1459, the young Henry Tudor had become a ward of William, Lord Herbert of Raglan, a staunch Yorkist, in whose household he had resided for nearly a decade. Probably the strongest influence on Henry's early life was Lord Herbert's wife, Anne Devereux, daughter of William Devereux of Chartley, who reared the boy as her own son and longed to see him married to her daughter Maude. Probably it was the care and affection he received from Lady Herbert that caused Henry to grow up to be an unusually well-balanced and emotionally stable individual. Yet when a new phase of the Wars of the Roses broke out in 1469, the Herberts' main residence, Harlech Castle, fell to the Lancastrians. Lord Herbert was executed shortly after the battle of Edgecote, and Henry then passed into the care of his uncle Jasper, who had just returned from a first period of exile on the continent. He was taken to London during the brief restoration of Henry VI, to whom he was introduced for the only time. The saintly nature of the last Lancastrian king made a deep impression on the future ruler, who subsequently made repeated efforts to secure Henry VI's canonization. When in the spring of 1471 the Yorkists recovered the throne, the young head of the House of Tudor, who was then residing in Wales, fled with his uncle Jasper to the ducal court of Brittany, where he spent the next thirteen years as a pensioner of Francis II.[34]

During his long years abroad Henry grew to maturity. He was somewhat taller than the average Englishman, being about 5′ 9″ in height. He never became a seasoned fighter like the two Yorkist kings, but he rode well and enjoyed most kinds of physical activity. Devoted to hunting and other outdoor sports, he was even as a man of fifty "slender but well built and strong." Although his hair was a chestnut brown, his complexion was fair, while his eyes were "small and blue." According to a contemporary who knew him well, his face was "remarkably attractive . . . and cheerful, especially when speaking,"[35] which suggests that his expression was often animated. During his long stay on the continent, Henry acquired an obvious preference for French customs and manners. Towards the end of his life many of his subjects grumbled about the way he had developed autocratic tendencies while in exile. Yet his foreign experiences also gave him a broader outlook than that of most Englishmen. He spoke French fluently, and because of his first-hand knowledge of European conditions, he eventually became a great diplomatist, holding his own even with the wily Holy Roman Emperor Maximilian I. He was an excellent judge of men with a deep understanding of human nature. But even though his mind was quick and retentive, it was an altogether conservative and conventional intelligence.[36]

Henry's claim to the throne, which his mother began to advance during the late summer of 1483, was warmly supported by Elizabeth Woodville, who was willing to clutch at any straw to overthrow the hated Richard III. Once assured of the dowager queen's aid, Lady Margaret hoped to acquire support from peers and other landowners who would call out their retainers and confront the king in battle. To coordinate this risky business, she relied on her capable steward, Reginald Bray, who sent messengers into East Anglia, Kent, Devonshire, and Wales. She also made use of her personal chaplain, Christopher Urswick, who sailed across the Channel to Brittany to inform Henry that the time had come to secure Duke Francis's aid for an invasion of England. If the pretender could attack with a powerful force from the continent at the same time rebel troops were converging on London from several different directions, Richard's defeat would be ensured.

One of the most important participants in the uprising was to be the Duke of Buckingham, Richard's principal lieutenant in Wales and the West Country. Buckingham was known to be disaffected because of the king's failure to honor his pledge to return the great Bohun inheritance to him.[37] Aware of Buckingham's deep annoyance in this regard, Lady Margaret sent her steward to confer with him and John Morton, a staunch Lancastrian until Edward IV's recovery of the throne in 1471. Bishop Morton had been arrested at the time of Lord Hastings' execution in June 1483 and was now the duke's prisoner at Brecknock Castle. Morton at once told Bray he would do whatever he could to persaude his captor to support a rebellion on Henry Tudor's behalf. That the bishop's efforts succeeded can be seen from the fact that, on 24 September, Buckingham himself sent a letter urging the pretender to return from abroad in order to assert his rightful claim to the throne.

The rebellion was scheduled to begin on 18 October. Before that time arrived, Richard learned of the plot and took energetic counter measures. On 11 October, just before entering Lincoln on his way back to London, the king addressed a letter to the Lord Mayor and aldermen of York, who were informed that Buckingham and a host of others were about to betray him. He then directed the northerners to "send unto us as many men defensibly arrayed on horseback as ye may goodly make, to our town of Leicester, [by] the 21st of this present month." On 15 October Richard openly denounced Buckingham as a traitor and summoned all his subjects to take up arms against him. A reward of £1000 was offered for the duke's capture, while lesser amounts were promised for his accomplices.[38]

The uprising began on 18 October as originally planned, but without the element of surprise it had little chance of success. By stationing their retainers at Gravesend, the Howards were able to prevent a junction between the rebels of East Anglia and those of Kent and Surrey. In the West Country Henry was openly proclaimed by Peter Courtenay, Bishop of Exeter, and his brother Walter of Powderham, who were in league with the Marquess of Dorset and Bishop Woodville of Salisbury. The Courtenays were also assisted by such prominent Lancastrians from Devonshire and Cornwall as Sir Robert Willoughby, Sir Thomas Arundell, Richard Edgecombe, John Halliwell, John Trevelyan, and Richard Nanfan. But when the king sent an army against them, their resistance crumbled. Several of the ringleaders fled across the Channel to join Henry in exile, while others were captured and executed.[39]

Even more shortlived was Buckingham's sector of the rebellion. The duke had planned to lead an uprising in Wales and then march south in order to merge his forces with those being mobilized in the vicinity of Exeter by the Courtenays. But his strategy was wrecked by a great storm that swept over the region and caused floods to occur everywhere. Rivers burst their banks and the Severn became impassable. When they were unable to cross, Buckingham's retainers sensed the certainty of defeat and melted away. While he was desperately trying to ford the swollen river at Weobley, Sir Thomas Vaughan and his brothers, who had feuded for years with the Tudors, seized and plundered his stronghold at Brecknock Castle. With nowhere to turn Buckingham was captured a few days later by the sheriff of Shropshire, who took him in chains to Salisbury. Buckingham begged long and hard for a chance to explain everything to the king. But Richard refused to see him, and on 2 November he was beheaded in the marketplace.[40]

Several days earlier Henry had set sail for England with a dozen ships provided by the Duke of Brittany. But the same storm that ruined Buckingham's plan scattered his squadron, and he reached the western coast with no more than three vessels. At Poole he found the harbor too well guarded to land. On arriving at Plymouth he was invited ashore by men who claimed to be in Buckingham's service. Yet the pretender suspected a trap had been set for him, so he doubled back to Brittany, convinced there would be ample opportunity to confront Richard at some future time.

Although the king's supporters joked about the ease with which the rebellion had been suppressed, the uprising had revealed the burning hatred most Englishmen felt for Richard and caused Henry to emerge as a viable alternative to him. The pretender had proven himself to be courageous and resourceful, although his cautiousness and common sense had prevailed in the end. Respect for him mounted rapidly; and even though he had been "an obscure exile" and even "an irrelevance to English politics" only a few months earlier, he now emerged as a serious contender for Richard's throne.[41] Moreover, Henry's ranks soon swelled with men fleeing the kingdom to escape the royal wrath. Among those who made their way to his camp in Brittany were Richard Edgecombe, Sir Thomas Arundell, and the Courtenay brothers, all of whom had been active in the vicinity of Exeter; Sir Edward Poynings and Sir Richard Guildford, organizers of the rebel movement in Kent and Surrey; John de Vere, thirteenth Earl of Oxford, who escaped from Hammes Castle and put his vast military experience at the pretender's disposal; Sir James Blount and Sir John Fortescue, Captain and Chief Porter of Calais, respectively; and such well-to-do landowners as Sir John Bourchier, Sir Giles Daubeney, Sir William Berkeley, Sir William Brandon, Sir John Cheyney, and John, Lord Wells, step-uncle to the pretender. In addition, the Marquess of Dorset made a brief appearance before moving on to sample the attractions of Paris. Two prominent clerics who came out in open support of Henry at this juncture were John Morton, who had made his way from Brecknock Castle to Flanders, and Richard Fox, a doctoral student at the University of Paris for the last several years. Shortly after Fox arrived in Brittany, he introduced Henry to an ambitious French priest, Bernard André, better known as "the blind poet of Toulouse," who was to become the Tudors' first paid propagandist.

Because a significant number of his new adherents were former Yorkists, and because he suspected the Wars of the Roses might never be terminated otherwise, Henry decided to make a public declaration of his intention to marry Elizabeth of York and thereby unite the two branches of England's royal family. During a ceremony in Rennes Cathedral on Christmas Day 1483, he solemnly swore that, should he overthrow Richard III and obtain the throne that was rightfully his, he would take the chief Yorkist heiress for his wife, which would be the first step towards a permanent end of the dynastic conflict of the last thirty years.

Meanwhile Richard was far from idle in England. He presented generous rewards to those who had assisted him during the recent crisis; and early in 1484 he travelled through Kent, offering large sums for the capture of rebels still at large. This was but a few days before the only parliament of his reign opened on 23 January. Under the watchful eye of William Catesby, the king's nominee for Speaker, the parliament of 1484 not only sanctioned the way Richard had obtained the throne but also approved fifteen measures suggested by him. Several bills sought to provide protection for English traders against mounting foreign competition, while two acts were passed to modernize archaic legal procedures.

The most important measure, however, was a statute declaring benevolences to be illegal and stating that no Englishman would be required to pay them "nor any like charge" in the future. On the basis of this act, it has been claimed that Richard was prepared "to turn his back on the abuses of the past, and rely on Parliament for all extraordinary grants."[42] Yet it seems more likely that he was simply trying to curry favor, in order to stem the tide that was shifting so rapidly in Henry's direction. This impression is strengthened by the king's acceptance of a measure repealing a statute of Edward IV's reign which had established ways of keeping tenants on Duchy of Lancaster lands from evading the financial obligations of wardship.[43]

From Richard's point of view, the most pressing task of the parliament of 1484 was to punish those who had conspired against him several months earlier. Accordingly 104 individuals were attainted by means of four different bills. That such extreme action was taken against so many suggests that Richard was now "in the grip of something like panic."[44] In addition to the pretender and his uncle Jasper, those attainted at this juncture included Buckingham, the Marquess of Dorset, and the Bishops of Salisbury, Exeter, and Ely. Steps were also taken to punish Elizabeth Woodville by declaring invalid her marriage to Edward IV and revoking all earlier grants made to her; and similar measures were enacted against Lady Margaret Beaufort. Technically Henry's mother was not attainted, as is generally maintained, but was disabled from owning any real property, all her estates being confiscated by the Crown. But because Richard was wary of alienating Lord Stanley, whose support he felt he must retain in order to survive, he soon made a lifetime grant of them to Lady Margaret's husband.[45]

The Stanleys were not the only powerful family to profit from the king's largesse. In his determination to safeguard himself, Richard alienated lands worth in excess of £250,000, which had produced yearly rents of more than £12,000. His prodigality in this regard equalled that of an earlier usurper, Henry IV; yet he derived little benefit from his generosity, for it was obvious that he was trying to buy political support. Furthermore, while many aristocrats profited from his rule, through the grant of an estate, an office, or an annuity, too many of the rewards he parcelled out went to the Howards, the Stanleys, and the Percys, on whose support he felt his regime primarily depended. This inevitably made it appear that his favor was reserved for a small circle of his closest friends, most of whom belonged to the peerage. Below the rank of baron, only Sir Richard Ratcliffe received a grant of lands worth in excess of £500 a year.[46] Consequently the great majority of his subjects were unsympathetic to his plight; and when the final crisis enveloped him, they remained impassively on the sidelines.

Yet during the spring of 1484 it was not altogether clear that Richard's cause was doomed. The last embers of Buckingham's rebellion had been stamped out, and parliament had willingly done his bidding, even establishing a precedent by granting him tunnage and poundage for life.[47] For this reason Elizabeth Woodville should not be judged too harshly for accepting an accommodation with him. By this juncture the widow and five daughters of Edward IV had been reduced to penury and were dependent on the charity of the monks in the Abbey. Besides, it was all too tempting for the dowager queen to accept the official line that Buckingham had been responsible for all the harm that had befallen her family. There is also a distinct possibility that the poor woman's mind had been unhinged by the tragic events of the last ten months. Within a few more years she was to be lodged in Bermondsey Abbey, which doubled as a royal nursing home in the fifteenth century, and it was there that she would die in 1492. At any rate, when Richard made overtures to her in March 1484 and offered to guarantee the safety of herself and her daughters, she readily accepted them. This was a great stroke of good fortune for him; and after establishing an annuity of £233 for her support, he paraded his sister-in-law and five nieces around the court as if to say that he could not have participated in the murder of the two princes.

Yet within a few more weeks, all of Richard's worldly successes turned to ashes. On 9 April 1484, exactly a year since Edward IV's death, his beloved son Edward, Prince of Wales, died at Middleham Castle. This was a crushing blow to Richard, who must have felt that God was mocking him. His illegitimate son, John of Pontefract, had no chance whatever of succeeding him, and everything he had striven for now seemed to have been in vain. As he instinctively knew, many of his subjects were likely to conclude that Providence had turned away from him altogether, which meant that his hopes of survival had been irreparably weakened. Richard's spirit remained unbroken, however, and within a short time he decided to name a new heir-apparent. At first he was tempted to designate the Earl of Warwick, only son of his late brother George, Duke of Clarence. But Warwick was a sickly child, and to choose him would be to raise questions about his earlier assertion that he believed Clarence to have been illegitimate. In the end his choice fell on another nephew, John de la Pole, Earl of Lincoln, eldest son of his sister Elizabeth, who was the wife of the Duke of Suffolk.

If the death of the Prince of Wales was a cruel stroke to Richard, it was an even more depressing blow to his wife Anne. Never strong or robust, Anne had been unable to give her husband the several sons he so obviously wanted. Her chances of giving birth again were poor at best, and the sudden death of her only child caused her outlook to become permanently clouded. She entered a period of decline, and on 16 March 1485 she died.

That Richard was relieved by his wife's passing is indisputable, for he could now remarry and father another legitimate son. As a result, rumors were soon rampant that he had arranged the death of his queen, who had died by a poisoner's hand. These reports took on added weight when he foolishly announced that he might marry his niece Elizabeth of York, as a way of forestalling the pretender's plan to merge the claims of Lancaster and York. So impolitic was this scheme that several of the king's closest advisers rushed to him and insisted that he adopt a different course. Catesby and Ratcliffe argued heatedly that even his most devoted followers in the North "would charge him with procuring the death of his Queen . . . in order to enter an incestuous relationship, and that he must deny any such scheme."[48] Shortly afterwards twelve eminent theologians assembled in his presence and predicted that the pope would never grant the dispensation necessary for such a marriage. Because of the concerted opposition of his own followers, Richard made an unprecedented appearance at the Guildhall on St. John's Day. Before the Lord Mayor and various other dignitaries of the capital, he solemnly swore that he had had no part in his wife's death and that he had no intention of marrying Elizabeth of York. Anyone guilty of spreading such pernicious lies would be severely punished. Yet according to a reliable eyewitness, the king made this declaration more to appease his dwindling circle of supporters than to satisfy himself. Certainly he was in no hurry to send his niece away from court, which was necessary to protect her reputation. Not until mid-June was she instructed to take up residence at Sheriff Hutton, in Yorkshire.[49]

From his exile in France Henry loudly criticized Richard's plan to marry Elizabeth of York. Probably Henry did not know about the king's appearance at the Guildhall, nor of the intense pressure being exerted upon him by his advisers, for the pretender regarded the threat as a serious one, at least momentarily. During the spring of 1485 Henry was living as a pensioner of Charles VIII of France rather than at the ducal court of Brittany, which he had fled because of Richard's efforts to extradite him to England. Duke Francis was as friendly to Henry as ever, but during the summer of 1484 he had fallen ill and lost control of his greedy Treasurer, Pierre Landois. In return for a substantial payment, Landois agreed to assist in the apprehension of Henry and his supporters, now several hundred strong. Shortly before the pretender was to be arrested, rumors of the plot reached Bishop Morton in Flanders, who had at once sent a message warning Henry of the danger. Only an hour before Landois' horsemen set out to capture him, Henry and five servants put on disguises and crossed the border into France, leaving most of the English exiles behind. When Duke Francis subsequently recovered from his illness, he rebuked the Treasurer for his actions and gave permission for the other Englishmen to join their leader at the French court. The good duke even provided funds to help defray the cost of their journey.[50]

Once Henry appealed to the French government, he received assurances of generous aid, and in November 1484 the Council of State voted 3000 *livres* to help with the equipping of his troops. Charles VIII and his elder sister, Anne of Beaujeu, who was serving as regent for the fourteen-year-old king, regarded Henry as a valuable tool to be used in the interests of their country. Richard III had long been hostile to France and was known to favor a resumption of the Hundred Years' War. In 1475 he had loudly criticized Edward IV's decision to negotiate a peace treaty with Louis XI, and early in 1483 he had vigorously supported the call for another expedition to the continent. Should Richard ever feel secure on the English throne, he was likely to emulate the campaigns of Henry V, the hero of Agincourt. From the French point of view it was therefore essential to encourage divisiveness in England, and what better way to do that than by aiding Henry? Moreover, should the pretender succeed in overthrowing Richard, the threat of an English attack was bound to fade, for not only did the Tudor claimant have strong French preferences but he would also be morally indebted to those who had helped him in his hour of need.

During the winter of 1484–85 the French authorities gave increasing support to Henry, and serious preparations for a new assault on England began. Aided by such capable administrators as Fox, Poynings, and Morton, the pretender planned a cross-Channel operation with great care and thoroughness. In the Earl of Oxford and his uncle Jasper, he had military commanders who could provide the experience of battle that he himself lacked, while his other adherents were able to furnish information about conditions and loyalties in all parts of the countryside. In the words of an authority on the period, "This was indeed a government in the making, at present more a general operational staff than a civilian administration, but in command of talents which could manage the affairs of a kingdom."[51]

By the beginning of 1485, Richard was aware of what was being planned for him and was taking appropriate counter measures. Indeed as early as December 1484 he had directed commissioners throughout the realm to be ready for an invasion at any time. During the spring of 1485 he apparently felt the attack would come somewhere along the southern coast, for in May he appointed Francis, Lord Lovell to command a fleet at Southampton. Yet he did not ignore the possibility of a landing in Wales and had a system of signalling lamps set up in the hills of Pembrokeshire, particularly in the vicinity of Milford Haven.[52]

Richard's defensive measures proved to be extremely costly and compelled him to turn to his richer subjects for assistance. Yet because he had promised the parliament of 1484 that he would never resort to benevolences or "any like charge" in the future, his commissioners encountered serious resistance when they requested sums of up to £200. As a consequence the king's agents had no choice but to promise that any sums advanced would be guaranteed by privy seals redeemable within eighteen months. The loans were nevertheless denounced as a "malevolence," and little more than £20,000 was raised in this fashion.[53] That so little money was forthcoming at this critical juncture is clear proof that Richard's popular support had all but collapsed.

By the last week of July Henry had completed the mobilization of his troops and ships at the Norman ports of Rouen and Harfleur. His expeditionary force consisted of between 400 and 500 hard-core supporters, refugees like himself from England, and at least 1500 infantrymen provided by the French Crown. They embarked on 1 August and, backed by a "soft south wind," landed six days later on the Welsh coast near Milford Haven. Their first task was to secure Dale Castle, which they did with no apparent difficulty. Early the next morning they set out for Haverfordwest, ten miles to the north, where they spent several days waiting for the arrival of Welsh reinforcements. Henry was of course the head of an old Welsh family, and the Lancastrians had always been more popular in Wales than the Yorkists. In addition many Welshmen believed Henry to be a descendant of the ancient House of Cerdic, which had ruled over the Saxon kingdom of Wessex; and there was a widely accepted prophecy that a great Welshman would arise one day and conquer England, after which he would end the restrictions imposed on the Welsh people by their English rulers since 1399. Before his departure from France, Henry had addressed letters to the magnates of the region as a way of securing pledges of their support. The greatest of the Welsh chieftains, Rhys ap Thomas, who had been Richard's principal lieutenant in Wales since Buckingham's execution, had promised to raise 4000 men on Henry's behalf. Yet when the pretender appeared, there was no rush to join him. Not until 12 August, by which time a worried Henry had promised viceregal powers in Wales to Rhys should his cause triumph, did the Welshman ride in with his retainers. Then the other magnates of the area, including Richard Griffiths, John Morgan, and Sir Walter Herbert, followed suit; and it was at last safe for Henry to continue his march into England.[54]

After passing through Aberystwyth and Macynlleth, the pretender arrived on 15 August at Shrewsbury, which refused to admit him for a day. This was the only resistance he would encounter before coming face-to-face with Richard's army. Henry's ranks continued to swell, particularly after Gilbert Talbot, the powerful uncle of the Earl of Shrewsbury, came over to him with 500 men at Newport. But Henry was alarmed by the failure of his step-father Lord Stanley and his brother Sir William to declare themselves. The Stanleys dominated the northwest midlands, along the Welsh frontier, and their support was crucial for the success of Henry's campaign. Yet the Stanleys were notorious for hedging their bets: in 1459 Lord Stanley had almost been impeached for his failure to support the Lancastrians at Blore Heath. In an effort to persuade the Stanleys to commit themselves, Henry addressed several anxious letters to his mother and her husband in which he divulged his plan to cross the Severn and march with all possible speed towards London. Although the Stanleys were, as usual, determined to be on the winning side, whichever that might be, Sir William arrived for a private talk with Henry after he reached Stafford on 17 August. There is no record of what was said on that occasion, but the younger Stanley obviously refused to pledge himself or his brother to a definite course of action. The next day the pretender met and conversed with both brothers at Atherstone, which suggests that they were now giving serious thought to aiding Henry. However, Lord Stanley's eldest son had just been taken hostage by Richard, so he was in no position to join openly with the pretender. Despite the Stanleys' temporizing, the rebel forces were significantly strengthened that same day when Sir John Savage rode into their camp with "a choice band." It must have been about this point, too, that a thousand Scotsmen arrived to fight on Henry's behalf. Because of Richard's conquest of Berwick in 1482, the English monarch was hated by James III, who was eager for a chance to overthrow him. James even believed that after Richard's deposition, Henry would voluntarily return Berwick to Scotland!

Meanwhile, at Nottingham Castle, where he had been in residence since mid-June, Richard had learned that the long-feared invasion was at last underway. On 11 August the king directed his principal supporters to call out their retainers and meet him within a week at Leicester. Because of his failure to move more rapidly, Professor Chrimes feels that Richard initially believed his challenger would be bottled up in Wales, either by Rhys ap Thomas in the south or by the Stanleys in the north. Not until he was informed that Henry's army had reached Shrewsbury did he realize the campaign would not be restricted to the Welsh contryside, and only then did he become seriously alarmed.[55] By 19 August the king was at last ready to move and set out with his troops in the direction of Leicester. On Sunday afternoon the 21st he arrived at the base of Ambien Hill, two miles to the south of the little town of Market Bosworth. Within a short distance of his position were encamped the five armies of the two opposing sides—Henry's, the Stanleys', the Duke of Norfolk's, the Earl of Northumberland's, and now his own. A pitched battle the next day was bound to occur.

Because no eyewitness account of the encounter is known to exist, any attempt to reconstruct what happened on 22 August can only be an exercise in historical imagination. From later records it appears that fighting began at an early hour, with Henry's troops charging across a marshy area towards the king's position on the slopes of Ambien Hill. Although the battle lasted less than three hours, it was bitterly fought, with heavy casualties on both sides. Richard had about 10,000 men in his command, while Henry had but half that number and the Stanleys, 3000. Exactly how many men Norfolk and Northumberland had brought with them has never been determined. Once the issue was joined, Northumberland, whose father and great-grandfather had died in combat, kept his troops safely at the rear, which was a severe blow to the royal cause.[56] Worse, the Stanleys remained on the sidelines until the climax of the fighting: when they saw Henry had a good chance to win, they threw their troops into the breach and thereby assured his victory. Of those on whose active support Richard had counted, only the Howards fought wholeheartedly on his behalf. But Norfolk was killed early in the day, while the Earl of Surrey was wounded so badly that he begged to be put out of his misery.

As for Richard himself, he knew that this was his last opportunity to save himself and his throne. Should his troops win a tactical victory, it would still be impossible for him to carry the day again if Henry escaped with his army intact. The night before the battle Richard had revealed his desperation in a rousing speech to his men. After branding the pretender "a Welsh milksop," he declared that "as for me, I assure you . . . I will triumph by victory or suffer death for immortal fame."[57] Richard therefore fought demonically. He threw himself into the fray and made strenuous efforts to reach and kill his challenger. He unhorsed Sir John Cheyney, "a man of great force and strength," and ended the life of Sir

William Brandon, the rebel standard bearer. But before he could accomplish his primary objective, Henry's guardsmen closed about him, and he was brought down fighting manfully to the end. His body was treated as disrespectfully as he had come to be regarded. Stripped completely naked, it was trussed across a horse's back and transported to Leicester, where it was displayed in the Grey Friars' Church for two days, so no one could later claim that he was still alive. Then his body was interred in the local cemetary where a decade later his conqueror erected an alabaster monument to his memory.[58]

Once the fighting and subsequent pursuit of Richard's troops ended, Henry and his men prepared to give thanks for their victory in the little church of Stoke Golding, the spire of which could be seen from Ambien Hill. As they moved off in that direction, the golden circlet that had been attached to Richard's helmet was found in the dust by Reginald Bray, who took it at once to Lord Stanley. Sensing the drama of the moment, Henry's step-father rode briskly to the pretender's side and bade him dismount and kneel. Then he placed the circlet on his head and acclaimed him Harry the Seventh, King of England and Wales. The reign of the first Tudor monarch had begun.

II

The Reign Begins

The England that Henry VII ruled after 1485 was a thinly settled land of not more than 2.25 million people. This was a smaller population than two centuries earlier, before the appearance of the Black Death and the great decline that occurred after 1348. During the mid-fifteenth century the population had begun to grow once again, but in 1485 it was still considerably lower than it had been at Edward II's deposition in 1327. Because the pressure on the land was so slight, England's per capita wealth was greater than it would have been otherwise. In 1497 an Italian visitor maintained that "the population of this island does not appear to me to bear any proportion to its riches." In addition he declared that anyone travelling through the countryside could not fail to be impressed by its "great wealth." Yet he did not understand that in an age of primitive agricultural techniques, when acreage yields were less than a twelfth of what they are today, the low population density was one of the main causes of England's prosperity, which he attributed rather "to the great fertility of the soil."[1]

That the England of Henry VII was a relatively prosperous land is confirmed by much other evidence. In 1497 another Italian visitor noted that Englishmen "delight in banquets and variety of meat and food, and excel everyone in preparing them with excessive abundance. They eat frequently . . . and are particularly fond of young swans, rabbits, deer, and sea birds. They often eat mutton and beef, which is generally considered to be better here than anywhere else in the world." Similar views were reported in 1499 by the Milanese ambassador, who informed his government: "I stay on in this country, eating ten or twelve courses at each meal, and spending three hours at table twice a day." Still another foreigner, who arrived from the continent in 1501, was amazed by the range of goods available in the shops of London. The city abounds, he declared, "with every article of luxury . . . but the most remarkable thing is the wonderful quantity of wrought silver. In one single street, named the Strand, there are fifty-two goldsmiths' shops, so rich and full of silver vessels, great and small, that in all the shops of Milan, Rome, Venice, and Florence put together, I do not think there would be found as many of the magnificence as there are to be seen in London."[2]

Such statements about the country's wealth are now accepted, although until recently there was a strong tendency for historians to discount them. Between 1334 and 1500, according to R. S. Schofield, the assessed taxable wealth of England increased by more than 200 per cent, even though the population was still lower at the end of the period than it had been at the beginning. Moreover, wage rates were consistently high throughout the fifteenth century, which caused Thorold Rogers to characterize that period as "the golden age of the peasant laborer." Not until the second decade of the sixteenth century did real wages take a downward turn, causing serious hardship for the lower classes. Although the tin industry had been depressed since the 1390s, the wool trade was flourishing as never before, and increasing numbers of broadcloths were being exported to the continent. Yet the quantity of raw wool sent abroad each year had declined since 1399, which explains the stagnation of such ports as Boston and Lincoln. Towns like Colchester and Lavenham, however, which were dependent on their exports of woven cloth, tended to show steady growth and used a portion of their increasing wealth to build substantial new parish churches or to enlarge and beautify existing structures. In most urban areas the richer inhabitants wore unusually fine clothing, at least according to continental standards; and as early as 1363 sumptuary laws had been passed to keep the lower orders from garbing themselves too elaborately.[3]

Although town life was increasing in importance at this time, the greater part of the population still lived in the countryside and made its living through agriculture and closely related activities. Indeed there were probably a dozen countrymen for each town dweller at the close of the Middle Ages. The few urban areas that can legitimately be called towns were little more than over-grown villages of between 500 and 1000 persons; while the leading provincial centres, such as York, Norwich, and Bristol, had fewer than 10,000 inhabitants. The only city of real consequence was London, which had a population of between 50,000 and

60,000 in 1485. If there was much of a tendency towards greater urbani-
zation during the Tudor period, it was because of the rapid growth of
London, the population of which was increasing faster than that of the
country as a whole. Yet even here, it was not until after the dissolution of
the monasteries and the acquisition of their properties by private de-
velopers that there was a pronounced tendency for the capital to expand.
During the latter part of the sixteenth century, London's population grew
to almost 200,000; and by the end of the Tudor period, one out of every
five Englishmen was living somewhere within the Thames valley.

This increasing concentration of population in the southeast was for-
tuitous, for roads and bridges were extremely primitive until the 1550s,
when local officials were at last made responsible for their maintenance.
Throughout the medieval and early modern periods, Englishmen were
largely dependent on the network of roads and highways built many
centuries earlier, during the period of Roman occupation. That network
consisted of approximately 5000 miles of paved thoroughfares radiating in
all directions from the capital; and although they had fallen into decay
after the last legions were withdrawn in the fifth century, the Roman
roads continued to be the keystone of the internal transportation system
until the building of turnpikes and canals in the eighteenth century.
Because of the poor condition of the roads it was inevitable that, during
Henry VII's time, the rate of overland travel would be painfully slow. As
Professor Russell has written, "A normal time for messengers between
London and Exeter was a week, while people taking heavy loads north
from London would expect, if not attacked by robbers or bogged down, to
spend the first night in Hertfordshire." Clearly Henry VII was often
inconvenienced by the poor state of the nation's roads, for when he died in
1509 he bequeathed £2000 to improve the highways and bridges between
Richmond, Windsor, Southwark, and Canterbury.[4]

Although overland travel was dangerous and time-consuming, there
was a tendency, at least in one sense, for internal communications to
improve. For this was the age of William Caxton and the introduction of
printing by mechanical means. After the establishment of Caxton's press
at Westminster in 1476, dozens of foreign printers settled in England; and
within several decades the new process had spread throughout the countryside. Printing was both a cause and an effect of the rising level of
literacy. And as Englishmen became more closely knit in a cultural sense,
the political unity of the realm was enhanced, to the great benefit of the
central government. Furthermore the spread of printing gave the king and
his ministers a valuable tool that earlier regimes had lacked. Manifestoes
and proclamations could be circulated more easily than in the past.

Broadsides could be published in sufficiently large numbers to garner support for radical changes of policy. The age of the political pamphlet and the party press was in fact approaching.

If Henry VII profited from the spread of printing by the new mechanical means, for which he deserves little credit, he was aided even more by the conservative backlash that had set in by the time of Bosworth. Most Englishmen longed to see a permanent restoration of law and order. They or their forefathers had witnessed repeated acts of brutality for more than a century; and even if but a small percentage of the population had actually participated in the Wars of the Roses, the middle and lower classes were more fearful of a violent and unrestrained aristocracy than of a powerful monarch. Furthermore, as Professor McFarlane once observed, "The loyalty of the propertied classes . . . was engaged more by the hope of effective rule than by attachment to a particular dynasty."[5] In addition most Englishmen seem to have grasped the connection between the well-being of their country and the fortunes of the central government. For whenever the latter was strong, the realm tended to be unified and peaceable, with the result that the king's commands reverberated through the chancelleries of Europe. But whenever royal power declined, the forces of disorder asserted themselves and England's role in international affairs suffered accordingly. Patriotism therefore required all good Englishmen to support a revival of the king's authority.

Edward IV had attempted to capitalize on the longing for peace and order, but inadvertently he had compromised his own position by marrying a woman too far beneath him to be acceptable to his greatest subjects, thereby paving the way for his younger brother's usurpation of the throne. Once Henry VII seized power, he took full advantage of the popular longings by making a suitable marriage and comporting himself as a unifier and stabilizer. Former Yorkists who were willing to accept him were treated with dignity and consideration, for the new king was not a vengeful man. Rather he hoped that all his subjects would join him in renouncing the lawless ways of the past and promoting a new spirit of unity and concord. Fortunately for him—and for the country—the overwhelming majority of his subjects were determined that he should succeed. Less than a fourth of England's temporal peers had fought against him at Bosworth; and of those who did, a great many had been killed or captured, including Norfolk, the Earls of Surrey and Northumberland, and Lord Ferrers. In addition such Yorkist stalwarts as Catesby, Ratcliffe, and Brackenbury had perished, either during the encounter or shortly afterwards. Although the Earl of Lincoln and Viscount Lovell had escaped, the opposition party had been greatly weakened, if not shattered.

Only a few diehards were left to continue the struggle, in a desperate attempt to overthrow Henry and accomplish a Yorkist restoration. Unfortunately for their hopes, the new king was a pragmatic man with a clear understanding of the hazards of politics, and he always kept a watchful eye over his former enemies and their activities.

Clearly the first Tudor monarch had profited from the years he had spent in exile. His insight into other men and their motives was extraordinarily great. Recognizing that nothing but success would justify his seizure of the throne, he made concerted efforts to secure the best possible counsel and appointed only capable and experienced men to the main offices of government, although he retained the final word and always served as his own chief minister. He brought little administrative experience of his own to the throne in 1485 and naturally made a few mistakes, particularly in regard to the management of the royal finances. But because of his intelligence and application, he was an exceptionally fast learner and mastered his craft within a few years. In short, Henry was an uncommonly successful king because of his own qualities of mind and heart. Of course the movements of the age favored a restoration of strong kingship, but in the last analysis his attitudes and abilities were the decisive factor. For it was still an era of personal monarchy, when the occupant of the throne was expected to rule as well as reign. The king alone set the tone of his government, and whatever qualities he brought to his office had a bearing, for good or ill, on every aspect of life and society.

Immediately after Bosworth Henry demonstrated his willingness to reward those who had aided him against Richard III. While still on the battlefield he knighted eleven men, including Gilbert Talbot and Rhys ap Thomas. The latter, whom he had begun to address fondly as "Father Rhys," was also named Constable and Chamberlain of Brecknock Castle, Chancellor of Haverfordwest, and a member of the royal Council. Within a brief time Henry also knighted his mother's steward, Reginald Bray, who had done so much to make his victory possible, and conferred an annuity of 100 marks along with the Earldom of Bath on Philibert de Shaundé, leader of the French forces at Bosworth. In addition he revived the Earldom of Devon for Sir Edward Courtenay; awarded a barony and the mastership of the royal hounds to Sir Giles Daubeney, who had fought with exceptional valor at Bosworth; and granted an annuity of £100 along with the castles of Glamorgan, Abergavenny, and Haverfordwest to his uncle Jasper, who also recovered the Earldom of Pembroke. These rewards were generally applauded as appropriate and well deserved, and they suggest that Henry made effective use of the patronage at his disposal from the very beginning of the reign.[6]

Before leaving the midlands for London, Henry sent a trusted deputy to Sheriff Hutton to take charge of Elizabeth of York, whom he intended to marry in due course, and Edward, Earl of Warwick, now the premier male representative of the House of York. Both were subsequently escorted to the capital, where Elizabeth was reunited with her mother and sisters, while Warwick was for safety's sake lodged in the Tower. Shortly after the royal emissary departed on his mission, Henry sent out a circular letter informing his subjects that he had in fact defeated and killed Richard III, which should be regarded as God's judgment on him. It must have been about this time, too, that he ordered the release of all prisoners taken during or after Bosworth, except for Surrey and Northumberland. No one was to be mistreated or deprived of his possessions, provided that he swore to abide by the king's peace. Anyone refusing to give such a pledge was to be hanged straightaway.[7]

By the beginning of September expressions of support were pouring in, for, since Richard II's deposition in 1399, Englishmen had invariably accepted a *de facto* king. Lord Hastings' eldest son arrived to swear homage and allegiance, while at Oxford the various halls and colleges proclaimed their pleasure at the outcome of Bosworth. Although the university had given a gracious welcome to Richard III in 1483, it now delighted in Henry's triumph. Indeed, in the words of its chief historian, "Richard's conqueror seemed superior to Hannibal and recalled Alexander to academic minds."[8] Meanwhile, in London, preparations were underway for a magnificent reception in his honor. At a special meeting of the Common Council on 31 August, it was decided that he should be greeted by 435 persons chosen to represent all the guilds and clad in raiment of "bright murrey." The Lord Mayor and Court of Aldermen were to be dressed in scarlet, while their armed escort was to be clothed in "tawney medley."[9]

On his way to the capital Henry rested for a few days at St. Albans, after which he made his triumphal entry into the city on 3 September. Hailed at Shoreditch by throngs of cheering townspeople, he listened attentively to windy speeches given by local officials and to Latin verses recited by Bernard André. Then he rode behind his trumpeters to the north door of St. Paul's, where he offered to the Dean of the cathedral the banner of St. George and the other standards that his troops had used at Bosworth. After attending a *Te Deum* for his victory, he crossed the churchyard to the palace of the Bishop of London, where he spent the next several days.[10]

Decisions now had to be made concerning appointments to key positions in the government. Although Henry was naturally determined to secure the most important offices for his loyal supporters, he hoped to preserve continuity with the past by retaining able and trustworthy men who had served the Yorkist kings. As a result there was a skilful, and unexpectedly successful, mingling of Lancastrian and Yorkist personnel during the early years of the reign.[11] This was possible because the bureaucracy and the political nation had never been completely polarized by the rival claims of the two Houses.

The great office of Lord Chancellor was conferred on John Alcock, Bishop of Worcester, who had superintended the administration of Wales and the Duchy of Lancaster for Edward IV, while the equally significant post of Lord Treasurer was awarded to Thomas Rotherham, Archbishop of York and a former Lord Chancellor. The latter was retained for less than a year, however. In July 1486 he was succeeded by John, Lord Dinham, who had been Richard III's steward and principal surveyor for Cornwall. As Lord Privy Seal, Henry nominated Peter Courtenay, Bishop of Exeter; and for his personal secretary he selected Richard Fox, who was soon to be elevated to the episcopal bench. When in 1487 Fox was named to succeed Bishop Courtenay as Lord Privy Seal, the position of king's secretary was entrusted to Oliver King, who had served in that capacity during the last years of Edward IV. John Radcliffe, Lord Fitzwalter, became Steward of the Household, while Sir William Stanley was named Lord Chamberlain. John de Vere, Earl of Oxford, who had led the Tudor vanguard at Bosworth, was made Lord Admiral and Constable of the Tower. In addition he received such profitable sinecures as keeper of the Tower menagerie. Henry's uncle Jasper was granted several handsome rewards, being nominated Chief Justice of Wales, Constable of all the royal castles in the Welsh marches, and steward of the manorial courts within the same area. In March 1486 he was additionally granted the important office of Lord Lieutenant of Ireland. To maintain order in the North, particularly along the Scottish border, Henry selected the Earl of Northumberland, head of the great Percy family. Although Northumberland had been imprisoned immediately after Bosworth, Henry was now convinced of his loyalty and appointed him warden of both the east and the middle march.[12]

Although there was no purge of Yorkist personnel after Bosworth (which would have encouraged the divisiveness that Henry hoped to avoid), it would be wrong to assume that most office-holders were confirmed in their present positions. Sir James Tyrell, one of the Chamberlains of the Exchequer, was immediately discharged as was John Gunthorpe, a priest who had doubled as Lord Privy Seal and Dean of the Chapel Royal before 1485. Another priest in Richard III's service, Edmund Chaderton, who had been Treasurer of the Chamber, was removed to make way for one of Henry's strongest adherents, Sir Thomas Lovell, who was also appointed Chancellor of the Exchequer, an important position left vacant by Catesby's death. At the same time Richard III's Chancellor of the Duchy of Lancaster, Thomas Metcalfe, was dismissed so his office could be awarded to another loyal supporter, Sir Reginald Bray. Still another Yorkist discharged within a few weeks of Bosworth was Richard Langport, Clerk of the Council since 1455: on 30 September 1485 his place was assigned to John Bladiswell.[13]

Yet a number of Yorkists in middle- or lower-level positions were retained by the new king. One such individual was Alfred Cornburgh, who had been a royal functionary since 1455, serving first as a Yeoman of the Chamber and then as Under-treasurer of the Exchequer. Henry confirmed Cornburgh in the latter post and, in 1486, named him Keeper of the Great Wardrobe as well. Two other Yorkist officials employed by the new king were Thomas Roger, Clerk of the Navy to both Edward IV and Richard III, and Sir Richard Empson, who was reappointed Attorney of the Duchy of Lancaster, an office he had held between 1477 and 1483.[14] Perhaps Henry's wisest decision was to retain all twelve judges of the three great courts of common law. In this way he assured his subjects that he would respect the independence of the courts and would see to it that the law was administered fairly and impartially.

While Henry was deciding on those who would serve in his government, other important decisions had to be made. Preparations were already underway for the coronation, scheduled for 30 October; and in mid-September writs were sent out for a parliament to meet on 7 November. Once these steps had been taken, Henry established a permanent guard of archers that subsequently became known as "the Yeomen of the Guard." Although most historians hold that Henry created a totally new institution (albeit modelling it on the palace guard of Louis XI of France), there were actually numerous English precedents for it. The Plantaganet kings had normally kept a corps of guardsmen known as "the Yeomen of the Crown"; and during the 1390s Richard II had maintained a band of 312 Cheshire archers in his frantic quest for security.[15] Moreover, because Henry's guard consisted of only fifty men at first, it was on about the same scale as the armed bands employed to protect the families of great noblemen. During the years after 1500 Henry quadrupled the guard's membership and set aside £1200 annually for its maintenance. But that was relatively late in the reign, when he had become obsessively fearful for the safety of himself and his family. Those taken into this service, at least at the outset, were commoners who had joined him in exile and distinguished themselves at Bosworth. Paid at the rate of 6d. a day, they were equipped with long- and crossbows and were sworn to defend the royal family with their lives, should that ever prove necessary. They dined together as a body and, at royal expense, maintained an elaborate table, which helps to explain why they soon became known as "beefeaters." They made their first appearance on the morning of Henry's coronation.[16]

Before that time arrived Henry made another effort to pacify the realm by offering clemency to Yorkists who would come in and make peace with him. On 24 September he sent heralds into all parts of the realm to announce the grant of a general pardon. Among those who seized this unparalleled opportunity were the Earl of Lincoln, the late king's intended heir, and his father, the Duke of Suffolk. After taking the proper oaths, they were welcomed by the whole court and accorded the respect to which they felt entitled. Lincoln and his father were not the only Yorkists to swear allegiance to Henry at this juncture. Elizabeth Woodville's only surviving son, the Marquess of Dorset, returned from the continent about this time and spent several days at Westminster. Although Dorset had been left behind as a hostage for Henry's French borrowings,[17] he knew there was nothing to be gained by remaining angry, and his willingness to come to terms was gratefully acknowledged by the monarch. As for the dowager queen, whose daughter Henry intended to marry, she was received at court with all the panoply owing to one of such exalted rank. Although Henry refused to restore all the properties confiscated from her by Richard III, he reserved several manors for her maintenance and, in general, acted dutifully towards the woman who would soon be his mother-in-law. He recognized her brother Richard as third Earl Rivers and, on 16 September, appointed another of her brothers, Edward, Governor of the Isle of Wight. During subsequent months he made repeated efforts to arrange a marriage alliance between the dowager queen and James III of Scotland, whose two sons were prospective husbands for two of her daughters. Nothing came of this interesting proposal, but it was seriously discussed until June 1488, when the Scottish monarch was murdered by his rebellious subjects.[18]

On Sunday the 30th day of October Henry was at last crowned in Westminster Abbey. The coronation was a splendid affair, deliberately intended to surpass the festivities attendant on Richard III's enthronement. The preparations had been supervised by a commission headed by Bishop Courtenay and the Earls of Oxford, Pembroke, and Nottingham. No expense was spared for the occasion, with cloth of gold being purchased at the extraordinary price of £8 a yard. Purple velvet for the king's robes cost 40s. per yard and crimson satin, 16s. Ermine, sarcenet, and buckram were bought in large quantities, as were shoes and boots, saddles and spurs, swords and banners. Substantial sums were also spent for ostrich plumes, gold and silver fringe, and the dozens of bolts of red velvet needed for the hundreds of dragons and roses that served as the principal decorative motif.[19] The coronation festivities began on the preceding Thursday, when Henry elevated his uncle Jasper to the Dukedom of Bedford and conferred the Earldom of Derby on Thomas, Lord Stanley. He also created six new Knights of the Bath and handed out a few other rewards to his supporters. Then he dined at Lambeth Palace with the venerable Archbishop of Canterbury, after which he was escorted to the royal apartments in the Tower. He spent most of the next day in meditation and prayer, although he also created twelve more Knights of the Bath, who included Lord Fitzwalter, Sir Reginald Bray, and the current Lord Mayor of London, Sir Hugh Bryce.[20]

On Saturday the 29th there was a great procession through the streets of the city to Westminster, and the next day the coronation itself occurred. The sword of state was carried by Lord Derby and the jewelled Crown by Bedford, while Henry's train and spurs were borne by the Earls of Oxford and Essex, respectively. The eighty-year-old archbishop was too infirm to handle anything more than the anointing and crowning, so most of the elaborate ritual was performed by the Bishops of Durham and Ely, although it fell to Bishop Courtenay to ask the will of the people. The mass was celebrated by Bishop Kempe of London, the only person invited to sit with Henry during the banquet that followed the ceremony. Bedford served as high steward for the feast, with the Earl of Ormonde handling the duties of carver and the Earl of Arundel presiding at the cupboard. Once the first course had been brought in, Sir Robert Dymmock rode into the hall on a courser draped with red and white silk. After a lavish salute to the king, he threw down a challenge to any and all persons who wished to contest Henry's title to the throne. The second course was served, after which minstrels appeared to entertain the guests, who included the mayor and aldermen of London as well as the benchers of Chancery, the barons of both the Exchequer and the Cinque Ports, and various mitred abbots and other clerical dignitaries. Shortly before the banquet ended, the Garter King-of-Arms gave thanks for the king's largesse that day; and according to a specialist on Tudor pageantry, "one can well imagine Henry retiring that night very satisfied with his day's work." Perhaps because of the extreme length of the festivities, the tournament scheduled for the day of the coronation was postponed for two weeks.[21]

By the time the coronation tournament took place, the first parliament of the reign had opened at Westminster and Thomas Lovell, the new Treasurer of the Chamber, had been elected Speaker. The first order of business was to clarify Henry's title to the throne, which was a complicated matter owing to the fact that he had been attained by Richard III's parliament. Shortly before the session opened, Henry referred this thorny question to the twelve judges at Westminster who ruled that, because Henry had taken it upon himself to be king, his previous attainder was automatically reversed: no parliamentary act to remove the ban against him was therefore necessary. Although such a judgment may have appeared specious to most Englishmen, it actually had much to commend it. After all, high treason was by definition an act committed against the sovereign, and it would be absurd to hold that Henry, who was now recognized by almost everyone as the rightful king, had offended against himself.[22] Yet the Lords and Commons clearly had qualms about the judges' terse ruling. For even now Henry did not claim to have been the true monarch at the time he was attainted, nor had he done anything before embarking from France to suggest that he was endowed with regal powers. To accept the judges' decision as sufficient would therefore mean that almost any successful usurper would henceforth be able to demand parliamentary recognition. Accordingly, the two Houses decided to pass a declaration that would clarify and strengthen his claim to the throne. Intended to prevent future problems that might result from ambiguity, this parliamentary declaration announced that it was hereby:

. . . ordained, established, and enacted, by the authority of the present Parliament, that the inheritance of the Crowns of the realms of England and of France, with all the preeminence and dignity royal to the same pertaining . . . be, rest, remain, and abide in the most royal person of our now sovereign lord King Harry the VIIth, and in the heirs of his body lawfully coming, perpetually with the grace of God so to endure, and in none others.[23]

Parliament's declaration was passed by men so pleased with their new king that they wanted to ease his burdens in every way possible. It should be noted, however, that only eighteen of twenty-nine temporal peers summoned to the parliament of 1485 were actually present. It is also apparent that Henry was accepted because he was already a *de facto* monarch and because individuals with better hereditary claims than his had been eliminated. Yet, paradoxically, he was to succeed in reestablishing the principle of indefeasible hereditary right, which had been so grievously weakened during the preceding century. And since his time none but his direct descendants have occupied the English throne.

While settling the matter of the king's title, parliament was voting to return the estates confiscated from Lady Margaret Beaufort in 1484. The Earl of Oxford was also aided in the recovery of properties lost to the Yorkist kings, while similar restitution was made to Edward Stafford, the seven-year-old son of the late Duke of Buckingham. Yet because of the new duke's youthful age, he became a royal ward and was placed in the household of Lady Margaret Beaufort, where he remained until he came of age in 1498. His estates, worth in excess of £6000 a year, were temporarily divided between Lady Margaret and his mother, Catherine Woodville, who was soon to become the wife of Jasper Tudor.[24]

Henry naturally believed that his greatest enemies should be attainted; and since parliament was willing to concede that his reign had begun the day before Bosworth, he could logically argue that all those who had belonged to Richard's army were guilty of high treason. Yet when he proposed legislation against several dozen individuals, he provoked a storm of protest. Both chambers were anxious to bring a halt to the lawlessness of the past and to pave the way for a new era of political harmony; but on humanitarian grounds they recoiled from the idea of so many executions. For his part, Henry had to consider his own safety; and if he failed to insist on the customary action against known enemies, he might foster the notion that he was weak and irresolute. The fact that Richard III had attainted more than 100 persons during the aftermath of Buckingham's rebellion would make any laxity on his part stand out the more sharply and would encourage future plotting by making him appear uncommonly merciful. Despite strong opposition he therefore insisted that some twenty-eight men be attainted. These naturally included the late king and Norfolk as well as Surrey, Lords Ferrers, Lovell, and Zouche, and such functionaries as Catesby, Ratcliffe, and Brackenbury, many of whom were already dead. Henry is often criticized for his harshness in 1485, but it is difficult to see how he could have adopted a more sensible course, taking as he did a middle ground between great severity and undue laxity. Even after parliament grudgingly did his bidding, he continued to make overtures to the Yorkists as a way of securing their allegiance; and by 1495 all but eight of the attainders of his first parliament had been reversed.[25]

Henry was also concerned to strengthen the royal finances, which he rightly saw as the first step towards a permanent expansion of royal power. To assist him in this, parliament passed a bill authorizing him to confiscate all royal estates alienated since 2 October 1455. Had this act of resumption been passed in its original form, it would have doubled— perhaps even tripled—the landed wealth of the Crown; but in order to ensure its passage, Henry had to agree to the inclusion of 461 exceptions, which robbed it of almost all effectiveness.[26] Why then did Henry persevere and insist on its passage? Such earlier rulers as Henry IV, Edward IV, and Richard III, all of whom had deposed reigning kings, had given away large tracts of crown lands as a way of buying political support. Did Henry intend to put his subjects on notice not to expect similar grants from him? Perhaps he could recover only a fraction of the lands alienated since 1455, but at least he could alert the upper classes not to expect further grants from the royal demesne.

More important in a practical sense than the act of resumption was parliament's decision to vote Henry the customs duties for life. Apparently he did not suggest this, although he was of course grateful that the two chambers wished to make him such a grant. Richard III had been voted tunnage and poundage in 1484; but no previous king had received such a lifetime grant from his first parliament: Edward IV had been voted the duties by his *second* parliament, four years after his accession. Thus a new constitutional practice was just being established, and it seems unfair to criticize Henry for not requesting a lifetime grant of the duties in 1485, as several historians have done. At any rate, the new king derived a handsome profit from the generosity of his first parliament. His steady rule led to a strengthening of economic conditions throughout the realm and this coincided with the increasing continental demand for English wool. As a consequence England's foreign trade grew substantially during the course of the reign, causing Henry to receive more in the way of customs revenues than any of his Lancastrian or Yorkist predecessors.[27]

Because of the obvious need to reestablish order and stability, the Lords and Commons swore a special oath to abstain from certain lawless acts in the king's presence on 19 November. Such an oath was not without precedent. In 1392 an assembly of notables had pledged to commit no misdeeds in the future and to rely wholly on the courts for redress against their enemies. Similar oaths had been sworn in 1429, 1433, 1461, and on at least one other occasion during Edward IV's reign. In 1485 the Chief Justice of the King's Bench, Sir William Hussey, was particularly irate that such oaths were often broken as soon as they were taken. During a meeting of the judges before parliament opened, Hussey delivered a stern lecture on "the wickedness of taking oaths only to break them." He also warned that the laws of the realm "would never be well executed until the lords, both spiritual and temporal, combine to observe them"; and he demanded that particularly stiff penalties be imposed on upper-class criminals so that other individuals "would take warning from them."[28]

Largely because of this pressure from the Chief Justice, the members of parliament consented to abstain from such illegal acts as: (1) the sheltering of felons and hindering their arrest; (2) the granting of bail to known criminals; (3) the taking of bribes and other unlawful payments; (4) the retaining of other men in their service, either through illegal indenture or special oaths; (5) the intimidating of juries; and (6) participating in riots and other illegal assemblies. After this special oath was sworn, first by the Commons and then by the Lords, Henry directed the sheriffs to administer it to all prominent inhabitants within their jurisdictions.[29] Unhappily the oath of 1485 was no more effective than its predecessors. Henry was nevertheless determined to persevere in his campaign against lawlessness; and in 1487 he secured parliamentary authorization to establish a new tribunal, in order to strengthen the administration of justice.

Before the parliament of 1485 disbanded, several measures of lesser importance were passed. One provided for the construction of a bridge to link the Isle of Thanet with the mainland, while another required the dissolution of the Court of Requests, a tribunal that had safeguarded the interests of the poor during the Yorkist period. A precursor of the seventeenth-century Navigation Acts forbade the importation of Gascon wines in foreign-owned ships, while several measures placed restrictions on alien merchants in England, particularly those of the Hansa. To appease the king, who was devoted to the chase, unlicensed hunting in the royal forests was made a felony. Although Henry's reign would not be known for the passage of important religious legislation, a statute of 1485 authorized the bishops to punish in whatever manner they deemed suitable all clerks, priests, and others in holy orders found guilty of fornication, incest, "or any other fleshly incontinency."[30]

The last important business of the session was transacted on 10 December, just before the prorogation was announced. Once the members had assembled in Henry's presence, the Speaker presented a petition passed by the Commons. As discreetly as possible the king was reminded of his promise to marry Elizabeth of York. The crowns of England and France had now been settled on him and the heirs of his body, so it was high time for him to honor his pledge to unite the claims of Lancaster and York. After the petition of the lower House had been delivered, the lords spiritual and temporal rose in their place and unanimously acceded to it. Thereupon Henry made a gracious speech and declared anew his intention of marrying the chief heiress of York.[31]

Most historians are baffled by Henry's slowness to honor the pledge he had made at Rennes Cathedral two years earlier. Professor Chrimes suggests that the king probably wished to make Elizabeth's acquaintance before rushing into matrimony with her. Because contact between them was impossible before Bosworth and difficult while the initial decisions of the reign were requiring so much of his time, the marriage was of necessity delayed.[32] R. L. Storey emphasizes, however, that both Henry and his intended wife were descended from John of Gaunt, which meant that their relationship fell within the prohibited degree of consanguinity. Shortly after Bosworth application was made to Rome for a dispensation that would allow them to marry, but not until 16 January 1486 did Henry learn from the papal legate to the British Isles, the Bishop of Imola, that Innocent VIII intended to grant the dispensation; and only two days later the marriage took place, with Archbishop Bourchier officiating.[33]

It is no longer fashionable to maintain, as almost all historians until recent times did, that Henry wanted to delay the marriage in order to establish the idea that he owed the throne only to himself and not to the position of his wife. Yet there still seems to be some validity to such a proposition, if not for quite the same reasons given by earlier writers. Historians of the late nineteenth and early twentieth centuries stressed the fact that Henry was a forceful man who would never agree to be his wife's "gentleman usher." Consequently he had to emphasize his own claim to the throne, in order to keep the reins of power in his own hands. Such an explanation now seems specious, for women of the period were invariably dominated by their husbands, and Henry would naturally make the most important decisions for his wife, even if he were only her consort. Nevertheless Henry did have a valid reason for wanting to postpone his marriage to Elizabeth of York. Had their marriage been solemnized before the coronation or while his first parliament was in session, there would doubtless have been confusion in the public mind, with many people believing that he owed the throne to his wife. This would have been extraordinarily dangerous for him since Elizabeth's four sisters—Cecily, Anne, Catherine, and Bridget—would undoubtedly marry and have children one day. If the queen's sisters were thought capable of transmitting a claim to the throne, pretenders might eventually abound in all corners of the realm, particularly if Henry and Elizabeth had no sons of their own. Thus the only rational course was to deny that any heiress of York, even the king's intended wife, had an inherent right to the throne; and this naturally compelled him to delay the wedding and stress the sufficiency of his own claim.

That such considerations predominated in Henry's thinking in 1485-86 can be seen from his subsequent actions. Although contracted for political reasons, his marriage to Elizabeth of York soon proved to be uncommonly successful. Almost a decade younger than her husband, Elizabeth was tall and fair, with long golden hair. Not only was she strikingly attractive, but she was "intelligent above all others," at least in the opinion of Polydore Vergil.[34] Because of the queen's breeding and common sense, she was content to remain in the background and never meddled in political affairs. In short, Elizabeth proved to be an ideal consort for her husband, who soon began to dote on her. Furthermore, she did not fail in her wifely duty to provide him with a succession of children, and, as early as September 1486, she was delivered of a son, Arthur, whose name emphasized his Welsh descent. Despite Henry's obvious satisfaction with his wife, he refused to allow her to be crowned until almost two years had elapsed: her coronation did not occur until 25 November 1487. It is inconceivable that Henry, who was normally so considerate of others, would have postponed his wife's coronation for so long a time, at the risk of offending and possibly dishonoring her, without a good political reason for doing so. And the only convincing explanation is that he was still concerned to stress his own claim and deny that of the queen and her sisters.

Henry's treatment of his four sisters-in-law confirms that this was indeed his strategy. Until July 1488 he hoped to arrange for two of them to marry into the royal House of Scotland, so they would be safely out of the realm. But the battle of Sauchieburn, followed by James III's murder and the accession of the anti-English James IV, wrecked that plan and caused Henry to conclude that he must dispose of them within England. Bridget was persuaded to enter Dartford priory, where she lived as a nun until midway into the reign of Henry VIII. Catherine was betrothed to William, Lord Courtenay, eldest son of the Earl of Devon, one of Henry's strongest supporters; while Cecily became the wife of John, Lord Welles, step-uncle to the king and a trusted comrade-in-arms. The last sister, Anne, was married in February 1495 to Thomas, Lord Howard, eldest son of the Earl of Surrey, who had gained the king's confidence by 1489, when he was released from the Tower and granted extensive powers in the North. Thus all four sisters were disposed of in such a way that neither they nor their children would pose a threat to the new dynasty.[35]

While taking these steps to safeguard his young House, Henry was establishing ceremonial guidelines for his court. By most present-day readers he is remembered as a grudging and parsimonious king who was more concerned to amass great wealth than to enjoy whatever spendable income he had. Such was true of only his last six years, however, for during the greater part of the reign he stressed the importance of pageantry and ceremonial. He was well aware that his subjects expected him to look and act the part of a powerful monarch and to preside over a court that excited wonder and admiration. In an age before the Crown had a standing army or police force, it was imperative that the king use other means to maintain his rule. As a consequence Henry was careful to dress appropriately and to project an attitude of confidence and security. In a dispatch written several years after Bosworth, the Milanese ambassador gave the following description of his appearance during a recent audience at Woodstock: "His Majesty, in addition to his wonderful presence, was adorned with a most rich collar, full of great pearls and many other jewels in four rows, and in his bonnet he had a great pear-shaped pearl, which seemed to me something most rich."[36] Only a few weeks later Henry conversed with a new ambassador from Venice, who subsequently informed his government that he had been received "in a small hall, hung with handsome tapestry." The king was dressed in "a violet colored gown, lined with cloth of gold, and a collar of many jewels, and on his cap was a large diamond and a most beautiful pearl." As they conversed Henry leaned casually against "a tall gilt chair, covered with cloth of gold"; and once the ambassador was dismissed, he paid his respects to the queen, "whom he found at the end of a hall, dressed in cloth of gold."[37]

For the first fifteen years of the reign, Henry revelled in the pomp and majesty of his position, which was probably inevitable owing to the privations he had suffered between 1471 and 1485. His marriage to Elizabeth of York was solemnized with a grandeur exceeded only by that of the coronation. Equally elaborate festivities occurred when he finally allowed his wife to be crowned in the Abbey and at the time Prince Arthur was baptised in Winchester Cathedral by Bishop Alcock. Neither was any expense spared in November 1489 for the ceremony that marked Arthur's investiture as Prince of Wales and Earl of Chester, nor at the time Arthur was made a Knight of the Garter in May 1491.[38]

A particularly lavish ceremony occurred on All Hallows Day 1494, when the king's second son, Prince Henry, who had been born at Greenwich in 1491, was created Duke of York. On that occasion the king appeared in his finest robes, with the crown of state squarely upon his head, and "the trumpets did blare forth with out the cloister gallery." Both his wife and his mother were included in the royal party, which also consisted of Cardinal Morton, the Archbishop of York (who was not in his ceremonial vestments, however), the Dukes of Bedford and Buckingham, the Marquess of Dorset, and a great retinue of earls, lesser peers, knights, and influential commoners. Henry marked the occasion by knighting thirty-three men, after which his private secretary, Oliver King, read aloud the patent of the prince's creation. A high mass was then celebrated in the Chapel Royal by eight of the bishops. Jousting and other amusements were held later in the day for the thousands of onlookers who had gathered in expectation. That these festivities extended over a three-day period suggests that Henry not only valued but also enjoyed the tournaments and other spectacles that he staged from time to time, although it is also true that he usually remained on the sidelines and rarely took an active part in them.[39]

Henry also liked to give periodic banquets to which hundreds of persons might be invited. According to Polydore Vergil, his hospitality was always "splendidly generous," while another European visitor maintained that he kept "a sumptuous table, as I had the opportunity of witnessing twice . . . when I judged that there might be from 600 to 700 persons at dinner."[40] During the Christmas revels of 1493-4, Henry held a particularly lavish feast at Westminster to which the Lord Mayor and numerous other dignitaries of the capital were invited. The Great Hall was hung with rich Arras tapestries, and an elaborate masque was performed by twenty-four ladies and gentlemen of the court. Immediately afterwards the king's table was set with sixty dishes "of divers confections, and the Queen[was served] with as many, and the Mayor and his brethren with twenty-four."[41]

Henry had a great love of sports and games and competed regularly at tennis, chess, cards, and dice. Because he hoped to perpetuate the legendary skills of England's archers, he persuaded two of his parliaments to pass legislation freezing the price of longbows and creating obstacles to the increasing use of crossbows. He enjoyed bullbaiting and cockfighting, but his greatest passion was for the chase, which caused him to prefer a country life and to maintain a stable of fine horses. He also had a large kennel of spaniels and greyhounds, and, because he liked to hawk as well as hunt, he kept a number of falcons and other birds of prey. Yet his favorite pet was a spider monkey, which amused a group of courtiers one day by destroying the memoranda book in which he kept notes about both personal and governmental matters, which is evidence in itself of his rather methodical nature.[42]

Despite his fondness for physical activities and elaborate amusements, Henry was a quiet man with an obvious intellectual bent. He had a deep love of books and established a palace library at Sheen, which he stocked with richly bound works in Latin, French, and English. Such European-born scholars as Pietro Carmeliano, who served as his first Latin Secretary, benefited from his generous patronage, as did a number of accomplished poets, including Bernard André and John Skelton. He employed a band of minstrels and gave handsome rewards to those who composed ballads and quatrains for their use. He twice rewarded Robert Fayrfax, one of the best composers of the age, with payments of £20 each.[43] His account books show that he made periodic purchases of flutes, organs, and other musical instruments for his favorite palaces and castles. Certainly he never employed as many court musicians as his granddaughter Elizabeth I, who kept between sixty and seventy musicians on her payroll. But he did utilize a sizable band of musicians, among whom one of the most prominent was the celebrated singer William Cornish, who in 1502 received 13s. 4d. " 'for setting of a carral upon Christmas Day.' "[44]

Henry's devotion to architecture was as great as his love of music. With his friends Sir Reginald Bray and Bishop Alcock of Worcester, he was an important patron of the kingdom's artisans and workmen. He favored the perpendicular, or late Gothic, style, which reached its optimum development about this time, and donated large sums for the completion of the great new chapel at King's College, Cambridge, which had begun half a century earlier by Henry VI. He made extensive renovations to Baynard's Castle, the London residence of the Plantaganet kings; and he enlarged and modernized the Placentia Palace at Greenwich, which had originally been constructed by Humphrey, Duke of Goucester and subsequently became a favorite retreat of both Henry VIII and Elizabeth I. When the old palace at Sheen was destroyed by fire at Christmas 1497, he set to work immediately and built a much finer dwelling, which he renamed Richmond and took four years to complete. The Great Hall of the new palace was 100 feet in length, while the enclosed gallery, which set the style for aristocratic country houses during the next two centuries, was twice as long. In January 1502 he began the construction of his masterpiece, the majestic extension to the eastern end of Westminster Abbey, which was completed only a few weeks before his death and in which both he and his wife were buried.[45]

Although poorly educated in a formal sense, and with an incomplete knowledge of Latin that was unique to his dynasty, Henry was nevertheless a man of sound intellect and judgment. His approach to politics and government was invariably sensible and rationalistic, and, according to Bacon, his subjects were deeply impressed by his wisdom, "whereof everyone stands in awe." Diligent and hardworking, he selected his ministers with great care and forethought; and in the view of his first biographer, "he was not afraid of an able man, as Lewis the Eleventh [of France] was; but contrariwise, he was served by the ablest men that were to be found, without which his affairs could not have prospered as they did."[46] Less affected by flattery than most men, the king inquired of the Bishop of Meath one morning how he regarded a complimentary address just delivered by a new foreign ambassador. " 'There was no fault in it,' answered the bishop, 'except that it praised your Majesty too much.' "

" 'Truly,' said the king, 'we were of that opinion ourselves.' "[47] Perhaps it was such honesty and candor, along with the freedom he gave his ministers to express their true opinions, that inspired Bacon's encomium to his life and work—"a wonder for wise men."

III

Conspiracies and the Council

Within a few weeks of his marriage to Elizabeth of York, Henry decided to make a progress through the Midlands and the North. Such a journey was likely to be hazardous, for Yorkist feeling was still strong throughout the region. The city of York had long been a centre of resistance to the Lancastrians, and, on learning the outcome of Bosworth, the municipal authorities had passed a declaration stating that Richard III, "late mercifully reigning upon us, was through great treason . . . piteously slain and murdered, to the great heaviness of this City." It is possible, as Professor Kendall once suggested, that the local burgesses might have risen in favor of the Earl of Lincoln had Henry not circulated a false report of his death shortly after Bosworth.[1]

A journey into Yorkshire would therefore be a hazardous undertaking, but Henry was not without courage and knew he must not let the sullen opposition of his enemies continue as a malignant growth within the body politic. Fortunately for the prospects of such a journey, Miles Metcalfe, Recorder of York and leader of the Yorkist irreconcilables, died in February 1486. So alarmed had Henry been about the intrigues of Metcalfe and his brother Thomas, Richard III's Chancellor of the Duchy, that he had exempted both men from the general pardon granted the late king's other supporters. Since October 1485 Henry had repeatedly urged the Common Council of York to discharge Miles Metcalfe from his post, but it had ignored all his directives. Thus, when the Recorder's death became known in London, Henry was greatly heartened and concluded it was as safe as it might ever be to begin his northern progress.[2]

Because his wife was already pregnant, Henry decided it would be too risky to take her along, although her presence might have been a deterrent to his enemies. Henry and Elizabeth said their farewells to one another about the beginning of March, and he then proceeded by way of Waltham to Cambridge, where he received a joyous welcome. After spending several days in the university town, he passed through Huntingdon and Stamford before entering the gates of Lincoln, where he observed Easter in time-honored fashion. He attended mass and even-song each day during Holy Week and, while distributing alms, washed the feet of a poor beggar for each of his twenty-nine years. Before resuming his journey he heard disquieting reports that Francis, Lord Lovell and two other avowed enemies, Humphrey Stafford and his brother Thomas, had escaped from sanctuary at Colchester and disappeared. Whether they intended to lead an insurrection against him was not immediately apparent. Henry refused to heed suggestions that he return straightaway to London, but he took the precaution of summoning his uncle Jasper and the Earl of Northumberland, who soon arrived with their retainers and bolstered his escort by several thousand men.[3]

The wisdom of securing reinforcements was underscored when Henry arrived at Nottingham and learned that a rebellion was underway between Middleham Castle and Ripon. He was also informed that the Stafford brothers were planning an assault on Worcester, which they hoped to capture and use as a citadel against him. Once he reached Pontefract the reports became gloomier still: Lovell, it was said, expected to enter York from the north and raise the local citizenry against him. These rumors soon proved unfounded, however, for the rebels were unable to enlist more than a few hundred adherents. It was widely known that they had been attainted by the parliament of 1485, although they loudly insisted that they had secured pardons, displaying forged letters patent to that purpose.[4]

On 22 April Henry at last entered his northern capital. Dressed in ermine and cloth of gold, he was attended by a number of bishops, lords, knights, and influential commoners. Although he had been warned to expect a cold reception, he was greeted at Tadcaster Bridge, the southern limit of the York franchises, by a delegation of aldermen, the two sheriffs, and twice their usual complement of twenty horsemen. At Micklegate Bar, the main gate to the city proper, an elaborate pageant was staged in his honor. The mayor's welcoming speech included not only the customary assurances of loyalty but also "explicit disclaimers of other allegiances and even of anti-Henrician activity prior to Bosworth Field." Doubtless Henry was not deceived by such patent falsehoods but was not displeased to hear the city fathers make them. The way from Micklegate Bar to Ouse Bridge was hung with rich cloths in compliance with an order given by the Common Council. After crossing the river, the procession turned left into Cony Street and arrived at the Guildhall, where another pageant took place.[5]

After several days in York Henry sent his uncle Jasper off to confront Lord Lovell and his motley supporters. As the duke moved northward he announced his nephew's willingness to pardon all those who submitted immediately, which prompted most of the viscount's men to lay down their arms. Lovell had no option but to flee and took refuge with Sir Thomas Broughton, leader of the Yorkist diehards in Lancashire. Later he was hidden by friends in the Isle of Ely, but ultimately he sailed across the Channel to the Hainault city of Tournai, where Margaret of Burgundy, widow of Duke Charles the Bold and a sister of the two Yorkist kings, had her court. According to Polydore Vergil, Margaret "cherished such a deep hatred of King Henry, that it seemed she would be content with nothing short of his death." Consequently her palace became, in Bacon's notable phrase, "a sanctuary and receptacle of all traitors against the king."[6]

Once Jasper Tudor returned with word of Lovell's flight, Henry seized the initiative and marched against the Stafford brothers and their followers at Worcester. As he neared the city the rebels broke camp and fled, obtaining sanctuary with the abbot of Culham, in Oxfordshire. By this juncture Henry had decided to challenge the church's right to serve as a refuge for traitors against him. On his orders the Stafford brothers were removed from the monastery on 13 May and transported to Westminster, where they were tried before the King's Bench. Although the abbot of Culham appeared on 28 June to plead for the sanctuary rights of his monastery, which dated from the eighth century, the king was determined to make an example of the two brothers. Yet the judges had qualms about what they were expected to do; and only after lengthy deliberations in the Exchequer Chamber did they rule that sanctuary was not pleadable in such cases, since treason was a common-law offense over which no spiritual agency, not even the papacy, had jurisdiction. Only the king could pardon treason, so sanctuary offered nothing more than temporary protection in such cases. Early in July Humphrey Stafford was executed at Tyburn, although Henry relented at the last minute and commuted the sentence of Thomas Stafford on the grounds that he had been corrupted by his elder brother. During subsequent weeks several of the Staffords' closest associates were condemned by tribunals at Worcester and Birmingham, over which Henry maintained a careful watch throughout.[7]

Although most historians criticize Henry for infringing the rights of the church, he had no recourse unless he was prepared for dangerous rebels to remain at large. Furthermore the pope understood the reasons for his actions and refused to take umbrage. On 6 August Innocent VIII issued "a very just and honorable bull" in which he condemned the most common abuses associated with sanctuary. Henceforth church property could be watched closely so that, at the end of forty days, suspected traitors would automatically fall into the hands of royal officials. Moreover, suspected felons who emerged from sanctuary only to commit additional crimes could be forcibly removed from their refuge and would never be entitled to the privilege of sanctuary again. Early the next year the pope took further action and decreed that sanctuary would no longer be allowed to fraudulent debtors. Henry was delighted by Innocent's strong support of his action; and he quickly dispatched the Bishop of Hereford and nine other emissaries to tender his thanks and make a formal offer of his homage and allegiance.[8]

Meanwhile Henry had completed the first progress of his reign. He departed from Worcester the morning after Whitsunday and, on nearing Hereford, received a gracious welcome from the mayor and his horsemen. The municipal officials had commissioned three pageants in his honor, all of which were "comparatively flat and ordinary," however. From Hereford he travelled on to Gloucester, where only simple festivities on his behalf were staged, and thence to Bristol, on the outskirts of which he was met by the sheriff and a vast throng of citizens on horseback. After several days of lavish entertainments there, he rode eastward to Sheen, where he took a royal barge back to the capital. He arrived in London on 5 June, exactly a month after a violent demonstration against his government occurred. Early in May a group of malcontents armed with standards reminiscent of an earlier time gathered at Westminster to proclaim their dissatisfaction with recent events. When they were unable to storm the palace, they rode off to Highbury, hoping to overwhelm a royal contingent encamped there. Nothing came of this affair, but it shows how, almost a year after Bosworth, there were still periodic disturbances, even in the Home Counties.[9]

During the summer of 1486 Henry enjoyed a badly needed respite of peace and contentment, and on 20 September he was delighted by the birth of his son Arthur at Winchester. But his cup of tranquility was not yet filled to overflowing, for rumors of another and more dangerous plot against him were soon in the air. As early as November observers were predicting that more would soon be heard of the Earl of Warwick, only son of the late Duke of Clarence and thus a nephew of the two Yorkist kings. The Lovell and Stafford plots had revealed the futility of conspiring against Henry without having a possible Yorkist replacement for him. And that replacement could only be the premier male representative of the White Rose faction, which meant that the sickly Earl of Warwick would have to be put forward, if only to be eliminated at a later time. Such apparently were the conclusions of John de la Pole, Earl of Lincoln, Richard III's favorite nephew and intended heir. Lincoln and his father, the Duke of Suffolk, had made their peace with Henry the previous autumn, having been among the eighteen peers who took the parliamentary oath of 19 November to abstain from illegal acts. But the glittering prospect of the throne was something that Lincoln could not renounce altogether, and during the winter of 1486–87 he laid the basis for a new conspiracy.

Henry had incarcerated Warwick in the Tower shortly after Bosworth, and Lincoln probably assumed that his young cousin had been murdered, just as the two sons of Edward IV had been killed during the summer of 1483. Certainly it was not altogether fanciful for Lincoln to conclude that Warwick's earthly existence had been terminated, since no one had been allowed to see him for a year or more. At any rate Lincoln began to search for someone to impersonate his cousin, someone of the right age and demeanor, for whom a miraculous escape from the Tower could be claimed. Exactly when Lincoln made contact with Richard Symonds, a 28-year-old clerical resident of Oxford, is unclear, although it was probably a known Yorkist troublemaker, Bishop Stillington of Bath and Wells, also a resident of the university town, who served as the intermediary between them. What is certain is that Symonds had a protégé, a lad of eleven or twelve by the name of Lambert Simnel, whom he had long tutored. Simnel was a precocious boy; and although he was of comparatively low birth, his father having worked as a cobbler, baker, and organ-builder, he had acquired a graceful and cultivated air. Symonds suspected that he might be able to use his charge one day to advance his own career; and because he aspired to a bishopric, he first thought of portraying Simnel as one of the Princes of the Tower. When he learned of Lincoln's search for someone to impersonate Warwick, Symonds quickly altered his plan so it would accord with the earl's scheme.

Once they began to conspire together, Lincoln and Symonds agreed that their charge should be taken to Ireland, where Yorkist feeling was still quite strong. The father of the two Yorkist kings, that Richard of York who had died in 1460, had been an exceptionally popular Lord Lieutenant of Ireland during the 1440s and 1450s, largely because his preoccupation with English politics had led him to grant virtual self-government to the Irish people. In 1450 he did nothing to prevent the Irish parliament from passing a declaration that it alone could legislate for Ireland. Consequently memories of Richard of York lived on long after he and his two kingly sons were dead; and as Lincoln correctly predicted, someone claiming to be Richard's grandson and rightful heir would be strongly supported by the Irish people.[10]

When the imposter, accompanied by Symonds and several of Lincoln's retainers, landed at Dublin in January 1487, he was hailed by crowds that included several of the magnates of the land. Among these were most of the bishops and, more importantly, Gerald Fitzgerald, eighth Earl of Kildare. Since 1479 Kildare had held the great office of Lord Deputy, while his brother Thomas had been Lord Chancellor nearly as long. Yet it was because of his family connections that Kildare was the most powerful man in Ireland. Through his mother Joan, daughter of the seventh Earl of Desmond, he was closely related to the Fitzgeralds of Munster, who dominated the eastern sections of Kerry and much of western Cork. His first wife, Alice Fitz-Eustace, who lived until 1495, was a daughter of Roland Fitz-Eustace, Lord Portlester, who had served as Lord Treasurer of Ireland since 1454; while his sister Eleanor was married to Conn More O'Neill, greatest of the Ulster chieftains. Kildare also had close ties with the O'Donnells of Ulster and the O'Hanlons of northern Leinster. He himself controlled the southern and central parts of the latter province; and from his stronghold at Maynooth, several miles west of Dublin, he exerted a powerful influence over every facet of Irish life and politics.[11]

Although a man of great natural ability, Kildare was apparently rather gullible and seems to have been persuaded with little or no effort that Simnel was the real Earl of Warwick. He therefore took the imposter under his wing and gave him invaluable assistance. Yet not all the Irish lords followed Kildare's lead. The Archbishop of Armagh and the Bishop of Clogher refused to have anything to do with the conspiracy; and in Waterford and Kilkenny, Simnel faced concerted opposition from the Butlers, Kildare's bitterest rivals. However, with the support of "the Geraldines," as the two branches of the Fitzgerald family were known, the imposter and his mentors were able to organize an elaborate plot. Messengers were sent across the Channel to England to secure pledges of assistance from Sir Thomas Broughton and other Yorkist diehards in Lancashire, while Sir Thomas Bodrugan promised to raise Cornwall and Devonshire at the appropriate moment. Even Elizabeth Woodville and the Marquess of Dorset were drawn into the web of intrigue. Henry had treated his mother-in-law and her son considerately, but they were nevertheless dissatisfied with their lot, since they lacked real influence at court. An emissary was also dispatched to Tournai, where Viscount

Lovell had been living for some months as a pensioner of Margaret of Burgundy. Lovell was delighted to learn of the new conspiracy, while Margaret at once agreed to provide substantial aid. She raised 2000 mercenaries under the command of Martin Schwartz, a German soldier-of-fortune, to whom she pledged further assistance, should that prove necessary.[12]

Before Schwartz and his men could embark for Ireland, Henry learned of the plot and took effective countermeasures. In February 1487 he summoned a number of prelates, lords, and rich commoners to meet with him and the Council at Sheen. There he secured approval for immediate action against Elizabeth Woodville, who was stripped of her estates and incarcerated in Bermondsey Abbey, where she lived on an annuity of 400 marks until her death in 1492. As for the Marquess of Dorset, he was detained on suspicion of treason and kept under close surveillance, although he was not actually punished until several more years elapsed.[13] In order to demonstrate the absurd nature of the Simnel plot, Henry paraded the real Earl of Warwick through the streets of London on 19 February. On that day Warwick was taken from the Tower to St. Paul's Cathedral, where convocation was in session and he was immediately recognized. After attending mass he conversed with several leading courtiers, including his cousin Lincoln, who must have been startled by this development.

Subsequently Henry directed the coastal officials to arrest anyone seeking passage to Flanders or Ireland without good reason. In addition he sent Christopher Urswick to survey the ports of Lancashire to determine whether they were capable of handling such transport ships as might come from Ireland. Early in March Henry was particularly anxious to interrogate Bishop Stillington, whom he suspected of abetting the conspiracy. Shortly after Bosworth he had granted the bishop a free pardon for his past activities; but he had remained suspicious of Stillington's loyalty and in 1486 required the Yorkist to post a bond of £1000 as security for his future actions. By the spring of 1487 Henry was convinced that the bishop was involved in the new conspiracy and had probably served as the liaison between Symonds and Lincoln. He therefore ordered Stillington to appear before him, which caused the prelate to go into hiding. On 14 March Henry sent an armed band to Oxford to arrest him and any others who had "conveyed him from place to place and hid him." Despite threats about a possible loss of their privileges, the university authorities refused to hand him over, maintaining in their defense that Stillington was afraid of being assassinated on the way to the capital. Eventually the bishop fell into the hands of Henry's agents, who questioned him at length and then imprisioned him at Windsor. How long he remained in captivity is unclear, although by May 1489 he was again in residence at Dogmersfield, his episcopal palace south of London.[14]

By mid-March it must have been apparent to most observers that Henry was in command of the situation and was unlikely to be overthrown. But the conspirators were too deeply involved to think of turning back and, moreover, there were remarkably few cool heads among their ranks. Shortly after Warwick's appearance at St. Paul's Cathedral, Lincoln eluded the watch on the ports and sailed for the continent. On his arrival at Tournai he convinced his aunt, the dowager duchess, that the plan must go forward, despite the increasingly heavy odds against it; so the outfitting of Schwartz's troops continued, and late in April they at last set sail for Ireland. After a voyage of about a week, they landed at Dublin on 5 May, where they were greeted by the imposter, the priest Symonds, and the Earls of Kildare and Desmond. Within a few days they decided that Simnel should be crowned as King Edward VI; and during a ceremony in Christ Church Cathedral on 24 May, a jewelled wreath borrowed from a nearby statue of the Virgin Mary was placed on his head. The "coronation sermon" was preached by John Payne, Bishop of Meath; and when the time came for "Edward VI" to be shown to the crowd, he was hoisted onto the shoulders of Darcy of Platten, the tallest Irishman of the age. Once the ceremony ended Simnel was escorted through the streets of Dublin to the castle, where a feast in his honor was held.[15]

Kildare, who was now widely regarded as "tutor and protector" to the imposter, summoned a parliament to meet, which at once recognized Simnel as the rightful king. About the same time a council of war met and laid plans for an invasion of England. Thomas Fitzgerald resigned the Great Seal so he could go along, but Kildare manufactured reasons to stay behind. On 4 June an armada of sorts set sail from Howth, and the next day it landed on the Lancashire coast near Furness. Commanded by Lincoln, Lovell, and Schwartz, the imposter's troops were immediately joined by Sir Thomas Broughton and fifty other horsemen, although Broughton's efforts to raise the entire region had failed.

As soon as Henry learned of the imposter's landing, he set out from Norwich, where he had been keeping watch over the eastern ports, for the Midlands. On reaching Kenilworth he summoned his most trusted supporters to join him immediately at Coventry; and within a few more days he was able to march northward with 4000 men. Once he arrived at Nottingham his army was bolstered by the arrival of 5000 troops under George, Lord Strange, eldest son of the Earl of Derby; and shortly afterwards a Welsh contingent captained by Rhys ap Thomas rode in. Henry now had a numerical superiority of at least two to one; and in addition his two main generals, Bedford and Oxford, were considerably more experienced than their rebel counterparts. It is apparent, too, that Henry's troops were far better armed and equipped. Neither were they beset by the numerous problems that inevitably confront a multi-national force, such as the one they would soon be facing. All in all, the advantages were squarely on Henry's side, and only blunders of a colossal kind would keep his cause from prevailing.

The king refused to leave anything to chance, however; and once he learned that his enemies were moving southward by an easterly and not by the principal westerly route, he evacuated Nottingham for Radcliffe, so he would be in a position to march up the Fosseway and halt their progress. At first Lincoln seems to have planned a lightning march for the walled safety of York, but such a maneuver would expose his flank to crossfire from the Earl of Northumberland's men. He therefore set out for Southwell, where, on 15 June, he wheeled eastward and crossed the Trent at Fiskerton Ford, several miles below Newark. That night he pitched his camp along a ridge crossed by the Fosseway, by which Henry's troops were now rapidly advancing.[16]

On 16 June the battle of Stoke, the last real encounter of the Wars of the Roses, occurred. A little before 9 A.M. the vanguard of the royal army, commanded by Oxford, marched up from the south to engage the rebels, who occupied a strong position on Rampire Hill overlooking the river. Because Henry refused to commit more than half his men to the fray, the battle was fought by armies of approximately equal size. It was a stiff encounter lasting three hours or more. Fighting began when Oxford's line reached the foot of the hill and Lincoln gave the signal to attack. In the first turbulent moments of the engagement, when the rebels rushed down the slopes to throw themselves on their enemies, the royal vanguard was severely shaken. But the center of the king's line did not crumble; reinforcements were quickly brought up to stiffen its resistance; and the superiority of Henry's armor and weaponry soon revealed itself. During the course of the fighting, Lincoln, Schwartz, and Sir Thomas Broughton perished, as did nearly 4000 of the men they had brought with them. Thomas Fitzgerald also died on the field, but Symonds and the Bishop of Meath were captured, while Lord Lovell was never seen again: probably he drowned while fording the Trent in his heavy breastplate, although legend holds that he starved to death after hiding and being walled up in the cellar of his house at Minster Lovell. The king's losses were almost as

great as those of the rebel host. Yet his two commanders, Bedford and
Oxford, survived the engagement unscathed; and shortly after the fighting
ended, the imposter fell into his hands.[17]

Henry was naturally elated by his victory, believing it signified there
was no longer cause to worry for the safety of his throne. Once the tumult
ended he handed out more generous rewards than usual. Thirteen new
bannerets were created, while fifty-two of his partisans were knighted,
including Thomas Lovell, Chancellor of the Exchequer and Treasurer of
the Chamber.[18] When the imposter and his advisers were brought before
him, Henry demonstrated the remarkable clemency of which he was
capable. Because Simnel was a poor innocent whose actions had been
guided by others, the king spared his life and ordered that he be given
employment in his kitchens. The would-be monarch became a scullion,
although he occasionally waited upon Henry above stairs, especially when
the latter wanted to impress visiting dignitaries. In later years Simnel
became a falconer, and for the remainder of his life he was a devoted
servant of the Crown. Symonds, who had done so much to foment the
conspiracy, was thrown into a dungeon, where he languished for several
decades. How long he lived, and whether he ever recovered his freedom,
are questions yet to be answered by historical investigation. When the
Bishop of Meath was brought in, he grovelled and begged pitifully for his
life. Because Henry was willing to allow most men one serious offense,
and because the bishop had no record of previous disloyalty, he granted
him a full pardon. That such clemency was not misplaced was proved by
the bishop's subsequent behavior, for he quickly became one of Henry's
staunchest adherents. As for the other survivors of Stoke Field, several
dozen were hanged, although the gibbets were not nearly so busy as after
most rebellions. Many of those who had fought on Simnel's behalf were
required to pay with their purses rather than with their lives, for with
faultless logic Henry argued that they had been the cause of his recent
expenditure, and a number of heavy fines were therefore assessed.

In regard to Ireland, where the limitations of royal power now stood
clearly exposed, Henry had some difficult decisions to make. If he
attempted to punish every Irishman who had rallied to Simnel's cause, he
might provoke a rebellion encompassing the whole island. But if he took
no steps whatever, he would foster the notion that he was completely
without resources and that his Irish subjects could plot against him in
perfect safety. On 5 July 1487 he therefore requested that the pope
excommunicate all Irish clerics who had participated in the imposter's
coronation. Innocent VIII was as anxious as ever to cooperate with the
English monarch, and in January 1488 he issued the requested bull.

Before that time arrived Henry publicly commended the loyalty of the burghers of Waterford, who had repulsed a lengthy siege by Desmand and the Geraldines. In his dispatch of 20 October 1487, the king also directed the Common Council of Waterford to take energetic measures against Kildare and to apprehend " 'as many of our said rebels as ye shall attain unto by sea and land, with all manner of their ships, goods, and merchandise, as ye shall find to be carried or conveyed . . . to our said city of Dublin, and to the parts thereabouts.' "[19]

Henry's action caused Kildare, who desperately wanted to continue as Lord Deputy, to send conciliatory letters to London in an effort to explain away his support of the imposter. Although Henry was not deceived by Kildare's protestations, he knew there was no alternative to continued reliance upon the earl, since no one else was capable of maintaining a semblance of law and order in Ireland. Therefore, after a delay of several months in order to cause Kildare some nervousness, Henry wrote to inform the earl that, while he would be severely reprimanded for his past conduct, he would be granted a full pardon in the end, provided he swore to behave himself in the future. Late in May 1488 Henry sent a special emissary, Sir Richard Edgecombe, to Ireland to treat for " 'the sound rule of peace . . . and to administer oaths of fealty and allegiance, and to imprison rebels and traitors.' " With a force of some 500 men, Edgecombe landed at Kinsale on 27 June and at once accepted submissions from Viscount Barry, Lord de Courcy, and thirty-seven others. Then he journeyed to Waterford, pardoning along the way all those who came in and swore allegiance, and thence to Dublin, where he received a warm welcome from the mayor and various other dignitaries. Yet Kildare refused to appear for almost a week and ultimately demanded that the king's emissary confer with him at his house outside the walls of Dublin. The Englishman reluctantly agreed, and on 12 July he was received by the Deputy and 200 heavily armed retainers in the Great Hall of St. Thomas Court. After two days of negotiations, which culminated in the delivery of Kildare's pardon, the earl returned to his stronghold at Maynooth, where he entertained Edgecombe two days later. The Englishman urged Kildare to visit Henry in England, at either Westminster or Sheen, but the Irishman responded that nothing could induce him to leave his native land. Neither would he give a bond for his future behavior, as Edgecombe was pressing him to do. After a few additional days in Dublin, the king's emissary rode north to Drogheda, where he accepted submissions from a delegation of Ulster landowners. Once forty or so of them had treated with him, he ruled that his work of pacification had succeeded, and on 30 July he and his men sailed back to England.[20]

Meanwhile, on the 9th of the previous November, the second parliament of the reign had opened at Westminster. This was but six days after Henry's return to the capital from northern England. During the weeks following the encounter at Stoke, the king paid a second visit to York, where he knighted the Lord Mayor and enjoyed sumptuous entertainments. After a round of talks with local dignitaries, whose loyalty he was more hopeful than ever of securing, he visited Pontefract, Durham, Newcastle, and Ripon in turn. Once he was reasonably sure of his acceptance throughout the region, he returned to London, where on 3 November he knighted the Lord Mayor and Recorder, William Horn and Thomas FitzWilliam, respectively.[21]

Henry's second parliament, which remained in session until 18 December, was called primarily to handle the problems resulting from the Simnel conspiracy. John Morton, who was now Archbishop of Canterbury as well as Lord Chancellor, delivered the opening sermon on the text: "Depart from evil and do good; speak peace and pursue it."[22] The king's nominee for Speaker, John Mordaunt, a barrister of the Middle Temple who had distinguished himself at Stoke, was duly elected, after which a government spokesman called for the attainder of twenty-eight leaders of the plot. Whether there was any opposition to this proposal, comparable to the resistance that had materialized during the previous parliament, is unclear. Probably there was not, for Henry had demonstrated both his political mastery and his exceptional fairness during the past year, while the men who had fought against him at Stoke were clearly more guilty of treason than those who had opposed him at Bosworth. In addition Archbishop Morton, one of Henry's closest advisers, was now presiding over the debates in the upper House. Thus the king's control over parliament was appreciably greater than it had been in 1485, and there is no record of any opposition to his demand for the attainder of his enemies.

Henry was determined to recover most of the money he had spent during the previous six months; and since he could legitimately appeal to parliament in emergency situations, he quickly let it be known that he expected a financial grant. The two Houses responded with commendable generosity and, within a few days, voted him two tenths and fifteenths, which were ostensibly intended for the defense of the realm. This grant was expected to produce £120,000 but probably did not yield that much. Most Englishmen objected to paying taxes for any purpose and usually found reasons to keep from doing so. Meanwhile the convocations of Canterbury and York, which were both in session, had offered the king a tenth of the assessed valuation of all benefices. If the proceeds of the clerical contribution are added to the receipts of the parliamentary grant,

Henry's coffers were probably enriched by at least £100,000. And if the fines imposed on the surviving rebels are added in, the king obviously received sums far in excess of what he had had to pay out. Indeed he derived a handsome profit from the Simnel conspiracy, although he doubtless preferred less hazardous ways of raising money for his needs.[23]

In 1487 Henry hoped to secure legislation that would enable him to strengthen the administration of justice, since he was especially anxious to promote better law-enforcement. As Polydore Vergil observed of him, "He cherished justice above all things; as a result he punished violence, manslaughter, and every other kind of wickedness whatsoever."[24] Accordingly he persuaded his second parliament to authorize him to establish a completely new tribunal that was to consist of the Lord Chancellor, the Lord Treasurer, the Lord Privy Seal, the two Chief Justices, and at least one temporal and one spiritual peer. At the time he created it, Henry envisaged a judicial board of preeminent authority that would take energetic measures against maintenance, embracery, retaining, and the various other offenses that had been condemned by the parliamentary oath of 1485, which had proved to be a dead letter.[25]

In some ways the new court was similar to Chancery, since cases were initiated before it by bills or "informations," while its deliberations took place behind closed doors without the participation of a jury. The new tribunal functioned for more than a decade but then entered a period of rapid decline, and by the end of the reign it had disappeared altogether. This was owing largely to the fact that its jurisdiction conflicted with that of the Council, which had had judicial duties for several centuries.

During the late Middle Ages the Council had often heard cases of a legal nature, usually while meeting in the Star Chamber, a large room built by Edward III near the Receipt of the Exchequer. The Council consisted of the main officers of both church and state and was frequently attended by the king himself—theoretically the Council could not meet unless he was present, although this was not true in practice. Because of the high rank of its leading members, the Council could not be swayed or intimidated by over-mighty subjects in the same way the lesser courts often were. Thus it was an ideal agency to handle the thornier cases, particularly those pertaining to the ownership of land or in which the coercion of jurors was alleged. The Council was also well suited to settle disputes between wealthy landowners and other powerful individuals who scorned to accept the judgments of local courts. It is important to note, however, that the Council's legal activity rarely conflicted with the work of the common-law courts. On the contrary, by restraining the violence endemic in English society for generations, the Council paved the way for a restoration of the rule of law, which in turn made possible a resurgence of the jury system and the common-law courts, which might otherwise have collapsed and disappeared.

Because of Henry's role in this important process, he should be seen as one of the main preservers of England's medieval inheritance. Had his efforts to strenthen royal power not come when they did, only a generation before the Reformation swept over an unsuspecting Europe, his successors would probably have lost control of events and failed to keep individuals with radical Protestant beliefs in check. Had Henry VIII and Elizabeth I lost their power in this regard, the English people would doubtless have divided into two hostile factions, as the French people did during the 1550s and 1560s; and in that event England might well have suffered a ruinous War of Religion, comparable to those endured by many of the peoples of central and western Europe. Had this actually happened, there would have been an inevitable movement towards absolutism, as there was in France and most of the German principalities, and in time England's medieval inheritance might have been swept completely away. As Cardinal Richelieu, that great seventeenth-century French statesman, once noted, the only alternative to anarchy was absolutism,[26] a political truth that would have applied to England had religious strife disrupted the fabric of national life for a generation, as was the case across the Channel. Thus Henry VII's work, coming at the precise moment it did, enabled his successors to maintain religious peace among their subjects and to preserve such hallowed institutions as trial by jury, the common law, and parliament.

Because Henry's work of strengthening royal power was accomplished primarily by means of the Council, an analysis of that important institution is necessary at this point.

During Henry VII's time the Council was comparable to the cabinet of a modern Prime Minister and advised the king on every aspect of government and administration. From time to time it considered such subjects as taxation, commercial policy, the coinage, piracy and coastal defense, agriculture, the upkeep of the country's roads and bridges, the affairs of London and its numerous gilds, the governance of Wales, Ireland, and the church, and the conduct of foreign policy. Thus the range of its activity was extraordinarily broad, and the Council was virtually omnicompetent under the king. But it was never more than an advisory body, and the monarch was always free to disregard its advice, although Henry VII was well aware of the hazards of doing so without good reason. Indeed he tended to be unusually solicitous of his councillors' views and rarely accepted advice from men outside their ranks. Yet he continually stressed the Council's dependence on him, making it clear that no policy could be adopted without his approval.[27]

The names of 227 councillors appointed during the reign are known to us at present. Of that number only a few dozen attended with any regularity, since average meetings rarely included more than twenty members. In regard to Henry's most active councillors, sixteen had been employed by Edward IV; nineteen had belonged to Richard III's Council; and thirteen had served both Yorkist kings. In addition, fifteen others were closely related to Edward IV's councillors, while almost all had risen to prominence during the Yorkist period.[28] Of the various groups represented on the Council, the largest consisted of clerics: sixty-one churchmen, or slightly more than 25% of the Council's total membership, enjoyed the rank of councillor at some point between 1485 and 1509. The next largest group was comprised of bureaucrats or civil servants, who totalled forty-nine in all. Courtiers and peers numbered forty-five and forty-three, respectively; while the smallest category consisted of lawyers, only twenty-seven of whom were appointed during the reign.[29]

Although men trained in the law were but a small minority of the Council's membership, they were a stronger element than their numbers alone would suggest. For the two Chief Justices, the Chief Baron of the Exchequer, and the three leading Sergeants-at-Law were invariably appointed and were as active as their colleagues in discussing the main affairs of state. Indeed Henry VII attributed great weight to the views of the judges; and as Professor Pollard once observed:

The judges did, in fact, in Tudor times fulfill to some extent the function of the Supreme Court under the constitution of the United States, and Bacon's encomium of the consultation of judges by the crown was a deduction from his historical study of Henry VII's reign. It was the judges who decided that Henry could not pass an act of attainder without the consent of the Commons, and Henry accepted their verdict as final.[30]

Between 1485 and 1509 there was a tendency for the Council to grow in size. During the autumn of 1485 it consisted of only two bishops, five peers, and nine others, but by the end of 1486 those who occasionally attended had increased to thirty-three, while in the period 1505-9 more than forty individuals were sometimes present at the same time.[31] Of the 227 men known to have taken the oath of councillor, only one—Sir William Stanley—was removed from his post, and then only because of his conviction for treason. Thus councillors served for life, although at no time were they all present simultaneously. Indeed many of Henry's councillors attended less than a dozen meetings, while others were considerably more active. There was in fact an inner ring of the most important councillors, just as there had been in Yorkist times; and it was this inner ring that actually assisted Henry with the day-to-day affairs of government.

The Council's inner ring was a fluid body whose membership varied according to the place individual councillors enjoyed in the king's esteem at any precise moment. In 1497 the Milanese ambassador described Lord Daubeney, Sir Thomas Lovell, and Sir Reginald Bray as the most powerful men in the realm,[32] so it would be safe to assume that they belonged to the inner ring at that juncture. Richard Fox, Lord Privy Seal between 1487 and 1516, was clearly a member of it as was William Warham, Archbishop of Canterbury and Lord Chancellor after 1503. Of the temporal peers, whom Henry had no desire to exclude (despite the teachings of Victorian historians), the Earls of Surrey, Oxford, Derby, and Ormonde were active members of the inner ring for long periods, and so too was Jasper Tudor, Duke of Bedford, until his death in 1495. Administrative officials who belonged to it at one time or another included Sir Richard Edgecombe, Sir Edward Poynings, Sir Richard Guildford, Sir John Heron, Sir John Riseley, Sir Richard Empson, and Edmund Dudley.

Probably the most influential councillor of the entire reign was John Morton, who, within two years of Bosworth, was appointed Archbishop of Canterbury as well as Lord Chancellor. Morton was a short and unprepossessing man, but he had a quick mind, an unfailing sense of duty, and a reputation for unimpeachable integrity. According to Sir Thomas More, who knew him well, he was "a man of great natural wit, very well learned, and honorable in behavior, lacking in no wise ways to win favor."[33] Morton had been reared in the West Country, in the vicinity of Lady Margaret Beaufort's ancestral estates; and until 1471, when he at last came to terms with Edward IV (who made him Bishop of Ely eight years later), he had been a fervent Lancastrian. At no time, however, did he support Richard III. He was arrested during the Council meeting on 13 June 1483, after which Lord Hastings was beheaded; and following the collapse of Buckingham's rebellion several months later, he fled to the continent. Henry valued his opinions highly and, in 1493, arranged for him to become a Cardinal. Until his death in 1500, Morton was unquestionably the king's most trusted advisor, although in some ways his function was that of an elder statesman.[34]

During recent times there has been much confusion about the work of the Council, and particularly about its judicial sessions in the Star Chamber. It should be noted that a *court* of Star Chamber did not emerge before the death of Henry VII, even though the statute of 1487 which created the tribunal that had disappeared by 1509 was described as "pro camera stellata" (*camera stellata* is the Latin equivalent of "star chamber") by a nameless Elizabethan scribe. From the latter part of the Tudor period, most historians erroneously assumed that the so-called Star Chamber Act of 1487 established the court that played such an important part in England's government from the time of Cardinal Wolsey until its abolition by the Long Parliament in 1641. Yet such early legal scholars as William Lambarde, William Mill, and William Hudson, who wrote during the reigns of Elizabeth I and James I, were convinced that the Court of Star Chamber evolved quite naturally from the Council's judicial work and was not founded by a precise legislative enactment. Furthermore a modern authority has warned that it is pointless to waste very much time on "the abortive question of the court's [*i.e.*, the Star Chamber's] antiquity."[35]

Misunderstandings also persist to this day about the cases referred to, and the procedures employed by, the Council in Star Chamber. Contrary to popular notions, almost all of the approximately 300 cases known to have been adjudicated by the Council while Henry VII was on the throne were initiated by private suits and not by government process. Only about 10% of the litigation considered by the Council during Henry VII's time was in fact of a criminal nature, and such offenses as felony and treason were studiously avoided, largely because the Council was powerless to impose capital punishment, which was reserved for the common-law courts and parliamentary acts of attainder. Moreover, the Council in Star Chamber generally consisted of seven or eight bishops along with several other councillors, and this also limited the king's desire for it to play an active part in the prosecution of crime, for which a smaller and more stable group that included several legal experts would naturally have been required.[36]

Because "official prosecutions in Star Chamber were the exception rather than the rule," known felons seldom appeared before the court. On the rare occasions they did, their testimony was used to clear up some technicality "before a case at common law could begin" or their presence served to remove an obstacle to the proper functioning of some other court.[37] If criminal actions comprised only a fraction of the Council's legal work, what sorts of cases did it routinely consider? Embezzlement, fraud, forgery, defamation of character, disputes over municipal franchises, quarrels about villeinage or commercial transactions, complaints about the malfeasance of sheriffs—these were the kinds of cases that the Council normally heard. Yet in more instances than not, disputes about the ownership or possession of land lay at the heart of complaints addressed to the Council, although riotous behavior was usually the ostensible source of dissatisfaction. As John Guy has explained:

The most frequent complaint [addressed to the Council] was that defendants came riotously with force of arms and evicted the plaintiff from his house or land; and, as might be expected, an unquiet title invariably lay behind the case. In addition about half the purely civil (i.e. non-disguised) suits in Star Chamber were also about land and its management. These comprised questions of title and possession, tortious enclosure, copyhold tenure, nonpayment of rent and illegal distraint.[38]

Although the Court of Star Chamber of Elizabethan times used an *ex officio* oath that caused men to incriminate themselves, this was not true of the Council in Star Chamber during Henry VII's reign. In fact, between 1485 and 1509 the Council generally operated in a surprisingly humane fashion and allowed most defendants several chances to testify, although by the 1590s only one appearance was permitted. A large proportion of the cases considered by the Council prior to Henry VII's death received no final judgment but were remitted for settlement to the King's Bench, albeit with instructions as to how they should be handled. Concerning those few instances when judgment was actually rendered, punishments tended to be moderate and sensible. Fines were often imposed but seldom very heavy ones: in cases of riot they rarely exceeded £10. More serious crimes naturally merited steeper fines, as when in 1502 Sir Henry Vernon and his eldest son were ordered to pay 400 marks for abducting a young heiress. Imprisonment was also a frequent method of punishment, but almost never was physical mutilation decreed, comparable to the brutal manglings ordered by the Court of Star Chamber during its last decade of existence. All in all, the Council in Star Chamber of Henry VII's time was a remarkably gentle tribunal, and there is no evidence of ruthlessness or extortion on its part.[39]

Whenever he was in London, Henry presided over the work of the Council, as he clearly did from 7 to 9 June 1486. On numerous occasions, therefore, he functioned as a judge. Yet because of his preference for outdoor pursuits, he went on frequent progresses and spent long periods away from the capital. Although he was always accompanied on his travels by several trusted councillors, with whom he could confer at a moment's notice, most of the Council's membership remained behind at Westminster, where, during his absences, someone else had to direct their work. By the mid-1490s Cardinal Morton, a septuagenarian who rarely ventured beyond the precincts of Westminster and Lambeth, was too infirm to discharge this duty; and it was probably for this reason that a new official, the Lord President of the Council, made his appearance in 1497. Although the Lord President enjoyed high status, Bishop Fox being the first holder of the office, his post never evolved into a truly important one, for he was never made responsible for an administrative department comparable to the Exchequer or Chancery. The only duties of the Lord President were to preside over the Council whenever the king was away and to occasionally supervise the work of the tribunal known as the Court of Requests.

Whenever he was in the countryside, Henry received frequent petitions requesting him to settle disputes between two or more subjects. Many of these petitions he handed over to Bishop Fox, his reliable Lord Privy Seal, who normally accompanied him on his travels. By 1493 so many suits were being delegated to the trusty bishop that Henry nominated several assistants to help him, and in this way he quietly revived the Court of Requests, which had been dissolved by an act of his first parliament.[40] The Court of Requests had first appeared during the Yorkist period in order to handle "poor men's causes" and the periodic complaints directed against royal officials. Such a tribunal was needed because of the heavy expenses involved in pursuing cases through the ordinary courts of law, with their stiff fees and frequent postponements. Shortly after his usurpation of the throne, Richard III had established a standing committee of the Council to dispense justice quickly and cheaply to the poor; and in December 1483 John Harington was appointed "clerk of the Council of the said requests and supplications."[41] Despite the usefulness of such a tribunal, the parliament of 1485, which was dominated by the upper classes, saw fit to abolish it; and only after eight years had elapsed did Henry VII contrive to revive it. In the words of one authority, "the court of requests [as reestablished in 1493] was emphatically the court of the Lord Privy Seal."[42] Yet whenever the offices of Lord Privy Seal and Lord President of the Council were held by different men, the holder of the latter post would preside over the court in the Lord Privy Seal's absence.

Because Henry VII and Bishop Fox both tended to be peripatetic during the 1490s, the Court of Requests was migratory also. In 1494 it heard cases not only at Westminster but also at Sheen, Woodstock, Langley, Canterbury, and Windsor. The next year it sat at Nottingham, Leicester, and even Collyweston, Lady Margaret Beaufort's country house in Northamptonshire. Only in the decade after 1509 did the court become stationary and meet on a regular basis in the capital, owing to Cardinal Wolsey's preferences.[43] Like the Star Chamber, the Court of Requests eventually aroused the jealousy of men trained in common-law precepts, and during the early Stuart period it was gradually reduced to impotence by prohibitions issued by the common-law judges, who forbade private individuals to appear before it. Yet during the sixteenth century, the court performed a valuable service for the lower classes. This was because its procedures was faster and cheaper than those of the common-law courts and because it was seldom swayed by the aristocratic biases that typified most of the common-law judges. Thus, in disputes over livestock, prices, tools, or rent, a man of limited means was far more likely to receive a fair judgment from the Court of Requests than from the King's Bench or the Common Pleas.[44]

Although Henry VII and the other rulers of his House were monarchs of a practical bent and did less than they might to restrain the economic ambitions of their greater subjects (and they would have been foolhardy to pursue an aggressive policy in this regard), few historians would deny that they had some concern for social justice and believed they had a responsibility to protect their poorer subjects from outright victimization. Thus even though Tudor England was basically a gentry state, it never degenerated into naked class oppression. And for this, Englishmen of the period were primarily indebted to the founder of the dynasty, who revealed his sympathy for the poor in a variety of ways. Not only did he reestablish the Court of Requests, which his first parliament had abolished, but he periodically sought to enforce the laws against enclosure, an upper-class movement that had gained momentum since the 1450s and was especially detrimental to the well-being of poorer families.[45] Furthermore he secured the passage of two statutes specifically designed to help men of limited income. The first, enacted in 1489, established procedures to be used by poorer men whose complaints were being ignored by local officials; while the second, passed six years later, authorized the Lord Chancellor to grant free writs and legal assistance to defendants without means.[46] These statutes were less effective than the king had hoped, since their enforcement depended on the cooperation of unpaid local officials who rarely shared his sympathies. But his attitudes in this regard still serve as a worthwhile example to legal aid societies in our own day.

IV

Financial and Foreign Policy

As an administrator Henry is best remembered for his management of the royal revenues. Since the appearance of Bacon's biography of him in 1622, historians have been awed by his success in strengthening the financial position of the Crown. Knowing all his policies would fail unless he was rich, Henry was determined to enjoy that "felicity of full coffers" which his first biographer attributed to him; and by the end of his reign he had more than doubled his ordinary annual income, from £52,000 to approximately £113,000. As a result he was the first English king in more than a century to be completely solvent. In addition he was the only monarch of his own age who was consistently able to pay his own way.

Although Henry was incomparably "the best business man ever to sit upon the English throne,"[1] his achievement, impressive as it was, should not be exaggerated. He cared little for innovation and, in regard to methods of financial management, simply followed in the footsteps of his predecessors. He was not interested in modernizing the existing machinery of government but only in making it as efficient as possible and exploiting whatever sources of revenue it provided. Moreover, by the time he died, his total income did not exceed that of previous English kings. During the fiscal year 1374–5 Edward III had enjoyed total receipts of £112,187, while during the 1390s Richard II had generally realized £120,000 per year, or £7000 more than Henry could normally expect over a century later. In comparison to the revenues of contemporary rulers, Henry's income was even smaller. The kings of France enjoyed almost £800,000 a year during the first quarter of the sixteenth century, while the

Emperor Charles V, who was also king of Spain from 1516, had an annual income of £1,100,000. But whereas Henry's rivals squandered their revenues on the Italian Wars and other expensive campaigns, he never sought glory for himself on foreign battlefields; and while they were battering one another and driving themselves into bankruptcy, he was following a neutral course and saving his money for more sensible ends. Only once in twenty-four years did he engage in continental war, and that conflict was of such brief duration that he spent considerably less on his troops than parliament granted him. Thus Henry made efficient use of every penny that came his way, although he realized, of course, that a magnificent court was necessary to convince Englishmen and foreigners alike of his wealth and power. At no time, however, did he allow expenditure to get out of hand, for he was determined to amass a large treasure on which he could rely should an emergency occur. By the last year of his life he had invested more than £250,000 in jewels, plate, and other valuables; and early in 1509 a foreign observer characterized him as "the richest lord that is now known in the world."[2]

If Henry eventually became the most affluent ruler of his age, the situation at his accession was far from propitious. Revenue had declined since the palmy days of the 1470s; trade had so decayed after Edward IV's death that a mere £20,000 was realized from the customs duties in 1485; and shortly after Bosworth the methods used so expertly by the Yorkist kings to manage their finances were inadvertently scrapped. Thus not only did the new monarch have to find funds to tide his government over until he could stabilize the situation, but he also had to reestablish the machinery that had enabled his predecessors to solve the financial problems bequeathed to them by the improvident Henry VI. Luckily for the new king, he soon found a first-rate administrator in Sir Reginald Bray, who gave him invaluable assistance in this important work. Bray, who became Chancellor the Duchy of Lancaster in September 1485, was well versed in methods of revenue management, having supervised Lady Margaret Beaufort's ancestral lands during the Yorkist period. Thus he had a wealth of experience of the kind that Henry himself lacked, and the latter allowed Bray a free hand in all business pertaining to the Duchy, the most important part of the royal demesne, with extensive holdings in London, Calais, Wales, and thirty-three of the English counties.[3] Together Henry and his minister formed a capable team; and until Bray's death in 1503, he was unquestionably the king's chief financial adviser.

The most pressing task confronting Henry after Bosworth was to ensure that sufficient funds would be available for routine operations. This meant that short-term loans would have to be contracted until the royal finances recovered from the disruptive effects of Richard III's usurpation. Officials like Bray himself, Alfred Cornburgh, Under-treasurer of the Exchequer until his death in 1487, and John, Lord Dinham, who became Lord Treasurer in July 1486, were often called upon to advance sizeable amounts for the king's needs. Altogether £10,127 17s. 4d. was raised by means of loans in 1485–6, with various groups and individuals assisting the government. The corporation of London provided £2000 (which was only half the sum requested of it, however), the Archbishop of Canterbury made available £100, while the Bishop of Winchester furnished 100 marks. During the autumn of 1486 commissioners scoured the countryside for additional loans. The average sum requested was unexpectedly small, with wealthy Londoners being asked to contribute no more than £5 and residents of outlying areas rarely more than 20s. Although the total amount secured was inconsiderable, the loan of 1486 was important as "the first of the forced loans which figure so prominently in the Tudor period."[4]

If Henry often appealed to his richer subjects for middling or small sums, he was careful to see that all loans contracted were repaid by the agreed date. As a consequence the Crown's credit was never higher; and after the first year of the reign, the corporation of London, a particularly important source of loans, felt no qualms about advancing large amounts. In 1487 it lent £4000, and in July 1488 it provided an additional £2000. By August it had lent £5700 more, in two separate transactions; and in 1490 it made a further £2000 available for the king's needs.[5] By the time the loan of 1490 was negotiated, Henry's financial position had greatly improved, a £5000 surplus on the ordinary account becoming apparent by the end of 1489; so within a short time the Crown was able to dispense with short-term borrowings. During subsequent years the royal revenues continued to expand, and as early as 1492 Henry was in a position to invest large sums in jewels and plate. Within four more years he was able to turn his back on borrowings of any kind, and for the remainder of the reign he was blessed with large budgetary surpluses. In contrast to Edward IV, with whom he is often compared, Henry was able to balance his budget far more rapidly, since the Yorkist king had not been completely debt-free until seventeen years after his accession. Not only was Henry fully solvent within seven years of Bosworth, but he also raised royal revenue to considerably higher levels than his Yorkist predecessor, who was solvent for a brief time but "achieved nothing more."[6]

That the Crown's financial position improved so dramatically after 1485 was owing primarily to Henry's own efforts and diligence. For at least the first fifteen years of the reign, he took a regular part in administrative affairs, in order to secure as much revenue as he legally could. In 1498 a somewhat critical foreign visitor, who was convinced he was avaricious, declared that "he spends all the time he is not in public or in his council, in writing the accounts of his expenses with his own hand."[7] Clearly Henry was determined to be rich in order to be secure, and to that end he eventually revived the Chamber system, which had fallen into disuse within a few months of Bosworth.

For the management of their finances, the Yorkist kings had relied on the Chamber of the Household, a considerably smaller office than that leading department of state, the Exchequer. The Chamber had the advantage of a much simpler accounting routine, modelled on that of the Duchy of Lancaster, which made it far more responsive to the royal will. During the 1460s and 1470s an increasing percentage of the king's revenues had passed through the Chamber, causing the Exchequer to decline to the role of a minor accounting office. Yet those same factors that gave the Chamber its strength—its disregard for bureaucratic red tape and its close dependence on the monarch—ensured that it would be particularly susceptible to political turmoil and disruption. A crisis at the highest level of government was bound to affect the Chamber's routine operations, and this was certainly true during the aftermath of Bosworth. Once Richard III was overthrown and Henry mounted the throne, the Chamber system came to a grinding halt and the Exchequer recovered its earlier predominance. Most of the royal revenues were re-entrusted to the older department, with its complicated routine and interminable delays, originally devised as a means of preventing fraud but now seen only as a way to frustrate effective government. Within a few years Henry realized that, in order to be master in his own house, he would have to revert to the administrative methods employed by his Yorkist predecessors.[8]

In his supervision of the Chamber, Henry relied primarily on two men: Sir Thomas Lovell and Sir John Heron. Lovell, who served as Chancellor of the Exchequer for the entire reign, doubled as Treasurer, or effective head, of the Chamber until 1492, when he was promoted to the Treasurership of the royal household. Even before Lovell's elevation, Heron was handling many of the routine duties of the office, so he naturally succeeded to the headship of the Chamber. Heron served with distinction in this post for nearly thirty years, until his death in 1521. The king worked closely with both men, but particularly with the latter, whose account books he regularly inspected. As late as 1502 Henry was "still checking and signing Heron's individual receipts and totals to the extent of . . . five or six signatures per page."[9] That Henry himself audited the

Chamber accounts was largely owing to the fact that an increasing percentage of his revenue was passing through the office. Before 1487 only a negligible proportion of the king's income was entrusted to its management, but during the next two years it handled an average of £17,000 annually, or some 25% of the Crown's total receipts. By the early 1490s the Chamber had become responsible for approximately £27,000 a year, and within another decade its receipts and issues had soared to more than £100,000 annually. By the time the king died in 1509, more than 90% of the Crown's ordinary income was being administered by this one office.[10]

Doubtless the most important revenues paid to the Treasurer of the Chamber were the rents from the crown lands, which accounted for slightly more than a third of the king's ordinary income. In the supervision of the royal demesne, the Chamber officials were especially proficient. Indeed it was for that purpose that Edward IV had developed the office in the first place, deliberately copying the managerial techniques of the greatest landowners of the age. Inevitably, then, the receivers-general of the crown lands were responsible to the Treasurer of the Chamber and his assistants; and most authorities hold that the crown lands were particularly well managed during the Yorkist and early Tudor periods. Some historians even maintain that this was the "golden age" of the crown estate. Certainly Henry VII was anxious to increase the revenues from this source; and while he was on the throne, the rents from the crown lands rose by more than 200%, from approximately £12,000 in 1485–6 to more than £41,000 in 1508–9.[11] A large portion of this increase was owing to Bray's skilful management of the Duchy of Lancaster, which paid only £666 to the Chamber in 1488 but almost £4500 a decade later. By 1508, at which time Sir Richard Empson was Chancellor of the Duchy, its payments amounted to £6566.[12]

The growing receipts from the crown lands cannot be attributed solely to more efficient estate management, however. Between 1485 and 1509 there was a marked tendency for the royal demesne to grow in size, which automatically increased the Chamber's revenues. At the time he became king, Henry acquired two extensive tracts which had been forfeited to the Crown as a result of Richard III's death and attainder: the estates that had formerly belonged to the Earldom of March and that half of the great Beauchamp inheritance which had been the dowry of Richard's wife Anne Neville. In 1487 Henry was pleased to learn that Anne Neville's mother, the Dowager Countess of Warwick, had settled most of her lands on him; so when she died in 1492, the Crown was further enriched. By that juncture Henry had acquired, also by way of reversion, the estates owned by Richard Woodville, third Earl Rivers, who died without heir in March 1491.[13]

Probably Henry's most ethically doubtful acquisition of land came by way of an agreement he made in 1489 with William, Lord Berkeley, whom Richard III had created Earl of Nottingham. Although Nottingham had obtained the western part of the vast Mowbray inheritance as a result of Richard's usurpation of the throne, he was an early supporter of Henry VII, whose coronation he helped to arrange during the autumn of 1485. The earl longed for a more elevated place in the peerage than he currently occupied; and because he had no children, it was easy for him to disinherit his younger brother Maurice, who had annoyed him some years earlier by marrying the daughter of a Bristol merchant, and to bequeath his extensive properties to the king. In return for this Henry agreed to confer on Nottingham the title of first Marquess of Berkeley, which he did on 28 January 1489. Thus when Lord Berkeley died in 1492, Henry inherited an estate that included well over seventy manors in western England as well as scattered tracts in Ireland. Maurice was of course outraged by this arrangement; and until his death in 1507 he left no stone unturned in his campaign to recover his rightful inheritance. By means of "legal chicanery and influence in high places," Maurice managed to recover some forty-one manors, but that still left Henry with a net gain of at least thirty.[14]

While Henry was involved in these legal wrangles with Maurice, he was acquiring even larger properties. When in 1495 the Dowager Duchess of York died, her estates, reputedly worth £1200 a year, escheated to the Crown; and after Sir William Stanley's conviction for treason during the same year, Henry was able to claim estates worth more than £1000 annually. Altogether 138 persons were attainted for treason between 1485 and 1509; and although almost all of these actions were eventually reversed, Henry invariably required some new manor or estate as the price of his consent. Moreover, whenever his own relatives died, he took steps to ensure that the Crown was the principal beneficiary. His uncle Jasper's death in 1495 enabled him to acquire properties worth at least £3000 a year; and when in 1503 his wife Elizabeth of York died, Henry recovered the lands that had been set aside eighteen years earlier for her jointure. By all these means he significantly enlarged the royal demesne, which was at least a third more extensive at the time of his death than it had been during Yorkist times.[15]

If the rents from the crown lands increased steadily after 1485, their relative importance was almost stationary, since the king's total income was growing so rapidly. From the time he mounted the thorne, Henry was determined to secure every penny to which he was legally entitled; and to that end he concentrated on the full range of possibilities open to him. As early as December 1486 he announced that all landowners with incomes of at least £40 a year must fulfill the statutory requirement of knighthood. The sheriffs were to report the names of "all persons having £40 in lands or revenue"; and all such men were to assemble in his presence on 4 February 1487 to receive their knighthoods. Those who disregarded this command did so "at their uttermost perils" and on pain of a £200 fine. Similar proclamations were issued in March and December 1500 and again in December 1503.[16]

Whether Henry raised much revenue in this fashion is doubtful. An occasional fine may have been collected, but his real aim in requiring his richer subjects to apply for knighthood was to bring additional lands into a feudal relationship with the Crown "as a matter of recent record."[17] From the time he became king, Henry planned to utilize the opportunities provided by the feudal system, and particularly the incidents of wardship and escheat, to which the tenants-in-chief of the Crown were still subject. But if Henry was going to take full advantage of the possibilities offered by the feudal system, he had to know exactly who his tenants-in-chief were. He had to establish which lands were held directly from the Crown, or *in capite*, although such information was often deliberately concealed from him. In addition, if he was going to enjoy a sizeable revenue from this source, he had to find a way to convert rich but independent landowners into tenants-in-chief, thereby reversing a long-standing trend.

Paradoxically the last problem was the one for which there was the easiest solution. As Professor Elton has observed, Henry almost from the outset exploited "every device for turning a mesne tenant into a tenant-in-chief," thereby increasing the number of landowners in a feudal relationship with the Crown. Whenever his subjects sought to alienate their estates, either through sale or voluntary gift, he insisted that they retain a portion of any lands held directly from him, and in this way he created new tenants-in-chief with little difficulty. Pressure was also exerted on co-heirs, who were compelled to subdivide their lands in such a way that each retained some acreage *in capite*.[18] The Yorkist kings had occasionally used such methods, but their methods were feeble when compared to Henry's.

In his attempt to discover concealments, Henry was also following in the footsteps of Edward IV and Richard III. Between 1471 and 1485 the Yorkist kings had appointed numerous commissions to investigate feudal tenures throughout the realm, in order to ensure a substantial return on their feudal rights. After Bosworth Henry revived these commissions on an expanded scale, and during his first year he directed them to uncover "concealed lands" in Middlesex, Surrey, Kent, Leicestershire, and ten other counties. As a result of these and similar commissions appointed in later years, a substantial extension of the king's feudal rights was achieved within a decade.[19] At the same time such surveys were being made, Henry was making frequent use of enquiries known as *inquisitions post mortem*, which were intended to discover whether a prominent landowner who had recently died had held any lands *in capite*. Families afraid of being confronted by a staggering obligation to the Crown regarded such enquiries with horror; and of the last fifty *inquisitions post mortem* conducted for which detailed evidence is available, slightly more than half revealed the existence of minor heirs whose true ages had been concealed from the king.[20]

That substantial sums were at stake is proved by the fact that, during the winter of 1485–6, Henry received 500 marks for the wardship of young Gyles Arlyngton, which the Crown had assigned to the Earl of Oxford. Two years later the wardship and marriage of Henry Beaumont, heir to a rich viscountcy, brought 800 marks from Bishop Fox and Sir William Hody, Chief Baron of the Exchequer. Yet it would be wrong to assume that every wardship was quite so remunerative. The one pertaining to Humphrey Hill was granted in 1487 to Richard Harp, Receiver General of the Duchy of Lancaster, for a mere £20.[21] Whether there was any tendency for the price of wardships to rise during the course of the reign cannot be ascertained from the materials presently available, although there are scattered indications that there was indeed such a tendency. Early in the reign, for example, Henry sold the wardship of Elizabeth Trussell to George, Earl of Kent for £266. After the earl's death several years later, Henry sold the same wardship to John, Earl of Oxford for £1333. Regardless of whether there was an increase in the average price of wardships, the king's income from this source showed steady growth over the years. In 1487 he received only £353 from wardships, but seven years later he netted £1588. Towards the end of the reign he obtained far more from this source, collecting £6163 in 1507 alone.[22]

Until 1503 Henry was aided in the management of this important business by Sir Reginald Bray, who helped to determine which estates of minor heirs should be sold to others and which should be retained and administered by the Crown. Many such lands were in fact retained and managed by royal officials. Within a year of Bosworth Henry appointed three special receivers to oversee all lands belonging to royal wards in the five northernmost counties of England; and fourteen years later he directed the Bishop of Carlisle to supervise all wardships and marriages in the same region. By 1505 the king's income from estates administered in wardship exceeded £5000 a year.[23]

Although revenue from this source increased steadily after 1485, it never attained quite the level Henry hoped it would reach. This was because of the device known as "a use," or more properly "an enfeoffment to use," which had become widespread since its introduction in the mid-fourteenth century. A use was a form of trusteeship by which a tenant-in-chief would convey his lands to relatives or friends, who would administer them for the benefit of an heir who was not yet of age. In this way an estate could be kept from passing directly to a minor heir and thus into the hands of the king, while the heir was coming of age. The trustees appointed to supervise the lands would fulfill the conditions resting on the land, so the king would have no justification for demanding that the land should revert to him during the heir's minority. Uses were thus tailor-made to help landowners circumvent the problem of minor heirs and thus assisted them in evading one of their primary obligations to the king.[24]

Edward IV had been unable to assert his control over uses, and while he was on the throne there were at least a dozen tenants-in-chief whose heirs and properties escaped wardship. In desperation Edward IV convinced his last parliament to prohibit the device on lands subject to the jurisdiction of the Duchy of Lancaster, but for obvious political reasons the statute of 1483 was repealed the next year by Richard III's only parliament. Thus the problem of uses was still a critical one when Henry VII mounted the throne. The new king secured legislation from his first parliament to strengthen the authority of the courts in this regard. Henceforth suits could be brought against "tenants to use" (men who held land in trust for someone else), whereas in the past such men had been immune from legal action. In 1487 Henry persuaded his second parliament to abolish certain types of uses pertaining to movable goods. But these two statutes were hardly sufficient to protect the king's financial interests. When in 1489 the fourth Earl of Northumberland was killed in a riot, his estates should have passed to his eldest son, who was still a minor, and thus to the Crown. But Northumberland had established a use for his son's benefit, so his lands, reputedly worth £1575 a year, escaped the king's reach. By the time the fifth Earl of Northumberland came of age in 1498, Henry had lost revenues amounting to more than £14,000.[25]

The prospect of so much lost income caused Henry to seek more effective lesgislation from his third parliament. The new statute, one of the most important of the reign, was enacted in 1490 and stipulated that a minor heir of a tenant-in-chief who died intestate was now to be subject to wardship regardless of whether a use had been established for his benefit. If the heir of an intestate landowner had already attained his majority, he would be expected to pay a customary relief, or inheritance tax, to the king. Despite these provisions, which were clearly to the Crown's benefit, the act of 1490 has been characterized as "a timid and tentative statute," for it could be circumvented by any landowner farsighted enough to draw up a will, and all landowners now had strong inducement to do just that. But despite the measure's shortcomings, it established the direction royal policy would take until 1536, when Henry VIII coerced the two Houses into passing the notorious Statute of Uses, which prohibited the device altogether until it was partially reallowed by the Statute of Wills of 1540. Furthermore the act of 1490 applied to the whole realm, whereas Edward IV's shortlived statute had pertained only to lands falling within the purview of the Duchy of Lancaster. In addition Henry VII's measure was clearly the most effective legislation that could be hoped for at the time, given the fact that Henry's possession of the throne was not yet uncontested. It would have been dangerous, perhaps even suicidal, for him to have pressed for a stronger act, thereby flaunting the interests of his most powerful subjects.[26]

Because parliament was dominated by the propertied classes, the two Houses would have been reluctant in any case to pass stronger legislation against uses. Yet the Lords and Commons were not unwilling to make Henry an occasional grant of taxation. Between 1485 and 1509 he enjoyed a parliamentary revenue of £281,999, or slightly less than £11,750 for each of his twenty-four years on the throne. This compares quite favorably with the yearly average of approximately £11,000 that Edward IV had obtained during his reign.[27] Yet despite the members' generosity, most of Henry's subjects felt that he should not become overly dependent on parliamentary support. The average Englishman hated paying taxes for any reason, and twice during the reign—in 1489 and 1497—massive protests occurred when royal officials sought to collect taxes already granted by parliament. Besides, any questions about the constitutional maxim that the monarch should "live of his own" during peacetime had been resolved in 1467, when Edward IV had promised his third parliament that he would henceforth pay the ordinary expenses of his household and government out of his own pocket, requesting financial grants only during wartime or in the wake of domestic upheavals.[28] Because Edward's promise was considered binding on his successors, Henry was in no position to insist on parliamentary support except under emergency conditions. Events nevertheless enabled him to make several appeals for money during the course of the reign: in 1487, during the aftermath of the Simnel plot; in 1489–90, because of an impending war against France; and in 1497, as a result of a recent Scottish attack on northern England and a popular insurrection in Devonshire and Cornwall. In 1504 he made a final appeal to parliament and secured a feudal aid worth almost £31,000 for the knighthood of his son Arthur and the marriage of his daughter Margaret.[29]

If Henry could count on parliamentary aid under exceptional circumstances, he could also rely on benevolences, which were similar to forced loans with the important difference that they did not have to be repaid. Because one of the king's main responsibilities was to defend the realm, he could appeal to his richer subjects for financial assistance whenever an attack was pending, which he could do indirectly through a parliamentary grant or in a more direct way by means of a benevolence. If not resorted to too often, benevolences could be extremely remunerative, for the individual sums collected were limited only by the subjects' wealth and generosity. For example, the benevolence of 1491-2 produced almost £48,500 for the war against France, or only £475 less than the three parliamentary subsidies voted between 1487 and 1497.[30]

Henry also received substantial sums from the church, although clerical property was taxed more lightly before the Reformation than it was to be afterwards. Several times during the reign, usually when parliament was about to make a grant, the convocations of Canterbury and York voted a substantial financial contribution. In 1487 and 1496, for example, the clerical assemblies offered Henry a tenth of the assessed valuation of all benefices within the realm. On other occasions the Crown was allocated a flat sum. Early in 1489 the two convocations granted £25,000 for the impending war against France; and in 1497, shortly after the Scottish attack on northern England was repulsed, the clergy of Canterbury contributed a generous £40,000 towards Henry's war chest.[31] In addition the king secured money from the church by making occasional use of the odious Renaissance practice of simony. At one point he secured 1000 marks from a successful applicant for the deanery of York; and on another occasion he required £300 for the archdeaconry of Buckingham.[32] Considerably more profitable was the device of keeping bishoprics vacant for months or years, in order to obtain their revenues. During the summer of 1492 the Chamber received £1800 from the unfilled diocese of Bath and Wells; and two years later the Crown obtained an additional £1200 from the temporalities of Durham and of Bath and Wells, the latter of which was vacant once again. In 1495 an even larger sum was received from the properties of the unfilled bishopric of Lincoln.[33] Henry raised more revenue in this way than any of his predecessors but not nearly so much as his granddaughter Elizabeth. Whereas he allowed only a few dioceses to remain vacant for over a year, the Virgin Queen kept them unfilled for much longer periods of time in order to acquire their revenues. While she was on the throne, the see of Oxford had no incumbent for forty-one years, the bishopric of Ely was vacant for nineteen years, and the diocese of Bristol went without for fourteen.[34]

If Henry's granddaughter exceeded him in this rather unsavory business, he surpassed her in another way. Whenever a new bishop was invested with his temporalities, he was required to pay a third of his first year's income to the Crown. Henry at once saw that if he moved his bishops from one diocese to another, he would be entitled to this initial payment on numerous occasions. Between 1485 and 1509, therefore, his bishops were involved in what appeared to be an unending game of musical chairs. Thomas Savage, who was elevated to the episcopal bench in 1493, was moved only three years later from Rochester to London, from which he was translated in 1501 to York. Richard Fitzjames followed in Dr. Savage's footsteps and occupied two of the posts previously held by him. In 1497 Fitzjames began his progress at Rochester, where he remained until his 1503 transfer to Chichester, from which he was moved three years later to London. During the seven years he served on the episcopal bench, Henry Deane occupied three different sees in turn: Bangor, Salisbury, and Canterbury, where he died in 1502. Two men who first became bishops during the Yorkist period were twice translated by Henry. Richard Redman, who was named to St. Asaph in 1471, was moved in 1495 to Exeter and six years later to Ely; while Edmund Audley, Bishop of Rochester from 1480 until 1492, served at Hereford during the decade 1492-1502 and at Salisbury between 1502 and his death in 1524. Undoubtedly the most peripatetic bishop of the age was Richard Fox, who, after being consecrated at Exeter in 1487, was translated to Bath and Wells in 1492 and only two years later to Durham. In 1501 Fox was promoted to the much greater see of Winchester, which he held until his death in 1528. On each of his transfers, Fox had to pay the Crown a third of his first year's income from his new office, a not inconsiderable amount since the bishoprics of Durham and Winchester were worth approximately £3000 and £4000 per year, respectively, at this time. Fox's last two positions were of course among the richest bishoprics in the British Isles, but many other English sees enjoyed substantial revenues. According to one authority, "twelve of the seventeen archbishops and bishops were among the forty wealthiest prelates in Christendom." The dioceses of Exeter and Salisbury, for example, were currently rated at £1566 14s. 6d.

and £1027 7s. 11d. per year, respectively, a third of which was owed to the Crown whenever a new bishop was consecrated.[35]

Exactly how much revenue Henry derived from the church each year is far from clear. J. J. Scarisbrick maintains that he received an average of at least £12,500,[36] but Professor Chrimes challenges such an unequivocal assertion. The financial records of the period are not only incomplete but also misleading and, in some cases, even contradictory. Until detailed studies are made by specialists, "the value of the clerical contribution must remain speculative."[37] Yet it would obviously be safe for us to conclude at this point that Henry enjoyed a substantial yearly income from this particular source.

Even more difficult to determine than the revenue Henry derived from the church is the amount he received every year from the profits of justice, or proceeds of the judicial system. Moderate fines were generally imposed by the Council and the prerogative courts but considerably heavier ones by the courts of common law. In 1505, for example, the Common Pleas ordered the fifth Earl of Northumberland to pay £10,000 for his offense in ravishing a royal ward, Lady Elizabeth Hastings, which may have been Henry's way of recovering most of the income he had lost during the earl's minority. Although the fines imposed by the courts were paid to the Treasurer of the Chamber, it would be impossible to calculate their average yearly value, since fines were often reduced through subsequent negotiation. Yet Henry punished almost all criminal acts, including treason, by means of heavy financial exactions; so it seems likely that he enjoyed a greater revenue from this source than any other ruler of the century.[38]

Another device Henry used to particularly good effect was the practice of requiring powerful individuals to post bonds for their future behavior. Scores of men were compelled between 1485 and 1509 to acknowledge substantial debts to the Crown, which they would forfeit if they committed the slightest misdeeds. Richard III had used this procedure to promote loyalty to his government and had extracted bonds from at least ten men. From the time he mounted the throne, Henry continued and widened the process, demanding a surety of £10,000 from Viscount Beaumont of Powicke as early as December 1485. A similar bond was extracted the next year from the Earl of Westmorland; and in February 1487 sureties of £500 each were demanded from Sir John Waterton and Thomas Savile, whose quarrels were disrupting the peace of the northern counties. On 27 August 1487 several friends of Lord Scrope, a minor participant in the Simnel conspiracy, were required to post bonds totalling £7000 as a guarantee that

Scrope would not leave the precincts of Wallingford Castle "or any other castle or place which might be assigned to him."[39] This system of restrictive bonding is normally associated with the latter part of the reign, when it became particularly widespread and oppressive. But Henry made heavy use of it within a short time of Bosworth and, during his first decade on the throne, required bonds from at least 191 persons. By 1499 he had extracted sums ranging between £1000 and £10,000 from elevent different peers.[40]

The most important nobleman forced into financial thralldom in this way was the Marquess of Dorset, whom Henry suspected of complicity in the Simnel plot of 1487. In May 1491 fifty-two of Dorset's friends signed bonds ranging between £100 and £1000 that he would remain loyal, which meant that his circle would be severely penalized, if not altogether ruined, should he ever antagonize the king again. A year later, as Henry was about to embark on a military expedition to France, the marquess himself was obliged to sign a comprehensive agreement with the Crown. Not only did Henry take custody of Dorset's eldest son, but several of the king's officials assumed control of the marquess's estates, the revenues of which would revert permanently to the Crown should Dorset give offense in any way. Only if he was obedient and loyal for the remainder of his life would his son be allowed to inherit the estates.[41] After 1492 Dorset was too enmeshed to cause Henry any further worry, but other influential Englishmen still flirted with conspiracy, the particular bane of the upper classes in the opinion of most foreign observers. As a consequence the Crown received a substantial yearly revenue by way of forfeited bonds. During the fiscal year 1493-4, it obtained approximately £3000, which was only a fraction of what Henry received in later years. In 1503-4, for example, he collected a total of £30,824 18s. 4d. in this manner.[42]

A far more predictable source of revenue were the receipts of the customs duties, which accounted for slightly more than a third of the king's ordinary income by the end of the reign. Between 1485 and 1509 there was an increase of approximately 22.5% in the revenue derived from this source, which averaged about £33,000 per year during the first decade and slightly more than £40,000 annually during the last.[43] Because nothing was done before 1507 to augment the rates on imported goods, it would appear that this increased income resulted from expanded trade with the continent and the heightened vigilance of the customs officials, who were periodically encouraged "into greater efficiency than before." Because of intense pressure from the Crown, a number of smugglers were arrested, particularly when they tried to unload goods in the outports. In 1486, for example, a Spanish trader, Don Diego de Castro, was apprehended at Poole with a cargo of silks and spices valued at £122 2s. 6d. Since a smuggler's wares were equally divisible between the Crown and the arresting officers, the increased efficiency of the customs service played a part, if not an altogether significant one, in the steady growth of royal income.[44]

In order to maximize the receipts from the customs duties, Henry did everything he could to encourage England's foreign trade. Indeed many of his policies were designed to promote great commercial ties with the continent, for, as Bacon said of him, "he could not endure to have trade sick." In addition he knew that a slump in the country's foreign trade would make it more difficult to obtain loans from the corporation of London, should he need to do so again in the future. Although Henry took steps to stabilize the value of the currency, which was an undoubted stimulus to commercial growth,[45] his most important contribution to the expansion of trade was accomplished through the medium of diplomacy.

From the time he ascended the throne, Henry gave serious thought to the way foreign policy affected commercial conditions and particularly the wool trade, which was still the mainstay of England's rather limited participation in European economic life. Yet it should never be forgotten that Henry's foreign policy was erected on a second pillar as well, namely his determination to establish his dynasty on a basis of equality with the other great ruling families of the age. And whenever economic and dynastic considerations conflicted, he invariably sacrificed the former to the latter. During the course of his reign his diplomatic objectives were essentially defensive, his overriding aim being to safeguard the throne he had won so narrowly at Bosworth. Like one of his Stuart descendants, he was determined never to have to set out on his travels again; nor did he intend to suffer the same fate as Richard III. To a large extent all of Henry's policies stemmed from this one great objective; and if his actions in time seemed to define a system or method, this was only because he made consistent responses to the options open to him. The promotion of England's foreign trade was but one of the methods he used for the achievement of his broader aims. As trade expanded and the receipts of the customs duties grew, he acquired greater resources with which to maintain a strong defensive position. And as he concluded commercial treaties with other governments, his new-found friendships deterred his enemies from attacking him. Thus his commercial policy was not an end in itself, and several times during his reign "his merchants were more instruments, even victims, than beneficiaries of his foreign policy."[46] Nevertheless his actions did lead to an expansion of England's foreign trade, which rested on stronger foundations than ever by the time he died.

Shortly after Bosworth Henry announced his desire for peace with all and particularly with the kings of France and Scotland, who had assisted him against Richard III. In October 1485 he proclaimed a one-year truce with the French Crown, and two months later he appointed Oliver King, Archdeacon of Oxford, to meet with special emissaries from Charles VIII. These negotiations proceeded smoothly, and in mid-January 1486 a three-year truce was concluded. Meanwhile Henry and his advisers were conferring with the three Scottish officials who had come south the previous October to witness his coronation. Because of the lawless ways of the Scottish nobility, James III was as anxious as his English counterpart for cordial relations, and on 30 January 1486 Henry directed the Earl of Northumberland "to treat with such commissioners as James . . . may appoint to conclude a treaty of peace and abstinence from war, as well as by land as by sea." A truce to continue until 1489 was signed at Ayton in June 1486, and it was extended at regular intervals until 1495, when a Yorkist imposter appeared at the Scottish court and received generous aid from James's son and successor. Only a month after the signing of the truce of Ayton, Henry negotiated a commercial agreement with his old protector, Francis II of Brittany. At the same time he was considering overtures made by the Archduke Maximilian, ruler of the Low Countries, with whom he concluded a commercial treaty early the next year.[47]

During his first decade as king, Henry was particularly anxious to encourage English trade with Florence, Pisa, and the other city-states of northern Italy. During the 1460s Florentine galleys had called regularly at Southampton and the other ports of southern England, but during the second half of Edward IV's reign, English merchantmen had taken over most of the carrying trade. In 1472 an English ship docked at Leghorn for the first time, and thereafter English sailings for the Mediterranean increased rapidly. Inevitably, the efforts of England's merchants were opposed by the Venetian government, which aspired to total domination of the Mediterranean carrying trade. This was especially worrisome to the Florentines, who were unwilling to depend on an old adversary for their much-needed imports of raw wool. In 1489 Lorenzo de Medici suggested a commercial agreement by which England would acquire a monopoly over the wool trade, which could be achieved by the establishment of a staple, or exclusive outlet, at Pisa and a solemn undertaking by English merchants not to engage in trade with any other Italian ports. When Henry expressed an interest in the proposal, two Italian merchants who had longstanding ties with England, Christofano Spini and Tommaso Portarini, were sent to London to conduct the negotiations.[48]

Late in October the two Italians reported that they had received a

gracious welcome from Henry, who had referred their proposal to the
Lord Treasurer, the Lord Privy Seal, the Bishop of London, and several
other Councillors. The negotiations almost foundered, however, when the
English expressed fears about the likely Venetian reaction and demanded
the exclusion of all but their own wool from Pisa. Yet all difficulties were
smoothed away by the beginning of 1490, when a treaty along the lines of
the original proposal was concluded. It provided for the establishment of a
staple at Pisa, guaranteed safe-conducts to all English traders in northern
Italy for six years, and restricted England's wool sales to Venice to no
more than 600 sacks a year. Shortly afterwards two English merchants,
Thomas Hawes and Hugo Clopton, set sail for Pisa, where they leased a
warehouse and several smaller buildings, which served as the headquarters for the projected trade.[49]

Just as Henry feared the Venetian reaction was a harsh and determined
one. Within a few months the Doge and Senate struck back by prohibiting
the transport of Greek and Malmsey wines to Pisa, in order to deprive the
English ships of their return cargoes. This hostile act caused Henry to
impose a duty of 18s. a ton on all wines transported to England in
Venetian ships, which sparked a bitter tariff war. This conflict was
eventually won by England, largely because of Henry's determination
that his subjects should enjoy a share of the Mediterranean carrying trade.
But whether an English victory would have resulted had Venice's attention not been diverted by the outbreak of the Italian Wars in 1494, which
were to make northern Italy the storm center of European politics until
1529, is a question that no amount of historical speculation will ever be
able to answer.[50]

While he was encouraging commercial penetration of the Mediterranean, Henry was also promoting increased trade with several other
continental countries. In 1489 he renewed a treaty of friendship with
Portugal that had originally been concluded in 1378; and during the same
year he obtained trading rights for his subjects throughout Denmark and
at the staple town of Bergen, in Norway. He also gained permission for
English trawlers to fish in Icelandic waters, a particularly valuable concession since it could be used to exert pressure on the Hansa, the powerful
confederation of north German cities. Henry hoped to increase England's
trade with the ports along the Baltic, but all his efforts were resisted by the
Hansards, who refused to allow English merchantmen to call at Danzig,
Riga, or the other League cities. Henry also desired to curb the privileges
of the Hansa in England, where German merchants had enjoyed near-
monopolistic rights since the conclusion of the treaty of Utrecht in 1474.
Henry himself had confirmed the Utrecht agreement in 1486, less than a

year after Bosworth. But during subsequent years he steadily chipped away at the privileges accorded the League, insisting that England's foreign trade should not be dominated by aliens. He was not notably successful, however, since the Hansa was much too strong to be broken by unilateral English action.[51]

Henry also encountered occasional difficulties with Ferdinand and Isabella, co-rulers of the seven kingdoms that comprised the country known as Spain. Because Henry did not want Gascon wines or Toulouse woad to be transported to England in Spanish ships, his policies were of necessity opposed by the Spanish monarchs, who ultimately secured legislation hostile to English interests. The Spanish "Navigation Act" of 1494 forbade the exportation of all domestically-produced goods in foreign-owned vessels whenever Spanish ships were available, and in that way it impeded Anglo-Spanish trade during the following decade.

If England and Spain were commercial rivals, they were nevertheless willing to cooperate in diplomatic and military affairs, owing to a common animosity towards France. Ferdinand and Isabella hoped to recover the Pyrenean counties of Cerdagne and Rousillon, which had been conquered by Louis XI in 1462; and because of the precarious health of Francis II of Brittany, whose heir apparent was a girl of twelve, Henry was fearful of a French takeover of that strategic territory, which would lead to a great expansion of French power along the Channel coast. Thus England and Spain had good reasons for wanting an alliance with one another, an alliance that would be particularly gratifying to Henry since it would enable him to claim equality with two of the greatest rulers of the age.

Early in 1488 Henry suggested an eventual marriage between his young son Arthur and the three-year-old Catherine of Aragon, fifth and last child of Ferdinand and Isabella. The Spanish rulers were intrigued by the proposal and sent a special ambassador, Rodrigo de Puebla, to England to negotiate for both a marriage treaty and a new commercial agreement. Conversations during the summer of 1488 accomplished nothing definite because of the Spaniards' assumption that Henry was in a weak position and could be made to accede to all their demands. Once it became apparent that this was untrue, Ferdinand and Isabella became more reasonable; and in mid-December Henry appointed Dr. Thomas Savage and Sir Richard Nanfan to go to Spain and conclude an alliance along the lines already laid down in London.[52]

On 19 January 1489 Savage and Nanfan, accompanied by a host of attendants, embarked from southern England; but a great storm forced them back to their native shores, where they were detained for three weeks. Not until 16 February did they land at Laredo, on Spain's northern coast. A leisurely journey by horseback brought them to the royal camp at Medina del Campo, near Valladolid, where they arrived on 12 March. Two days later they were received by Ferdinand and Isabella in solemn audience. Dr. Savage's speech of greeting was answered by the Bishop of Ciudad Rodrigo, whose remarks were almost unintelligible since he was completely toothless. After a round of tournaments and receptions, serious talks began on 26 March, and the next day the treaty of Medina del Campo was concluded.

The treaty stipulated that the English and Spanish monarchs should aid in the defense of one another's territories and that neither Crown should assist or shelter rebels against the other. If either kingdom found itself at war with France, the other was to intervene immediately, and neither was to leave the war without the express consent of its ally. A joint campaign against the French was clearly envisaged, the stated objectives of which were Normandy and Aquitaine for England, Cerdagne and Rousillon for Spain. Catherine of Aragon was to sail for England and marry Prince Arthur as soon as the two children were of canonical age. The princess was to retain her place in the succession to the Spanish throne, and her marriage portion was set at 200,000 *scudos*, or slightly less than £40,000. Should Arthur die before Catherine, she was to have as her jointure one-third the annual revenues of all royal estates in Chester, Cornwall, and Wales, which receipts were to be augmented had she become Queen of England in the meantime.[53]

Once a few changes of wording were made to satisfy Henry, the treaty was ratified by the English Crown on 20 December 1490. Except for the last five or six years of the reign, it was to serve as the cornerstone of England's foreign policy until 1525, when Ferdinand and Isabella's grandson, Charles V, jilted Henry VIII's daughter Mary, thereby destroying the basis of Anglo-Spanish cooperation for the time being.[54]

Despite the treaty's obvious importance and the 35-year friendship it engendered, Henry is often criticized by historians for concluding such an agreement. In the treaty he pledged to assist Ferdinand and Isabella in the reconquest of Cerdagne and Rousillon, an eminently sensible goal, while they promised to help him recover Normandy and Aquitaine, a totally unrealizable objective. By 1493 they had achieved their aim while doing little or nothing to assist in the accomplishment of his, although both countries were briefly involved in a joint war against France. Most historians therefore feel that Henry was duped by Their Most Catholic Majesties, although there is no reason to believe that Henry himself ever felt that way. His attitude towards the Spanish rulers remained unchanged until just before Isabella's death in 1504, and at no time was he willing to scrap his basic strategy of cooperation with Spain against the more powerful France, which was theoretically sound. Furthermore he was never as thin-skinned as his more celebrated son and refused to allow personal feelings and petty insults to determine the course of his foreign policy. Neither should it be forgotten that the conclusion of the treaty of Medina del Campo marked a great diplomatic victory for him. In the eyes of all Europe he had now emerged as an equal of the powerful House of Trastamara, the leaders of which had agreed to marry one of their daughters to his son. The adventurer of 1485 had clearly arrived.

V

The French War and a New Imposter

Several weeks before the treaty of Medina del Campo was signed, Henry entered into an important agreement with the government of Brittany. Known as the treaty of Redon, this pact was concluded on 10 February 1489 and committed England to provide 6000 men to fight at Brittany's expense in the approaching war against Charles VIII of France, whose aggressive behavior foretold an eventual attack on the duchy's independence.[1] Henry hoped to retain the friendship of the French Crown but was not prepared to accept its absorption of Brittany, which had long enjoyed autonomy within France. Henry therefore sent two ambassadors, Sir Richard Edgecombe and Dr. Henry Ainsworth, to the continent to negotiate a military alliance with the duchy. He also raised 3000 troops to buttress a small volunteer force that had already sailed across the Channel. On the same day the treaty of Redon was signed, this small English army took control of St. Omer.[2] With these actions a diplomatic crisis began that was to hang like a sword over all of Henry's affairs for the next three years.

In order to understand this crisis, which ultimately led to an English invasion of France and to French support of a new imposter against Henry, a brief account of Franco-Breton relations prior to 1489 must be given. The ailing Duke of Brittany, Francis II, who had been Henry's protector for thirteen years, had long been concerned for the future of his House, since he had no sons and would be followed on the ducal throne by his daughter Anne, who was unlikely to be of age at the time of her accession. As early as 1486 Francis had sought to ease his daughter's path by finding a powerful husband for her. His choice fell on the Archduke Maximilian, son and heir of the Emperor Frederick III, who expressed an immediate interest in a marriage alliance. But Charles VIII and his elder sister, Anne of Beaujeu, the real head of the French government, denounced the scheme and made their displeasure known by besieging Nantes. When a border war broke out during the spring of 1488, Henry instructed Lord Scales and 500 English volunteers to sail across to Duke Francis's assistance. Although this timely aid was welcome, it was hardly sufficient for the purpose at hand; and because the troops promised by Maximilian did not materialize, owing to discord between him and the burghers of Ghent and Bruges (encouraged, apparently, by the French), the Breton forces were badly beaten by a French army at St. Aubin-du-Cormier on 28 July. Stoically, Francis II accepted his defeat and, in an agreement of 20 August, promised to do homage to the French Crown. He also pledged that neither of his daughters, Anne or Isabel, would marry without Charles VIII's permission; and he surrendered four towns as security that he would never again seek foreign aid against his rightful overlord. Three weeks after this humiliating capitulation, Duke Francis died, and the twelve-year-old Anne mounted the ducal throne. Charles VIII and Anne of Beaujeu at once claimed wardship of the new ruler, as they were legally entitled to do, and a union between France and Brittany became a distinct possibility, as all could see.[3]

Across the Channel in England, Henry now had to decide on the proper course to follow. Until this juncture he had maintained a pretence of neutrality, sending his almoner, Christoper Urswick, over the previous May with an offer of mediation and a proposal that Anne should marry his youthful ward, the Duke of Buckingham, who ₊was living in Lady Margaret Beaufort's household. But Henry's overtures were rejected out of hand, so he renewed the truce that he had concluded in 1486 with Charles VIII and told the French ambassador that Lord Scales's mission had been undertaken without his knowledge or approval. Once Duke Francis died, however, and the French government claimed wardship of the young duchess, the situation became appreciably more dangerous for England. Should Henry remain neutral despite the altered circumstances, incalculable advantages would accrue to England's oldest adversary. As Professor Wernham has written:

. . . the acquisition of Brittany . . . would give France control of almost the entire southern shore of the Channel and, in addition, [would] add to her dominions a maritime province with a vigorous sea-faring population and the best—indeed before the founding of Le Havre, almost the only—bases for an invasion of England or for preying upon English trade. It would therefore threaten important and valued English interests, which even so reluctant a warrior as Henry VII could not afford to neglect. If he made no attempt to ward off such a menace, he might ruin his credit at home and his prestige abroad and smooth the path for a more fortunate Simnel.[4]

Henry therefore raised 3000 additional troops and opened negotiations with Anne's protector, the Marshal de Rieux, for the treaty of Redon, which was concluded on 10 February 1489. At the same time he sent out writs for his third parliament, which opened at Westminster on 13 January. The ostensible reason for this parliament was to provide funds for the coming war, which Henry would not enter until assured of a sizeable grant. The financial position of the Crown was improving from month to month, but he had still not attained complete solvency, being partially dependent even at this time on short-term loans. Although the Breton government had promised to pay most of Henry's operating expenses, direct involvement in the conflict was bound to be costly, and Henry therefore requested a parliamentary grant of £100,000, which would enable him to keep 10,000 archers in the field for twelve months. By contemporary standards this was an enormous sum of money; but because the foreign situation seemed so dangerous, the Lords and Commons consented to it, albeit after a long and somewhat heated debate. The greatest rancor during the discussions occurred over the question of what percentage of the tax should be borne by the clergy and what percentage by the laity. After much bitter wrangling between parliament and convocation, it was agreed that the laity should be responsible for three-fourths of the grant and the clergy of the province of Canterbury for the remainder. The two Houses also agreed to the raising of additional taxes should the troops be needed for more than twelve months, provided that no more than £25,000 was collected during any subsequent year. The money was to be raised by means of a graduated tax on land, a method used several times since 1404 without any notable success.[5]

The discord that took place at Westminster was slight indeed when compared to the turbulence that occurred in the northern counties once Henry's agents sought to collect the taxes voted by parliament. During April a dangerous tax revolt broke out in Yorkshire, which compelled the king to shift his attention from foreign to domestic affairs, at least for a few months.

The northern counties had long been exempt from the usual forms of taxation, since they had a special duty to defend the border from Scottish attacks. During the parliament of 1489 pointed references were made to this northern obligation, and steps were taken to exempt the region once again. But royal agents were nevertheless active there, for Henry was determined to secure whatever revenue he could, even at the price of local dissatisfaction. When protests and other expressions of discontent mounted, Henry's principal lieutenant in the North, the Earl of Northumberland, gave his wholehearted support to the king's policy, in order to strengthen his waning influence at court. Since 1486 Northumberland had been warden of the east and middle marches and had held several other local offices as well. Yet in 1488 he was removed from the captaincy of Berwick because of government fears that his power was becoming too great. When Henry's tax agents encountered widespread opposition early the next spring, Northumberland gave unswerving aid to the Crown as a way of demonstrating his continued reliability.[6]

Yet when the first signs of dissatisfaction appeared in the North, the earl's attitude was hesitant and conciliatory, as he attempted to mediate between the disgruntled populace and the king. Only when ordered to assist the royal agents so they would not encounter resistance elsewhere did he render all the aid he could muster to a policy of which he was not the author but only an instrument. In this way he deflected criticism from the king to himself, and within a short time his neighbors came to regard him as the cause of all their misfortunes. On 28 April, while addressing an angry crowd at Cocklodge, his country house near Thirsk, he was cut down by John à Chambre and several other ruffians. That Northumberland's chief assassin was an ardent partisan of the House of Tudor, having received a lifetime position in Galtres forest after distinguishing himself at Bosworth, has caused some historians to conclude that Henry planned the attack on Northumberland as a way of ridding himself of a potentially dangerous subject. Certainly the king could be unscrupulous whenever stealth and guile alone would enable him to attain his objectives. But in this case there is absolutely no evidence to connect him with the earl's assassination, although he of course profited from the elimination of the head of the great Percy connection, his successor being a boy of eleven. Furthermore there was an outpouring of genuine grief at Westminster, as eulogies for the slain earl were composed by Bernard André, John Skelton, and several other court poets. Neither should it be forgotten that without Northumberland's own actions, there would have been no reason for the mob to fall upon him and his household servants.[7]

Once news of the earl's death spread throughout the North, a disgruntled cousin of the Percys, Sir John Egremont, sought to guide these happenings into political channels. A Yorkist who opposed all cooperation with the king, Egremont hoped to fan the grievances of the region into a full-fledged revolt against Henry. He sent letters to known malcontents throughout the North and entered York with his retainers. But according to an authority on these events, "plebeian insurrections which were as remote from London as this one, and which received no determined support from the gentry, had no hope of success."[8]

Once informed of Egremont's attempt to raise the region, Henry decided to go there in person, and on 10 May he summoned his subjects to help him in putting down the rebellion. Then he mobilized an army, the vanguard of which he entrusted to Thomas Howard, Earl of Surrey, who had just been released from the Tower. Surrey had been imprisoned after Bosworth, but the king now felt sure of his loyalty and believed he should have this chance to prove himself. With a small band of men the earl rode off towards the North and, on 22 May, overwhelmed the rebels in a battle near York. Sir John Egremont escaped to Flanders, where he took refuge with Margaret of Burgundy, but John à Chambre and several others were captured and executed. Because they were hanged before Henry arrived on the scene, the king was able "to play his accustomed role of the clement prince who spared the deluded." Yet a commission of oyer and terminer was subsequently issued to the Earls of Surrey, Derby, and Shrewsbury, along with several prominent commoners, to investigate conditions throughout the North in order to determine whether additional punitive measures were needed. Henry also directed Surrey and another influential Councillor, Richard Tunstall, to assist the work of the tax collectors throughout the region; and he additionally appointed Surrey his principal lieutenant there. The king had decided not to fill the wardenships of the east and middle marches, left vacant by Northumberland's death, but to take them into his own hands, as he had already done with the captaincy of the west march. To handle the actual duties of these important offices, Henry named Surrey his deputy and granted him extensive powers throughout the area. The king was increasingly impressed by the former Yorkist, who performed his duties so capably after 1489 that, upon the death of John, Lord Dinham in 1501, he elevated him to the great office of Lord Treasurer.[9]

During the spring and summer of 1489 Henry was still worried about the fate of Brittany and was devoting whatever time he could spare to diplomatic affairs. As early as 14 February, only four days after the treaty of Redon was signed, he concluded a defensive alliance with the Archduke Maximilian; and late the following month his two ambassadors, Savage and Nanfan, initialed the treaty of Medina del Campo, which committed Spain to support England in a joint war against France. Unfortunately for

Henry his newly acquired allies were too involved with other matters to give serious thought to the Breton problem. Maximilian was away helping his father, Frederick III, in a campaign against the Hungarians, while Ferdinand and Isabella were about to launch their final assault on the Moors of Granada and thus were unable to spare more than a few troops. Thus the 3000 archers led to the continent by Sir Robert Willoughby received almost no assistance, except from the Bretons themselves. Sporadic fighting during the next few months accomplished nothing of value, although English aid kept Dixmude from falling to the archduke's rebellious subjects and their French allies. Despite this timely support from England, Maximilian concluded a separate peace with Charles VIII in July; and French emissaries who arrived in London about the same time urged Henry to do likewise.

The English ruler must have been profoundly disappointed by the late summer of 1489. All his plans had miscarried, despite his recent flurry of diplomatic activity; and only £27,000 had been collected from his last parliamentary grant. Had he deserted the Duchess Anne at this juncture, no one would have been too surprised or offended. Indeed there are grounds for arguing that he should have reconciled himself to a French annexation of the duchy, which was all but inevitable. But Henry's outlook was in many ways old-fashioned. He never subscribed to the cynical and opportunistic methods practised by Maximilian and Ferdinand of Aragon, whereas honor seemed to dictate continued support for the daughter of his old benefactor, who had sheltered him for thirteen years. Henry therefore recalled his prorogued parliament in January 1490 and persuaded it to grant him additional financial support. Because he was willing to cancel the uncollected portion of the taxes voted the previous year, he was now allocated an extra tenth and fifteenth with which to finance his troops on the continent.

Yet at the very time he was securing this aid, Henry was giving fleeting thought to a possible peace settlement. The coalition he had put together the previous year had dissolved altogether, and he was under strong pressure from a papal nuncio, Lionel Chieregato, who had recently arrived from the continent. As the nuncio explained, Innocent VIII was anxious for England to conclude a peace treaty with France, so Charles VIII would be free to launch a campaign against Ferdinand I of Naples, who had been nibbling away at the Papal States for several years. Because of this prodding from Rome, Henry sent several ambassadors to the continent during the spring of 1490 to engage in peace talks, first at Calais and then at Boulogne. But these negotiations accomplished nothing because of contrary pressures on Henry to remain in the war. The Duchess Anne and her mentor de Rieux were especially anxious to prevent an English defection, and on 15 February they appointed special ambassadors to treat with him. He responded by sending additional troops to take possession of the towns that had been promised him by the treaty of Redon as security for the eventual repayment of all his expenses; and when a new Anglo-Breton agreement was negotiated the following July, he obtained an annuity of 6000 crowns in lieu of the ordinary revenues of Morlaix, which an English contingent then held.[10]

During the spring of 1490 the archduke also reappeared on the scene and sought to stiffen Henry's resistance. On 22 May Maximilian instructed his envoys to propose a joint attack on France, and after lengthy conversations a new military agreement was concluded by England and the archduke in September. This was quickly followed by a pact between the English Crown and Ludovico Sforza, Duke of Milan, who was increasingly fearful of a French attack on northern Italy. But at the very time this new anti-French coalition was forming, Ferdinand and Isabella were adopting a more neutral stance, which augured poorly for the future. During the summer of 1490 the remaining Spanish troops in Brittany, except for a small garrison at Redon, were recalled to southern Spain in order to participate in the final attack on Granada. This unpropitious development did not deter Maximilian, however, for before the year ended he and the Duchess Anne were married by proxy, and in January 1491 Anne publicly acclaimed herself "Queen of the Romans." (As heir apparent of the Holy Roman Emperor, Maximilian had several years earlier been granted the honorary title of "King of the Romans.")

Anne's marriage to the archduke led to an immediate defection by one of her strongest partisans, Alain d'Albret, which was naturally applauded by the French. Heretofore one of Anne's most ardent defenders had been the Gascon adventurer d'Albret, who had long been involved in a bitter quarrel with Charles VIII and Anne of Beaujeu. D'Albret had gone to the duchess's assistance in the unrealistic hope of gaining her hand in marriage; and when he learned that she had become the wife of Maximilian, he veered angrily back in the direction of his native land. In April 1491 he surrendered Nantes to a French regiment, which was the signal for a renewed attack on the duchy. Anne's troops refused to take the field until their arrears had been paid; and as for the archduke, "who always had too many irons in the fire and too little money in his pocket," he was in no position to send any aid. Consequently the French were able to seize Redon from its Spanish defenders and Guingamp and Concarneau from their English garrisons. Once these three towns had fallen, the French army settled down before the gates of Rennes, hoping to starve Anne and her advisers into submission.[11]

For their part, Anne and de Rieux implored Henry, whose troops still controlled Morlaix, to send over reinforcements at once. He immediately obtained additional funds from his wealthier subjects by means of a benevolence; and on 17 October 1491 his fourth parliament assembled at Westminster. Henry now proposed to go in person to the continent, for which even larger sums would be required. Although he had not spent all the money voted for military purposes since 1489, the Lords and Commons responded to his appeal by granting him two tenths and fifteenths. In addition he was authorized to collect a third tenth and fifteenth, should he remain abroad for more than eight months. Probably because of parliament's generosity on this occasion, Bacon characterized Henry's wars as "a mine of treasure, of a strange kind of ore, iron at the top, gold and silver at the bottom."[12]

Henry sent several hundred reinforcements to the continent during the autumn of 1491, but, like the archduke, he was in no position to provide more than token assistance to the Duchess Anne at this juncture. Serious trouble was brewing in Ireland, and the affairs of that island would soon require all of his time, at least until the spring of 1492.

Because of the undiminished influence of the Earl of Kildare, Henry had retained him as Lord Deputy after the collapse of the Simnel plot of 1487, in which the earl had been implicated. Yet the king was wary of the Irishman and watched his actions closely, lest he give assistance to another imposter. Probably Henry did not know that Kildare received a large shipment of muskets from Margaret of Burgundy during the winter of 1489–90. But the king was clearly aware of the bitter hatred between Kildare and the burghers of Waterford, against whom the Deputy had murderous designs. Waterford enjoyed a particularly high place in Henry's affections, since it had been the only Irish city to rejoice in his overthrow of Richard III. In 1488, during the course of Sir Richard Edgecombe's mission to Ireland, the common council of Waterford had urged the withholding of a royal pardon from Kildare, who was patently disloyal and ought to be hanged for his treasonous behavior. Although this advice was wisely ignored, the Deputy developed a burning hatred for the city fathers, whose power he was determined to break. The municipal officials naturally turned to the king for protection, and on 28 July 1490 Henry summoned Kildare to appear before him within ten months. As defiant as ever, the Deputy absolutely refused to leave Ireland and did not even send his excuses to the king until the ten-month period expired.

Shortly afterwards he summoned a parliament to meet at Trim, which at his urging passed a massive act of attainder against his Waterford enemies.[13]

This was only a short time before a new Yorkist imposter arrived in southern Ireland in November 1491. Claiming to be the younger son of Edward IV, this new imposter was actually a Flemish lad by the name of Perkin Warbeck. Born at Tournai about 1475, Perkin was the son of John Warbeck, or Osbeck, a minor functionary of that town, and Katherine de Faro, daughter of another functionary of the same town. While still a child, Perkin was taken by his mother to study at Antwerp, where, because of unsettled conditions, he remained only a few months. On returning to his birthplace, he was apprenticed to several masters in turn, until he attracted the notice of Sir Edward Brampton, who was so impressed with the boy's manner and appearance that he made him a footman to his wife.[14]

Born in Portugal about 1430, Brampton had emigrated to England during the late 1450s in order to escape the increasing persecution of Jews throughout the Iberian peninsula. On his arrival in England Brampton became active in political affairs and, in order to be accepted at court, converted to Christianity. Some of the chroniclers of the period even maintain that Edward IV stood god-father to him! Certainly Brampton was an ardent Yorkist and acquired a detailed knowledge of court life during the years 1471–83. In August 1482 he was appointed Governor and Captain of the Isle of Guernsey; and because he gave strong support to Richard III in 1483, he was granted £350 out of "the customs and subsidies on any goods and merchandise of his in the ports of London, Sandwich, and Southampton." The following year he was knighted, and about the same time he was awarded several manors and numerous smaller tracts in Northamptonshire. Whether he fought for Richard III at Bosworth has never been determined; probably he did, for his estates were confiscated soon afterwards. During the late summer of 1485 Brampton and his wife fled to the continent, at which point Perkin Warbeck must have entered their service. During the spring of 1487 the Bramptons, accompanied by their servants, set sail from Middleburg for Lisbon, where they remained for several years. It was during this period that Perkin developed a consuming interest in the affairs of the Yorkist court and learned all he could about Edward IV's younger son, whom he was soon to impersonate.[15]

How long Perkin remained with the Bramptons in Portugal in unclear. Sometime after 1489 they made successful overtures to Henry VII and, upon returning to England, recovered most of the lands they had lost as a result of Bosworth. Their rise in Henry's favor was rapid, probably because they were able to divulge Perkin's true identity to him, and in 1500 their eldest son was knighted at Winchester.[16] When the Bramptons embarked for England in 1489 or 1490, Perkin had already taken employment with Pregent Meno, a prosperous clothier from Brittany, who subsequently took him to Ireland. Because the imposter was tall and handsome, albeit somewhat squint-eyed, it was his job to model the fine silk clothing sold by his employer. Apparently he made a vivid impression on all who saw him, for the Irish at once concluded that he was of princely birth. Either he was a younger son of the Duke of Clarence (and thus a brother of the imprisoned Earl of Warwick) or an illegitimate son of Richard III. In the confession he signed after his capture six years later, Perkin maintained that he had revealed his true identity to John Walter, Lord Mayor of Cork. But Walter and his associates refused to believe he was anything less than a prince, in which they were encouraged by a fervent Yorkist, John Taylor.[17]

Originally a prosperous merchant of Exeter, John Taylor had been employed by the Yorkist kings as a customs inspector and minor functionary of their court. In 1489 he was accused of disaffection towards the new monarch; and although he received a full pardon in June of that year, he was ordered to leave the realm. He crossed the Channel and settled at Rouen, from which it was easy to remain in contact with Edward Frank and the other plotters who, in December 1490, sought to free the Earl of Warwick from the Tower.[18] When that conspiracy failed, Taylor departed for Ireland, where, as he well knew, Yorkist feeling was still undiminished. Apparently he was the first person to sense how Perkin could be used to impersonate the younger son of Edward IV; and in November 1491 he arranged for him to be paraded through the streets of Cork as "Richard IV."[19]

Once the plot began in earnest, Taylor and his associates attempted to secure assistance from the greater magnates of Ireland. Overtures to the Earl of Desmond were successful, for he quickly associated himself with the conspiracy and even offered to send messengers to James IV of Scotland on Perkin's behalf. But most of the Irish lords recalled the outcome of the Simnel plot of 1487 and refused to commit themselves. This was particularly true of Kildare, who was doubtful of the scheme and remained a safe distance from it. In a letter to the Earl of Ormonde in 1493, the Deputy insisted how he "never lay with him [the imposter], neither aided, comforted, nor supported him with goods in any way whatsoever."[20] It is possible of course that Kildare gave secret assistance to the conspiracy while leaving himself a convenient escape route, should it fail. But regardless of the truth of the matter, the new plot had little chance of success without the Deputy's wholehearted support, which he steadfastly refused to give. As a result the new imposter was not even to be crowned, in Dublin or elsewhere, despite his masquerade of nearly six years.

By December 1491 Henry had learned of the plot and dispatched to Ireland a special force commanded by Thomas Garth and Sir James Ormonde. Little is known about Garth, other than that he was a member of Lincoln's Inn and had once served as captain of Berwick, which prompted the Irish to dub him "the king's Captain." Ormonde, however, was an illegitimate son of John Butler, sixth Earl of Ormonde, who had died in 1478. Because the seventh Earl of Ormonde insisted on living in England, where he was a prominent member of the Council, the real leader of the Butler clan during the 1490s was a cousin of the seventh earl, Sir Piers Butler. As was doubtless to be expected, Sir Piers was not pleased by the reappearance of his illegitimate kinsman, a treacherous man who soon became known as "Black James." Had Sir Piers been able to secure assistance from the Geraldines, he would have been in a position to defeat Back James handily. But relations between the Butlers and the Geraldines, enemies over many years, were too strained for a reconciliation at this juncture, and Sir Piers was all but isolated. Moreover, Black James could count on support from the O'Briens of northern Munster, his mother's family, while he soon concluded a pact with the Burkes of Clanrickarde, who had an abiding hatred of Kildare. Thus even though Black James faced opposition from within his own House, he was able to defeat the imposter's partisans, and during the spring of 1492 he took possession of the Geraldine townships of Kilkenny and Tipperary.[21]

In March 1492 Perkin and the Earl of Desmond sent frantic appeals to James IV for aid; but because no Scottish support was forthcoming, Desmond retreated to the fartherest reaches of Munster while Perkin prepared to leave Ireland altogether. Early in 1492 a French emissary had arrived in southern Ireland with an invitation for the imposter to journey to Paris, where he would receive financial aid and a warm welcome from Charles VIII. The French Crown was willing to assist Perkin, who might be a valuable pawn in its difficulties with Henry over Brittany. The imposter therefore bade farewell to his Irish supporters, and, accompanied by Taylor and Loyte Lucas, the French emissary, he set sail for France. After an uneventful journey he arrived at the French court, where he was hailed as the rightful Duke of York and granted all the perquisites owing to one of such exalted rank. A mansion was set aside for his residence, and guardsmen under the Sieur de Concressault were assigned to watch over and protect him.[22]

If Kildare had done nothing to assist the imposter, neither had he done very much to oppose him, and Henry concluded it was at last time to appoint a new Lord Deputy. On 11 June 1492 he replaced Kildare with Walter Fitzsimons, Archbishop of Dublin, who had long been on friendly terms with the Geraldines, however. At the time of his ouster, Kildare reluctantly signed a bond for 1000 marks as a guarantee of his future loyalty. The appointment of a new Lord Deputy was not the only change Henry made in the Irish government at this juncture. Lord Portlester, who had served as Treasurer since 1454 and as Chancellor since 1487, was discharged from both of his positions. The first was conferred on Black James Ormonde, while the second went to Sir Alexander Plunket.[23]

These changes of government personnel were hardly sufficient to pacify Ireland, however, since Kildare was furious that both he and his father-in-law, Portlester, had been fired in this way. Fighting continued much as before, and during the summer of 1492 Black James attacked one of Kildare's strongest partisans, O'Connor of Offaly, and murdered his son. For this he was roundly criticized by Garth, who was at once imprisoned by Ormonde. Subsequently Black James ordered the execution of Garth's eldest son. These outrageous acts caused Henry to conclude that additional changes were needed in the Irish administration.[24]

Yet before he could find a final solution to Ireland's problems, Henry's attention was again diverted by the Breton problem, which was now approaching a climax. During the preceding year Henry had given whatever time he could spare to foreign affairs, even sending additional troops to the continent during the autumn of 1491. But that assistance had not kept the Duchess Anne and her ministers from capitulating to the French once and for all. The Breton treasury was empty, and Anne had no more jewels she could sell to raise money for her troops. Consequently she was unable to keep the French from overrunning the duchy and occupying its capital. As soon as Rennes fell, however, Charles VIII proposed a truce and offered his own hand in marriage. While the duchess pondered this unexpected turn of events, her suitor courteously withdrew to Touraine. Because the pope was increasingly anxious for Charles to launch a campaign against the Aragonese king of Naples, he favored the marriage and did everything he could to facilitate it. At his instance, Anne's confessor explained away her doubts about the earlier marriage she had contracted with Maximilian. As soon as all her questions had been answered, she made up her mind to become the wife of the king of France;

and on 6 December 1491 they were married, in fact as well as name, at Langeais.

Once the Duchess Anne became queen of France, there was no longer a compelling reason for the Anglo-French crisis to continue. Regardless of how it affected English interests, the French annexation of Brittany could not be reversed by any means short of a massive assault on Charles VIII. Henry had no intention of adopting such a course, since hostile moves by him might cause the French authorities to give greater assistance to Perkin Warbeck. Besides, Henry may have sensed that Charles's gaze was turning increasingly towards Italy, where he would soon intervene, so that a French absorption of the duchy might not be as hazardous for England as he had previously supposed. In contrast to these considerations, however, was the fact that he had continually preached the need for war since 1489. He had realized more than £48,000 from the benevolence of 1491; and from his third and fourth parliaments he had obtained more than twice as much. If he suddenly ended the struggle at this juncture, his credibility with his subjects would be totally destroyed and he could expect to be accused of dishonesty and hypocrisy. He was clearly caught in a trap of his own making, which meant that he felt compelled to launch a military demonstration of some kind against France.

Although it cannot be proved, Charles VIII may have understood Henry's dilemma. Until December 1491 Charles had supported James IV's efforts to strengthen the Auld Alliance by concluding a Franco-Scottish marriage alliance against England. But when the King of Scots abruptly reversed himself and made overtures to Henry during the winter of 1491–2, the French monarch did nothing to dissuade him.[25] Indeed Charles probably suggested such a course to James, since he was anxious to avoid a protracted campaign against England. Clearly Henry was too practical to think of reopening the Hundred Years War and making a serious effort to conquer France; and although he was the political heir of the Lancastrian kings, he was more likely to follow the example of Edward IV, who had ended his invasion of France in 1475 when Louis XI bought him off at Picquigny. Thus Charles VIII may have realized that while Henry could not avoid a show of force, it was likely to be a brief and relatively painless encounter.

As early as December 1491 Henry issued commissions for the hiring of fifty foreign ships along with a contingent of German archers. Yet the bulk of the English army was to be raised through indenture, for, like earlier kings of England, Henry was dependent on his richer subjects for a substantial field force. By February 1492 Sir William Paston and other prominent landowners in East Anglia were busily equipping themselves with horses and armor, and it was generally assumed that the expedition would set sail about Easter. For his part, Henry still hoped to secure foreign assistance, and on 6 April he staged an elaborate pageant to commemorate the fall of Granada, which failed to elicit a response from Ferdinand and Isabella. In addition he dispatched two emissaries to the continent to treat with Maximilian, but they soon reported that no help could be expected from that quarter. By this juncture large numbers of troops had been mobilized at Portsmouth, where three large breweries were constructed to satisfy their needs. Without an adequate supply of beer, the government held, the English fightingman would be unable to do his best.[26]

During the summer of 1492 last-minute negotiations took place at Calais and Etaples, as the two governments sought to find a face-saving formula that would render the invasion unnecessary. By August there were widespread reports of French landings along England's southern coast, which caused Henry to instruct the sheriff of Kent and the Lord Warden of the Cinque Ports to be ready to fight at a moment's notice. This was followed by an English expedition against the pirates of Sluys, whose nominal overlord, the Count of Ravenstein, was an old opponent of Maximilian. By mid-September so much time had elapsed that the end of the campaigning season was fast approaching, and Henry decided it was at last safe to depart. After naming his son Arthur to serve as regent during his absence, which could only be for a few weeks, he embarked for the continent.

On 2 October Henry landed at Calais with a force of 12,680 soldiers, nearly 3200 of whom had brought along their own horses. The troops were under the joint command of the Duke of Bedford and the Earl of Oxford, England's most experienced generals. In hopes of booty and adventure, the Earls of Shrewsbury, Suffolk, and Devon had come along, as had Lords Audley, Strange, Latimer, Powis, Dudley, Hastings, and Grey, all of whom were attended by scores of their own retainers. For more than two weeks the king and his army remained at Calais, where an elaborate code was drawn up to enforce discipline, apportion the duties of the main commanders, and divide whatever spoils were captured from the enemy. On 18 October the English army at last set out for Boulogne, the principal objective of the campaign, which had just been garrisoned by 1800 men and provisioned for a period of two years. The siege of Boulogne began on the 22nd and was conducted with no more energy than the earlier stages of the expedition. Within a few days the French commander, the Sieur d'Esquerdes, offered terms considerably more generous than those accorded Edward IV in 1475. Moreover, by this juncture English honor had been appeased by reports of an impressive victory at Sluys: on 13 October the castle had fallen to Sir Edward Poynings and his 2500 troops, although the town itself had been taken by Philip of Cleves. Thus there seemed little reason to continue the siege of Boulogne, which was bound to be a hazardous undertaking, so it was ended after only nine days. Because less than a dozen men had been killed or wounded during this mock campaign, there was remarkably little rancor associated with the peace negotiations that now opened. On 3 November final terms were agreed upon at Etaples, only a few miles from Boulogne.[27]

The treaty of Etaples, which concluded Henry's only European war, stipulated that the English should evacuate all French territory at once, excepting of course Calais, which they continued to hold until 1558. In return for this, the French promised to give no more assistance to Perkin Warbeck, nor to any other imposter who might subsequently appear, and to pay a large portion of Henry's military expenditure since 1489. Ultimately Henry was to receive a total of 620,000 crowns, which did not include the arrears of eight payments still owing under the treaty of Picquigny, or an additional 125,000 crowns. These sums were to be discharged at the rate of £2500 every six months until a grand total of £159,000 had been paid.[28] The peace was announced at Boulogne on 4 November, and five days later it was proclaimed in London by the Lord Mayor and Archbishop Morton, who shortly afterwards celebrated a *Te Deum* in St. Paul's Cathedral. Within three more days Henry returned to Calais, where he boarded a ship for Dover on 17 November.[29]

Upon his return to England Henry portrayed himself as a conquering hero, whereas the campaign had been unusually brief and no exploits of any importance had occurred. Because the invasion failed to break Charles VIII's grip on Brittany, most historians dismiss it as a dismal charade. Certainly it was not the glorious success that royal apologists proclaimed it to be, but it did accomplish two important results for England. First, because of the unusually humane manner in which it was conducted, it made possible a speedy reconciliation between the two countries. Indeed from 1492 until the end of the reign, there was remarkably little friction between London and Paris, and Henry made concerted efforts to keep from quarreling with the French Crown, which was now one of the basic elements of his foreign policy. And second, the Boulogne campaign led to a significant strengthening of Henry's financial position. All in all, the invasion cost him only £48,802, or a scant £318 more than he had realized from the benevolence of 1491. But in addition he had obtained more than £133,000 from the parliamentary grants of 1489-91;[30] and as a result of the treaty of Etaples, he was henceforth to receive an annuity of £5000 from the French Crown, an annuity that was paid quite punctually until 1511. Thus the brief war against Charles VIII was extremely profitable for him, since it enabled him to end his dependence on short-term loans and invest large sums in jewels and plate. Paradoxically, it was his oft-derided invasion of France that caused him to attain a position of complete solvency, which only the greatest of his predecessors had been able to do.

VI

Diplomacy and Intrigue

Although Charles VIII refused to surrender Perkin Warbeck as Henry had pressed him at Etaples to do, the French king did agree to expel the imposter from his dominions. Thus the would-be Plantaganet had to seek another refuge, and from the French court he journeyed north to his birthplace in the Low Countries, where he sought assistance from Margaret of Burgundy. The dowager duchess still hoped to overthrow the hated Lancastrians, and, after a lengthy interview with the new arrival, she recognized him as her nephew. Taking Warbeck under her wing, she provided him with a bodyguard of thirty halberdiers and tutored him in the ways of the Yorkist court, thereby reinforcing what he had already learned from Brampton and Taylor. She also ordered that planning begin for an eventual invasion of England.[1]

By the summer of 1493 Henry was aware not only of Warbeck's whereabouts but also of his true identity,[2] which he had undoubtedly learned from Brampton, who was back in England by this juncture. Hoping to force Margaret to sever her ties with the imposter, Henry dispatched Sir Edward Poynings and William Warham, "a cleric of great modesty, learning, and gravity,"[3] to the court of the Archduke Philip, son and heir of Maximilian I, who had just succeeded his own father as Holy Roman Emperor. The archduke's councillors gave serious thought to Henry's firmly-worded protest but ultimately ruled that they could not restrict Margaret's freedom of action on her own dower lands. Enraged by this, Henry decreed an immediate embargo on all trade between England and the Low Countries and shortly afterwards ordered the Merchant

Adventurers to transfer their cloth outlet on the continent from Antwerp to Calais. This action prompted the Burgundian government to retaliate by placing a ban on all English iron and woollen goods.

Such a resort to economic warfare hurt the subjects of both governments. Trade declined while unemployment mounted. The only gainers were the merchants of the Hansa, whose increased profits provoked the ire of suffering artisans in England. In September 1493 the king required the Hansards to post a bond of £20,000 for their promise not to trade illicitly; but this did not forestall a bitter attack the following month on the Steelyard, the headquarters of the Hansa in London and the centre of its English operations. This riot involved more than 500 apprentices and journeymen and lasted until the Lord Mayor arrived on the scene with a strong force. Scores of artisans were arrested and imprisoned, although the great majority were soon released and only the ringleaders were tried and punished.[4]

Knowing the imposter would probably seek Scottish aid, Henry took steps to cultivate better relations with James IV, who had received letters from Warbeck as early as May 1492, if not sooner. Late in May 1493 Henry directed Sir William Tyler and three others to negotiate a "real treaty" to replace the truce signed at Coldstream the previous November. The four emissaries were also to suggest that James look towards England for a bride: Henry had in mind a cousin of his own, a daughter of the Countess of Wiltshire, whom he falsely styled "the Princess Katherine." The Scottish ruler was not fooled by such a stratagem, however, and vowed that he would marry none but a real princess. Thus the negotiations foundered, despite Henry's offer of generous compensation for violations of the current truce; and the treaty signed at Edinburgh in June 1493 was little more than an extension, for another few years, of the existing peace. Although disappointed by the outcome of these negotiations, Henry gave handsome presents to the Scottish envoys who came south to witness his ratification of the treaty on 18 July. Lord Sempill and Sir Robert Carre received £20 each, while the Earl of Angus was given 200 marks and a valuable gilt cup.[5] Perhaps Henry was thinking of subsidizing a faction in Edinburgh that would look to England rather than to France for support. He may even have been plotting a possible *coup d'état* against James IV, should the latter openly assist Warbeck. In 1494 Henry requested Charles VIII to hand over John Stewart, the nine-year-old cousin of the King of Scots, who was currently living in Paris with his father Alexander, the treacherous Duke of Albany.[6] If Henry gave fleeting thought to the idea of setting up a rival to the Scottish throne, nothing came of the project, despite James's eventual support of Warbeck.

Meanwhile, during the previous year, the "Duke of York" had appealed to Ferdinand and Isabella for assistance. When they turned a deaf ear to his pleas, he accompanied Duke Albert of Saxony to Vienna in order to attend the funeral of Frederick III. Warbeck was hopeful of gaining support from the new emperor, Maximilian I, who was known to be embittered by Henry's embargo on Anglo-Burgundian trade. The imposter therefore received a gracious welcome at the Habsburg court and enjoyed an honored place between the Venetian and Sicilian envoys in the procession to St. Stephen's Cathedral. When in the summer of 1494 Maximilian paid a state visit to Antwerp, Warbeck was among those who accompanied him. On 6 October he was present at the investiture of the emperor's son Philip as Duke of Brabant, by which time he was residing in the *Hôtel des Anglais*, which had formerly housed the Merchant Adventurers and on the gates of which he displayed the royal arms of England. The imposter also sported a guard of twenty halberdiers who took as their chief badge the White Rose of York. This flaunting of his pretensions angered loyal Englishmen still in the city, who periodically retaliated by flinging mud and stones at his princely residence.[7]

How much of Warbeck's support was provided by Maximilian and how much by Margaret of Burgundy is unclear. Late in 1494 he acknowledged a debt of 800,000 crowns to the dowager duchess and made far-reaching commitments for the future. Should he ever obtain the throne for himself, he would not only repay his entire indebtedness to her but would also reimburse all the money she had spent on Lincoln's and Lovell's rebellions, restore all the property she had lost in England since Bosworth, and allow her to hold the town and castle of Scarborough for the remainder of her life. Only a month later Warbeck made equally extravagant promises to the emperor and his son at Mechlin. Should the imposter die before establishing himself on the English throne, his "claim" would devolve not on a Yorkist in England but on the Habsburgs, whose willingness to attach any value to such a pledge is difficult to understand. As Professor Elton has remarked, "Maximilian was himself good at making worthless promises, but one feels that on this occasion he had met his match."[8]

Although Henry was not informed of the agreements being made for the disposition of his kingdom, he was clearly worried about the possibility of conspiracy at home, which would strengthen the chances of a successful invasion. As early as February 1494 he had several suspected traitors arraigned at the Guildhall, and later the same year his agents penetrated a more important group of plotters, who, in addition to several laymen and two Dominican friars, included the Dean of St. Paul's Cathedral, William Worseley. The churchmen were spared, but Sir

William Mountford and two others were beheaded on Tower Hill, while their less influential associates were executed at Tyburn. Lord Fitzwalter and Sir John Radcliffe were sent to Calais and imprisoned there. Only when they tried to escape were they required to pay with their lives.

Undoubtedly the most powerful individual executed at this time was Sir William Stanley, brother of the Earl of Derby and one of the richest commoners in England. Stanley had played a major role at Bosworth and claimed much of the credit for Henry's elevation to the throne. Although he had been named to the important post of Lord Chamberlain, he felt that he had been insufficiently rewarded, since the coveted Earldom of Chester had been withheld from him. Whether Sir William took an active part in the plotting against Henry is unclear. Probably he did not but merely sought to hedge his bets, as he often did, so that he would emerge on the winning side, whichever that might be. This was brought to the king's attention by Sir Robert Clifford, a paid informer who received £500 from the Crown in December 1494. Because Henry was determined to make an example of men who were only lukewarm in their support, he had Stanley arrested on a charge of constructive treason; and on 6 February 1495 the Chamberlain was arraigned before the King's Bench. Sufficient evidence was produced to ensure his conviction, and ten days later he was beheaded. With Sir William's fall the other plotters became, in Bacon's memorable words, "like sand without lime, ill bound together . . . not knowing who was faithful." Not only did Henry destroy the last remnants of the conspiracy, but he also enriched himself in the process. The Stanley lands, reputedly worth more than £1000 a year, reverted to the Crown; and at Holt Castle in Denbighshire, royal agents found a cache of plate and jewels valued at almost £9500.[9]

More significant than his destruction of the English conspirators was Henry's decision to strike at whatever remained of Yorkist power in Ireland. The king was anxious to pacify the smaller island to the west so it would no longer be a haven for his enemies. During the summer of 1492 he had replaced Kildare with Archbishop Fitzsimons, who was incapable of maintaining law and order, however. In September 1493 Henry therefore named another new Lord Deputy: Robert Preston, Lord Gormanston, who was also a failure in the position. The bickering became more strident than ever, and within a few months Henry summoned all the greater magnates of Ireland to attend him at Westminster. Kildare, who was still the dominant figure in Dublin and most parts of Leinster, received an especially warm welcome at court, and during the spring of 1494 he attempted to recover the king's favor. Henry remained suspicious of him, however, and during a banquet one evening remarked loudly,

"My masters of Ireland, you will crown apes at length." This derisive comment caused consternation among the Irish lords, for, as they well knew, apes were a prominent feature of Kildare's coat of arms. Henry also alarmed his Irish guests by having them served by Lambert Simnel, whom they had accepted as their rightful monarch only a few years earlier. When Simnel appeared, the banquet hall grew deadly quiet, and no Irishman would accept food or drink from him. Yet the tension was eventually broken by Nicholas, Lord Howth, a jovial man who had not participated in the Simnel conspiracy. From his place across the table Lord Howth called out, "Bring me the cup if the wine be good, and I shall drink it off for the wine's sake and mine own also; and for thee, as thou art, so I will leave thee, a poor innocent." Henry was relieved that Lord Howth made sport of his joke, which had come so close to backfiring; and before the Irishman returned to his native land, he was rewarded with £300 in gold along with the robes he wore that evening.[10]

Although Kildare gave assurances for his future loyalty, Henry refused to reemploy him at this juncture, the wisdom of which soon became evident. Upon returning to Ireland the ex-Deputy was incensed to learn that Black James Ormonde had dismissed his kinsman, the Earl of Desmond, from the constabulary of Limerick. Thereupon Kildare broke his oath to live peaceably and took up arms once again. Meanwhile, in Ulster, Hugh O'Donnell of Tyrconnell was involved in some suspicious dealings with James IV, which made the whole island seem ripe for a fresh attempt by the imposter.

Knowing how dangerous it would be to rely on a native Irishman under these circumstances, Henry concluded that he must resort to new men as well as new methods. On 3 September 1494 he therefore appointed his three-year-old son Henry to succeed the ailing Duke of Bedford as Lord Lieutenant of Ireland, and the next day he named one of his most capable advisers, Sir Edward Poynings, to serve as Lord Deputy. To assist Poynings in his work of pacification, the king selected Henry Deane, Bishop-elect of Bangor, for the great office of Lord Chancellor; and for the equally significant post of Lord Treasurer, he chose Sir Hugh Conway.

Within a few weeks Poynings set out on his celebrated mission, and in mid-October he landed at Howth with 700 men. After attending to preliminaries, he marched off towards the North, where many of the disaffected had fled. Along the way he was attacked by the O'Hanlons, who, as he soon learned, were in league with Kildare and the Geraldines. This caused him to fall back on Drogheda, where he had summoned a parliament to meet on 1 December. This parliament, one of the most important in Irish history, passed a series of laws which established a new relationship between England and Ireland. The most important of these, soon to become known as "Poynings' Laws," put the Irish parliament under the firm control of the English Crown. Indeed Chapter 9 specified that no parliament could henceforth meet in Ireland until the Deputy asked leave of the king and submitted a list of the proposals he intended to introduce. This list would be considered by the king and his councillors at Westminster, and, if its provisions were deemed acceptable, a license would be issued under the Great Seal to hold a parliament in Ireland, but only for the ends set forth by the Deputy and approved in advance in England. Equally important, Chapter 39 stipulated that henceforth all laws passed by the English parliament would apply to Ireland, despite declarations by the Irish parliament in 1409 and 1450 that it alone could legislate for Ireland.[11]

Other provisions of the laws enacted at Drogheda also strengthened England's grip on Ireland, either by increasing the Deputy's authority or by striking at the military power of the native Irish. A powerful court, soon to become known as the Court of Castle Chamber, was established at Dublin under the Deputy's sole control. Elaborate procedures were outlined for the maintenance of governmental authority whenever a Deputy was absent from the scene. Steps were also taken to improve the financial position of the Irish administration, in order that it might eventually become self-supporting. Accounting procedures in the Irish Exchequer were tightened up; an Act of Resumption recalled whatever royal lands had been alienated since 1327; the lordship of Trim and Connaught was declared annexed, as were the Earldoms of March and Ulster; the king was granted a five-percent duty on all imports except those managed by the burghers of Waterford, Dublin, and Drogheda; and henceforth the constables of the seven principal royal castles were to be Englishmen rather than Irishmen. Although all citizens were allowed to keep firearms appropriate to their rank, no one was to procure artillery without a license. Neither was anyone to accept livery or wages from a lord or gentleman. Severe penalties were prescribed for agitators who stirred the native population to violence, and such traditional war cries as "Butlerabo" and "Cromabo" were outlawed. Yet, as a precautionary measure, it was decreed that the Pale should be fortified, a wide ditch to be dug around its perimeter.[12]

Once the Drogheda parliament completed its work, Poynings resumed his efforts to pacify the Irish countryside. Kildare, who had been attainted just before the session ended, was arrested in February 1495 and sent the next month to England. Within a few more weeks the Deputy went to the aid of Black James Ormonde, who was attempting to recapture Carlow

Castle from Kildare's brother James and the Geraldines. Probably because of this difficult undertaking, Henry sent over additional troops in June, which meant that the Irish army was stronger than ever when the imposter reappeared six weeks later.

That Warbeck made a second bid for power during the summer of 1495 was owing largely to the complex international circumstances then prevailing. Only a year earlier Charles VIII had sent an army across the Alps in order to assert his claim to the Neapolitan throne, which had been occupied since 1435 by a junior branch of the House of Aragon. Although long anticipated, the French advance down the Italian peninsula was virtually uncontested. On 17 November Florence opened its gates to the invaders; by the end of December Rome had capitulated; and on 22 February the French troops entered Naples in triumph. But the other rulers of the time soon joined together to withhold the fruits of victory from France. In March 1495 envoys from Milan, Spain, the Papal States, and the Empire gathered at Venice and established the "Holy League," the stated purpose of which was to expel Charles VIII's armies from Italy. Although England was not represented at Venice, the signatory powers expected Henry to clamor for membership in the League and to seize the occasion to attack France from the rear. As much a dreamer as ever, Maximilian even insisted that Henry should be denied admission until he promised to cross the Channel in force. Had Henry sought entry into the League at this juncture and proclaimed himself an ally of Maximilian, the latter would doubtless have withdrawn his support from Warbeck. But the pragmatic Henry knew how risky it was to attach any faith to the emperor's professions, and besides there was no compelling reason for him to sacrifice his good relations with Charles VIII, with whom he had been on friendly terms since 1492. The French invasion of Italy did not endanger English interests. On the contrary, by focusing the attention of other rulers on the Mediterranean, it might be expected to divert them from a possible attack on his realm. Thus from Henry's point of view, Charles VIII's involvement in Italy was something to be encouraged rather than opposed; and although he became a nominal member of the Holy League in July 1496, in order to placate Ferdinand of Aragon, he made it clear that he would not declare war on France. Rather he announced that he still desired to be the good friend of Charles VIII, who was delighted and responded by signing a new commercial treaty with him in May 1497.

Because of Henry's refusal to dance to the emperor's tune, Maximilian resumed his support of the imposter and together they brought to completion the long-smouldering plan for an invasion of England. In May

1495 Margaret of Burgundy dispatched a long letter commending the project to Pope Alexander VI; and within a few more weeks the emperor assured the Venetian ambassador in Vienna that Warbeck would soon be firmly seated on the English throne and that one of his first acts would be to declare war on France. Henry's agents on the continent clearly knew that something was afoot, although they failed to discover where the blow might come. Since a cross-Channel operation might well be coordinated with a Scottish attack on northern England, the king directed the Earl of Surrey and several other Northerners to see that all able-bodied men living within the precincts of the border were in readiness to beat back a possible invasion. Yet Henry did not neglect diplomacy, for once again he proposed a family compact, this time offering James IV the hand of his own daughter Margaret, which shows how dangerously he regarded the situation.[13] Probably because of these well-considered moves, Warbeck received no aid from Scotland until he himself appeared at James's court.

Early in June the imposter sailed across the Channel with some fourteen ships. But the inhabitants of Kent were on their guard, and the 300 invaders set ashore at Deal were quickly defeated by the sheriff, Sir John Peachey, who sent them off to London "all railed in ropes, like a team of horses in a cart."[14] Warbeck himself remained safely aboard; and when he realized that the attempt had failed, he sailed off to try his luck again in Ireland. On reaching the coast of Munster, he made contact with the Geraldines, who promised to assist him in an attack on Waterford. On 23 July he appeared off the city with eleven ships, and shortly afterwards Desmond arrived with 2400 men. But even though they were totally surrounded, the inhabitants of the city mounted a stout resistance and held out until a relieving force under Poynings and the Lord Mayor of Dublin arrived. Three of Warbeck's ships were captured, and on 3 August he sailed away again in fright. Accompanied at first by Desmond and several others, he was pursued only as far as Cork. Ultimately he made his way to Ulster, where, after conferring with Hugh O'Donnell, he crossed the straits to southern Scotland. After a series of hazardous adventures, he arrived at the court of James IV about the end of November.[15]

Even if the Scottish king questioned the identity of this newcomer, he had a good reason to assist him. Since 1482 the English government had held the great border fortress of Berwick, which Henry VII had no intention of surrendering. If the English ruler could be deposed, his successor might prove more cooperative, particularly if the return of Berwick was made a prior condition of Scottish support. Consequently, when the imposter arrived at Stirling, he received a gracious welcome and was introduced around the court. Clothes and apartments were provided for him along with a pension of £1200 a year. Because James IV wished to believe Warbeck's claims, he publicly accepted him as the rightful king of England. In addition he arranged for him to marry a cousin of his own, Lady Catherine Gordon, the beautiful sister of the Earl of Huntley. The imposter soon fell deeply in love with his Scottish wife; and it is hard to begrudge him the brief happiness he experienced during the spring of 1496.[16]

Meanwhile Henry was taking steps to fortify himself so he would not be caught off guard. In October 1495 his fifth parliament opened at Westminster and enacted a series of measures he proposed. Sir William Stanley and several others executed earlier in the year were attainted and their estates declared forfeit to the Crown. Yet Yorkists who had made their peace with the king were assured that the past was safely dead and buried: no proceedings would be initiated against them for any offences committed before Bosworth Field. Closely associated with this was the measure known as the "De Facto Act," which was designed to keep men from hedging their bets, as the Lord Chamberlain had done. Henry was determined to have his subjects' whole-hearted loyalty; and at his urging parliament decreed that, in the unlikely event an imposter gained the throne, no one would be prosecuted for supporting the reigning, or de facto, monarch. Whether this measure would have provided the protection intended is doubtful, since no parliament has ever been capable of binding its successors. But the De Facto Act was useful for its psychological value, because it seemingly prohibited legal action against men who remained loyal to the present occupant of the throne. It therefore kept the weak-in-heart from making overtures to Warbeck, and in that way it served a worthwhile purpose.[17]

Probably because he still hoped to avoid hostilities with Scotland and wanted no repetition of the circumstances of 1492, when he had been compelled to invade France, Henry did not request a financial grant from parliament. Nevertheless the Lords and Commons assented to the collection of any arrears remaining on the benevolence of 1491, while convocation willingly voted to contribute ten per cent of the assessed valuation of all benefices within the realm. Because the Northerners would probably resist a demand for war taxation, a fixed imposition on that region was established for the upkeep of the fortifications at Berwick and Carlisle.

Shortly after the session ended, Henry brought a halt to the economic warfare that had raged with the Low Countries since the autumn of 1493. Embargoes and counter-embargoes had hurt the commerce of both countries, although Anglo-Burgundian trade had never completely died out. It is possible, as several scholars in fact maintain, that the rather primitive

economy of England was more seriously affected than the more sophisti-
cated one of the Low Countries and that Henry was on the verge of giving
way. But, as it turned out, the Archduke Philip took the initiative at this
juncture and proposed a resumption of full commercial ties. Moreover, the
archduke had already withdrawn his support from the imposter, who was
now ensconced at the Scottish court. In January 1496 the Burgundian
government sent Lord Beures and several other high-level emissaries to
London; and after a month of talks the treaty characterized by Bacon as
the "Intercursus Magnus" was signed on 24 February.

Although the new treaty did not refer to Warbeck by name, it stipulated
that neither government should henceforth aid or shelter rebels against the
other. In addition the Burgundian representatives at last agreed to restrict
the dowager duchess's freedom of action should she continue to engage in
conspiracy. Even more important than these clauses were the economic
provisions of the treaty, which Professor Wernham has aptly called "the
Magna Carta of the English traders' position in the Netherlands." In the
future English merchants would be allowed to sell their wares in all parts
of the archduke's dominions with the sole exception of Flanders. They
would not be obligated to pay tolls or duties in excess of those collected
during the previous fifty years; and they would receive fair and speedy
justice in the archduke's courts, in accordance with precise rules pertaining to fraudulent transactions, recovery of debts, inspection of cargoes,
and other matters likely to provoke discord. As Professor Wernham has
observed, "If Henry sacrificed trade to his dynastic necessities in 1493, he
amply repaid the debt in 1496."[18]

After the conclusion of the Intercursus Magnus, Henry concentrated on
ways of dislodging the imposter from the Scottish court. Although James
IV had ignored his earlier marriage proposals, Henry renewed his offer of
his daughter Margaret's hand, which would be contingent, however, on
the expulsion of Warbeck. Between 5 May and 2 September 1496, Henry
issued three separate commissions to treat for a marriage alliance between
the two Crowns. The Bishops of Durham and Carlisle, the Earl of Surrey,
and several other Northerners were instructed to go to Stirling in order to
confer with James IV. Should a treaty be concluded, the Bishop of
Durham and at least one other English emissary were to sign it on Henry's
behalf.[19] In order to show his support for these diplomatic efforts,
Ferdinand of Aragon, who longed to see England in the Holy League,
dispatched a special ambassador, Don Pedro de Ayala, Bishop of the
Canaries, to Scotland with instructions to promote the match in whatever
way he could.

Despite this combined Anglo-Spanish offensive, which paved the way for England's admission to the League in July, James IV honorably refused to divest himself of the imposter. Rather he speeded up his preparations for war, and in mid-September he and Warbeck struck across the border with 1400 men. Styling himself "Richard IV," the imposter sought to keep the Scottish troops from harming any civilians they happened to meet and offered a reward of £1000 along with a substantial revenue from land to the person who brought him the head of Henry VII. As was probably inevitable, the Scottish army was unable to resist the opportunity to plunder. Within a few days the enterprise broke down altogether, after only a few miles had been traversed. No uprising of the local population occurred on behalf of the would-be deliverers, which was crucial to the success of the attack. Rumors soon drifted in that an English force had set out from Carlisle to meet the Scots, although Surrey was in fact just completing his mobilization. Knowing how dangerous continued occupation of English soil was likely to be, James IV directed his troops to recross the border. By 21 September he and Warbeck were safely back at Coldstream.[20]

Because of the Scottish invasion, Henry could appeal once again to his wealthier subjects for financial aid. On 24 October a special assembly of notables met at Westminster to consider the need for an army to resist the continuing threat from the North. This assembly of peers, clerics, lawyers, and merchants remained in session for two weeks and authorized Henry to raise whatever money he could by means of a new benevolence. Yet many Englishmen refused to open their purses, even in this time of present danger. Others would contribute only a fraction of the sums demanded of them. Dame Elizabeth Elsyng, for example, was rated by the commissioners at £40 but would not pay a penny more than £5, for which she was severely reprimanded by the Council. When the corporation of London was asked to provide £10,000, it succeeded in raising only £4000. Yet the yield from the country as a whole was an encouraging £57,388 10s. 2d., or almost £10,000 more than from the benevolence of 1491.[21]

Even this sum might prove inadequate, so within a brief time Henry summoned a parliament to meet, as the assembly at Westminster had urged him to do. In January 1497 the sixth parliament of the reign opened; and after a lengthy account of James IV's misdeeds by Cardinal Morton, the Lords and Commons voted two tenths and fifteenths, or £120,000, for the maintenance of "two armies royal for a substantial war to be continued upon the Scots." The first tenth and fifteenth were to be paid at the Exchequer by 31 May, while the second grant was to be deferred until the 8th of November following. Any sums collected by means of the benevolence of the previous year would be deducted from the amounts that would otherwise be owed under this allocation. In addition, steps were taken to ensure that the burden did not fall inequitably on the poorer property-owners, who were largely exempted from the second tenth and fifteenth. It was also agreed that, should the war be a long one and the armies require additional funding, Henry would be allowed to raise an additional £120,000. But should the conflict come to a speedy end, whatever remained to be collected on these grants would be cancelled immediately. While parliament was agreeing on the precise terms of its financial aid, convocation was voting Henry £40,000 with which to prosecute the war.[22]

Once assured of adequate financial support, Henry decreed that all Scots must abjure the realm by the Feast of the Purification (2 February). Then he mobilized an army under the Earl of Surrey, who set out at once for the border. After inspecting the fortifications there, Surrey and his men crossed into southern Scotland, burning houses and farm buildings in a brief raid. Meanwhile, in the precincts of London, steps were being taken to create a more powerful force under Giles, Lord Daubeney, the new Lord Chamberlain. Although Daubeney and his men departed for the North in order to attack James IV, they were compelled by an insurrection that threatened to engulf the capital to redirect their steps before that assault could begin.

In the southwestern counties and particularly Cornwall, there were widespread complaints about the demand for war taxation. Scores of irate householders protested that it was not their duty to finance a campaign against the King of Scots. Because the people of the North had a special responsibility for border defense, they had long been exempted from most forms of direct taxation, so it was incumbent on them to shoulder the burdens of a war which was, in any event, only "a small commotion" which would end "in a moment." The Cornish protestors were led by Thomas Flamank, a lawyer who provided arguments justifying the up-rising, and Michael Joseph, a blacksmith who made a direct appeal to the poor farmers and miners of the Southwest. Within a few days Flamank and Joseph had gathered a band of more than 15,000 men. They had no intention of challenging the king himself but resorted to the constitutional fiction that his ministers alone were to blame. If only new councillors could be appointed, governmental policy was bound to change for the better and the demand for additional taxation would doubtless be with-drawn. Thus the obvious strategy was to make a peaceful protest to Henry, who undoubtedly wished to be apprised of their views.[23]

Early in May the rebels set out from Bodmin, the shire town of Cornwall, for London. After crossing the Tamar they marched through Devon and Somerset, doing injury to no one. But when the corporation of Bristol refused to admit them, they fell upon a royal tax collector at Taunton and killed him. Upon reaching Wells they were joined by Lord Audley, an impoverished nobleman who was still annoyed by the failure to take any booty on the Boulogne campaign of 1492. Still unopposed, the Cornishmen tramped on through Wiltshire and Hampshire until they arrived at Winchester, whence they took the Great Road north towards London. By this juncture Henry had posted sentries throughout the city and lodged his family in the Tower for safety. By 13 June Lord Daubeney was poised at Hounslow Heath with between 8000 and 10,000 men. Meanwhile the king had gathered a smaller army at Henley-on-Thames, which he merged with the Chamberlain's force after moving his head-quarters to Lambeth.

After a brief skirmish in Surrey, the rebels demanded that Flamank and Joseph lead them into Kent, the home of such folk heroes as Wat Tyler and Jack Cade, for which reason the county was generally considered the citadel of English freedom. But for the last three decades Kent had enjoyed a high degree of prosperity and was not disposed to admit the Cornishmen. Furthermore the local landowners, led by Lord Cobham and the Earl of Kent, had gathered troops enough to block their way. Thereupon the rebels became dispirited, particularly when they learned that Henry would not parley with them until they laid down their arms. The weak-in-heart began to steal away, while a cadre of self-appointed peasant leaders offered to surrender Audley and Flamank in return for a general pardon. It was with a deep sense of foreboding that the Cornishmen encamped at Blackheath on 16 June, the tenth anniversary of the battle of Stoke.

Early the next morning Daubeney launched a fierce attack. The Chamberlain himself led the vanguard of the royal army, while the Earl of Oxford commanded the centre. Because of the early hour the royalists achieved a tactical surprise, and briefly it appeared that the rebels, fighting on foot and without adequate weapons, would be routed within the hour. But they rallied and put up a stout defense, capturing large numbers of the vanguard, including Daubeney himself. But they were no match for Oxford, England's finest general; and when he charged their exposed flank, they were quickly overrun. More than a thousand Cornishmen perished, whereas the king's losses did not exceed 300. All the rebel leaders were captured or slain, the most important survivors being sent off to London to be tried for treason. As befitted his noble rank, Lord Audley was beheaded on Tower Hill, whereas Flamank and Joseph were hanged, drawn, and quartered at Tyburn.[24]

Shortly after the battle ended, Henry knighted several of his commanders along with the sheriffs, mayor, and recorder of London. Then he returned to the capital by way of Borough High Street, where he was joyously acclaimed by citizens delighted to know that the threat to the city and its inhabitants was over. After a thanksgiving service in St. Paul's Cathedral, he was reunited with his wife and children in the Tower. As inclined as ever towards mercy, he allowed the release of most of the prisoners taken at Blackheath once they had surrendered their effects to their captors. Yet he subsequently sent a commission headed by Amias Paulet into the West Country to impose fines on several dozen participants in the rebellion. In this way he added approximately £9000 to his coffers.[25]

Fortunately for the king, the imposter and his Scottish protector did not take advantage of the Cornish revolt to launch another attack on northern England. Consequently, while order was being restored in the Southwest, Henry made renewed overtures to James IV. Again he suggested the conclusion of a marriage alliance, which was to be contingent, however, on the expulsion of Warbeck and the payment of a large indemnity. James's response to these terms, which he considered insulting, was to strike across the border in July and besiege Norham. But Surrey was standing in readiness with 10,000 men and forced the Scottish invaders back across the Tweed. With a romantic flourish James challenged the English general to hand-to-hand combat, with the victor's prize to be Berwick. Surrey refused to consider the King of Scots' proposal, which he rejected with heavy sarcasm; and when the Englishman saw that he could not lure his adversary into a real encounter, he contented himself with the destruction of the outworks of Coldstream Castle and the harassment of Scottish peasants living nearby.

Neither the English nor the Scottish king wanted the war to continue indefinitely; and although James still refused to surrender the imposter, he wished to terminate his role as Warbeck's official benefactor. Even before the attack on Norham, he had insisted that "Richard IV" try his luck again in Ireland; and to speed him on his way, he even provided him with one of his own ships for the voyage. Thus there was no longer a compelling reason for the two monarchs to persist in their opposition; and through the good offices of Bishop Ayala, a seven-year truce was signed at Ayton on 30 September.

Meanwhile, late in July, the imposter had landed at Cork, where he received a warm reception from the mayor, John Atwater, and Black James Ormonde, previously Henry's strongest Irish supporter. Ormonde's recent change of sides had been caused by his bitterness over the Geraldines' return to favor, symbolized by Kildare's reappointment as Lord Deputy,[26] which demonstrated once again how riven Ireland was by local rivalries. Unfortunately for Warbeck's prospects, Black James was killed only nine days after his landing by an enemy within his own House, Sir Piers Butler. Even though Warbeck continued to have the backing of Atwater and Lord Barry, a rich landowner of the neighborhood, the death of his strongest proponent meant that his cause in Ireland was doomed. Which way was he now to turn? Expelled from France by Charles VIII, likely to be arrested by the archduke if he returned to the Low Countries, no longer welcome at the court of James IV—the future must have appeared bleak indeed to the young man who had set out to see the world a decade earlier. The only chance seemed to lie in a surprise descent on Cornwall, where the embers of rebellion might be fanned back to life. Early in September Warbeck and a hundred Irish supporters therefore set sail for western England. Almost intercepted at sea by a squadron of ships from Waterford, they made their way to Whitesand Bay near Land's End, where they disembarked on 7 September.[27]

Once ashore Warbeck sent his young wife, who had loyally remained at his side since their departure from Scotland, to the security of the monastery at St. Michael's Mount. Then he set off for Bodmin, which he entered at the head of a sizable force, his ranks having swelled along the way with local malcontents. Greatly heartened, he again proclaimed himself "Richard IV" and convoked a council of war. It stressed the necessity of capturing a fortified town in the West Country that could be used as the headquarters for a later march on London. Exeter seemed to offer the best chance of success, and on 17 September Warbeck and 8000 partisans appeared before its walls. Throughout the assault the rebels were fed and sheltered by the local country people; but because they were inadequately armed and equipped, their attempt to take the city by storm was a hopeless undertaking. A clever plan was devised to set fire to the northern and eastern gates, but it was defeated by Exeter's inhabitants, who were fiercely loyal to the king.[28]

Unable to storm the city and with 400 of his men killed in the attempt, Warbeck withdrew to Taunton, which was even more reluctant to admit him. By this juncture Henry had learned of his challenger's movements and directed Daubeney to lead his troops into the Southwest. Furthermore the landowners of the region were beginning to mobilize their retainers; and the fleet sailing down the Channel under Lord Willoughby de Broke would soon be able to prevent an escape by sea. In desperation Warbeck rode out of camp on the night of 21–22 September and galloped with a few trusted supporters for the Hampshire coast, where they hoped to catch a ship for the continent. But it was already too late. The southern ports were blocked, and the imposter had no choice but to take refuge in Beaulieu Abbey. Within a few days his dejected followers surrendered to the king's mercy, and, sensing that his masquerade was at last over, Warbeck did the same. He was conducted back to Taunton, where on 5 October he made a full confession and acknowledged his true identity. Shortly afterwards he was transported in chains to Exeter and commanded to repeat his confession in the presence of the king and his own disspirited wife, who had just been brought in from St. Michael's Mount.[29]

Henry was unusually merciful to the young couple now in his power. Although Warbeck had caused him many anxious moments during the last six years, the king took no legal steps against him and placed him under the loosest possible surveillance. Had the imposter been content with this arrangement, he might have lived out his days in far greater comfort than Lambert Simnel was doing. But he chafed at even the most gilded imprisonment, and when he tried to escape in June 1498, Henry had no choice but to take harsher measures against him and had him thrown into the Tower.[30] As for Warbeck's wife, who resumed her maiden name shortly after her capture, she was accorded the utmost respect and invited to become a lady-in-waiting to Elizabeth of York. She resided at court for more than a decade and ultimately married James Strangeways, a gentleman of the king's bedchamber. After his death some years later, she took two more husbands in turn, both of whom she lived to bury, since her death did not occur until 1537.

The king was almost as merciful to the men of Devonshire and Cornwall who had supported Warbeck's last attempt to capture the throne. Never one for savage reprisals, he ordered only a few executions and, in general, allowed the guilty to pay with their purses rather than with their lives. Fines were assessed on Warbeck's most active partisans, and, once the royal commissioners completed their work, Henry was another £5699 richer. As a consequence he derived a handsome profit from the events of 1497, since his outlay to suppress the Cornish revolt and repulse the Scottish invasion had not exceeded £60,000. Yet he had received grants of £150,000 from parliament and convocation, while the fines collected in the West Country amounted to £14,699. Thus he realized a net gain of nearly £105,000, or almost as much as he had obtained from his earlier campaign against Charles VIII. Since 1492 he had been completely solvent, spending less every year than he took in; and for the remainder of the reign there would be large budgetary surpluses, which put him in a stronger financial position than any other occupant of the English throne.[31] From the summer of 1497 foreign ambassadors made pointed references to his growing wealth. In September of that year the Milanese envoy, Raimondo de Soncino, informed his government that Henry "has upwards of six millions of gold [£1,300,000], and it is said that he puts by annually five hundred thousand ducats."[32] These figures were of course greatly exaggerated, as Bishop Ayala of the Canaries recognized. In July 1498 the Spanish ambassador reported to Ferdinand of Aragon that "the king of England is less rich than is generally said. He likes to be thought rich, because such a belief is advantageous for him in many respects." But even the sceptical bishop soon changed his mind, for during the next year he observed that Henry's revenues "augment every day. I think he has no equal in this respect."[33]

Regardless of how much money Henry was able to put aside each year, he no longer had any reason to worry about the financial position of his government, at least during peacetime. Nor did he have cause to be concerned about the stability of the realm, which was quieter than ever by the end of 1497. Indeed there was such a marked absence of conspiracy during the next few years that foreign ambassadors commented admiringly on the extent of Henry's power. In 1498, for example, the Milanese envoy informed his government that "the kingdom of England was never in such tranquillity or so loyal to his Majesty as now, both nobles and people being in great obedience to the King."[34]

There remains to be said only a few words about Henry's policy towards Ireland during these years. Sir Edward Poynings continued as Lord Deputy until December 1495, when he was recalled and rewarded for a job well done with the Wardenship of the Cinque Ports. To succeed Poynings, the king turned back to Kildare, who had been a prisoner in England since the preceding March. During his time in captivity, the Irishman had realized that Henry was much too strong to be overthrown and that, because of the king's sensible attitudes, it would not be as hard to work with him as he had formerly supposed. For his part, Henry was deeply impressed by Kildare's natural wit and quickness. When directed at one point to choose an advocate for his coming trial, the earl announced that he would be served by none but the king, since in his view there was no one of greater ability in the country. Assuming that Henry had been offended by such temerity, the Bishop of Meath declared, "All Ireland cannot rule yonder gentleman," to which the king replied, "Then he is meet to rule all Ireland."[35]

Because Kildare's wife had died in November 1495, Henry arranged for the earl to marry a cousin of his own, Elizabeth St. John, daughter of Oliver St. John of Lydiard Tregoze. Once this family compact had been sealed in the summer of 1496, Kildare appeared before the monarch and his Council at Salisbury and vowed to do everything in his power to pacify Ireland, even promising to find a solution to the quarrels between the Geraldines and the Butlers. Thereupon the Irishman received a pardon for his past offenses and was reappointed Lord Deputy. Although Henry required him to leave his eldest son in England as a hostage, the earl and his new countess departed for Ireland during August; and on 21 September he took the oaths of office during a great public ceremony at Drogheda. That the king made no mistake in restoring Kildare to power was amply proved during the summer of 1497, when Warbeck made his final appearance in Ireland. For the first time the Geraldines rallied to the Tudor cause; and just as the earl and his forces were about to sweep down on Warbeck, the imposter took fright and sailed away to Cornwall.[36]

For the remainder of the reign Henry had no cause to worry about the situation in Ireland. Although he did not inquire into Kildare's private dealings, the Deputy honored his promise not to feud with the Butlers. Shortly after his return to Ireland Kildare selected an old associate, Archbishop Fitzsimons, now on cordial terms with the Butlers, for the great office of Lord Chancellor, which received wide popular approval. Subsequent quarrels within the Butler and O'Neill clans eased Kildare's task of maintaining peaceful relations between the various family groups. Most important of all from Henry's vantage point were the Deputy's efforts to lessen Yorkist feeling throughout Ireland. Because of Kildare's unrivalled popularity, he was able to carry most of the Irish people along with him, and within a few years Henry's fears about Yorkist conspiracy there had dissappeared altogether. Thus, according to his own lights, the king's Irish policy was a complete success. In April 1503 he summoned Kildare to attend him once again in England and accorded him lavish marks of favor and respect. The earl's son Gerald, who had lived at court for the past eight years, was granted lands worth more than £800, after which he was married to Lady Elizabeth Zouche, a distant cousin of the king's. After three months of tournaments and receptions at Westminster, Kildare returned again to his native land with his son and new daughter-in-law, weighted down "with great honor and new Instructions."[37]

Criticisms that Henry erred in granting Kildare too much power and that he missed a golden opportunity to subdue Ireland for good by recalling Poynings in 1495 are without much substance in fact. No Englishman would have been accepted as Deputy for more than a few years; and despite the reforms of William Hattecliffe and other English officials who went to Ireland in the spring of 1495, the Irish administration was never in a position to pay its own way. It is true that Henry's campaign to strengthen the royal finances was a brilliant success; but his efforts in this regard would have been hopelessly undermined had he become embroiled in a long and expensive war in Ireland. The treasure he bequeathed to Henry VIII in 1509 was nowhere as great as Bacon and his other early biographers maintained; and it was completely depleted within a few years of his death as a result of the French War of 1512-14 and his son's programme of rapid naval expansion.[38] Thus the first Tudor king's resources were not without limit, which meant that he had little choice but to rely on Kildare, the only Irishman of the age who was strong enough to rule the island on a long-term basis. That Henry saw the situation clearly and played along with the earl until he won his confidence helps to explain the extraordinary success of the government's policy towards Ireland during the early Tudor period, whatever its long-term effects may have been. That some historians have attacked Henry for failing to foresee the developments of a later age, and particularly the way the Reformation drove the English and Irish peoples into opposite camps, seems shortsighted and unfair, to say the least. Regardless of what steps Henry might have taken to prevent future conflict, the relationship between the two islands was far simpler during his lifetime than it was to be a century later; and from his vantage point his most pressing task was to win the trust of Kildare and the Geraldines, in order to end Yorkish plotting once and for all. Thus he should not be blamed for concentrating on limited, sensible, and moderate goals. In all that he attempted in regard to Ireland, he succeeded admirably.

VII

Welsh and Local Government, Legislation and Parliamentary Matters

If in time Henry solved the problem of Yorkist Ireland, he brought peace and stability to Wales far more quickly. Naturally he had advantages in regard to Wales that he could never expect to enjoy in Ireland. He himself was the head of an old Welsh family, which gave him powerful connections in all parts of the principality and the marches.[1] At one time or another during the reign, he controlled at least fifty of the 136 marcher lordships, including the twenty-two that comprised the Earldom of March, inherited from the Mortimers by way of the Yorkists; and this gave him greater power in the borderlands than any of his predecessors.[2] In addition he had the unswerving support of Rhys ap Thomas in Carmarthenshire and of Jasper Tudor in the northern sections of the principality. On the latter's death in 1495 all his estates, including those of the Earldom of Pembroke, reverted to the king, who soon granted them to his second son, Prince Henry. The execution of Sir William Stanley in 1495 also led to a substantial increase of royal power in Wales. The lordships of Bromfield, Yale, Holt, and Chirk were incorporated into the royal demesne; and until the Duke of Buckingham came of age in 1498, the king also controlled the lordships of Newport, Caurs, and Brecknock. In 1504 Henry negotiated a special indenture with Buckingham and various other landowners in South Wales, by which they signed bonds as pledges of their future loyalty.[3] Thus Henry had extensive resources of power and patronage, and it should come as no surprise that the Welsh countryside was relatively quiet during his reign. There was of course some local fighting even after 1504, but the region clearly became less turbulent with the passage of time. Even more significant from Henry's vantage point, no imposter or Yorkist pretender ever appeared there; and at no time during the reign was any fundamental dissatisfaction with the dynasty expressed.

That Wales was relatively peaceful between 1485 and 1509 was owing, at least in some degree, to the sympathy Henry expressed for the aspirations of his Welsh subjects, who on their part claimed him as a native son. His triumph at Bosworth was considered a victory for Wales also; and shortly after 1485 scores of ambitious Welshmen crossed the border into England, where better job opportunities existed for them than at any time since 1399. Throughout the Tudor period numerous Welshmen, including Williamses, Thomases, Herberts, and Morgans, were employed in the royal household. Other important positions in the capital were also open to them. Sir Richard Exmewe became a prosperous merchant and served in 1492 as Warden of the Goldsmiths' Company and in 1517 as Lord Mayor. Of course not all the Welsh newcomers settled in the vicinity of London. Henry Vaughan proceeded no farther than Bristol, where he was soon elected mayor, while Sir David Owen settled in Hampshire and was eventually named constable and chief carver of Winchester Castle. In so far as later developments are concerned, the most important Welshman to settle in England at this juncture was David Cecil, who, after distinguishing himself at Bosworth, founded a Northamptonshire family that achieved greatness in only two generations: his grandson William, the first Lord Burghley, served as Elizabeth I's chief minister for forty years.[4]

Before 1485 the main positions in the Welsh church had always gone to Englishmen, a practice that now ceased. Not only did Henry VII appoint Welshmen to the four bishoprics in their native land, but he also selected them for important positions in both England and Ireland. John Morgan became Dean of Windsor, whereas Henry Deane, who had achieved fame as Prior of Llanthony, was named Lord Chancellor of Ireland in 1494. About the same time Deane was appointed to the Bishopric of Bangor, from which he was translated early in 1501 to the important English diocese of Salisbury. Less than a year later he was selected to become both Archbishop of Canterbury and Lord Chancellor. Poor health compelled Deane to resign the Great Seal in July 1502, however, and early the next year he died at Lambeth. Occasional rewards and distinctions were also conferred on various other Welshmen. Rhys ap Thomas, for example, was inducted into the Order of the Garter in 1505, an honor that no Welshman had enjoyed for more than a century.[5]

In regard to the day-to-day administration of Wales—as in so much else—Henry VII followed in the footsteps of his Yorkist predecessors. In November 1489, at the time of his son Arthur's investiture as Prince of Wales, he established a special council to manage the prince's estates in Chester, Cornwall, and Wales and to supervise administrative matters not only in the principality but also in the border counties of Shropshire, Hereford, Gloucester, and Worcester. Entrusted with comprehensive powers, this council was remarkably similar to the one Edward IV had established in 1471 for his eldest son, the ill-fated Edward V.[6] Until his death in 1495, Jasper Tudor was clearly the leading member of the revivified council for Wales; and in March 1493 he and Prince Arthur received a joint commission from the king to superintend the execution of justice throughout Wales and in the four border counties.[7] After Jasper Tudor's death two years later, Bishop Smith of Lincoln emerged as the dominant figure on the council, of which he was the official president until 1512. Doubtless he was present at Chester on 4 August 1499, when the prince arrived on an extended visit and the townspeople presented a mystery play, "The Assumption of Our Lady," for his entertainment.[8] By this juncture Henry VII had sent his heir apparent to live in the border area, so that he could secure first-hand political experience, which should be a good preparation for the duties that would eventually befall him.

As long as Prince Arthur lived, there was little to distinguish the Council of Wales from the advisory council of any great landowner. But after his death in 1502, the council quickly assumed more modern characteristics and became "a professionalized and articulated part of the royal government," answerable only to Henry and his ministers at Westminster.[9] That the Council of Wales became more bureaucratic in nature after 1502 was owing largely to the fact that, while the king insisted on keeping it in existence, he would not allow his second son, Prince Henry, to participate in its work. The king was deeply concerned about the safety of his only surviving son (his third son, Prince Edmund, had died in 1500), and he was determined to keep his new heir apparent, who was created Prince of Wales in 1504, under his watchful eye at court. Thus Prince Henry was never allowed to reside at Ludlow Castle or Tickenhill Place, in Worcestershire, as Prince Arthur had done. Yet Henry VII clearly understood the importance of retaining a Council for Wales and the border area, and as a consequence it did not disappear as its

Yorkist precursor had done between 1484 and 1489, when there had briefly been no Prince of Wales.

Little is known about the council's work during the years 1502-12, when Bishop Smith handled most of its routine duties. Presumably it was composed of the same ten men who had belonged to it before Arthur's death, and much of its work was apparently of a judicial nature.[10] In 1512 Geoffrey Blythe, Bishop of Coventry and Lichfield, succeeded in the presidency of the council, in which post he served until 1524. Except for a few years during the late 1520s and a comparable period during the Great Rebellion of the seventeenth century, the council never lapsed until its formal abolition in 1689, during the aftermath of the Glorious Revolution. Thus the council was an integral part of England's government during the greater part of the Tudor-Stuart period; and although a forerunner of it had existed between 1471 and 1484, it owed its permanent establishment, and much of its formal organization, to Henry VII.

Although Henry built on Yorkist foundations in regard to the governance of Wales, he refused to continue the arrangements they had made for northern England. Between 1471 and 1483 Richard of Gloucester had served as Edward IV's viceroy in the North, in which capacity he had been aided by a staff of lawyers, clerks, bailiffs, and scribes. Upon his seizure of the throne in 1483, Richard had appointed his favorite nephew, the Earl of Lincoln, to the position he had held and had established a special council to assist him, which was endowed with broad judicial and military powers.[11] Thus, before the end of the Yorkist period, there was a bureaucratic institution in existence in northern England, which must be regarded as a precursor of the more famous King's Council of the North, established by Henry VIII and Cromwell in 1537, during the aftermath of the Pilgrimage of Grace.

On his assumption of the throne in 1485, Henry VII decided it would be dangerous to continue Richard III's arrangements for the North and at once revoked the authority granted to Lincoln, who was subsequently killed at Stoke. In his management of northern affairs, the first Tudor monarch deliberately kept any agency or individual from acquiring too much power. Despite his insistence on the need for shared or dispersed authority, Henry had of necessity to depend more heavily on some men than on others; and from time to time he granted extensive powers to such noblemen as Henry Percy, Earl of Northumberland (ob. 1489); Thomas Howard, Earl of Surrey (ob. 1524); and Thomas, Lord Dacre of Gilsland (ob. 1525). Each of these men had an advisory council to assist him, in the manner of the time; but the power wielded by these bodies was inconsequential when compared to the authority enjoyed by the councils that had assisted Gloucester and Lincoln before 1485. From time to time Henry also granted special powers in the North to other trusted individuals, including the Bishops of Durham and Carlisle, his capable mother, Lady Margaret Beaufort, and such royal ministers as both the Chancellor and the Attorney of the Duchy of Lancaster. In 1498 Prince Henry was officially named Lieutenant of the North Parts, and several councillors were appointed to assist him. But this was a temporary expedient of no lasting significance; so it cannot be maintained that Henry VII made an important contribution to the government of the northern counties. Indeed, if this yardstick is applied, his reign was "a period of retrogression when compared with that of the Yorkists."[12]

That Henry VII refused to make any systematic arrangements for the North was probably owing in some part to his confidence in, and increasingly heavy dependence upon, the Justices of the Peace. For purposes of local government in all parts of his realm, Henry was content to rely primarily on the J.P.s, who were invariably appointed from the ranks of the richer gentry, although a law of 1439 allowed them to have yearly incomes of as little as £20 from freehold land. The J.P.s were never paid a salary by the Crown, but they were nevertheless happy to serve for the honor and status associated with their position and in order to have a potent influence over local affairs: an influence they were reluctant to see exercised by their enemies. According to Professor Bindoff, Henry VII gave more thought to the selection of J.P.s "than any other king before or since. He certainly helped to make nomination to the [local] commission of the peace the recognised first step in a gentleman's public career, and the competent discharge of its duties the condition of his further progress."[13] While he occupied the throne, Henry VII heaped great new responsibilities on the Justices and even granted them a supervisory and restraining power over their main local rival, the sheriff, now declining to the role of a ceremonial functionary. Almost all historians agree, therefore, that the office of J. P. achieved great new importance after 1485. To cite Professor Bindoff again, "the J.P., if not born, certainly came of age under the Tudors, who saw in his office the ideal instrument for their purpose."[14] Because each of Henry VII's seven parliaments conferred additional duties on the J.P.s, only the most important statutes of the period that pertained to them can be reviewed here.

In 1485 the Justices were directed to arrest all persons suspected of poaching under cover of darkness or in disguise. Two years later their power to grant bail to individuals awaiting trial was confirmed, but with the proviso that they must not release "known" burglars and murderers.

The same statute of 1487 also required them to investigate false returns made during the course of official inquests and to punish all jurors convicted of neglecting their duties.[15] Henry's third parliament, which assembled in 1489, enacted a measure that requried the J.P.s to take vigorous action to prevent such crimes as arson, murder, extortion, counterfeiting, and "many other enormities and unlawful demeanings." According to the provisions of this statute, the Justices were to proclaim at the beginning of each of their quarterly meetings, on pain of a 20s. fine, that the existing laws were sufficient to maintain peace and order, if only those laws were properly enforced. Anyone who impeded the Justices' work in this regard was to be reported to the king's officers at Westminster, and a J.P. who shirked his duties was to be punished by his fellow Justices, or in the unlikely event they refused to act, by the king and his Lord Chancellor.[16]

In so far as the granting of additional duties to the J.P.s is concerned, the parliament of 1495 was the most important of the reign, for it increased their responsibilities in numerous ways. Not only were they empowered to regulate beggars, vagabonds, and ale-house keepers, but they were also directed to punish laborers and artisans who refused to work for the official wage rates determined by them. In addition two or more Justices, provided at least one belonged to the quorum of the county commission, were authorized to punish merchants and traders who used false weights and measures, and they were also to take disciplinary action against mayors and bailiffs who failed to enforce the commercial standards decreed by parliament. Local officials guilty of extortionate practices were to be fined 40s. each and their names reported to the Exchequer. In order to prevent riots and other unlawful assemblies, the parliament of 1495 ordained that the Justices should hear cases against petty offenders without the participation of a jury, which was widely criticized, however, as an infringement of the subject's rights; and in 1510 the first parliament of Henry VIII repealed this portion of the statute of 1495.[17]

The last two parliaments of Henry VII increased the Justices' duties in additional ways. In 1497 the J.P.s were authorized to hear complaints against royal tax collectors, in the appointment of whom they were now to have a voice, and to assist in the assessment on local propertyowners of all subsidies, tenths, and fifteenths. In 1504 the two Houses directed the J.P.s to see that all sheriffs, mayors, and other local officials accepted the legal coin of the realm at face value. The Justices were also required to appoint searchers to ensure that brass and pewter products measured up to the prescribed standards of fineness. In addition the parliament of 1504 took steps to guarantee that the J.P.s always took proper legal action against individuals suspected of poaching or riotous behavior.[18]

Whether the Justices made a sincere effort to fulfil their manifold duties has long been a matter of dispute. According to Professor Chrimes, the king and his advisors never felt secure that their "principal instruments for the enforcement of law and order in the localities could be relied upon. . . . Henry VII's government did not notably succeed in solving the perennial problem that had beset its predecessors—how to enforce the law of the realm."[19] However, this view is not shared by most historians. G. R. Elton maintains, for example, that the Justices' independence of the central government has generally been exaggerated; while D. M. Loades and R. L. Storey contend that, by the time Henry VII died, the J.P.s were wielding their powers "to an extent they had not dared earlier in the fifteenth century, notably in their enforcement of the statutes against livery and maintenance."[20] The views of an Italian traveller in England in 1501–2 are clearly worth citing at this point. Although this Italian visitor believed that "there is no country in the world where there are as many thieves and robbers as in England," he was nevertheless impressed by the activities of the J.P.s, for whom there was no equivalent in his native land. In his opinion, "It is the easiest thing in the world to get a person thrown into prison in this country; for every officer of justice, both civil and criminal, has the power of arresting any one, at the request of a private individual, and the accused person cannot be liberated without giving security, unless he be acquitted by the judgment of . . . twelve men."[21] Thus even though the Justices did not evolve into "irreproachable pillars of public order," England enjoyed more efficient local government than almost any state in Europe. And because the wealth of the Tudor rulers was not inexhaustible and they were never able to maintain a standing army, it is doubtful whether they could have found a more dependable agency than the county commission or the individual J.P.

If the Justices' authority was greatly strengthened between 1485 and 1509, this was not the principal objective of Henry's legislation, which was geared primarily to other matters. Indeed only twenty-one of the 192 acts passed during the course of the reign pertained to the duties and responsibilities of J.P.s. Thus the overwhelming majority of the king's enactments were concerned with other problems, such as needed alterations to the common law. Of the various statutes that related to the common law, nine dealt with questions of procedure, seven with changes in the land law, and four with technicalities of the criminal law. Perhaps the most important in the last of these categories was an act of 1487 which made it a felony to abduct or aid in the abduction of an heiress, many of whom were kidnapped and forced to marry against their will at this time.[22]

Although it is often held that the Tudor rulers followed a paternalistic social policy, only a few of Henry VII's measures dealt with problems that were primarily social in nature. And of the few that did, the most important were passed early in the reign in an unsuccessful effort to regulate two closely related evils: enclosure and depopulation. The enclosure movement had gathered momentum since the 1450s but was still restricted primarily to Kent, Hampshire, the Isle of Wight, and half a dozen midland counties. It involved the consolidation of scattered strips of farmland into larger and more compact units, the conversion of arable land into sheep runs, and the seizure of lands formerly reserved for the whole community by the more powerful landowners. Although enclosure enabled a few men to double or even triple their yearly incomes, the movement was extremely detrimental to the bulk of the population, since it reduced the demand for peasant labor, led to a substantial increase of vagabondage and rural unemployment, and prevented small cottagers from using the common lands to pasture their farm animals or to forage for firewood, thatch, nuts, and berries. Thus the enclosure movement benefited one section of society at the expense of another, which Henry VII and his ministers naturally deplored; and it also led to the depopulation of areas where sheep runs became prevalent, since only a few hands were needed to tend the burgeoning flocks of sheep. As the movement continued, such coastal regions as Kent, Hampshire, and the Isle of Wight became more thinly populated than ever, which caused mounting alarm on the part of the government. For if England should again be invaded from the continent, the relatively few inhabitants of those counties where an attacking force might well land would be unable to stave off the assault until royal troops arrived on the scene, which meant that the chances of a successful invasion were appreciably greater than in the past.

Whether Henry VII was chiefly influenced by humanitarian or by strategic considerations is difficult to determine. Probably it was by the latter, since the statute of 1495 that empowered the J.P.s to regulate beggars and vagabonds demonstrated virtually no understanding of the reasons for their plight.[23] Furthermore, when the king first proposed legislation to correct the problem, he stressed the dangers of depopulation rather than the evils of enclosure. Yet in Henry's defense it ought to be remembered that no government of the time had the resources to solve such a complex socio-economic problem; and the few that made a sincere effort to do so, such as the Duke of Somerset's regime between 1547 and

1549, were quickly overthrown. As long as the upper classes profited from enclosure and were simultaneously responsible for the enforcement of anti-enclosure legislation, owing to their control of local government, there was no chance that the movement could be halted, let alone reversed. Not until the 1550s, when the European wool trade suddenly contracted and England's yearly exports declined by over twenty per cent, did the situation begin to correct itself.[24] Thus Henry should not be criticized too severely for failing to adopt measures that were clearly beyond his ability to implement.

If Henry wasted little energy trying to halt enclosure and depopulation, he nevertheless made a few gestures in that direction. Early in 1489 he secured a statute to prevent the further consolidation of scattered strips of arable land into more compact units on the Isle of Wight. By this act severe penalties were prescribed for men who engrossed strips worth in excess of ten marks a year. Henry also persuaded his third parliament to pass a statute against the enclosure movement in general. After a preamble that denounced the harmful consequences of both depopulation and enclosure, this act decreed that all farms of twenty acres or more should be maintained as separate agricultural units, "as were convenient and neces- sary for . . . upholding of tillage and husbandry." Occupiers who failed to heed this new requirement would forfeit half their yearly profits to either the king or the owner of the fee.[25]

Just as Henry took occasional steps to restrict the enclosure movement, he periodically sought to regulate the practice of retaining. For centuries the principal landowners of the realm had retained other men in their service as a way of providing themselves with armed supporters. But the small armies that resulted endangered the peace of the realm, and as early as 1392 a parliamentary act had directed the J.P.s to punish all violent deeds committed by the armed retainers of noblemen. Yet it was not until 1468 that an attempt of sorts was made to limit the institution itself.[26] Moreover, there is no evidence that anyone was ever prosecuted under the act of 1468, either by the Yorkists or by the Tudors. Indeed no monarch of the period gave any real thought to an outright prohibition of the practice, since the Crown had no army of its own and necessarily depended for military power on the levies of its greater subjects. When in 1489 Henry VII was about to send troops to the aid of Anne of Brittany, Lord Willoughby de Broke offered to provide "as his personal retinue 4 knights, 26 *hommes d'armes*, and 970 archers." Similarly, when Henry VIII invaded northern France in 1513, he was accompanied by the Earl of Northumberland, who brought along 500 heavily armed tenants from his Yorkshire estates.[27]

Until recently most historians believed that retaining declined and disappeared as a result of policies implemented during Henry VII's reign. Yet research during the last thirty years has shown that the practice continued until the very end of the Tudor period. In 1588, at the time of the Spanish Armada, the Earl of Pembroke offered Queen Elizabeth the services of 800 of his followers, including 300 horsemen, all equipped at his own expense. Even John Whitgift, Archbishop of Canterbury between 1583 and 1604, kept numerous retainers, 100 of whom accompanied him on his first official trip into Kent. In February 1601 the archbishop's retainers were of great assistance to Queen Elizabeth in putting down the rebellion fomented by the Earl of Essex.[28]

If Henry VII did not seek to abolish the practice of retaining, he at least hoped to bring it within manageable bounds. Four statutes passed between 1487 and 1504 attempted to regulate and control it;[29] and during the course of the reign several prominent landowners were prosecuted for illegal retaining. These included Thomas Neville of Gloucestershire and William Bassett of Worcestershire, both of whom were required to pay heavy fines to the Crown. In 1502 Sir Edward Stanley of Yorkshire was ordered to post a £200 bond for his offence of illegally retaining more than fifty men; while a proclamation addressed soon afterwards to local officials throughout the Southwest forbade any Englishman to retain another individual in his service, since, as Henry now contended, he had "reserved from the beginning of his reign the attainder to himself of all his subjects."[30]

The climax of Henry's efforts to control retaining came in 1504 with the passage of the famous Statute of Liveries. This measure was not as original in concept as many historians maintain, since it restated many of the clauses of the 1468 act and codified the more recent restrictions against retaining. The new statute began by declaring that, despite earlier legislation, "divers persons have taken upon them[selves] to give and some to receive liveries and to retain and be retained . . . and little is or hath been done for the punishment of the offenders." Because the J.P.s were often reluctant to act, they were henceforth absolved from prosecuting offenders in their quarterly meetings but were expected to report any breaches of the law to the Council or the Court of King's Bench for action by one of them. As in 1468, the fine for every sign or token illegally accepted was to be 100s. for each month an individual so retained "hath taken or accepted the same." Similarly, the penalty for men who gave such designations to others was to be 100s. a month for each individual illegally retained. Seemingly the Statute of Liveries prohibited all forms of livery, with the exception of those reserved for household servants, since it did not reenact the lawful service clause of the 1468 act. Yet the new legislation empowered the king to issue licenses to his greater subjects, on whose retainers he would still depend for military power during wartime. In this way the Statute of Liveries enabled him to regulate the extent of his subjects' retaining and made him the real beneficiary of the institution. As an added safeguard, the measure stated that men who procured licenses to keep retainers could not use them in whatever manner they pleased and that all military service was ultimately owed to the king.[31]

The act of 1504 gave Henry a powerful weapon to use against any peer who engaged in suspicious dealings. George Neville, Lord Burgavenny was the first person to be prosecuted under it. In 1497 Lord Burgavenny had shown suspicious sympathy for Flamank, Joseph, and the other Cornish rebels when they sought to enter Kent, and in 1506 there were reasons for believing that he was in collusion with the Earl of Suffolk, a Yorkist imposter who had caused Henry much trouble since 1499.[32] Lord Burgavenny was therefore charged with illegally retaining 471 men from the central hundreds of Kent, to which he pleaded guilty and was ordered to pay £70,650. Subsequently he signed three different bonds, totalling £100,000, as pledges of his future loyalty. These three bonds were cancelled within a short time of Henry VII's death in 1509; and three years later, on the eve of the Anglo-French war of 1512–14, Lord Burgavenny was licensed by Henry VIII " 'to retain as many men as he can get in Kent, Sussex and Surrey and elsewhere . . . and he shall give them badges, tokens, or liveries as he thinks convenient.' " When in May 1514 he assembled his retinue at Canterbury, it consisted of 948 men, "whom he led as chief captain and lieutenant of the king's army."[33] Lord Burgavenny was only one of numerous landowners who provided troops during the war of 1512–14. In 1513 the king directed David Owen and several other gentlemen to mobilize as many men as they could, notwithstanding " 'any act, statute, or ordinance heretofore made to the contrary, concerning retainers.' " Yet once the war ended, the second Tudor king reverted to his father's policy and made the act of 1504 the basis of his attitude towards retaining. He nevertheless continued to depend on his subjects' levies whenever hostilities threatened. In 1544, for example, he instructed the Earl of Huntingdon "to accompany him to France and to bring along 150 footmen, including 29 archers, and also 70 horsemen."[34]

Like the Statute of Liveries, many of Henry VII's enactments were far from original: in general their purpose was to reinforce earlier legislation. It is surprising, therefore, that Bacon considered Henry VII the most important lawgiver since the time of Edward I. In a memorable passage, the king's first biographer maintained of his legislation that it was

. . . deep, and not vulgar; not made upon the spur of a particular occasion for the present, but out of providence for the future, to make the estate of his people still more and more happy, after the manner of the legislators in ancient and heroical times.[35]

Bacon's assessment has been restated in recent years by Professor Gray, who contends that Henry's best statutes are notable for their "breadth of outlook."[36] Yet many scholars dispute such a judgment. The great eighteenth-century jurist, William Blackstone, for example, maintained that Henry's laws were intended primarily for the benefit of the Exchequer.[37] A contemporary authority on Henry's reign, R. L. Storey, insists that "the principal aim of his legislation was to enable the common law machinery to function effectively, particularly against crime and riot." Professor Storey nevertheless refuses to consider Henry "a great law-reformer" and deplores the king's failure to sponsor any "really radical reforms."[38] Certainly the first Tudor king did not secure the passage of any fundamental measures, comparable to those enacted during the reigns of Edward I or Henry VIII; but we should never forget how difficult it is to achieve "really radical reforms" when there is no clearly felt need for them. Besides, even a dedicated reformer would have faced insuperable difficulties in early Tudor England, for, as one individual of the time maintained, "if the king should propose to change any established rule, it would seem to every Englishman as if his life were taken from him."[39] Most historians agree that what was really needed during Henry VII's lifetime was not a spate of new legislation but a determined effort to enforce existing statutes, a willingness to punish all criminal acts efficiently and impartially; and on this score it is impossible to criticize the king, who, according to Bacon, "did much [to] maintain and countenance his laws."[40]

If Henry VII was not one of the most important lawgivers in English history, his reign was nevertheless a period of considerable legislative activity that was of undoubted benefit to his subjects. While he was on the throne, 192 acts were passed in all, or an average of just over twenty-seven by each of his seven parliaments. This was almost exactly the same number as were passed by the later parliaments of Henry VIII and slightly more than were enacted by those of Elizabeth I.[41] But to what extent did Henry VII's legislation bear "the stamp of the king's wisdom and policy," as Bacon maintained? This is one of the thorniest questions surrounding any aspect of the reign, for two reasons. First, the history of parliament during the late medieval period has yet to be written; and second, two diametrically opposed views of the matter have been advanced in recent years by eminent authorities. The first, espoused by Professor Gray and many others, holds that the king himself was responsible for much of the legislation of the period. Indeed, Professor Gray contends that of the 192 statutes of the reign, 114 originated as public bills and 78 as private ones. As for the 114 public bills, only 17 were "passed at the request of the Commons," while nearly all of the truly important measures of the period, and especially those of any constitutional significance, arose from public bills for which the government was clearly responsible.[42] The second and more recent view has been advanced by Professor Elton, who insists that of the 36 penal statutes of the reign, the king's will "is professed to be behind only 15 . . . while 14 rested on commons' petitions and 7 grew out of requests put forward by sectional interests." Professor Elton has concluded, therefore, that "much has been put down to Henry VII that was only accepted, not initiated, by him."[43]

Regardless of the truth of the matter—and a definitive statement cannot be made until much additional research is accomplished—Henry exercised firm control over the deliberations of all his parliaments. That he was able to direct the work of his successive Lords and Commons with no apparent difficulty was owing to several different factors. First, he himself was a capable if not a brilliant parliamentarian who intuitively knew when to compromise and when to stand firm and insist on having his own way. Second, the Lords and Commons had as yet no life of their own and could assemble only when and for as long as he chose. There was no question about his right to prorogue, adjourn, or dissolve the two Houses whenever he wished; and unless he required new legislation or a grant of taxation, he was under no compulsion to summon them. Because Henry was completely solvent after 1492 and there was no real need for new legislation, the reign was not one of frequent or over-long parliaments. Indeed the seven parliaments that met between 1485 and 1504 sat for but fifty-nine weeks in all, or for an average of less than 2½ weeks during each of the twenty-four years of the reign.[44]

Although Henry's parliaments occasionally balked at his legislative proposals, an organized opposition did not come into existence for more than a century after his death. Even if such an opposition had coalesced while he was on the throne, it would have had little leverage or bargaining power to use against him, since he managed to balance his budget so quickly after Bosworth. Because he enjoyed regular budgetary surpluses by 1497, he was able to adopt an even more independent stance in relation to parliament during the second half of the reign. Between 1485 and 1497, six parliaments had met in all; but during the period 1497–1509, only one assembled, during the spring of 1504, for a session of nine weeks. The seven years that elapsed between the parliaments of 1497 and 1504 were the longest interval that had yet occurred without a parliament since the assembly had evolved during the mid-thirteenth century. Although two or three parliaments had generally met during each year of the fourteenth century, the length of time between sessions began to increase after the deposition of Richard II in 1399; and this culminated during the early Tudor period, when parliament was summoned less regularly than at any time before the era of Charles I's Personal Rule.

To ensure his control over parliament, Henry was careful to see that capable and experienced officials presided over the debates in both chambers. The four Lord Chancellors of the reign—Alcock, Morton, Deane, and Warham—were all eminent members of the episcopal bench; and with clerics of their prestige on the woolsack, Henry had no reason to worrry about the debates in the House of Lords.[45] In regard to the lower chamber, where the Speaker was technically an elected official, Henry never failed to secure the position for his own nominee, who was invariably paid £100 at the close of the session. (Rather interestingly, this was only half the sum Edward IV had generally granted his Speakers.)[46] During the Lancastrian period the same man had frequently served as Speaker during successive parliaments; but while Henry VII occupied the throne, a new Speaker was elected by each new assembly. All of Henry's Speakers were prominent lawyers and included such distinguished officials as Sir Thomas Lovell, Chancellor of the Exchequer and Treasurer in turn of the Chamber and the king's household; Sir Richard Empson, Attorney and subsequently Chancellor of the Duchy of Lancaster; and Edmund Dudley, under-sheriff of London from 1496 until 1502 and, beginning in July 1506, Lord President of the Council. During Henry's third parliament, which met in 1489, the Speaker was a former Yorkist, Sir Thomas FitzWilliam, Recorder of London, who had gone over to the new dynasty immediately after Bosworth.[47]

Although Henry never sought to pack the Commons with his own supporters, he did not ignore the need for parliamentary management, which helps to explain why he rarely vetoed bills that were submitted for his signature. Vetoes had often been used during the preceding century, and they were to be employed again with great regularity by Queen Elizabeth.[48] But during the time of the first Tudor monarch, the routine proceedings of parliament were so completely dominated by his ministers that he seldom felt compelled to avail himself of the veto power.

Nevertheless, he did occasionally amend or add provisos to bills at the time he signed them into law without referring them back to the two chambers. This was an accepted constitutional practice of the time. Between 1453 and 1483 a number of measures had been altered by unilateral royal action, without any consideration of the members' wishes. In 1465, for example, Edward IV had added two clauses to a subsidy bill that had been submitted to him by the Lords and Commons without seeking their approval. Exactly how often Henry VII utilized this arbitrary procedure is difficult to determine, and only a few important changes should apparently be ascribed to him. Yet on at least one occasion, "his action was so arbitrary that the unfortunate clerk of the parliaments did not know to which [bill] a proviso should be attached."[49] The monarch retained his power to amend bills in this fashion until the 1530s, when, because of the growing complexity of legislation owing to Henry VIII's break from Rome, his right to do so lapsed.

Henry VII also exercised two other powers over parliament that his successors lacked or chose to use more sparingly. He himself could introduce legislative proposals, which he did on one occasion in 1497, when he personally delivered in a bill that was at once read and debated by the Lords. In addition he had an undisputed right to punish the members of either House for failing to attend regularly scheduled parliamentary sessions.[50] How to guarantee regular attendance after 1485 was a minor problem compared to what it had been during earlier eras. Parliament was now an established part of the constitutional machinery, and a steadily increasing number of country gentlemen aspired to sit there. The tendency for borough seats to be contested by wealthy members of the gentry had already begun, and as a result the middle-class element in the Commons was declining. Yet even as late as 1529, the lower chamber still had a large bourgeois contingent, approximately half the total membership. Not until the reign of Queen Elizabeth did the floodgates truly open and the gentry elbow their way in in force, thereby converting the Commons into the kind of body the upper chamber had always been—a rich man's club.[51]

Because of the somewhat lower social status of the average member of the Commons during Henry VII's time, and because this was more than a generation before the advent of the "educational revolution" of 1560–1640, the debating skills and analytical abilities on display in the lower House were of a lesser magnitude than was subsequently to be the case. Yet it would be wrong to denigrate the abilities of every member of parliament during the early Tudor period, for many had a wealth of practical experience acquired over long political careers. Edmund Dudley, for

LEGISLATION AND PARLIAMENTARY MATTERS   *139*

example, was a member of the lower House in 1484, 1485, 1487, 1489, 1491, 1495, probably in 1497, and again in 1504, when he served as Speaker.[52] Of course it would be erroneous to assume that the average member sat as regularly as Dudley, but many were present on more than one occasion, and most were capable of framing bills and petitions. Perhaps it was for this reason that Henry treated the average member with unusual tact and consideration while he was on the throne. Only once, when he called for an exceptionally large feudal aid in 1504, did any real friction develop between him and parliament; and on that occasion he agreed to a reasonable compromise and was cordial to all but his leading critics.[53] In addition most Englishmen were delighted by his campaign to revitalize the powers of the central government and thereby provide them with the benefits of order and stability. He had adopted a programme they had long wished to see implemented, and as a consequence there was an identity of outlook and purpose between him and the average Englishman. And this, in conjunction with his own considerable talents, assured a harmonious relationship between Crown and parliament for all but a brief period during the reign.

VIII

Naval Affairs and the Age of Exploration

The reign of Henry VII was not one of the great periods of English naval history. Its achievements were modest when compared to the rapid growth of the fleet during Henry VIII's time or the daring exploits of Sir Francis Drake and the Elizabethan seadogs. Furthermore when the First Tudor king died in 1509, the navy was considerably smaller than it had been during earlier eras. Whereas Henry V had owned thirty-four vessels in 1422 and Edward IV at least fifteen in 1481, Henry VII bequeathed only seven men-of-war to his son.[1] Yet whatever the early Tudor navy lacked in quantity was offset by its improved quality. Not only were Henry VII's ships larger and better equipped than earlier ones, but the naval administration was organized along more professional lines. Thus although his contribution was not a brilliant one, it provided a firm foundation for his successors to build upon.

During the greater part of his reign, Henry VII was assisted in the management of naval business by three trusted advisers: Sir Reginald Bray, Sir Richard Guildford, and Sir Thomas Lovell. Bray, for example, supervised the construction of a powerful new warship, the *Sovereign*, which was built at Southampton in 1489–90. Constructed out of the spars and timbers of the *Grace à Dieu*, an obsolete ship that Henry had inherited from the Yorkist kings, the *Sovereign* was a four-masted vessel of between 600 and 700 tons, or more than three times as large as the average ship of the period. It was also considerably better armed than most vessels of the age, since it carried 225 serpentines, cast-iron guns that weighed 250 pounds apiece. Also completed in 1490, the *Regent*, which was built under the direction of Sir Richard Guildford, was an even larger ship than the *Sovereign*, although it was equipped with eighty-four fewer serpentines. Constructed in a shipyard on the Rother, then a tidal river in Kent, the *Regent* was patterned after the *Columbe*, a French vessel that Henry had seen and admired before 1485. Like its sister ship the *Regent* was a four-masted vessel and was one of the most expensive ships of the age to construct, costing almost £1000 in all.[2]

The counsel of advisers like Bray and Guildford was often supplemented by technical advice from the Keeper of the King's Ships, a bureaucrat stationed at Southampton who attended to such matters as the payment of workmen and the purchase of naval stores. Shortly after Bosworth Henry reappointed Thomas Roger, originally a merchant of the capital, to the post he had held since 12 December 1480. The king must have been pleased with Roger's work, for in December 1486 he increased his per diem wage while travelling on official business from 2s. to 3s.[3] Roger served as chief clerk of the navy until his death in 1488. Then the position was assigned to William Comersall, who was removed in 1495 to make way for Robert Brygandyne. Brygandyne had been a royal employee since at least 1490, when he was granted an annuity of £10. Doubtless his work was highly regarded, for as late as 1523 he was still toiling away at his duties.[4]

Brygandyne's greatest contribution to the administrative side of the navy was to assist with the development of Portsmouth as a fortified naval station, capable of meeting the needs of a permanent navy. This work was well advanced by 1494, when £2068 11s. 1d. was issued to William Cope, "in part payment of the charges of building a tower and bulwark there."[5] The first dry-dock in the British Isles was also constructed at Portsmouth. This installation was conceived by Bray, who in July 1495 arranged for Brygandyne to handle the duties formerly assigned to John Nest, the first foreman of the project. Although Brygandyne had no previous engineering experience, the dry-dock was completed without incident and was ready for use by May 1496. Yet within another year the dockhead was discovered to be in danger of collapsing, so a program to repair and strengthen it was launched in July 1497. This took eleven weeks to complete but cost the Crown no more than £12 10s.[6]

Although a few technical improvements occurred during the course of the reign, the naval thinking of the period did not progress to any significant degree. As yet England's naval leaders did not conceive of battles between the ships themselves but still thought in terms of infantry actions at sea, with the outcome being determined by hand-to-hand combat between the troops aboard once the process of ramming and boarding occurred. This is why the crew of the *Sovereign* consisted of 600 soldiers and sailors but only 40 gunners. It also helps to explain why, during the Anglo-French war of 1512–14, the *Regent* had an active complement of 700 men. Even the *Caravel of Ewe*, acquired in 1495 and one of Henry's smallest warships, had a complement of 170 men.[7] Because archers were still an integral part of any action at sea, the *Sweepstake* and the *Mary Fortune*, both completed in 1497, were equipped not only with oars but also with sixty sheaves of arrows.[8] This may have been inevitable as long the breech-loading serpentines of the period, the best guns of the age, could be fired only twice during the space of an hour. Although their range was approximately 1300 yards, the serpentines of Henry VII's ships were unable to pierce the hulls of enemy vessels, since their main function was to destroy sails and rigging, after which the serious business of ramming and boarding began. Because of this, it has been observed that, "In no respect was the navy of Henry VII more medieval in character than in the armament of the ships."[9]

Despite the essential soundness of such a view, a few harbingers of later developments already existed. In 1501 the 141 serpentines aboard the *Regent* included twenty-four brass ones,[10] and these were precursors of the more effective weaponry of the future. Heavier and more reliable brass guns would enable Henry VIII and his naval architects to build more modern vessels in the 1540s and thereby to inaugurate a new era in the history of naval warfare, when the outcome of battles was determined by the ships themselves and not by the troops they had aboard. This became feasible as soon as brass guns, which fired a deadlier and more accurate charge, were standard equipment aboard all of England's warships; but the process of conversion had clearly begun before the end of Henry VII's reign. Similar improvements, also pointing towards the future, were made in regard to sails and rigging. According to one naval historian, Henry VII's largest ships showed "an enormous advance in the number of masts and yards, and in their sail area," over vessels constructed during the Lancastrian and Yorkist periods.[11] Efforts were also made before 1509 to improve the food and drink provided for the crews, and by the last decade of the reign the cost of victualling a ship had risen from 12d. to 14d. for each seaman per week. Yet wages remained abysmally low, since the average sailor received only a shilling a week for shore duty and a scant 3d. extra for any time spent at sea. Boys who served as pages were paid even less, receiving as little as 6d. weekly.[12]

Henry VII's most important contribution to the development of the navy was not made through the construction of new ships and harbor installations or even through a series of technical and financial advances. Rather it was made in the less direct fashion of increased support for England's overseas trade and merchant marine. Reference has been made in an earlier chapter to some of the methods Henry used to foster greater English trade not only with the Low Countries but also with France, Spain, northern Italy, and the Baltic states. Not all of his efforts succeeded of course, but by the time he died in 1509 the volume of England's foreign trade was greater than it had ever been, causing a recent historian to observe that "Henry's claim to be the Father of British Trade is a very strong one." Moreover, this same authority maintains that whenever a substantial volume of sea-trade arises, "Naval Power will almost inevitably develop in order to protect it. Indeed, it is questionable whether any lasting Navy has grown up for any other reason than trade protection, direct or otherwise." By the same token, whenever naval fleets are constructed for other reasons, "they will very soon wither and die . . . if there is no volume of maritime trade behind them."[13] Certainly the earlier centuries of English history offer ample proof of the essential soundness of such a view. Such kings as Alfred the Great, John, and Henry V had built large numbers of warships for their own special ends; but because of the absence of a substantial volume of overseas trade, their fleets had declined and disappeared within a few years of their deaths. Such was not to be the case after Henry VII died, however. Because of the extent to which he increased English trade abroad, his successors were acutely aware of the need to build even more warships; so while Henry VII should not be regarded as the "Father of the British Navy," he might well be considered its "Grandfather."[14]

Henry VII's right to this lesser title appears even stronger when one recalls his efforts to develop larger numbers of merchant craft, which he naturally expected to requisition for the Crown during wartime at the nominal rent of a shilling a ton per month. Almost from the time he took the throne, Henry offered substantial bounties to those who would construct or purchase ships of not less than eighty tons—he saw no need to encourage the construction of smaller vessels, or "coast crawlers." Such financial inducements to bolster the size of England's merchant marine were not without precedent. In 1449 Henry VI had instituted a similar programme; and while on a visit to Bristol in 1474, Edward IV had promised generous rewards to anyone who would undertake to build a new ship.[15] Yet when Henry VII resorted to his predecessors' methods in 1488, he attained considerably greater success, since he was willing to allow tax credits not only for ships constructed in English dockyards but also for vessels purchased abroad. Occasionally he granted as much as 5s. a ton—or £20 for an eighty-ton ship—which was the same rate that Henry VIII and Elizabeth I subsequently allowed. In 1488, for example, he granted a rebate of £26 13s. 4d. to Nicholas Browne of Bristol, who had recently purchased a foreign ship of 140 tons, out of the customs duties Browne owed at the conclusion of the first voyage with his new ship. Three years later he extended a similar tax credit to three Bristol merchants who had constructed a commercial vessel of 400 tons; and in 1502 he granted £20 to Hugh Elyot and his two Bristol partners, who had just acquired a French-built ship of 120 tons.[16] Since a three-masted vessel of substantial tonnage could be built for approximately £110 at this time, the king's bounty was an effective stimulus to the construction of a larger merchant marine, although there is little reason to believe that this expansion was limited to England's eastern ports, as several historians maintain.[17]

If Henry VII ought to be remembered as "the Grandfather of the British Navy," he is just as entitled to be regarded as "the Grandfather of British Colonization of North America." Deeply interested in the geographical discoveries of the age, Henry gave substantial support to John and Sebastion Cabot and to many lesser-known men who participated in the exploration of the New World; and had his example been followed by his immediate successors, England's domination of the North American mainland would have become an accomplished fact long before it was.

Henry's first opportunity to participate in the process of trans-Atlantic discovery occurred during the winter of 1488-9, when Bartholomew Columbus, brother of the great Christopher, appeared at the English court. During the past few years the two Columbuses had been trying to gain support from a king or prince for a trans-Atlantic voyage. In 1484 or 1485 Christopher had sought help from John II of Portugal; but that monarch was intent on reaching the Far East by way of South Africa and refused to give the explorer any assistance.[18] Within a few more years the elder Columbus decided to pin his hopes on Henry VII of England; and in 1488 he sent his brother Bartholomew, a chartmaker in Lisbon for more than a decade, to London. After a hazardous journey, during which he was beaten and robbed by Easterling pirates, Bartholomew arrived in the English capital during the winter of 1488-9. Several months elapsed before he secured an audience with the king, who was at once intrigued by the map presented to him and the accompanying Latin verses that purported to explain what the map revealed. Henry expressed a desire to be of assistance and was polite and agreeable to the younger Columbus, with whom he conversed on several occasions. But ultimately he referred the matter to a committee of the Council, which objected to it on the grounds that the project was based on an exaggerated notion of the breadth of Asia and thus on a mistaken view of the Atlantic's size. Thus the proposal was rejected in England for exactly the same reasons it was turned down elsewhere, although the Anglo-French crisis of 1489-92 probably contributed to Henry's decision to withhold his support. At any rate, after several frustrating years in London, Bartholomew departed for Paris, hoping an appeal to Charles VIII would bring better results. He was still at the French court in 1493 when news arrived that his elder brother had just returned from a trans-Atlantic voyage backed by Ferdinand and Isabella. Thereupon Bartholomew packed his bags and set out for the Spanish court at Valladolid.[19]

Henry VII is usually criticized for his failure to support the Columbus brothers, since most historians feel that his decision cost England dearly in the trans-Atlantic competition that new began. G. R. Elton takes a different view, however, and contends that:

> . . . even if the king had been at liberty in 1490 to listen to the Genoese visionary, it does not follow that England lost what Spain gained. If Columbus had sailed from Bristol in 1490, as John Cabot did seven years later, he would have reached the inhospitable shores of Nova Scotia (as Cabot did) and not the promising islands of the Caribbean: the winds would have seen to that.[20]

Although Elton's reasoning is undeniably correct, the king had sincere regrets when he learned of Columbus's discoveries and the lucrative trade that was likely to fall to Spain. When several years later John Cabot appeared in England and proposed to make a similar voyage, Henry quickly gave financial support to him, since he was determined to seize this second opportunity.

John Cabot, who occupies such an important place in the naval annals of his adopted land, was characterized by a contemporary as "a Venetian by birth and a most skillful mariner."[21] Yet Cabot actually seems to have been born in Genoa, from which he moved about 1461 to Venice, where he was admitted to full citizenship fifteen years later. A merchant by trade, Cabot made several voyages to the ports of the Black Sea as well as the eastern Mediterranean but ultimately concentrated his efforts on the Near Eastern spice trade and supposedly made a journey, disguised as a pilgrim, to Mecca. While travelling along the shores of the Red Sea, Cabot was told by Arab traders that their wares came from the northeastern parts of farthest Asia, which fired his imagination. That Cabot prospered in the spice trade there can be no doubt, for in 1484 he made a generous settlement for the benefit of his wife Mattea.[22] Exactly when he and

Mattea moved with their three sons to Spain is unclear, although by 1490 the family was established in Valencia, where Cabot was employed as a technical adviser to the government on the construction of new harbor installations. In 1493 his plan for a new jetty was rejected because Ferdinand of Aragon would not provide the necessary "matching funds," and thereupon his job as a consultant ended. This was only a short time before Columbus returned from his first voyage and proclaimed that he had discovered the island approaches to farthest Asia. Cabot may have met and talked with Columbus at Barcelona; but whether he did or not, he was clearly sceptical of Columbus's claims, believing the Genoese explorer had not sailed far enough and that the lands he described bore no relation to Marco Polo's thirteenth-century account of Cathay and Cipango. Cabot therefore decided to make a voyage for himself; and since he had virtually no prospects in Spain, he departed for Portugal, where John II still had no intention of financing a trans-Atlantic voyage. Then he set out for England, where he arrived in 1494 or 1495, settling in Bristol with Mattea and their three sons, Ludovicus, Sebastian, and Santius.

Early in 1496 Henry VII made a progress through western England and stopped over for a few days at Bristol, at which time Cabot secured an audience with him. To the eager monarch Cabot explained that by sailing west in a higher latitude than Columbus had done, he would have appreciably greater chances of success, since the distance between Europe and the Far East would be considerably shortened. Should he in fact reach the eastern tip of fartherest Asia, he would then be able to coast towards the southwest, until he arrived at Cipango or Cathay. Thus, in Cabot's view, the time spent on the open sea would be but a small portion of the toal voyage, which would greatly lessen the hazards and enable England to become thereby an active participant in the Far Eastern spice trade.[23]

Henry was impressed by Cabot's proposal and, on 5 March 1496, authorized him and his sons "to sail to all parts, regions, and coasts of the eastern, western, and northern sea." Granted under the privy seal, the king's patent was remarkably similar to earlier commissions extended to explorers supported by the Portuguese Crown, since, like John II, Henry did not intend to commit himself to continuing support until he was sure the venture would succeed. Once the Cabots returned with proof that they had actually reached fartherest Asia and not just a fishing bank off some large island, Henry would decide what assistance to render. Yet he voluntarily gave the Cabots £50 for their initial voyage; and in his grant of 5 March, he authorized them to govern any territories they discovered to the north, west, or east of Iceland—but not to the south, where the Spaniards and the Portuguese were now entrenched.[24]

Although Henry hoped that his support of a trans-Atlantic voyage would not antagonize the two Iberian kingdoms, there was little chance that an English-backed expedition would be accepted by them impassively. Indeed the Cabots' arrival in England had already been reported to Ferdinand of Aragon by his watchful ambassador, Dr. Puebla. Ferdinand was intent on keeping other rulers from gaining any part of the anticipated trade with "the Indies"; and he was also fearful that a voyage by the Cabots would divert Henry's attention from European problems, and particularly the Italian Wars, in which he hoped the English monarch would soon intervene. Consequently Ferdinand informed Dr. Puebla in a letter of 28 March that, "We are of [the] opinion that this is a scheme of the French King's to persuade the King of England to undertake this so that he will give up other affairs. Take care you prevent the King of England from being deceived in this or anything else of the kind, since wherever they can the French will endeavor to bring this about."[25] Doubtless the ever-obliging ambassador lodged a complaint with Henry, as he had been instructed to do. But such a protest accomplished nothing, for the king saw no reason to prevent the Cabots from organizing a voyage.

Late in June 1496 John Cabot set out with a single ship that was inadequately equipped for a trans-Atlantic voyage. Within a few weeks it was buffeted by stormy seas; and there are indications that Cabot was either misled by his crew or became involved in a bitter quarrel with them, perhaps over whether to continue or not.[26] At any rate he was compelled to turn back and so accomplished nothing of value on his first attempt.

Back in Bristol he redoubled his efforts and, with the support of several merchants, procured a better ship, the *Mathew*, "a fast, able, and weatherly craft."[27] On 20 May 1497 he set out for a second time with a crew of nineteen or twenty men; and from Dursey Head, on the southern coast of Ireland, he sailed southward several degrees until he felt he had reached the latitude of the legendary "Isle of Brasil." After a voyage that lasted five weeks, he sighted land at daybreak on 24 June at a place he subsequently named "Cape Discovery" and declared to be due west of the French city of Bordeaux. Professor D. B. Quinn, on the basis of a statement made almost fifty years later by Sebastian Cabot, holds that the landfall occurred at the northeastern tip of Cape Breton Island. Yet this view is vigorously disputed by Samuel Eliot Morison, who not only insists that Sebastian did not go on the voyage of 1497 but also contends that the landfall took place 360 miles farther north, at Cape Degrat on Quirpon Island, which corresponds to the latitude the elder Cabot himself gave for his landing place. With admirable restraint the greatest student of the Cabot voyages,

J. A. Williamson, maintains that the landfall could have occurred at any of the innumerable capes between Maine and Labrador.[28]

Regardless of where land was originally sighted, Cabot and several of his men went ashore on 24 June and erected a large cross of wood or stone. They also planted banners bearing the arms of Henry VII, Pope Alexander VI, and St. Mark of Venice. Subsequently the *Mathew* cruised for a month along the shores of Newfoundland (which is just to the south of Quirpon Island), Cape Breton Island, and possibly New Brunswick, covering approximately 1200 nautical miles, according to Cabot's calculations. Once Cape Degrat was sighted (or resighted, if Professor Morison's thesis is correct), Cabot and his men set sail for home. After an easterly crossing of just over two weeks, owing to the prevailing winds, they sighted the rocky islet known as the Ushant, off Brittany, whence they turned northwards and arrived at Bristol on 6 August. All in all, the voyage was "remarkably lucky and efficient" and lasted less than three months.[29]

On his return to England, Cabot proclaimed that he and his men had reached the northeastern tip of fartherest Asia and had thereby discovered a safe, all-water route to Cipango and Cathay. After a brief reunion with his wife and sons in Bristol, Cabot hurried to Westminster to inform the king of his success. Henry was delighted and at once gave him a reward of £10 from the privy purse. Within a few more weeks the king settled a lifetime pension of £20 a year on him,[30] which enabled Cabot to procure better lodgings for his family in Bristol, near the bridge over the river Avon. On 23 August a Venetian trader in London, Lorenzo Pasqualigo, informed a friend that Cabot received a rapturous welcome wherever he appeared. According to the Pasqualigo letter, "vast honor is paid to him and he goes [through the streets] dressed in silk, and these English run after him like mad, and indeed he can enlist as many of them as he pleases, and a number of our rogues as well."[31]

Reports at once circulated about the nature of Cabot's next expedition. Pasqualigo believed that Henry had "promised him for the [next] spring ten armed ships as he desires, and has given him all the prisoners to be sent away, that they may go with him." Another Italian in London, Raimondo de Soncino, spread an even more elaborate tale, maintaining that Henry "means to send him out with fifteen or twenty ships."[32] Whatever the king's original intention, such a mammoth expedition was not envisaged when new letters patent were issued on 3 February 1498. According to this second royal grant, which supplemented but did not supersede the Cabots' previous commission, the explorer and his sons were authorized to impress six ships of not over 200 tons apiece, for which they should pay the same monthly rental as the Crown (*i.e.*, a shilling a ton per month). In addition they were empowered to enlist any seamen who desired to go along. For his part, Henry would provide one of his own ships, equipped and victualled for an entire year, which would assist with the establishment of a fortified commercial outpost, the principal objective of the expedition.[33]

During the spring of 1498 John Cabot completed the preparations for his third, and final, voyage. The merchants of Bristol were wildly optimistic about the chances for a valuable new trade and provided four ships laden with caps, laces, woollens, and "other trifles," which they hoped might appeal to the natives of the Far East. The ship made available by the king was also a commercial vessel, in which several merchants of the capital ventured "small stocks."[34] Yet somewhat surprisingly, much less is known about the voyage of 1498 than that of the previous year. Historians do not agree as to whether Sebastian Cabot went along, although he himself maintained in later years that he did in fact participate on the first leg of the journey. In point of fact, only five of John Cabot's shipmates of 1498 have been positively identified: Thomas Bradley and John Carter, who received a joint grant of £17 from the Crown on 1 April 1498; Launcelot Thirkill, principal owner of the vessel that Henry provided; Giovanni de Carbonariis, a Milanese cleric in England; and Father Fray Buil, that same Spanish friar who had caused so much discord during Columbus's second voyage.[35] Late in May the expedition set sail. After less than a month at sea the ship commanded by Thirkill and carrying Father Buil (and possibly also Sebastian Cabot) was so buffeted by gales that it had to double back to Ireland "in great distress." John Cabot and the four other ships continued on their way, however; and according to a letter that Bishop Ayala sent to Ferdinand of Aragon towards the end of July:

I have seen, on a chart, the direction which they took, and the distance they sailed; and I think what they have found, or what they are in search of, is what your Highnesses already possess. It is expected that they will be back in the month of September. I write this because the King of England has often spoken to me on this subject, and he thinks that your Highness will take great interest in it.[36]

Cabot and the four ships that continued on with him were never heard of again. They obviously reached the North American mainland, for portions of their cargo of caps, laces, and "other trifles" were found some years later among the Algonkian Indians.[37] From Newfoundland or Cape Breton Island, they undoubtedly coasted towards the southwest, where

Cipango and Cathay were believed to be situated. H. P. Biggar holds that they reached the entrance to Chesapeake Bay, while Boies Penrose maintains that they travelled at least as far as the Outer Banks of North Carolina.[38] Perhaps it was among the dangerous shoals of the Outer Banks that one or more of Cabot's ships capsized. If any of them escaped disaster, they probably continued their southerly coasting; and J. A. Williamson believes that at least one vessel made its way "through the Spanish islands into the Caribbean," where it either sank during a hurricane or was destroyed by Spanish gunfire.[39] Regardless of what may have happened, no reports of Cabot and his men ever reached England. Because of this Polydore Vergil maintained of the explorer that "he is believed to have found the new lands nowhere but on the very bottom of the ocean, to which he is thought to have descended together with his boat, the victim of that self-same ocean, since after that voyage he was never seen again anywhere."[40]

Despite the tragic outcome of Cabot's third voyage, Henry's support of trans-Atlantic exploration caused great dismay on the part of Manuel I of Portugal, who, after the successful completion of Vasco da Gama's great 1498 voyage to India, at last intended for his country to enter the New World sweepstakes. In September 1499 Manuel I sent several high-level ambassadors to England in an attempt to dissuade Henry from subsidizing additional voyages. The English ruler listened politely to the Portuguese arguments and gave £60 to "the ambassador of Portugal," £50 to "the doctor of Portugal," and £5 to the secretary of the delegation. But he refused to agree that the two Iberian kingdoms were entitled to a monopoly of trade with the Far East because of a bi-lateral treaty between them or a papal bull of 1493 to that effect.[41]

The chief organizer of the next English voyage was João Fernandes, a wealthy squire (or *lavrador*) from Terceira, the main island of the Azores, an archipelago that had long been under Portuguese domination. In October 1499 Fernandes obtained a patent from Manuel I "to search for and discover islands in the Portuguese half of the world." But after a voyage to Greenland in 1500, he was angered to learn that his chief rival, Gaspar de Corte Réal, had just received a more lucrative grant from the Portuguese Crown. Thereupon Fernandes transferred his allegiance to England, with which he had had commercial dealings for nearly a decade: in January 1493 he shipped a large consignment of goods from Bristol to Lisbon. Shortly afterwards Fernandes settled in western England and formed a syndicate with two other Azoreans who had preceded him to Bristol: Francisco Fernandes, who seems to have been a cousin, and João Gonsalves. These three Azoreans then associated themselves in turn with three English merchants: Richard Warde, Thomas Asshehurst, and John Thomas. On 19 March 1501 the resulting corporation petitioned the Crown for permission to make a trans-Atlantic voyage, and Henry granted their request that same day.[42]

Long and detailed, the letters patent issued on 19 March 1501 authorized the six partners to make a voyage of discovery in whatever direction they wished and to annex any lands they found which were heretofore unknown to Christians. More specifically, the six men were instructed to annex and govern all territories on the western side of the Davis Strait (the waterway between Greenland and Labrador), so long as they did not encroach on any lands discovered earlier by John Cabot. Although sovereignty over all territories discovered and annexed would naturally be reserved to the king, the grantees were authorized to make and enforce suitable laws, either in person or through a resident deputy; and for a period of ten years no other Englishmen would be allowed to trade or settle in the new found lands without their permission. Any foreigners who tried to force their way in could be expelled, even if their homelands were currently at peace with England. For everything but the payment of customs duties, the three Azoreans were to be treated as naturalized subjects of the English Crown. They could use any ports of their own choosing; and until 1505 they would be allowed to import foreign goods free of the customary duties in one of their ships once a year.[43]

Rather interestingly, in the patent granted to the Anglo-Azorean syndicate in March 1501, Henry VII commanded all explorers flying the. English flag to punish any of their men who committed criminal acts, and particularly those " 'who shall rape and violate against their will or otherwise any woman of the islands or countries aforesaid.' " According to Professor Morison, "This concern for the chastity of native women is unique."[44] Despite his attention to such a detail, Henry VII was not a prudish man, as Richard III had been, for he clearly enjoyed the ribald stories that the Earl of Kildare had told at Westminster in 1495–6. Yet he was also exceptionally considerate—even protective—towards the women who graced his court, his solicitous treatment of Lady Catherine Gordon being only one of numerous examples that might be cited.

Little is known about the first expedition sent out by the Anglo-Azorean syndicate, which set sail during the summer of 1501. Until additional evidence is discovered, it cannot be determined how many ships went along, nor precisely where the landfall took place. Perhaps it was on the coast of Labrador, the name of which is obviously derived from Fernandes's status as a *lavrador*. The only fact definitely established which relates to this voyage is that on 7 January 1502, Henry gave £5 to "the men of Bristol that found the Isle."[45]

During a second expedition, which departed in May or June 1502, one ship was commanded by Francisco Fernandes and a second by João Gonsalves, while João Fernandes may have been at the helm of a third. Exactly what part of the American coastline they reached is again unclear, although they apparently concentrated on finding a passage around or through the continental landmass to the Far East. If a ship commanded by João Fernandes actually went along, it seems to have been separated from the others and was probably lost in the ice. Certainly Fernandes and his English partner, Richard Warde, were never seen or heard from again after this juncture, which supports the idea that they went along but died during the course of the voyage.[46] The expedition had returned to England by the end of the summer, for on 26 September Henry granted annuities of £10 each to Francisco Fernandes and João Gonsalves. In addition he gave smaller sums to the mariners who brought him a bald eagle and several hawks from the New World.[47] Considerably more important than these feathered creatures were the three Algonkian Indians who were brought back in 1502. They caused a sensation at Westminster and were the object of disbelieving stares wherever they went. Within a short time they were seen by the London chronicler Robert Fabyan, who was so amazed by their primitive behavior that he noted how they were "clothed in beasts skins & did eate raw flesh, and spake such speach that no man could understand them, and in their demeanor [were] like to bruite beastes." Clearly Henry was intrigued by them, for he housed them at court for several years; and when Fabyan saw them again in 1504, they were dressed as ordinary Englishmen. On that occasion Fabyan tried to converse with them, but they refused to utter a single word, whether out of fright or inability he could not tell.[48]

Because João Fernandes and Richard Warde were both absent after 1502, the patent granted to their syndicate was of necessity redrawn. On 9 December 1502 Henry issued a new charter to the two surviving Azoreans and one of their English partners, Thomas Asshehurst, who now brought a rich Londoner, Hugh Elyot, into the resulting association. That Elyot became one of the patentees at this juncture signified an important advance, for he had ties with the leading mercantile groups of the capital, including the powerful Merchant Adventurers Company. Thus a wealthy London element with its infinitely greater resources was drawn in, and the new organization soon named itself "The Company of Adventurers into the Newfound Lands." By their original charter, the patentees were authorized to discover and annex heathen lands located anywhere in the world. Unlike previous explorers and syndicates backed by Henry, they were not restricted to lands that were currently unknown to Christians. By this juncture Henry had adopted the doctrine of effective occupation and would not deny the patentees the right to establish themselves in lands discovered by Spanish or Portuguese expeditions, provided that neither of those countries had effective control of the territories concerned.[49]

Whether a voyage took place in 1503 is unclear, although one probably did, for on 17 November Henry granted 20s. "to the one who brought hawks from the Newfound Island."[50] By the spring of 1504 preparations were underway for yet another expedition, and on 8 April the king presented 40s. "to a priest that goeth to the New Island." Although Henry also assisted with the purchase of supplies, advancing £50 for that purpose, the voyage of 1504 accomplished nothing of real value. How many ships went along and where the landfall occurred are questions that still await answers. Nothing of substance has actually been established about the expedition, except for the fact that on 25 August Henry presented £5 13s. 4d. to the sailors who brought him popinjays and bobcats from North America.[51]

By the winter of 1504–5 Henry had lost all faith in the Anglo-Azorean syndicate, which seemed incapable of developing a profitable trade with the New World. No commercial outposts had been established, and too many unproductive expeditions had been sent out. The patentees of 1501–2 had even failed in their campaign to lure fishermen to the Grand Bank. After December 1504 Henry gave no further aid to them; and after another abortive voyage in 1505 or 1506, the Anglo-Azorean syndicate ceased operations altogether.

Once he withdrew his support from the Anglo-Azorean syndicate, Henry pinned his hopes on John Cabot's son Sebastian, who was but twenty-three years old in 1505. Almost nothing is known about Sebastian's early life. Probably he was born in Venice before his father moved the family to Spain, although he later claimed that he had been born in Bristol. However, like most mariners, Sebastian was adept at spinning a good yarn, and it is dangerous to accept at face value anything he said or wrote on any subject. Sebastian may have participated in his father's voyage of 1497, but, except for his own testimony, there is little reason to believe that he sailed again in 1498, when four of his father's ships disappeared and were never heard of again. By 1505 Sebastian had made a name for himself as a surveyor and cartographer; and on 3 April Henry granted him an annuity of £10 out of the collections of the Bristol customs.[52]

Shortly afterwards Sebastian sought to organize a voyage to the New

World. But although he was known to enjoy the king's favor, he found it difficult to secure financial backing. Peter Martyr, who subsequently knew him well, maintained that the young explorer bore the entire cost of the expedition that finally embarked in 1508 or 1509. This seems unlikely, however, and is vigorously disputed by J. A. Williamson, who insists that most of the funds were provided by Hugh Elyot and Thomas Asshehurst, partners in the Old Anglo-Azorean syndicate. It is possible, too, that the venture was supported by William Clerk and the brothers Thorne, William and Robert, who had long been associated with Elyot and Asshehurst in London. In addition the king gave some assistance to the expedition, which was thus "a combined royal and mercantile undertaking."[53]

Sebastian's departure occurred sometime in 1508 or 1509, although the exact time of his departure and return cannot now be determined. It is also unclear how many ships he commanded. Peter Martyr and another sixteenth-century writer, Lopez de Gomara, maintained that he had but two vessels. Yet they also held that his crew numbered at least 300, which seems altogether unlikely: on John Cabot's voyage of 1497, the *Mathew* had carried a crew of not more than twenty men. Because of all the uncertainties surrounding Sebastian's voyage, Professor Morison questions whether it actually took place.[54] Other historians are not so sceptical, however. J. A. Williamson not only insists that it did in fact occur but contends that it was one of the most important of the early Tudor period, for two reasons. First, it enabled the younger Cabot to acquire a deeper knowledge of geography than his father, who had never grasped that America was a landmass of continental dimensions. And second, it extended the search for a North-West Passage and probably led to the discovery of Hudson's Bay a full century before the Dutch explorer saw it.[55] All the earliest accounts of Sebastian's first voyage agree that it lasted an entire year and that, during the month of July, his ships encountered so much ice that they "durst not pass any further." Several later writers have suggested than Sebastian's men became mutinous when he tried to push farther north and that he was compelled to alter his course. Thereupon the expedition coasted towards the South until it reached Cape Hatteras or even the Florida keys before returning to England.[56]

Back in Britain, Sebastian found that Henry VII was dead and that the new ruler was so preoccupied with European affairs that he had no time to give to exploring ventures. Thus "the first period of English discovery" now drew to a close, and in subsequent years there was "a notable falling off of interest by the English government and people in the New World."[57] Because the merchants of Bristol were bitterly disappointed by the failure to acquire anything more valuable than geographical knowledge, Sebastian prudently decided to live in London, where he remained until the outbreak of Henry VIII's first French War in 1512. Thereupon he reentered the royal service and was employed as a mapmaker on Sir Robert Howard's expedition to Gascony and Guienne. Shortly after arriving in southwestern France, he crossed the Pyrenees and won the favor of Charles I of Spain, who appointed him Pilot Major in 1518. Although he returned to England in 1520–1 to discuss the possibility of another American expedition, Sebastian lived primarily at the Spanish court for the next twenty-five years. He remained a pensioner of the Spanish Crown until the autumn of 1547, when the councillors of Edward VI at last provided funds to bring him back to England.[58]

As long as Henry VIII occupied the throne, there was no place at Westminster for a man of Sebastian's talents and aspirations. Except for several abortive voyages between 1517 and 1536, nothing was done during Henry VIII's reign to continue the work so hopefully begun by his father. Perhaps Henry VII did not give as much support to the explorers of the period as he might have done, although, according to Professor Morison, he was "second only to Ferdinand and Isabella in New World discovery" among the monarchs of his generation;[59] and certainly he never planned a voyage in the meticulous way that John II of Portugal planned Vasco da Gama's great 1498 expedition to India. Thus it would be wrong to maintain that he provided the impetus for the discoveries that occurred while he was on the throne. But during the years 1495–1509 he gave strong encouragement to those who were willing to brave the North Atlantic and evinced a sincere interest in their achievements. Moreover, he made it abundantly clear that he would not tolerate interference from Spain or Portugal and that he would give handsome rewards to those who developed commercial ties with the New World or discovered an all-water passage to the Far East. As a result numerous expeditions ventured forth, and by 1505 "English knowledge of North America . . . [was] greater than that of any other European country."[60] After 1509, however, England lost her lead to her continental neighbors, particularly France; and when an interest in exploration was at last rekindled during Queen Elizabeth's reign, a completely fresh start had to be made.

IX

Diplomatic and Cultural Developments

Although not often recognized as such, Henry VII's court was one of the most splendid of Renaissance Europe. Probably it was because English styles in painting, architecture, and literature lagged behind those of the continent and particularly of Italy that the court of the first Tudor ruler is generally considered to have been a backward and barren place. Yet if English artists and writers failed to remain abreast of foreign developments, the king himself was clearly fascinated by the political and cultural life of the main Italian states. In 1497 the Milanese ambassador called attention to the large number of "notable men" who represented him at the papal curia and kept him so well informed about current happenings throughout the peninsula "that we have told him nothing new." In addition the ambassador observed that, "The courtiers also have a great knowledge of our affairs, so that I could fancy myself at Rome." When in 1506 the celebrated writer-diplomat Castiglione arrived in England to receive the Garter on behalf of his master, Guidobaldo, Duke of Urbino, he was astounded by Henry's knowledge of the personalities and affairs of the leading Italian courts.[1]

The closeness of England's ties with Renaissance Italy was owing, at least in part, to the king's need to have several clerks to pursue his causes at the papal curia, where they could also clarify the procedures used by the English Chancery. As early as 1445 William Grey, subsequently to become Bishop of Exeter, was serving as Henry VI's proctor-ambassador in Rome, where he remained until 1453. During the 1460s Edward IV's chief spokesman at the papacy was James Goldwell, who was elevated to the see of Norwich in 1472. Less than six months after Bosworth, Henry VII appointed John Sherwood, Bishop of Durham, and two other clerics to represent him at the curia and "to prosecute all promotions to cathedrals which shall become vacant, and to endeavor to obtain that the recommendations of the Crown shall in all cases meet with success."[2]

Henry VII relied primarily on Italian nationals to handle his diplomatic affairs in Rome. These included Giovanni de Gigli, a native of Lucca, who had arrived in England by 1472 or 1473 as a collector of Peter's Pence. A doctor of both civil and canon law, Giovanni enjoyed the favor of Edward IV, who arranged for him to become Archdeacon of London as well as a prebend of St. Paul's Cathedral. During the winter of 1485–86 the Italian won the goodwill of the new monarch, who, after using him on a mission to Calais, recommended him for the Archdeaconry of Gloucester. By 1490 Giovanni had been reassigned to the papal curia, where he handled most of Henry's business and procured accommodations for Englishmen whenever they arrived on special embassies. So effectively did he perform his duties that the king arranged for him to become Bishop of Worcester in 1497, the temporalities of which he received on 18 July. Yet his tenure of his new position was unexpectedly brief, for he died the following summer. To succeed Giovanni as "solicitor of the King's causes in the court of Rome," Henry turned to his nephew Silvestro, also a native of Lucca, who was both a distinguished canon lawyer and a prominent man of letters. Late in 1498 Henry secured Silvestro's nomination as Bishop of Worcester, where he was enthroned by proxy in April of the following year. Until 1504 Silvestro continued to reside in the Eternal City; but when Pope Julius II decided to present a special cap and sword to Henry, Silvestro was selected to take them to the monarch at Richmond. For the next eight years he resided at the English court, where he was the official master of ceremonies. In 1512 he at last returned to Rome in order to attend a Lateran Council summoned to consider the most important affairs of the church.[3]

While Silvestro was absent in England between 1504 and 1512, his duties at the curia were entrusted to Adriano Castelli, who had succeeded the elder Gigli as collector of Peter's Pence in 1489. A native of Rome, Adriano was greatly respected by Henry VII, who nominated him in 1502 to the see of Hereford and, two years later, transferred him to the wealthier Bishopric of Bath and Wells. With the king's support, Adriano was made a cardinal in 1503; and shortly afterwards he was prompted by gratitude for Henry's favor and assistance to donate his palace in Rome for

" 'the use and accommodation of Englishmen . . . or for the use and accommodation of his majesty's ambassadors at the Roman Court.' " Although hated by Cardinal Wolsey, Adriano remained one of England's most trusted agents in Rome until 1517, when he was implicated in a plot against Leo X. At Wolsey's urging, Henry VIII repudiated him, whereupon Adriano became fearful for his life and fled to northern Italy, where he died in 1521.[4]

Although Italians played a prominent role in Henry VII's diplomatic corps, he did not rely on them exclusively, nor even for his most important foreign embassies. In such work he depended on such prominent Englishmen as: (1) Richard Fox, his long-time Lord Privy Seal, who came as close as any to being the king's Foreign Secretary; (2) Sir Richard Edgecombe, an important member of the Council who undertook several continental missions during the 1490s; and (3) John Gunthorpe, a priest who had been Lord Privy Seal as well as Dean of the Chapel Royal to Richard III. Although Gunthorpe was discharged shortly after Bosworth, he had been taken into the new king's service by the mid-1490s and conducted a number of embassies for the Crown before his death in 1508. Perhaps the most interesting member of Henry's diplomatic corps was John Stile, who, while on a mission to Ferdinand of Aragon in 1505, was instructed to remain in Spain as the king's resident. In many ways the choice of Stile to be England's first permanent ambassador to a secular court was a curious one. Deficient in both wealth and social connections, he was not particularly well educated, nor even intelligent. He made no effort to learn Spanish and relied on a garbled form of Latin as a means of communicating with the Spanish authorities. His salary was more promptly paid than that of Ferdinand's ambassadors, but it was always pitifully small, which meant that he never had the means to impress the Spanish ruler, who considered him a boor and deceived him repeatedly. Yet shortly after Henry VIII came to the throne in 1509, Stile was confirmed in his embassy; after being summoned home in 1511, he was sent back for a second tour of duty six years later. From this it would seem that Stile was really the precursor of a modern consul rather than an actual resident ambassador. Whenever high-level negotiations were about to begin, Henry VII, like all his Tudor successors, entrusted them to men of greater social status, to whom he granted full ambassadorial powers as well as generous rewards. This was also true of Ferdinand of Aragon, who sent a stream of grandees and bishops to preempt the most important duties of his resident in London, the rather plebeian canon lawyer, Dr. Puebla.[5]

Although Henry VII's contribution to the development of a permanent diplomatic service was not a significant one, he did a great deal to facilitate the spread of humanism in England. This was because he looked with exceptional favor on the foreign scholars at his court and regarded those who had been trained in the new humanistic methods as suitable candidates for responsible positions in his government. His attitudes in this regard were naturally resented by his own subjects, who wanted the most important jobs for themselves. As Bishop Ayala reported to Ferdinand and Isabella in 1498, "The King has the greatest desire to employ foreigners in his service. He cannot do so; for the envy of the English is diabolical, and, I think, without equal."[6] Despite the widespread prejudice against the employment of foreigners, scores of Italians attained positions in England between 1485 and 1509. These included Giovanni Battista Boerio, a Genoese doctor who was for some years the leading physician at court; Cornelio Vitelli, a Fellow of New College, Oxford, where he taught William Grocyn and other well-known humanists of the next generation; and, most important of all, Pietro Carmeliano, a native of Brescia, who had arrived in England by 1480, when Edward IV made him a clerk in the Rolls Office. Completely ignored by Richard III, Carmeliano began to prosper again within a few years of Henry VII's accession. By the early 1490s he had been named to the new post of Latin Secretary, which he held for the remainder of the reign. He handled much of the king's diplomatic correspondence, which he transacted in such an elegant Latin style that even the papacy was impressed. In addition he wrote several manuals for the study of grammar and rhetoric, which has caused him to be ranked with Bernard André as one of the principal founders of humanism in England.[7] Periodically rewarded with substantial sums from the privy purse as with lesser offices in the church, Carmeliano was eventually designated England's official Poet Laureate; and early in 1508 he wrote lengthy stanzas, in both English and Latin, to celebrate the betrothal of Henry's daughter Mary to the Archduke Charles of Austria. After the accession of Henry VIII in April of the following year, he was granted a sinecure worth £40 annually. He continued to reside at the English court until his death in 1527.[8]

Doubtless the most famous Italian employed by Henry VII, at least in the eyes of posterity, was Polydore Vergil. A native of Urbino, Polydore arrived at the English court in 1501 as a sub-collector of Peter's Pence, the yearly tribute paid by the English Crown to Rome since the ninth century. Because of his great intelligence and encyclopedic knowledge— Polydore had compiled a brilliant record at the universities of Padua and Bologna—he soon became a favorite of Henry VII, who arranged for him to receive a rich benefice in Leicestershire as well as to become a prebend in both Lincoln and Hereford cathedrals. In 1508 he was additionally named Archdeacon of Wells, although he continued to reside primarily at court. The king was particularly impressed by Polydore's understanding of history and urged him to make a study of the English past since ancient times. Begun in 1506, Polydore's *Anglica Historia* (which is an invaluable source for the period 1501–34) took three decades to complete and broke new ground in two ways. First, it rejected the Brute and Arthurian legends which had long been associated with the earliest periods of English history (for which reason it was long unpopular with English readers, however); and second, it devoted a separate chapter to each reign since the Norman Conquest, which quickly became the accepted format used by writers of English history.[9]

Although Italians were the most prominent foreign group at the English court, Henry VII did not restrict his patronage to them. Because of the fourteen years he had spent on the continent before Bosworth, he had a marked preference for French manners and fashions and offered employment to large numbers of Frenchmen. These included Etienne Fryon, one of the clerks of the signet as well as the king's official French Secretary; Quentin Poulet, a priest from Lille who served as keeper of the royal library at Sheen; and Giles D'Ewes (or D'Euze), one of the principal tutors to Henry's sons Arthur and Henry. In addition there was Bernard André, the famous "blind poet of Toulouse."

The most acclaimed literary figure of the entire reign, Bernard André was an Augustinian friar from southern France. He had been introduced to Henry before Bosworth and had immediately put his pen at the Tudor claimant's disposal. During the autumn of 1485 he was rewarded with a lifetime corrody at the Croyland monastery which had long been patronized by the Beaufort family. Within a few months of his arrival in England, André began to lecture at Oxford, and a short while later he was designated England's first Poet Laureate. From time to time he prepared pageants and masques for the entertainment of the court; and on 4 November 1486 he was awarded an annuity of ten marks by the king, who within a few more years asked him to assist with the education of Prince Arthur. A royal tutor until the prince's marriage in 1501, André received periodic rewards from the Crown, such as the £3 6s. 8d. he obtained from the privy purse on 3 December 1497. In April 1498 Bishop Smith of Lincoln, probably at the king's urging, named him to a sinecure at St. Leonard's Hospital, in Bedfordshire; and in December 1500 Henry himself presented André to the rectory of Guisnes, near Calais, where the poet died in 1522.[10]

Although André's influence was felt long after Henry VII's death— some historians hold that he prompted Henry VIII to write his celebrated book against Luther, *In Defense of the Seven Sacraments*—all of his own important writings had been completed by 1509. In 1486 he composed an ode to celebrate Henry VII's marriage to Elizabeth of York, and the next year he produced lengthy stanzas commemorating the king's victory over Lambert Simnel and the Earl of Lincoln. In 1489 he contributed an elegy in honor of the slain Earl of Northumberland as well as an ode celebrating the investiture of Henry's first-born son as Prince of Wales. Similar works flowed from his pen during subsequent years; and between July and September 1497 he composed his most famous work, a poem of seventy-nine stanzas entitled "Les Douze Triomphes de Henry VII." Conceived a few weeks before the king's capture of Perkin Warbeck, this poem predicted the imposter's eventual defeat and compared twelve episodes in Henry's early life to the twelve labors of Hercules. In addition, André maintained that Henry was an even greater figure than Hercules, for, unlike the legendary Greek hero, Henry had never succumbed to envy. Although rather strained in parts and clearly written for its propagandistic effect, André's "Douze Triomphes de Henry VII" pointed in the direction of the classicism of the New Learning, since the author successfully groped "his way out of medieval allegory into classical analogy." By many historians, therefore, André is paired with Pietro Carmeliano as one of the principal founders of humanism in England.[11]

André was almost as devoted to historical studies as he was to literature; and after leaving England for the rectory of Guisnes in 1501, he compiled annals of each year's principal events. These he submitted to Henry on a regular basis; and they earned for him a lifetime pension of £24, which the king established for him in 1505, as well as an annual free gift of £5 that he received each New Year's Day from 1506. Between 1500 and 1509 André also worked on an adulatory life of Henry, which he set aside when the king died, although he had covered no events later than 1497. Recognized in his own lifetime as Historiographer-Royal, André was a man of lesser talent than Polydore Vergil, whose *Anglica Historia* is a far more judicious work showing greater balance and critical ability, than André's *Historia Henrici Septimi*. However, André's historical work was more highly regarded by English writers of the following century, including the Elizabethan chronicler John Speed and the great Jacobean philosopher-statesman Francis Bacon, whose own biography of Henry VII appeared in 1622.[12]

Once André left England for the continent in 1501, the way was cleared for the rise of two native poets: Stephen Hawes and John Skelton. The lesser of the two, Stephen Hawes (1474–1523) was a graduate of Oxford who travelled widely on the continent, primarily in France and Italy. Upon his return to England, he was employed for many years as a groom of the king's bedchamber. He wrote long allegorical poems on conventional chivalric themes, including "The Example of Virtue," which he dedicated to Henry VII in 1504, and "Joyful Meditation," which celebrated the accession of Henry VIII five years later. Yet his most important poem was "The Pastime of Pleasure, or the History of Grand Amour" (1505), an allegorical romance that probably had a greater influence on Spenser's *Faerie Queene* than any other English poem, even those of Chaucer and Malory.[13] It would be wrong, however, to exaggerate the quality of Hawes's work, which generally consisted of old-fashioned rime royal as well as "dull excursions into the seven liberal arts." Despite its great length of nearly 6000 lines, "The Pastime of Pleasure" can only be characterized as turgid and uninspired. According to C. S. Lewis,

. . . there was more and better poetry in him than he could express. . . . There was a certain genuinely medieval fineness and simplicity about his mind if not about his art. He . . . [was continually] grasping at really good things beyond his reach. Accordingly, his failure excites sympathy rather than contempt—if indeed sympathy is needed for a man who lived in such a happy dream of love, chivalry, and wandering.[14]

A more talented writer who achieved a greater mastery of self-expression, if not of self-control, was John Skelton (ca. 1460-1529), undoubtedly the greatest English poet between the time of Sir Thomas Malory (ob. 1471) and that of Sir Thomas Wyatt (ob. 1542) and the only poet of the age who is still read for pleasure. Probably born in Yorkshire, Skelton seems to have been educated at Cambridge, although Oxford claimed him as one of its own sons shortly after Bosworth and was the first institution to designate him Poet Laureate: Oxford had accorded him this honor by 1490, whereas Cambridge did not grant him such recognition until 1493.[15] Skelton seems to have risen in the royal favor by first attracting the notice of Lady Margaret Beaufort, in whose household school he was employed until 1488, when he transferred directly to the king's service. In the spring of 1489 he wrote a violent diatribe against the assassins of the Earl of Northumberland, and less than six months later he rushed to Henry's defense and produced an equally violent work entitled "The Recule against Gaguin of the French Nation." This was only one of a number of poems contributed by such writers as Bernard André, Pietro Carmeliano,

Cornelio Vitelli, and Giovanni Gigli, who were horrified that Henry had been insulted in public by the French ambassador, Robert Gaguin, because of the king's unyielding opposition to the proposed match between Charles VIII and Anne of Brittany.[16]

By many critics Skelton is considered primarily a medieval poet, which is justified in part by the fact that he wrote a number of carols.[17] But although Alexander Pope's characterization of his work as "beastly" (owing to its almost total disregard of metre) stuck for many years, his compositions have been praised in our century by such distinguished men of letters as W. H. Auden and Robert Graves. Furthermore most recent scholars agree that his literary endeavors were influenced by humanism, a careful study of the classics, and a deep love of Latin literature. Indeed in his own day Skelton was considered an accomplished rhetorician; and sometime before 1490 he translated "Tully's Familiars" as well as the first five books of Diodorus the Sicilian. "Except for Chaucer's translation of Boethius a century earlier," Professor Carpenter writes, "Skelton's translation of *Diodorus* is the first such work of any length in the English language."[18]

For a decade or so Skelton's duties at court were poorly defined, but in 1498 he was appointed principal tutor to Prince Henry. Perhaps it was because of his important new responsibilities that he at last took holy orders. In March 1498 he became a subdeacon, the next month a deacon, and in June he was finally ordained priest by the Bishop of London. When on the 16th of the following November he performed his first mass, Henry VII gave him the generous gift of 20s., which was some three times the king's usual Sunday offering of a noble (6s. 8d.).[19] As tutor to Prince Henry, Skelton lived with his young charge at Eltham, the palace on the lower Thames that Erasmus visited in 1499 in the company of the youthful Thomas More, during the first of Erasmus's six visits to England. For the education of the prince, Skelton prepared a manual, *Speculum Principis*, in 1501, in which he emphasized the importance of both religious and moral instruction. Yet he also insisted that the prince receive a sound classical education and directed him to read works by Livy, Caesar, Ovid, Terence, Tacitus, and other Latin writers. Rather interestingly, however, he opposed the study of Greek literature, which was making rapid headway at the time, and was among those who called themselves "Trojans."[20]

On 2 April 1502 the lives of both Prince Henry and his tutor were forever altered when Henry VII's eldest son, Prince Arthur, died at Ludlow Castle. Thereupon more elaborate arrangements were made for the new heir to the throne, whereas Skelton's services were no longer required at court. A living was immediately found for him at Diss, an important rectory in Norfolk that was in Lady Margaret Beaufort's gift; and on 29 April the king gave him a farewell present of 40s. before he departed to assume his new duties. He remained at his country rectory, where he scandalized his parishoners by living openly with a mistress, until either 1511 or 1513, when he was called back to court by his old pupil, who now occupied the throne as Henry VIII.[21]

Almost all of Skelton's most memorable poetry (and much of his work has obviously been lost) was written between the time he became tutor to Prince Henry and the death in 1509 of Henry VII. His earliest poem of real value was his "Bouge [*i.e.*, rations, food allowance] of Court," which was probably composed in 1498 or 1499. This satirical work—and most of Skelton's poetry was satirical in nature—treated the problems and ultimately the horror of a young man who was becoming acquainted with the ways of "the real world." As C. S. Lewis has so well said, "Things overheard, things misunderstood, a general and steadily growing sense of being out of one's depth, fill the poem with a Kafka-like uneasiness."[22] The work for which Skelton will always be remembered, however, is his "Boke of Phylyp Sparowe," which has been called "our first great poem of childhood." This work of 1382 lines, which was probably written in 1507 or 1508, is a lament by a schoolgirl for her pet bird, which had recently died. Modelled in part on the second and third poems of Catullus, who many centuries earlier had bewailed the loss of a pet sparrow, Skelton's poem shows no great originality of concept, except in the sense that the religious rites for the dead bird are attended by 66 other feathered creatures. Yet in the short staccato-like lines and the riming couplets he used, Skelton succeeded in bringing both Philip Sparrow and his young keeper, Joanna Scroupe, vividly to life:

> Somtyme he wolde gaspe
> Whan he saw a waspe;
> A fly or a gnat,
> He wolde flye at that;
> And prytely he wold pant
> Whan he saw an ant.
> Lord, how he wold pry
> After the butterfly!
> Lorde, how he wolde hop
> After the gressop!
> And whan I sayd, Phyp, Phyp,
> Than he wold lepe and skyp,

And take me by the lyp.
Alas, it wyll me slo,
That Phillyp is gone me fro![23]

Because of his generous support of Skelton, Hawes, Polydore Vergil, Bernard André, and the various other literary figures at his court, Henry VII was clearly the most important patron of his era. By 1500, if not earlier, his interest in the arts was widely recognized and a knowledge of the classics had come to be regarded as a likely avenue to royal favor. Consequently a number of English scholars, men who journeyed abroad to complete their studies at continental universities, gathered in London during the last decade of the reign. In 1505 Erasmus, while on a lengthy visit to England, acknowledged that London had eclipsed both Oxford and Cambridge and become the country's most important educational center, where "there are . . . five or six men who are accurate scholars in both tongues [*i.e.*, Greek and Latin], such as I think even Italy itself does not at present possess."[24] Unfortunately for Erasmus, whose great achievements lay in the future, he never succeeded in winning Henry VII's favor; nor did many of the English scholars who went abroad during the first fifteen years of the reign receive as much support from him as they were to obtain from his son. (Yet it is worth remembering Professor Scarisbrick's contention that Henry VIII "gave no more than conventional patronage to any scholar.")[25] Regardless of how Henry VII's support of the most talented English students of his age compares with that of his successor, the founder of the dynasty was clearly aware of the most accomplished scholars among his own subjects. In 1505 John Colet became Dean of St. Paul's, whereas Thomas Linacre, upon his return from Italy in 1499 or 1500, had been taken into the royal household, first as a tutor to Prince Arthur and then as a physician to the king himself. Yet it is also true that the first generation of English humanists had to wait until the next reign for advancement, although hope of royal preferment is what drew them to London in the first place.

As long as Henry VII remained on the throne, the English court was a more interesting and cosmopolitan place, with a stronger international flavor, than it was to be in the time of his successor,[26] and foreign scholars were more likely to receive a warm welcome. According to Polydore Vergil, who arrived in England in 1501, he was "courteously received by King Henry, and ever afterwards was treated kindly by him"; and when Castiglione appeared at Westminster five years later, he also "was kindly received by Henry and handsomely entertained." Partly because of the periodic grants that came Polydore's way, the Italian cleric became one of the king's most devoted admirers, although it would be wrong to dismiss as fulsome praise all the kind words he wrote on behalf of his benefactor. In regard to Henry's intellectual ability and the nature of his court, he observed that:

His spirit was distinguished, wise and prudent; his mind was brave and resolute and never, even at moments of greatest danger, deserted him. He had a most pertinacious memory. Withal he was not devoid of scholarship. . . . He was gracious and kind and was as attentive to his visitors as he was easy of access. His hospitality was splendidly generous; he was fond of having foreigners at his court and freely conferred favors on them.

In Polydore's opinion, the king's only notable fault was the avarice to which he succumbed during the last years of his life.[27]

Polydore was not the only foreigner who made favorable comments about Henry's nature and abilities. In dispatches written after his capture of Lambert Simnel and Perkin Warbeck, the Milanese ambassador praised his inherent cautiousness, his tendency to deal openly and fairly with others, and his willingness to consider all sides of important questions.[28] Much the same view was held by Dr. Puebla, the Spanish ambassador to England during the greater part of the reign. From the time he arrived in the English capital, Dr. Puebla admired Henry for his "prudence and sagacity, the patient courage with which he faced his enemies, and the order and magnificence of his court."[29]

Unhappily, it is all but impossible to find either positive or negative statements made by native-born Englishmen. Even worse, too much emphasis is still placed on Lord Mountjoy's celebrated letter of 1509 inviting Erasmus to return to England once again, which, if read uncritically, distorts the situation at Henry VIII's accession quite badly.[30] In contrast, John Fisher, Bishop of Rochester for many years and a highly esteemed man himself, was deeply impressed by Henry VII's optimism and cheerfulness, as were most other English clerics, towards whom the first Tudor king was far more considerate than his son was to be. As for Henry VII's first biographer, Bacon considered him to be "a prince of great and profound judgment" as well as "this Solomon of England."[31]

Yet the most devoted of all Henry VII's admirers was probably Lady Margaret Beaufort. It might be objected that a mother's views are inherently too partisan to be of real value—although the reaction of Richard III's mother to his shabby treatment of her in 1483 is worth recalling, at least as a basis for comparison. Because Lady Margaret was believed by Polydore to be "a most worthy woman whom no one can extoll too much or too often for her sound sense and holiness of life,"[32] her relationship with her son deserves to be considered, if only in passing. After Bosworth Lady Margaret remained on exceptionally close terms with Henry, whose death occurred three months before her's. The king was often swayed by the views and opinions of his mother, the only woman he ever consulted about political matters (to the occasional annoyance of his wife, however); and in Lady Margaret's words, he was "my own sweet and most dear king and all my worldly joy." In a letter addressed to him on one of his birthdays, she hailed him as "my good and gracious prince, king, and only beloved son."[33] Because of the taciturn nature of the English people at this time, such expressions of affection are truly remarkable.

That such an unusual closeness existed between mother and son was owing to several factors, not the least of which was her earlier decision to subordinate her claim to the throne to his, which meant in effect that she had been his principal "kingmaker." In addition their closeness was partially a result of their deep mutual interest in the literary and educational developments of the time. As noted earlier, Skelton was employed in Lady Margaret's household school (doubtless as a tutor to the young Duke of Buckingham) until 1488, when he transferred to the king's service; whereas the Dowager Countess of Richmond had such a high regard for Bernard André, who dedicated several works to her, that he was widely known as "the king's mother's poet." Although she read and spoke fluent French, Lady Margaret was a great proponent of vernacular literature and commissioned the translation of several romances and devotional works into English. She herself translated a tract by Dionysius Carthusianus into her native tongue as *The Mirrour of Goulde for the sinfull soule;* and in 1503 she completed an English version of Thomas à Kempis's *The Imitation of Christ*, which had been started somewhat earlier by William Atkinson.[34]

In the history of higher education in England, Lady Margaret occupies a considerably higher place than her son, for she was one of the greatest of all patrons of Cambridge. She had a deep love of the younger university, which she hoped to raise to a level of equality with Oxford. At the beginning of the Tudor period, Cambridge was less than half as large as its sister institution; and while the latter drew students from all parts of the British Isles, Cambridge was quite provincial, attracting them only from eastern and central England. As a result of the benefactions of Lady Margaret and those who followed her example, such a situation no longer prevailed at the end of the sixteenth century. During the Tudor period Cambridge at last came of age and pulled even with Oxford, not only in size but also in quality; and in such disciplines as mathematics and the sciences, the younger university even forged ahead.

In her patronage of the university, Lady Margaret worked closely with John Fisher, who became her chaplain and main spiritual adviser in 1495. Lady Margaret had such a high regard for Fisher's ability and integrity that in 1505 she secured his elevation to both the Bishopric of Rochester and the Chancellorship of Cambridge, positions he was to hold until his execution by Henry VIII in 1535. With the assistance of her protégé, Lady Margaret obtained her son's permission in March 1497 for the establishment of two endowed lectureships, one at either university, for the teaching of sacred theology. Soon to become known as the Lady Margaret Professorships of Divinity, these were supported by the income of lands that produced yearly stipends of £20 each; and they remained the most prestigious teaching positions at both universities until the 1540s, when Henry VIII patterned his new Regius Professorships, with yearly stipends of £40 each, after them. In 1504 the king's mother established by charter a second new post at Cambridge, the Lady Margaret Preachership, whose main function was to encourage better preaching on the part of the secular clergy. The holder of this position was to be a resident Fellow of one of the Cambridge colleges, and at least once every two years he was to preach in each of twelve different parishes in the dioceses of London, Lincoln, and Ely. Almost as if in anticipation of one of the main demands of the Elizabethan Puritans, Lady Margaret called for the training of the parish clergy in the delivery of simple but eloquent sermons, which even the lowliest churchgoer would be able to understand and appreciate.[35]

Yet Lady Margaret's most important contribution lay in the enhanced support she obtained for several existing or newly established Cambridge colleges. At her prompting, and with considerable financial aid from her, Bishop Alcock of Worcester founded Jesus College in 1497, which was erected on the site of St. Rhadegund's nunnery, the buildings and revenues of which were conscripted for that purpose. In 1503, after the death of her daughter-in-law Elizabeth of York, Lady Margaret assumed the role of principal benefactress of Queens' College, which had been supported in earlier eras by Margaret of Anjou and Elizabeth Woodville; and in 1505 she began to give massive aid to Christ's College, which had recently been founded on the basis of a hostel known as God's House, to which Henry VII had given limited assistance. On 4 May 1505 she obtained a royal license to grant the advowson of Malton church, in Essex, to the master and scholars of Christ's College; and in November of the following year Henry granted her permission to settle properties worth £104 annually on the same college. These included three different manors, comprising about 3750 acres, in the counties of Essex, Cambridgeshire, and Leicestershire. In addition she persuaded the fabulously wealthy

Duke of Buckingham, who had lived in her household from 1485 until 1498, to confer several of his estates on Christ's College "for the good of his soul." In 1505 and again in 1506 Lady Margaret made lengthy visits to the university; and during the last three years of her life, she spent so much time there that a suite of rooms was reserved for her use above the Master's Lodge at Christ's College.[36]

In the will she drew up shortly before her death in July 1509, Lady Margaret made provision for a completely new college at Cambridge, which subsequently became known as St. John's. The executors of her will, who were naturally led by Bishop Fisher, were charged to see that an ample endowment for the new institution was established and suitable statutes for it devised. Although St. John's did not open its doors until 1516, it was to be the leading college at Cambridge for the next thirty years, until Henry VIII created that most munificent of all foundations, Trinity College, in 1546. That St. John's dominated the Cambridge scene for an entire generation was owing largely to the substantial financial provision made for it, not only by Lady Margaret's bequest but also through the subsequent exertions of Bishop Fisher, who obtained papal permission to suppress two nunneries, the properties of which were added to the endowment.[37]

Because of the diverse nature of Lady Margaret's cultural activities, it has been said that she "was more nearly the typical 'man of the Renaissance' than her son" and that even though her "influence and endowments were . . . religious rather than secular, they were outward looking and humanist, never scholastic."[38] Not the least significant of her contributions was the encouragement she gave to William Caxton, the father of English printing, and his successor, Wynkyn de Worde.

Printing had been established in England during the decade before Bosworth by William Caxton (1421-91) and his chief assistant Wynkyn de Worde (ca. 1455-1534), an Alsatian journey-man printer who was Caxton's original foreman. When Caxton opened his printshop near Westminster Abbey in 1476, his first task was to secure the patronage of Edward IV and his court, which was no great problem since he had earlier been in the employ of Edward's sister Margaret, Duchess of Burgundy. In 1477 Caxton published the first book to be mechanically reproduced in England, Earl Rivers's compilation of *The Dictes and Sayinges of the Philosophers*, a slim folio of seventy-six leaves. As a result of the publication of this book, the enterprising publisher won the support not only of Earl Rivers but also of his sister Elizabeth Woodville and her husband Edward IV, who was also pleased when Caxton subsequently offered the dedication of his edition of the legend of Jason and the Golden Fleece to the king's elder son. By a similarly skillful use of the dedications of the ninety-four other books he published before his death in 1491, Caxton won the support of Richard of Gloucester, George of Clarence, Bishop Russell of Lincoln, and various other notables of the period.[39]

The same tactics enabled Caxton to secure the patronage of the new dynasty during the years after Bosworth. Cleverly the printer and his foreman dedicated several works to Lady Margaret Beaufort, and in 1490 they offered the dedication of their *Book of Eneydos*, which was little more than a translation of the French *Roman d'Eneas*, to Prince Arthur. By 1490 Henry VII was clearly aware of the two printers, for in that year he asked them to make available to English readers another French work that he admired, which they willingly published as *The Book of Feates of Armes and Chivalrye*.[40]

By the early 1490s several other printers had established themselves in England. As early as 1478 Theodoric Rood of Cologne had set up a press in the High Street at Oxford, which he operated only until 1486, however, when he seems to have returned to the continent. In 1480 a second printshop in the capital was opened by John Lettou, who had probably been born in Poland but apparently mastered his craft in Italy. By 1482 Lettou had formed a partnership with a Belgian printer who had just settled in London, William de Machlinia, with whom he co-published a number of legal tracts. Yet within a few more years Lettou had dropped out of sight, leaving Machlinia in sole possession of the firm. By 1491 Machlinia too had either died or returned to the continent, probably after disposing of his inventory to William Pynson (ob. 1530), a Norman printer who had recently crossed the Channel. Between 1491 and the late 1520s Pynson and his chief competitor, Wynkyn de Worde, totally dominated the English printing industry, producing approximately seventy per cent of all the books published in England.[41]

After Caxton's death in 1491, de Worde assumed sole management of the printshop at Westminster, from which in the next decade he issued at least 110 books in average runs of 500 copies. Although de Worde was named official printer to Lady Margaret Beaufort in 1508 (at which time she persuaded Bishop Fisher to publish a volume of his sermons),[42] he was less successful than Caxton had been in attracting aristocratic support. Consequently he was dependent on the middleclass market of London proper; and during the winter of 1500-1 he moved the printshop from Westminster to a house in Fleet Street, just across from the entrance to Shoe Lane. Before declining health forced him to retire in 1532, he published almost 600 additional books, many of which he sold for as little as a penny apiece and of necessity printed hastily. As a result, "his reputation stands rather higher [today] than his work as a printer really deserves." Yet de Worde was also responsible for some beautiful books, many of which were illustrated with excellent woodcuts. In addition he deserves credit for saving several valuable manuscripts from destruction; he was the first printer in England to use both Italicized and Roman type; and though born and educated abroad, he did more to standardize English spelling and grammatical usage than Caxton had done.[43]

During his later years de Worde faced mounting competition from Pynson, a more exacting craftsman with appreciably higher standards. Like Machlinia before him, Pynson concentrated on satisfying the needs of the common lawyers and published treatises by Bracton, Littleton, Fortescue, and other well-known legal authorities. It was probably for this reason that in 1508 Henry VII appointed him to succeed William Facques, also of Norman birth, as official printer to the Crown, with a yearly stipend of 40s. Thereafter Pynson was responsible for the publication of all proclamations and edicts, and in 1515 Henry VIII increased his official stipend to 80s.[44]

It is curious that Henry VII, who was normally so quick to seize whatever opportunities came his way, was somewhat slow in grasping the full potential of printing. Not until 1504, for example, did he appoint William Facques to serve as the Crown's first official printer.[45] Yet if he did not immediately sense how the new techniques of mass production could be used to ease his political and administrative burdens, he did recognize within a year of Bosworth how printing might pose a serious threat to the new dynasty, for there was nothing to keep rebels from publishing manifestoes against him. Consequently control of the press was a major problem that concerned Henry and his successors until at least 1557, when a centralized agency, the Stationers' Company, was established with the right to supervise the distribution of all printed works.

At the outset Henry VII relied on Bernard André and his hirelings to supervise the activities of England's printers, an easier task than it might seem, for in 1500 no more than four towns had printshops.[46] After André left England for the continent in 1501, Henry entrusted control of the press to the Archbishop of Canterbury and the Bishop of London, who alone could authorize the publication of books and pamphlets as well as grant licenses for the importation of printed works from the continent. Yet Henry frequently bypassed his officials and allowed special privileges to the importers of foreign books. As early as 5 December 1485, for example, he authorized Peter Actors, a Savoyard who had settled in England at least a decade earlier and eventually became chief stationer to the Crown, to import any number of European books " 'and to dispose of the same by sale or otherwise, without paying customs' or 'rendering any accompt thereof.' "[47]

Peter Actors was undoubtedly the chief importer of foreign books during the last quarter of the fifteenth century. In 1479–80 he and two other stationers imported nearly 1500 books from the continent; and during the next few years their business increased steadily, since they were able to supply the needs of Thomas Hunte, chief stationer of Oxford University. After Bosworth Henry VII, who was chiefly interested in the beautifully printed and expensively bound works that could be procured only on the continent, availed himself of Actors' services on a number of occasions. On 14 June 1495, for example, Actors received £11 3s. 4d. out of the privy purse "for certain books upon a bill"; and on 16 August 1501 he was paid a further 14s. as reimbursement for five other books.[48] Foreign books were also purchased for the royal library by John Atkinson, Hugh Deans, and an unidentified Frenchman, who on one occasion received £56 3s. out of the privy purse and at another time, £10 15s. Yet the most active procurer of books for the king was probably the librarian at Sheen, Quentin Poulet, a French priest from Lille, whose yearly salary of £10 was a charge on the Bristol customs. On 30 March 1496 Poulet was paid £20 for books he had recently purchased on Henry's behalf, and on 26 July 1497 he received the enormous sum of £23 for a single work he had lately acquired. On 31 December 1501 a further £5 14s. was released to Poulet for thirteen additional books. Other payments to the librarian are recorded on 4 May and 8 December 1499, as are the release of large sums for bindings and book clasps. According to one scholar, Henry's library was remarkable for its "many costly bindings in velvet and silver." Books owned by him that are still extant and have been preserved in the British Museum "are sumptuous copies printed on vellum, with handpainted illustrations, and are now bound in red velvet, which may indicate that the original covers were of the same material."[49]

Just as Henry VII was a lover of fine books, he had a great liking for music, which was much more in evidence at the English court after 1485 than it had been during the Yorkist period. Whereas Edward IV had kept a musical establishment of only five players, the first of the Tudor rulers employed a sizable band of musicians: in 1508–9 there were nine trumpeters on his payroll as well as a variety of lutenists, organists, and drummers. In addition he retained assorted performers on clarions, viols, dulcimers, shawms, rebecs, fifes, tabors, sackbuts, recorders, and bells. Music was also provided from time to time by groups of itinerant foreign musicians, such as the "Frenche Pleyers" who performed at Westminster in both 1494 and 1495 and the "6 Mynstrells of France" who made a similar appearance here during the winter of 1508–9. On occasion beggars were allowed to sing before the king and queen, after which they were usually rewarded with a noble (6s. 8d). Clearly Henry placed great value on the ability to play and sing properly, for Prince Arthur was instructed by the court lutenists from 1494, whereas Henry VIII's skill at music, which can only have been acquired during his childhood, is legendary.[50]

Paradoxically, however, music was not valued at the time as something intrinsically important, as is the case today: a real concert never occurred during the reign of Henry VII. Rather music served as a buttress for important ceremonial occasions and was used primarily to call attention "to something worth *seeing*, as for example . . . the appearance of a course of a hundred dishes" during a royal banquet. The entrance of the king or queen or of some other notable personage, such as a foreign ambassador, was almost always accompanied by a fanfare from the royal trumpeters. In the same way weddings, baptisms, funerals, tournaments, processions, meetings of prominent individuals—even executions and "running at the ring"—were occasions when music was invariably performed. Yet as one authority has suggested, "It is possible that more musicians were regularly occupied in providing dance-music than for any other purpose."[51]

Music was naturally used for religious as well as secular purposes; and as a consequence one of the most important musical figures of the age was William Newark, Master of the Children of the Chapel Royal between 1493 and 1509. Newark presided over a choir that consisted of a dozen boys in addition to some twenty "singing-men" during the latter part of the reign. Probably the most accomplished of these singing-men was William Cornish, who wrote several Christmas carols and himself served as Master of the Children from 1509 until his death in 1523. Yet the most important composer of the period was undoubtedly Robert Fayrfax, who occasionally received large sums out of the privy purse, not only for his music but also for the spectacles he helped to stage from time to time. In October 1502, for example, he was paid £30 for three pageants he had recently mounted. Doubtless one of these pageants included the performance in Westminster Hall of a twelve-piece orchestra that consisted solely of ladies of the court, who attempted to play " 'on clarcordis, dusymers, clarysmballs and such other [instruments].' " Although this unusual entertainment has been described as a concert, Professor Stevens maintains that "it seems most unlikely that the performance was artistic in effect or intent." Rather it was simply a theatrical stunt which typifies that striving after novelty and sensation which was such a marked feature of court life at this time.[52]

Because of the search for more and more novel effects, court enter-tainments became increasingly elaborate as the reign progressed. Masques and other pageants assumed spectacular proportions, with the performers occasionally being wheeled into and around the Hall on a moving stage, from which they would descend to dance and frolic. Such mechanized masques were generally characterized as "disguisings." During the Christmas revels of 1493–4, the festivities were highlighted by such a disguising performed by twenty-four ladies and gentlemen of the court.[53] Quite naturally, perhaps, the most elaborate entertainments each year occurred at the height of the Christmas season; and for this reason a new court official—the Lord of Misrule—appeared during the decade after Bosworth to preside over the yearly Christmas celebrations. The Lord of Misrule was little more than an *ad hoc* functionary, although there is one such official listed for almost every Christmas of Henry's reign in the household accounts. The Lord of Misrule received a customary fee of twenty nobles (£6 13s. 4d.) and was the precursor of the later and more famous Master of the Revels.[54]

If the festivities of the yearly cycle reached a climax during the Christmas season, the celebrations of the *reign* culminated in November 1501, at the time of Prince Arthur's marriage to Catherine of Aragon. On that occasion truly sumptuous entertainments occurred; but it would probably be best to defer consideration of them until the next chapter.

X
The Zenith of the Reign

During the years immediately following his capture of Perkin Warbeck in 1497, Henry was vitally concerned with problems of foreign policy. By this juncture he had developed a strategy or approach that amounted almost to a system, the major principles of which were: (1) the avoidance of war, at almost any cost, with the Crown of France; (2) the maintenance of cordial relations with Ferdinand and Isabella of Spain; and (3) the development of greater English trade with the continent, and especially with the peoples of the Low Countries. Also among his primary objectives was the establishment of strong ties with both James IV of Scotland and the Emperor Maximilian, as a way of keeping them from aiding a new Yorkist imposter.

During the summer of 1498 Henry's pacific principles were put to the test when Maximilian slyly suggested that the death of Charles VIII and the accession of the relatively inexperienced Louis XII presented a golden opportunity for an invasion of France. Henry refused to consider such a cynical suggestion, however, since he knew the benefits that resulted from remaining on friendly terms with France. He therefore proposed that he and the new French monarch renew the treaty of Etaples of 1492, which Louis XII was happy to do in July 1498. That Henry's course was a sound one was amply proved the following month, when Ferdinand of Aragon concluded a military alliance with France.[1]

If it was relatively easy to cultivate the goodwill of Louis XII, Henry found it more difficult to secure the cooperation of the Archduke Philip, who had imposed a new duty on English cloth shortly after the conclusion of the Intercursus Magnus in February 1496. Henry had responded to that violation of the treaty by ordering the Merchant Adventurers to remove themselves once again from Antwerp to Calais. After lengthy negotiations a new agreement was reached in July 1497, by which the contested duty was removed. But when the archduke subsequently imposed restrictions on English traders operating within his dominions, the Merchant Adventurers refused to return to Antwerp until fairer conditions were allowed. They remained at Calais until late 1498, by which time negotiations were again underway and another settlement in sight. Signed at Calais in May 1499, this third agreement involved a return to the provisions of the Intercursus Magnus and a solemn pledge by the archduke to allow English merchants to trade in all his provinces excepting Flanders. For his part, Henry promised to reduce the duty charged on the raw wool sold by the Merchant Adventurers at Calais.

With the agreement of 1499 relations between the English and Burgundian governments took a sharp turn for the better, and in June 1500 Henry crossed the Channel with Elizabeth of York and a great throng of courtiers for a face-to-face meeting with the archduke. The interview took place outside the walls of Calais, in the nave of St. Peter's Church, which was elaborately decorated for the occasion. After a proposed Anglo-Burgundian alliance had been considered, a lavish banquet was held, followed by dancing and other amusements. These can only be considered harbingers of the more magnificent festivities that occurred on the Field of Cloth of Gold in 1520, when Henry VIII met in consultation with Francis I of France.[2] During the period after the meeting between Henry VII and the Archduke Philip, relations between England and the Low Countries continued to improve, and in 1502 the ban on English commerce was at last lifted. Unhappily the new cordiality was quite short-lived, for within a few more months a new trade war was imminent. This was owing to the support that the archduke and his father Maximilian were giving to a well-known Yorkist partisan, Edmund de la Pole, Earl of Suffolk, who had defied Henry by going into self-imposed exile on the continent.

The Earl of Suffolk was a younger brother of that John de la Pole, Earl of Lincoln, who had been killed at Stoke in 1487. Consequently Suffolk was the eldest surviving son of Elizabeth Plantaganet, sister of the two Yorkist kings, who had been married for many years to John de la Pole, Duke of Suffolk (ob. 1491); and as such he was a leading representative of the White Rose faction with a claim of his own to the throne. Henry VII was nevertheless quite fond of the earl, who was both a dashing swaggerer and a skilful competitor in the lists. Throughout the 1490s the king's treatment of him had been kind and generous to a fault. Suffolk was always cordially received at court; in 1492 he took a prominent part in the Boulogne campaign and was subsequently inducted into the Order of the Garter; and at one point the king paid him the extraordinary compliment of staying overnight at his country house in Oxfordshire. Yet there was an underlying tension between the two men, for Henry would not elevate Suffolk to the dukedom that his late father had enjoyed. As justification the king cited the family's rather straitened circumstances, owing to the confiscation of Lincoln's estates, which made it impossible for the earl to support a dignity higher than his current title. Besides, Suffolk had formally renounced his claims to the dukedom in 1491, when Henry awarded him a portion of his late brother's lands. A few years later, after the earl had killed another man in a brawl, he received a full pardon from the Crown; yet he was unable to forgive the indignity of being indicted before an ordinary court of law. During the summer of 1499 he suddenly bolted the realm, going first to Calais and then to St. Omer. Because Flanders had long been a breeding ground for Yorkist plots, Henry was doubtless tempted to take extreme measures against him. But the king refused to admit any alarm and simply requested the good offices of the archduke in persuading Suffolk to return to England. Although the king was not averse to the employment of drastic methods whenever they proved necessary, his pacific tactics succeeded, and within a few months the earl voluntarily reappeared at Westminster, where he was received as graciously as ever. When in the spring of 1500 Henry crossed the Channel for his meeting with the archduke, Suffolk was among those who accompanied him.[3]

The reconciliation was not to last, however, for by August 1501 the earl had fled to the continent once again. Accompanied now by his brother, Lord Richard de la Pole, he secured promises of assistance from Maximilian, whom he visited at Imst, in the Tyrol. The emperor declared that he would always help the heirs of Edward IV to obtain their rightful inheritance and persuaded the two Englishmen to settle at the free imperial city of Aachen until plans for an invasion of England could be formulated. This time Henry reacted vigorously to the news of Suffolk's flight. In November 1501 he had the earl and his brother outlawed at Paul's Cross and ordered the immediate apprehension of another de la Pole brother, William, who was still in England. Among those condemned for misprison of treason at this juncture was Sir James Tyrell, governor of Guisnes Castle, whom Suffolk had visited during his first flight to the continent. Shortly before his execution in May 1502, Tyrell signed a confession that he had directed the murder of the two Princes of the

Tower nineteen years earlier. Henry hoped that such a confession would assuage the rumors, still current in some circles, that the sons of Edward IV were still alive.

Meanwhile Henry had appealed to the emperor in an effort to secure Suffolk's extradition to England. Negotiations during the spring of 1502 led to the conclusion of a new commercial agreement between England and the Low Countries, by which Maximilian promised to expel all English conspirators from his as well as his son's dominions and to arrest any Englishmen who resisted. In return for this valuable concession, Henry contributed £10,000 towards a campaign Maximilian was planning to wage against the Ottoman Turks. Yet the emperor made no move to expel Suffolk, as he had promised to do. He no longer intimated he would support the earl in an invasion of England, and he encouraged Suffolk and his brother Richard to apply to Henry for a pardon. But he allowed the two Englishmen to live on at Aachen, where they were heavily in debt and increasingly fretful.

More successful than Henry's attempt to capture Suffolk, who eluded his clutches until 1506, were the king's negotiations with Ferdinand and Isabella. Henry was anxious to complete the arrangements for Prince Arthur's marriage to Catherine of Aragon, first proposed more than a decade earlier. On 1 October 1496 a new Anglo-Spanish marriage agreement, along the lines of the treaty of Medina del Campo but embodying amendments proposed by Henry, had been signed. That agreement had stipulated that Catherine should depart for England no later than 1 September 1500, by which time Arthur would have reached his fourteenth year. Her dowry of approximately £40,000 was to be paid in cash—the first half within ten days of the wedding, the remainder in two equal installments over the next two years. Henry ratified the new treaty in July 1497, and shortly afterwards Arthur and Catherine were betrothed at Woodstock. Once the Spanish monarchs had confirmed the treaty in 1498, application was made to Rome for a papal dispensation so that the two children could marry before reaching full canonical age. Alexander VI was as anxious as ever to remain on friendly terms with Europe's greatest secular rulers; and in May 1499 Arthur and Catherine were married by proxy at Bewdley, with Dr. Puebla taking the part of the absent princess.[4]

On instructions from the Spanish court, Dr. Puebla urged Henry during the spring of 1499 to end the continuing danger posed by Perkin Warbeck and the Earl of Warwick. Both men were under heavy guard in the Tower, but they might escape at any time and become the focus of a new plot against the king's life. This meant that the young House of

Tudor, of which Catherine would soon become a member, could not be considered altogether safe while either captive lived. Because there had been a minor plot in December 1498, during which a young Londoner named Ralph Wilford had masqueraded as Warwick, Henry conceded the wisdom of Dr. Puebla's advice. Yet he clearly had qualms about the actions he now planned to take and spent many sleepless nights worrying about the matter. In a letter of March 1499 Bishop Ayala informed a friend that, "Henry has aged so much during the last two weeks that he seems to be twenty years older." Not only did the king spend long hours in meditation and prayer, but he conferred on several occasions with William Paromis and other soothsayers, who hinted that his life might be in danger. As a consequence he concluded that both Warbeck and Warwick must be eliminated, which soon led to the worst judicial murders of the reign. Indeed, according to Bacon, Catherine maintained at the height of her subsequent troubles that, owing to Warwick's death, her marriage had been made in blood. Doubtless it was these events that caused Henry to be characterized by his first biographer as "a dark Prince and infinitely suspicious, and his time full of secret conspiracies."[5]

Although it cannot be proved, Henry apparently employed Thomas Astwood, one of the jailers in the Tower, as an *agent provocateur*. With the assistance of a fellow jailer, Robert Cleymound, Astwood won the confidence of his two charges, who never suspected that they would not be helped in escaping to Flanders, where troops were supposedly waiting for an attack on Henry. In this way the plot was deliberately brought within the bounds of high treason. Shortly before it was to be put in motion, the plan was "divulged" to Henry, who at once initiated legal proceedings against his opponents. No action was taken against Astwood and Cleymound, which supports the view that they were acting for the king, but on 16 November 1499 Warbeck and three others were hanged, drawn, and quartered at Tyburn. Several days later the unfortunate Warwick, who had languished in captivity since Bosworth because of his crime in being descended from Richard of York, was tried by a special tribunal headed by the Earl of Oxford. After publicly acknowledging his guilt, he was beheaded on Tower Hill on 29 November. Within another week a jubilant Dr. Puebla informed Ferdinand and Isabella that "not a drop of doubtful royal blood" was any longer to be found in England.[6]

Whatever fears the Spanish rulers had entertained for their daughter's safety should now have been satisfied. Yet for some reason of their own, they did not permit her to sail for England in 1500, as the treaty of 1496 had stipulated. However, because of a new bout of French aggression in Italy, they still wanted to be on friendly terms with Henry; so at their urging, Arthur and Catherine enjoyed a second proxy marriage in November 1500, with Dr. Puebla again substituting for the absent princess. Five months later Isabella at last conceded that every conceivable precaution had been taken for her daughter's safe departure. But the fleet assembled to take Catherine to England did not sail until 17 August;[7] and only four days out of port a sudden squall compelled it to double back to Laredo, at the eastern end of the Basque coast. More than a month elapsed before the damaged ships could be repaired, by which time an alarmed Henry had sent Stephen Brett, a well known Devonshire pilot, to look for the expedition. Brett was able to lead the little fleet, which sailed again on 27 September, around the rocky shoals off Brittany, and five days later the Spanish ships anchored at Plymouth. Catherine was welcomed ashore by the mayor and other local dignitaries, who accompanied her through the narrow streets to the church, where she gave thanks for her safe arrival. Because Henry had expected her to land at Gravesend, there were no official representatives of the Crown in the West Country to greet her. As soon as he learned of her landing, he sent a delegation of notables to extend his apologies and escort her to the capital.[8]

Meanwhile the leading individuals of western England had flocked to Plymouth to meet their future queen. With great ceremony Catherine was conducted to Exeter, where she was joyously acclaimed. Hundreds of commoners crowded in to catch a glimpse of her, and even her most menial attendants were lodged "as if they had all been grandees." After several days of lavish entertainments, the steward of the king's household, Lord Willoughby de Broke, arrived at the head of a deputation that included the Richmond King-at-Arms and the Somerset and Rougedragon heralds. Once Henry's greetings had been extended, a leisurely journey towards London began. As the procession neared Ambresbury, the princess was met and welcomed anew by a party that included the Earl of Surrey and several bishops and mitred abbots. Once Andover and Basingstoke had been left behind, Catherine and her burgeoning train arrived at Dogmersfield, the palace of the Bishops of Bath and Wells, fifteen miles south of London Bridge.[9]

Anxious to have a look at this princess sent him by the Spanish government, Henry set out from Richmond on 4 November with more than a dozen attendants. At East Hampstead he was joined by Prince Arthur, who had just ridden in from the Welsh marches, and together they covered the remaining miles that separated them from Dogmersfield. Once they arrived at the palace, however, Henry insisted on seeing Catherine alone. Only when he was convinced of her ability to bear children would he allow his son to be introduced to his future wife.[10]

Catherine remained at Dogmersfield until 9 November, when she was transferred to apartments at Lambeth Palace. Three days later she made her ceremonial entry into the capital, where she was greeted by an outpouring of genuine affection. As her litter crossed London Bridge, she heard welcoming addresses from maidens clothed as St. Catherine and St. Ursula. The route down Gracechurch Street and Cheapside was festooned with rich hangings and masses of red and white roses. In the doorway of a large house owned by a wealthy haberdasher stood the king and queen, who smiled broadly as she came into sight. Before her arrival at the Bishop of London's palace, where she and her train were to be lodged, she received a handsome gift of plate from the Lord Mayor, whose presentation speech was a prelude to an elaborate pageant depicting the seven virtues.[11] Londoners were deeply impressed by the splendor of the occasion; and in a letter written shortly afterwards, Thomas More described the scene for a friend.

Catherine, the illustrious daughter of the King of Spain and bride of our distinguished Prince, lately made her entry into London, amid a tremendous ovation; never, to my knowledge, has there been such a reception anywhere. The magnificent attire of our nobles aroused cries of admiration. But the Spanish escort—good heavens!—what a sight! If you had seen it, I am afraid you would have burst with laughter; they were so ludicrous. Except for three, or at the most, four of them, they were just too much to look at: hunchbacked, undersized, barefoot Pygmies from Ethiopia. If you had been there, you would have thought they were refugees from hell. Ah, but the lady! Take my word for it, she thrilled the hearts of everyone; she possesses all those qualities that make for beauty in a very charming young girl. Everywhere she receives the highest of praises; but even that is inadequate.[12]

Two days later the wedding itself occurred in St. Paul's Cathedral. The Archbishop of Canterbury, assisted by the Archbishop of Santiago, who had helped escort Catherine to England, presided at the high altar, where a nuptial mass was celebrated by sixteen prelates in all. The bride and groom were clothed in white satin, while the king and queen were dressed in more colorful raiment, wearing in brilliant display most of the £14,000 worth of jewels that had been bought just for the occasion. Once the ceremony ended, Henry hosted a lavish banquet at Baynard's Castle, where he created fifty-eight new Knights of the Bath, after which the newly-weds were gaily escorted to their bedchamber.[13] Ten more days of feasting, jousting, and elaborate entertainments directed by Fayrfax and Newark followed under the efficient coordination of Bishop Fox, the Lord Privy Seal. These occurred not only in the capital but also at Greenwich, to which the court was accompanied down the Thames by a water-pageant " 'with the most goodly and plesaunt mirthe of trumpetts, clarions, shalmewes, tabers, recorders and other dyvers instruments, to whoes noyse uppon the water hath not been heard the like.' "[14] There was a particularly sumptuous presentation one evening at Richmond when a pageant was wheeled into the Great Hall "in the form of a tower with two stories, in the upper part of which were eight disguised ladies, and in the lower eight knights. Before the latter descended to dance they let loose conies, or rabbits, which ran about the hall; the ladies let fly doves and other birds, and then came down to dance with the knights."[15]

Yet the most sumptuous productions of all took place in Westminster Hall, where one evening three successive pageants were wheeled into the presence of an admiring audience. The description given of these theatricals by Professor Boas cannot be bettered.

The first [pageant] was a castle drawn by four great animals. Eight disguised ladies looked out of the windows, and on each of the four turrets sat a boy, dressed like a maiden, and singing. The second was a ship, having as passenger a lady dressed like a Spanish princess, and manned by a crew who in 'theyr counteynaunces, speeches and demeanour used and behaved themselves after the manner and guise of Mariners'. The ship having cast anchor, Hope and Desire descended and announced that they were ambassadors from knights of the Mount of Love, which formed the third pageant. This contained eight goodly knights who made an attack upon the Castle, till the ladies yielded and came down to dance with them. During the dancing the pageants were removed, and after the disguisers had departed, some of the leading spectators descended into the hall and danced 'basse dances', which were measures of a slow and stately kind.[16]

It was undoubtedly on this occasion that Henry VII himself appeared among the dancers in the attire of a Spanish grandee.

Towards the end of these joyous celebrations, the emotional and psychological climax of the first Tudor reign, Henry wrote to inform Ferdinand and Isabella that their daughter had "been welcomed by the whole people." On 30 November, two days after Dr. Puebla delivered the first half of Catherine's dowry, Arthur himself sent a letter to the Spanish rulers in which he declared his great happiness and vowed to be a worthy son-in-law.[17]

By the first week of December 1501 Henry had decided that the young couple should reside at Ludlow, where the prince would resume his duties as governor of the Welsh marches. The elderly Sir Reginald Bray, who had only two years left to live, was not reappointed a councillor to the prince, but the latter was to be aided by two experienced bishops, Smith of Lincoln and Young of St. David's; and he was also to have the counsel of such capable Welshmen as Sir Henry Vernon, Sir William Udall, and Sir David Phillips. Among those who were to accompany Arthur and his bride to Wales were Catherine's chaplain and former tutor, Don Alessandro Geraldini, her duenna, Doña Elvira Manuel, and the duenna's husband, Don Pedro Manrique.

From London the royal train rode in stately procession past Abingdon and Kenilworth. After crossing the Severn, it proceeded by way of Bewdley to Ludlow, where Arthur and Catherine spent the winter of 1501–2 in quiet relaxations, a welcome relief no doubt from the hectic activities of the past few months. Exactly when Arthur fell ill, and from what affliction he suffered, is unclear. For several months the West Country had been racked by plague, while the particular bane of that era, the dreaded "sweating sickness," was also prevalent there. It was later held that the prince died of "a consumption," which suggests that he may have had tuberculosis and gradually wasted away. Certainly he had never been strong, and physically he was overshadowed by his wife, who was a head taller (albeit nine months older) than he. Whatever his illness, his condition became progressively weaker, and on 2 April he died.

A messenger was at once dispatched to inform the king and queen, who were in residence at Greenwich. Henry's saddened councillors decided he should hear the news from his confessor, who should be able to find suitable words of consolation. Despite the friar's text from Job ("If we receive good things from the hand of God, why may we not endure evil ones?"), Henry was deeply grieved, particularly since Prince Edmund had died in June 1500, and the future of the dynasty now hung by a single thread, the life of his eleven-year-old son Henry. Tearfully the king summoned his wife to his side. On learning the situation she did her best to comfort him, even declaring that she could still have another son. Later, however, in the privacy of her own apartments, she was so overcome by sorrow that Henry had to be called. When he found her weeping uncontrollably, he did what he could to soothe and reassure her.[18]

Meanwhile the prince's body lay in state on a catafalque in the Great Hall at Ludlow Castle, where the gentlemen of western England congregated to pay their last respects. After three weeks Arthur's corpse was removed to the nearby parish church, where a requiem mass was performed by the Bishops of Lincoln, Salisbury, and Chester. The Earl of Surrey substituted for the king as chief mourner. Also present at the funeral were the Earls of Kent and Shrewsbury, Lord Powys and Dudley, the eldest son of the Earl of Kildare, and various officers of the royal household. From Ludlow the prince's remains were transported to Worcester Cathedral, where they were interred in the choir. Catherine of

Aragon was unable to attend these sorrowful rites, for she was seriously ill at Ludlow, where there were brief fears for her life. After a lengthy convalescence, she was taken by easy stages to her mother-in-law's side at Richmond. When at last well enough to have her own household, she and her servants were installed in a vacant palace on the Strand that was owned by the Bishop of Durham.[19]

Five weeks later the news of Arthur's death reached Ferdinand and Isabella at Toledo. They immediately devised a strategy to bind Henry to them once again and directed their Lord Chamberlain, Hernan de Estrada, to depart for England at once. He was to demand the return of the 100,000 crowns already paid on Catherine's dowry, but simultaneously he was to insist on the fulfilment of all her dower rights, which entitled her to a third of the yearly revenues of all royal estates in Chester, Cornwall, and Wales. In addition he was to suggest that preparations begin for her eventual return to Spain. Yet once Henry was convinced the Anglo-Spanish alliance was about to be terminated, Estrada was to suggest a union between Catherine and Prince Henry.[20]

Why the Spanish rulers adopted such a devious strategy at this juncture can only be explained by a brief review of recent happenings in Italy. Some months earlier Louis XII of France had overthrown Ludovico Sforza and established himself on the ducal throne of Milan. Yet the French king realized that his Italian gains would be resented by Spain, so in November 1500 he sought to safeguard them by concluding the treaty of Granada with Ferdinand and Isabella. This treaty obligated the French and Spanish Crowns to cooperate in the partition of territories belonging to King Federigo of Naples. Louis' portion would be the city of Naples itself, the Terra di Lavoro, the Abruzzi, and several other northern districts, whereas the Spanish rulers would acquire Calabria, Apulia, and most of Federigo's southern provinces. In July 1501 a French army sacked Capua, which prompted the residents of Naples to capitulate shortly thereafter. King Federigo yielded to the French commander and was compensated for his losses with the French Duchy of Anjou. In March 1502 Federigo's son surrendered to the Spanish army at Taranto, after which the allies fell out and quarrelled over the remaining spoils. The treaty of Granada had not provided for all of King Federigo's territories, so there was ample room for bickering. The French armies had a momentary supremacy and won victory after victory. Only in Barletta were the Spaniards under their intrepid commander, Gonsalvo de Cordoba, able to stave off total disaster.

Thus the news of Arthur's death came at a particularly inopportune time for Ferdinand and Isabella. Because of the French gains in southern Italy, they desperately wanted to renew their alliance with England. Yet they were afraid that Henry would use their plight to wring better terms, and possibly a larger dowry, from them. Hoping to prevent this, they adopted a deliberately hard line and attempted to bluff him into believing they placed no particular value on their alliance with England. Indeed he would be lucky to secure its renewal on whatever terms they might allow.

Whether it was the Spanish strategy or Henry's inherent reasonableness that paved the way for a new draft treaty is unclear. Probably it was Henry's attitude, for in diplomatic affairs he rarely attempted to profit from the misfortunes of others.[21] Moreover, he still longed for a lasting marriage alliance with the House of Trastamara, which was crucial to his self-esteem; and he had no intention of returning any of the 100,000 crowns already paid on Catherine's dowry. Thus for a variety of reasons the relative importance of which cannot now be determined, a new marriage agreement was soon drafted. By September 1502 Estrada had formally proposed a union between Catherine and Prince Henry, and the English monarch and his advisers were giving serious consideration to it. Yet because Ferdinand and Isabella wanted the new treaty to include an English guarantee of their possessions in southern Italy, Henry would not accept it until it was significantly altered. Under no circumstances would he declare war on Louis XII and send troops to Normandy and Guienne, as he was being pressed to do; and not until almost a year elapsed was the new agreement completed, and then on terms considerably more favorable to Henry than to the Spanish rulers.

Before that time arrived another tragedy occurred to disrupt the harmony of Henry's personal life. Shortly after Prince Arthur's death, the king and queen had decided to try for another son, in order to strengthen the succession to the throne. Although Elizabeth of York was only in her mid-thirties, her new pregnancy was a difficult one, and she was seriously ill throughout the summer of 1502. During the winter of 1502–3, elaborate preparations were made for her approaching confinement, which was to take place at Richmond. But while on a visit to the Tower on 2 February, she was prematurely delivered of a daughter and died nine days later. The child was small and sickly and died within the month. Henry was inconsolable at the loss of his wife, who had been a strong support and a loving companion for over fifteen years. Indeed it was said of him that he "privily departed to a solitary place, and would no man should resort unto him." His grief was shared by the people of London, who had loved Elizabeth for her beauty and goodness. After her body had lain in state in the Tower, it was transported by means of a solemn cortege to Westminster Abbey, where it was entombed in the great new chapel Henry had begun to construct a year earlier.[22]

Despite his deep sense of loss, Henry was soon thinking of remarrying, if only to father another son and safeguard the succession. Within a few months he suggested to Ferdinand and Isabella that he himself should become Catherine's second husband. Isabella strenuously opposed this idea, not only because Henry was almost thirty years older than her daughter but because the princess would have no influence on the foreign policy of such an experienced king as Henry VII. Furthermore because the latter had a healthy son, who would doubtless inherit the throne one day, Catherine was unlikely to exercise very much power when she ultimately became a dowager queen, which might not be in the distant future. Isabella therefore insisted that the negotiations for a union between her daughter and Prince Henry continue; and as for a new wife for the king, he should look to the widowed Queen of Naples, a niece of Ferdinand of Aragon's, who was currently living with her elderly mother near Valencia. Henry VII was intrigued by this proposal and sent John Stile and two other Englishmen to determine whether the lady in question had a pleasing figure, whether her face and voice were attractive, and whether her breath was sweet and her teeth good. Eventually Henry learned that, although the widowed queen was comely enough, she was living as a pensioner of the Spanish rulers, since she had no revenues of her own and was unlikely to recover her position in southern Italy. Henry therefore concluded that Isabella had sought to dupe him, which caused his attitude towards Spain to become perceptibly cooler. But the new Anglo-Spanish marriage agreement had already been concluded by that juncture, so no lasting harm was done to the relationship between the two countries.[23]

Signed on 23 June 1503, the new marriage treaty was, in its most important respect, a rather curious treaty, for it rested on the assumption that Catherine's first marriage had been consummated, whereas the surviving evidence suggests just the opposite. Catherine's confessor, it is true, proclaimed shortly after Arthur's death that the marriage had been physically completed, but only as a way of guaranteeing that Catherine's dower rights in England would be respected. As soon as Catherine and her duenna learned of Don Alessandro's well-intentioned move, they denounced it in scathing terms and sent a detailed report of everything that had transpired to Spain. Isabella saw no reason to doubt the truthfulness of her daughter and Doña Elvira and recalled the confessor in disgrace to Spain. By October 1502 even Henry VII had been persuaded that

Catherine was still a virgin and issued a public declaration to that effect.[24] It is also significant that when Catherine at last remarried in 1509, she wore a white gown, the symbol of virginity then as now; and until her dying day in 1536 she never wavered from her contention that she and Arthur had never consummated their union. Because of her devoutly religious nature, it seems inconceivable that she would have lied about such an important matter, thereby endangering her soul.

Why then was the new marriage agreement based on the assumption that Catherine's marriage to Arthur had been consummated? For two reasons, primarily. First, Henry VII was naturally determined that there should be no questions about the legitimacy of any children born of the projected marriage; and since Arthur and Catherine had lived together for four months, he was afraid that, unless careful precautions were taken, future plotters against his House would stigmatize his grandchildren as bastards. Simply to recall how Richard III only twenty years earlier had used the alleged precontract between Edward IV and Lady Eleanor Butler as a way of discrediting his two nephews should be sufficient to dispel any notions that Henry's concern on this score was excessive. And second the ever-obliging Dr. Puebla, an authority on both civil and canon law, assured Henry that a papal dispensation could easily be obtained to remove the ban of affinity that would otherwise prevent a marriage between the princess and her former brother-in-law, the future Henry VIII. Thus it seemed better strategy for the king to maintain that Catherine's first marriage had been consummated, although he obviously believed otherwise, and to apply to Rome for a dispensation to remove the impediment resulting from the alleged consummation. Unfortunately for this well-thought-out course, the cooperative Alexander VI died before the requested dispensation could be granted; and after the brief pontificate of Pius III, the new pope, Julius II, obliged only after lengthy reflection on the matter. It is far from clear why Julius took so long before issuing the dispensation: whether he had questions about the alleged consummation of the marriage, or whether he suspected he was being asked to override not just a provision of the canon law but one of God's commandments, which no earthly agency—not even the papacy—had ever claimed to be able to do. At any rate, enough theological questions were left in doubt to justify Henry VIII's contention a quarter of a century later that his marriage to Catherine had been invalid from the beginning. Thus the agreement devised so skilfully by Henry VII as a way of guaranteeing the legitimacy of his grandchildren was eventually used by his successor to divorce the first of his six wives and so to pave the way for England's break from Rome.

The other provisions of the new Anglo-Spanish marriage agreement can be summarized quickly. As in 1496, Catherine's dowry was set at 200,000 crowns, of which Henry acknowledged he was already possessed of the first half. The marriage was to take place as soon as Prince Henry attained his fifteenth birthday, which would be on 28 June 1505, provided the remainder of Catherine's dowry was available to be paid over in London. The princess's rights as Arthur's widow were revoked, although she was promised an equal jointure at the time of her remarriage. Because the position of the Spanish troops in southern Italy had recently improved—Gonsalvo de Cordoba overwhelmed a French army in April 1503—there was no need for an English guarantee of the Spanish rulers' Neapolitan possessions, which Henry would not have given in any case. On balance, therefore, the marriage agreement was considerably more favorable to England than it was to Spain. Most of Henry's ideas and proposals were incorporated, although it was Catherine's and not her parents' interests that were sacrificed. As Professor Mattingly once noted, the princess "could not remarry for at least two years, and then not unless her dowry was ready; meanwhile, having renounced all her dower rights, she was obliged to live in England on the bounty of the English King."[25]

Once the new marriage agreement was signed, Catherine and Prince Henry were betrothed during an elaborate ceremony at the Bishop of Salisbury's palace. This was but a few days before Henry VII was scheduled to send his daughter Margaret north to Scotland for her approaching marriage to James IV.

Henry VII was even more hopeful of the long-term benefits that would accrue from a dynastic alliance with Scotland than he was about those that would result from the alliance with Spain. Indeed he believed a marriage between his daughter Margaret and James IV would lead to improved relations between the two countries, causing the King of Scots to conclude that he could safely terminate the Auld Alliance with France. Such optimistic hopes were soon to prove illusory, however, owing to the longstanding Scottish fears of England and to the determination of Louis XII to perpetuate the Auld Alliance, symbolized by his offer of common nationality to all Scots residing in France. But despite the obstacles to his policy, Henry VII persevered for more than a decade; and although the good relations he temporarily achieved with James IV declined and disappeared even before his death, his statesmanlike approach paved the way for an eventual union of the English and Scottish Crowns, which was accomplished in 1603 by his great-great grandson, James VI and I.

Shortly after the conclusion of the truce of Ayton in 1497, Henry had renewed his proposal for an eventual marriage between James IV and the Princess Margaret, then a child of nine. Although the outlook seemed propitious at first, Anglo-Scottish relations cooled again in June 1498, owing to a resurgence of border raiding. Both Henry's wife and mother objected to his plan to betroth the little princess to a lusty bachelor fifteen years her senior; but the king's wishes ultimately prevailed, and in August 1498 serious negotiations commenced. In July of the following year a treaty was concluded at Stirling which obligated the two kings to maintain peaceful relations for as long as either of them lived. This treaty was ratified on 8 September by Henry, who subsequently directed Bishop Fox to open negotiations for a formal marriage agreement.[26]

Once he arrived at the Scottish court, Fox made it abundantly clear that a union between James and Margaret could not take place until the princess was of a marriageable age, to which the Scottish ruler willingly assented. Yet James insisted on the provision of a substantial dowry, comparable to what would be appropriate for a Spanish infanta. Fox and his master refused to be influenced by rumors deliberately spread that James might yet choose to marry a German princess, and under no circumstances would they agree to provide more than half the sum being demanded of them. The only other obstacle to the marriage agreement was eliminated in July 1500, when Alexander VI granted a dispensation to remove the ban of affinity resulting from James's and Margaret's common descent from John Beaufort, Marquess of Somerset.[27]

The negotiations continued at a leisurely pace during the following year, with numerous envoys making the difficult journey between London and Edinburgh. Although Henry issued safe conducts to James's ambassadors in May 1501, not until the following October were the Archbishop of Glasgow, the Bishop of Moray, and the Earl of Bothwell instructed to go to Westminster to negotiate both a marriage alliance and a treaty of "perpetual peace." The three Scotsmen set out within a short time and arrived at the English court on 20 November, at which time Henry was still preoccupied with the celebrations attendant on Arthur's marriage to Catherine of Aragon. Yet on 28 November he directed the Archbishop of Canterbury, the Earl of Surrey, and Bishop Fox to confer with the three Scottish ambassadors on all matters pertaining to Anglo-Scottish relations, including the projected marriage agreement.[28]

The negotiations now proceeded at a quickened rate, and on 24 January 1502 three separate treaties were signed in the queen's Presence Chamber at Richmond. The first was the treaty of perpetual peace, which bound the two monarchs not to make war, nor to allow war to be made, on one another, just as neither ruler would shelter rebels or aid imposters against the other. Henceforth both kings would deal openly and fairly with one another, despite any prior agreements they had with other governments; and the great border fortress of Berwick would neither be assaulted by the Scots nor used by the English to launch an invasion of the Scottish lowlands. The second agreement signed on 24 January was an indenture designed to bring a permanent halt to the border raiding of the past. According to its most important clause, Englishmen guilty of assaulting Scotsmen within the precincts of the border were to be surrendered to the appropriate Scottish authorities for punishment, according to the custom of the border. Since the most deadly raids of the last few years had been perpetrated by Henry's subjects, it was not felt necessary to include a similar clause pertaining to Scotsmen guilty of attacks on their southern neighbors.[29]

The third and most important of the three treaties signed at Richmond was of course the marriage agreement, which stipulated that Margaret's dowry was to be £10,000 sterling, or £30,000 Scots, which was to be paid in three equal installments, the first being due at Edinburgh within a week of the wedding and the other two to be handed over at stated intervals within the next two years. At Henry's expense Margaret was to be escorted by 1 September 1503 to Lamberton Kirk, near Berwick, where she would meet her future husband, to whom she should be married within the next fifteen days. She would be allowed to have as many as twenty-four English attendants, and her husband was to support her in a fashion appropriate to her rank, granting her pen money of at least £1000 Scots per year. As her jointure, estates were to be settled on her that produced annual revenues of at least £6000 Scots. Should Henry VII be displeased with the lands earmarked for this purpose, he would have until 15 July 1503 to lodge a formal complaint.[30]

Two days after the three treaties were signed, an elaborate ceremony took place at Richmond. Margaret and the other members of her family participated in a high mass, at the conclusion of which she and James IV were married by proxy. Then the Earl of Bothwell came forward and, on behalf of his master, delivered several valuable presents to the princess, including a tiara of diamonds, emeralds, and rubies. Three days of tournaments and pageants followed, during which Margaret was formally addressed as "Queen of Scots." She was given her own separate establishments at Westminster and Windsor and served on dishes made especially for her use and emblazoned with the royal arms of Scotland.[31]

Despite the joyful nature of these festivities, the tension between the two kings persisted, for James IV was annoyed by the phrasing of the marriage agreement and the two accompanying treaties. He particularly objected to the way Henry had been styled "King of France," which was bound to offend Louis XII, and repeatedly demanded alterations. Henry refused to take umbrage, however; and because both monarchs were anxious for the marriage agreement to be completed, they temporarily ignored the friction that still existed between them.

On 27 June 1503, two days after the betrothal of Prince Henry and Catherine of Aragon, the English ruler and his daughter set out for Collyweston, Northamptonshire, Lady Margaret Beaufort's country house, where Henry had arranged to entrust the princess to the Earl and Countess of Surrey. The Lord Treasurer and his wife were to escort Margaret north for her marriage, which was to take place by the middle of September. After several days of feasting and other entertainments at Collyweston, the fourteen-year-old princess bade farewell to her father on 8 July. Their parting must have been a sorrowful one, since she revered him and he loved her dearly. But Margaret had the high spirits that typified her family; and once her train rode off towards the North, she gaily plied the Treasurer with questions about her future husband. The procession passed through such midland towns as Grantham, Sirousby, and Doncaster before entering the portals of York, where the princess was welcomed by the mayor and given a handsome present of plate. From York, Margaret and her attendants travelled on to Durham, where they rested for several days. Then they proceeded to Newcastle and enjoyed a lavish banquet hosted by the Earl of Northumberland. After Berwick's ramparts had disappeared from view, they crossed the border into Scotland, to a resounding salute provided by James's cannon. Once the princess and her train reached Lamberton Kirk on 1 August, they were met by the Archbishop of Glasgow and a great throng of wildly cheering Scotsmen.[32]

Two days later Margaret met her future husband at Dalkeith, where he came to woo her in the French fashion—bareheaded. The princess and Lady Surrey performed a basse dance for him, after which he paid lavish compliments to all the ladies present. The festivities were resumed the next day at New Battle Castle, where Margaret danced again and James performed on the lute and the clavichord. It is even recorded that he stole a kiss from his wife-to-be! The wedding occurred on 8 August, the day following Margaret's ceremonial entry into Edinburgh. The rites were conducted by the Archbishops of Glasgow and York in Holyrood Abbey, after which James entertained at a sumptuous wedding dinner. Unhappily the seating arrangements were poorly handled and did nothing to endear him to his bride: she was obliged to wait until the second serving, by which time he had already dined with Surrey and the two archbishops.

Indeed Margaret was so offended by the attention James lavished on his male companions that she sent off a blistering letter of complaint to her father.[33]

Most historians hold that Margaret was the author of her subsequent misfortunes in Scotland. Certainly she could be proud and willful and was convinced that her new country was inferior in every way to her native land. But in all fairness to her, it has to be admitted that James IV was a difficult and unaccommodating man. On occasion he could be courtly, charming, and vivacious; but as often as not he was mean, capricious, self-centred, and thoughtless. That he paraded his mistresses before his young wife was cruel and heartless, to say the least. In addition he was an incorrigible spendthrift, paying over £2000 for wine alone during the week of his wedding; and when he occasionally tried to economize, he berated his wife for her expenditures. After a stormy first year together, James and Margaret learned to tolerate one another, but they never fell in love. Although they had a son in 1507 (who lived but a few months), it was not until 1512 that their heir, the future James V, was born. During September of the following year Margaret's husband was killed on Flodden Field by his old adversary, the Earl of Surrey, who was subsequently created Duke of Norfolk by a grateful Henry VIII.

Because Margaret's marriage to James IV was anything but happy, it did less to heal the wounds between the two countries than Henry VII had hoped. During the years 1504–9 relations between England and Scotland were again strained, owing mainly to James's desire to transform his country into a major European power, which caused him to adopt a programme of rapid naval expansion. When his warships interfered with English merchantmen plying the waters of the North Sea, angry complaints poured in to his father-in-law. The continuation of border raiding also kept passions inflamed, particularly after several English marauders attacked and killed Sir Robert Ker, a prominent Scottish official. In 1506–7 war seemed about to break out when the English and Scottish governments took opposite sides in the bitter quarrel between the Duke of Guelders and his Burgundian overlord. Because the Duke of Guelders was nominally allied to both France and Scotland, the crisis caused James to think about a possible revival of the Auld Alliance. During 1508 there was so much trafficking between Edinburgh and Paris that Henry became alarmed. Rightly or wrongly, he detained two Scottish peers, the Earl of Arran and his brother Lord Patrick Hamilton, who were travelling back to Scotland without safe conducts. Although the two Scotsmen, both of whom were famous jousters, were graciously entertained at Richmond and Windsor, James IV was furious about their detention; and had Henry not been careful to maintain friendly relations with Louis XII throughout this period, his actions might well have led to war.[34]

Clearly Henry's policy towards Scotland was less successful than his efforts to pacify Ireland. Despite his obvious desire for friendship with Scotland, much blood was yet to be spilt before James VI came south to claim the throne of his Tudor forebears. But without the marriage of Margaret Tudor to James IV a century earlier, the union of the Crowns could not have been accomplished when it was. Morever, it should never be forgotten that the force which ultimately brought the two countries together was religion. Once the Reformation triumphed on both sides of the border, Englishmen and Scotsmen came to feel that they had common aims as well as a common destiny, which led in turn to greater cultural and economic cooperation. And when in 1560 Queen Elizabeth provided military assistance to the Scottish Protestants, thereby prompting them to look to London rather than to Paris for support, the old link between Scotland and France was permanently severed. Thus is is doubtful whether any policy, regardless of how skilfully framed and executed, could have overcome the traditional animosity between the two kingdoms until Henry VIII broke with Rome and initiated a course he knew not where it might ultimately lead.

XI

Decline and Exit

By the time Elizabeth of York died in 1503, Henry was a prematurely aged man. Only a few weeks past his forty-sixth birthday, he impressed most of his contemporaries as considerably older, largely because of the cares and worries that had sapped so much of his energy during the last decade. Owing to poor eyesight, he tended to squint; and according to Polydore Vergil, who knew him well, "his hair was thin and white; his teeth few, poor and blackish; his complexion sallow." Yet he was far from ugly, for, as Polydore also maintained, his appearance "was remarkably attractive and his face was cheerful, especially when speaking." Moreover, he never became obese, as his son Henry VIII did, but remained "slender, well built and strong" until the last year of his life.[1]

Although Henry VII continued to be "gracious and kind" to those who frequented his court, a marked change came over his behavior during these years. The death of his wife so soon after the funerals of his sons Edmund and Arthur could not have left his outlook unaffected. Furthermore the companions of his early years, those who had helped raise him to the throne, were now dying off or were already dead. His uncle Jasper's death in 1495 was followed by that of Cardinal Morton in 1500. Shortly afterwards Sir Thomas Brian, Chief Justice of the Common Pleas for the last fifteen years, expired. Early in 1501 came the obsequies for John, Lord Dinham, who had been Lord Treasurer since 1486; and in 1503 occurred the demise of Sir Reginald Bray, Chancellor of the Duchy and Henry's principal financial adviser since Bosworth. Within three more years Sir Richard Guildford, Master of the Ordnance and Comptroller of the king's household, died while on a pilgrimage to the Holy Land. And in 1508 came the funeral for Giles, Lord Daubeney, who had not only fought bravely for Henry at Bosworth but also led the charge against the Cornish rebels at Blackheath in 1497.

With such frequent reminders of his own mortality, Henry became increasingly withdrawn and contemplative. Always a religious man, he spent additional hours in meditation and prayer and, during the summer of 1506, travelled with his mother and Prince Henry to Cambridge, where he donated 100 marks to the university and contributed £100 towards the rebuilding of Great St. Mary's.[2] Thence he journeyed to the shrine of Our Lady of Walsingham, in Norfolk, where he devoted several days to spiritual affairs. Doubtless it was his stress on such matters that caused Polydore to observe how "he was the most ardent supporter of our faith, and daily participated with great piety in religious service. To those whom he considered worthy priests, he often secretly gave alms so that they should pray for his salvation."[3] Because Henry was often morose or preoccupied with religious questions, the laughter and gaiety that had pervaded his court during earlier years was conspicuously absent after 1503. The king still enjoyed such amusements as dice and cardplaying, and whenever he was in the countryside he liked to hawk and hunt. But only rarely did he host a banquet or tournament, and seldom was any attempt made to recapture the merriment of Prince Arthur's wedding day.

Yet the court was far from devoid of pageantry during these years. The new Master of Ceremonies, Silvestro de Gigli, who served from 1504 until 1512, was careful to see that important occasions were properly celebrated, while Henry himself still acknowledged the importance of display and "knew well how to maintain his royal majesty in all which appertains to kingship at every time and in every place."[4] Shortly after his wife's death, Henry summoned the Earl of Kildare to England and for three months staged lavish amusements in honor of him and his son Gerald, who was shortly to be married to Lady Elizabeth Zouche. When the Margrave of Brandenburg arrived late in 1503 to receive the Garter on behalf of Maximilian I, sumptuous entertainments were held at Baynard's Castle and at Windsor. In February 1504 a particularly lavish ceremony marked the investiture of the king's only surviving son as Prince of Wales, during which eight new Knights of the Bath were created. Two years later, when the Archduke Philip and his wife Joanna visited England, feasting and dancing, jousting and wrestling, took place at Westminster and Windsor. Late in 1506 festivities on a similar scale occurred when Castiglione arrived to accept the Garter for the Duke of Urbino; and when in 1508 the Earl of Arran and his brother were detained on their return to

Scotland from the continent, extravagant amusements took place at Richmond and Windsor for their entertainment.[5]

The Prince of Wales rarely took an active part in these festivities, for Henry VII was deeply concerned about his heir's safety and well-being. Indeed the king was increasingly worried about the succession to the throne and seldom permitted his son out of his sight. According to an ambassador's report of 1508, the seventeen-year-old prince slept in a room adjacent to the royal bedchamber, by which alone it could be entered. Whenever Prince Henry ventured into the park at Richmond, he was accompanied by several specially appointed attendants; and during scheduled exercise periods in the tiltyard, he was watched from a nearby window by his apprehensive father. By this juncture the Yeomen of the Guard had been increased to 200 men, since the king was obsessed by fears that he or his son might be assaulted. That Henry VII was so protective of his son caused most observers to doubt the wisdom of such a regime, which was so different from the way Prince Arthur had been reared. Yet in 1504 a Spanish emissary, the Duke of Estrada, commented approvingly on the king's devotion to his son and maintained that "certainly there could be no better school in the world than the society of such a father as Henry VII. He is so wise and attentive to everything; nothing escapes his attention."[6] Four years later, however, when Anglo-Spanish relations were noticeably cooler, another Spanish ambassador, the Count of Fuensalida, was considerably more critical of the king's treatment of his son. Fuensalida maintained in fact that, because no one was allowed to converse with the prince, "he never spoke in public except to answer a question from his father."[7] Yet Fuensalida clearly exaggerated the prince's isolation, for he had two youthful companions, Charles Brandon and Edward Neville, who accompanied him on most occasions. But it is also true that the king never thought of sending his son off to Ludlow, as he had done with Arthur, when he attained his twelfth year. Henry VII was determined to keep the prince by his side, even if his emotional development was stunted thereby and he lacked first-hand information of the duties that would eventually befall him.

The king's concern for his son's safety was heightened by reports of a conversation that occurred at Calais in 1503 or 1504. Several prominent men, including the Treasurer and Master Porter of Calais, Sir Hugh Conway and Sir Sampson Norton, had a long discussion one night and predicted that the king would die or be assassinated by the end of 1507, before Prince Henry attained his majority. According to the king's informant, there was much talk about the possible accession of the Duke of Buckingham or the Earl of Suffolk but no consideration whatever of

Prince Henry's claims. Conway is said to have declared that he and his principal lieutenants, Sir Anthony Browne and Sir Nicholas Vaux, were prepared to support either Buckingham or Suffolk but not the Prince of Wales.[8] Because of this and similar conversations that may have been reported to him by Bernard André, Henry VII had every reason to be alarmed about the situation that would confront his son should he die before the prince celebrated his eighteenth birthday. Moreover, he was not the only ruler to be concerned about the situation in England. When in April 1509 the first Tudor monarch died and the accession of his son was announced, Ferdinand of Aragon sent an offer of immediate military assistance, should the new king be confronted by a rebellion or a rival claim to the throne.[9] Thus Henry VII's treatment of his second son, which was altogether different from the relative freedom he had allowed Prince Arthur, must be viewed against his growing fears about the possibility of a disputed succession.

Although many Englishmen might have been content with the accession of Buckingham, Henry VII had no cause to doubt his loyalty. The same was hardly true of the king's attitude towards Suffolk, who was still in self-imposed exile on the continent. Although the earl and his brother Richard were living in penury at Aachen, owing to Maximilian's failure to send them any aid, Henry was determined to nullify any threats from that quarter; and as early as 22 February 1503 he had the two de la Poles excommunicated at Paul's Cross and ordered the confiscation of all their estates in England. The same treatment was decreed for Sir Robert Curzon, governor of Hammes Castle near Calais, who had helped relay messages between Suffolk and the emperor. Yet Curzon ultimately recovered the king's favor, probably by providing information about the earl's whereabouts. When in 1506 Curzon returned to England, he was granted an annuity of £400 along with a full pardon for his past offenses.[10]

Although Suffolk finally received 2000 gold florins from Maximilian in July 1503, he had grown tired of Aachen and soon stole away, leaving his brother Richard to fend off their angry creditors as best he could. Suffolk failed in his efforts to secure assistance from the Elector Palatine of the Rhine, who, at the urging of Louis XII of France, turned a deaf ear to his pleas. Eventually the Yorkist claimant set out for Friesland, where he hoped to obtain support from Duke Albert of Saxony, who had assisted Perkin Warbeck a decade earlier. But on his way north he was arrested by agents of Duke Charles of Guelders, an unscrupulous princeling who imprisoned him at Wageningen. In desperation Suffolk bargained for his freedom, which he offered to buy with funds that a Spanish merchant in Antwerp had allegedly agreed to lend him. But the suspicious Charles would not release him until all the money he had been promised was actually paid over. So Suffolk remained in confinement, while his captor reflected on the very best way to use this pawn so luckily fallen into his hands.[11]

Meanwhile, during the early months of 1504, Henry was taking additional steps to neutralize the threat posed by Suffolk and his brother. The seventh and last parliament of the reign convened on 25 January; and after passing such measures as the Statute of Liveries, it proceeded to attaint fifty-one men (the largest number so condemned by any parliament of the reign),[12] who naturally included Suffolk and his brothers Richard and William. That Sir Robert Curzon was not among those attainted at this juncture would seem to confirm the hypothesis, first advanced by Bacon, that he was now serving as a royal informant. Yet other evidence suggests that Henry was still unaware of the precise whereabouts of his Yorkist adversary. Indeed the king was so worried about a possible invasion from the continent that he abruptly reversed his long-established policy towards the Hansa. Recalling how Edward IV had recovered the throne in 1471 by means of Hanseatic support, Henry persuaded the parliament of 1504 to renew the rights and privileges that the Hansa had enjoyed in England since Bosworth.[13] Yet the king's fright was of brief duration; and once he gained custody of Suffolk two years later, he resumed his earlier course of chipping away at the Hansa's privileged position.

Henry's determination to avoid a disputed succession is best illustrated by his efforts to capture Suffolk; but many of his other actions during these years were prompted by the same intense desire to pave the way for his son's peaceful accession. Because he had long equated money with power, he was convinced that a bountiful treasury would be the most practical legacy he could leave the prince. Accordingly he appealed to his seventh parliament for a sizable financial grant; but because the realm was at peace and the constitution required him to "live of his own" during such circumstances, he was in no position to demand a subsidy or even a tenth and fifteenth. Therefore Henry suggested that the members grant him two feudal aids, claiming as justification that he was entitled to recoup the expenses of Prince Arthur's knighthood in 1489 and the dowry he had provided Princess Margaret in 1503.

When Henry revealed that he expected a grant of at least £90,000, a furious debate took place in the Commons. Margaret's dowry had been only £10,000, while the expenses of Arthur's knighthood cannot have been a fourth as much. Why the king wanted such a large sum was never explained to the members, since he was not about to tip his hand and reveal his fears about the succession. Thus it was inevitable that his request would be opposed. The leader of the forces ranged against him was Thomas More, a "beardless boy" of twenty-six, who addressed the lower House with such eloquence that it refused to vote more than £40,000. In the end the king acknowledged his error in demanding too much and announced that he would be content with £30,000. But he was so annoyed by More's speeches that he deliberately picked a quarrel with his father, who was imprisoned in the Tower until he paid a fine of £100.[14] Such actions as these help to explain why Henry acquired a reputation for avarice during the last years of his life. Despite the valiant efforts of Professor Elton to acquit him of the charge, he was clearly guilty of a number of disreputable if not illegal practices. Probably Polydore Vergil, who was far from an unfriendly witness, puts the situation best. Within a short time of Henry's death, Polydore maintains, the king "laid aside all moderation and sank into a state of avarice. . . . It is not clear whether at the start it was greed, but afterwards greed became apparent."[15]

Just as Henry sought to procure as much money as he could from the parliament of 1504, he resorted to numerous other devices during these years to raise additional revenue, often without showing any sense of restraint. In October 1504 he demanded £2000 in return for a special charter of liberties requested by the boroughs of the three Welsh counties of Anglesey, Merioneth, and Carmarthenshire. When in 1507 he confirmed the charter of 1504, he required an additional £2300.[16] Like Edward IV, who had dabbled in commercial ventures, Henry was ready to invest in promising business pursuits; and in 1505–6 he realized £15,000 from the importation and sale of alum, a commodity necessary for the dying of cloth. In July 1507 he issued a new Book of Rates for the port of London, which led to an automatic increase of the customs revenues. From time to time he leased his warships to merchants engaged in overseas trade; and between 1505 and 1509 he made interest-free loans of almost £88,000 to individuals who pledged to import large quantities of European goods, on which the normal customs duties would have to be paid for as long as the loans remained outstanding. In 1506 he waged a fierce legal battle to recover £4000 that had been embezzled by Robert Fitzherbert, a former official of the customs service. Throughout this period the king profited from the revenues of vacant bishoprics and abbacies, receiving £6049 10s. 6d. from this source in 1504 and £5339 2s. 1d. the next year. Henry also demanded occasional contributions from the Hansa, since he no longer feared its support of an imposter against him. In 1508 he ruled that the Hansards had broken their pledge not to trade with the Low Countries during a brief stoppage of trade that occurred three years earlier and insisted that they pay him a penalty of £20,000.[17]

In his zeal to obtain as much revenue as he possibly could, Henry encountered a strong spirit of opposition, particularly on the part of the citizenry of London. Late in 1506 there was an open clash between him and the municipal authorities, who, in protest to his financial exactions, refused to accept his candidate for sheriff, Sir William FitzWilliam. The king retaliated by sending one of his most trusted officials, Edmund Dudley, Lord President of the Council since July, into the city to nullify the first election. Dudley did as the king instructed, and shortly afterwards FitzWilliam was proclaimed sheriff, to the great irritation of the municipal corporation, which never forgave this interference in its affairs. For his part, Henry was annoyed at having been defied and began to look for excuses to punish his chief critics in the capital. During the winter of 1507–8 he accused three former Lord Mayors—Sir William Capel, Sir Lawrence Aylmer, and Thomas Kneysworth—of misconduct in office, which generated additional hard feelings. The chief target of the king's attack was Capel, Lord Mayor in 1503–4, who had allegedly winked at the activities of known counterfeitors and was fined £2000, which he steadfastly refused to pay, insisting that the charges against him were utterly false. The other dignitaries convicted along with Capel, Aylmer, and Kneysworth included several aldermen and former sheriffs, who also refused to pay their fines and were imprisoned in the Tower until Henry's death in 1509. Then they were released by the new monarch, who wisely agreed to remit their fines, owing to the obvious need to reestablish friendly relations with the municipal corporation.[18]

Just as Henry VII often bilked the most affluent citizens of London, he secured large sums from peers and wealthy commoners around the kingdom. In July 1505 he demanded £5000 from Lord Fitzwater in return for the reversal of his son Robert's recent attainder. Lord Fitzwater seems to have paid the king no more than £2000, which was nevertheless an extraordinarily large sum by the standards of the time.[19] Lord Dudley, who had been indicted for "various felonies" early in 1504, signed an agreement with the Crown on the 26th of November following, by which he promised to pay £600 as the cost of a full pardon.[20] A much larger payment was extracted from the Earl of Northumberland after being convicted in 1505 of ravishing Lady Elizabeth Hastings, a royal ward. Northumberland's fine was originally set at £10,000, although it was subsequently reduced to £3000, payable in yearly installments of 500 marks each. Still another agreement, concluded in 1507, required the earl to surrender his Yorkshire estates to royal bailiffs, who would administer them until a total of £5000 had been received at the Exchequer by way of yearly payments of 1000 marks.[21] According to a story told by Bacon but not provable by documentary evidence, the king was entertained several years before his death at Castle Hedingham, the country seat in Essex of the Earl of Oxford. On that occasion the earl, in obvious hopes of impressing his sovereign, was attended by scores of armed retainers, all dressed in his own livery. The king showed no visible displeasure at the time; but once he returned to London, he initiated legal proceedings against the earl, who was accused of violating the Statute of Liveries of 1504. Subsequently Henry sent one of his leading councillors, Sir Richard Empson, into Essex to collect a fine of 15,000 marks from the unfortunate earl.[22]

Even if Bacon's account of Henry's harsh treatment of the Earl of Oxford is without foundation, the king was clearly guilty of draconian measures against George Neville, Lord Burgavenny, who was imprisoned in the Tower in May 1507. Accused of illegally retaining some 471 men from the central parts of Kent during the preceding thirty months, Lord Burgavenny was tried before the King's Bench and ordered to pay the enormous fine of £70,650. Because even the richest individual of the time would have been ruined by such a fine, hard bargaining began at once; and on 5 November 1507, twenty-six of Burgavenny's associates signed bonds totalling more than £3200, which they would immediately forfeit should the nobleman ever commit a disloyal act. Six weeks later the harrassed peer himself entered into a recognizance with the king, by which he would have to pay 5000 marks should he ever reappear in the shires of Kent, Surrey, Sussex, or Hampshire without a special license from the Crown. Finally, on 24 December 1507, Burgavenny concluded a last agreement with Henry, to whom he acknowledged a total indebtedness of £100,000 "or thereabouts." He also recognized the king's right not only to imprison him but also to confiscate all his revenues until the entire sum was discharged. Luckily for Burgavenny, however, Henry's resolve was not unshakable; and within a short time he declared that he would be content to receive £500 a year during the next decade, provided that the peer gave him no further trouble.[23] While the Kentish nobleman was experiencing such problems, James Stanley of Yorkshire was being confronted by similar difficulties. Stanley, whose troubles with the law had begun in 1496, was accused of illegally retaining dozens of yeomen, shearmen, and common laborers, all of whom had accepted and displayed his chief badge, a silver eaglesfoot. By 1509 Stanley had been ordered to pay the unbelievably high fine of £145,610, whereas the individuals taken into his service were ordered to pay £58,644.[24]

During the last years of Henry's reign, bonds and recognizances were used not only to punish or restrain various criminal acts but also to ensure the loyalty of officials with military duties. When in 1503 Lord Mountjoy was appointed Keeper of Hammes Castle, he was obliged to sign an indenture for 10,000 marks; and he was additionally required to find a substantial number of guarantors who would pledge an equal amount that he would hold the castle safely to the king's use, surrendering it to another royal appointee whenever ordered to do so in writing.[25] Bonds and recognizances had occasionally been used by previous monarchs but never to the same extent as by Henry VII. During the Yorkist period only one peer had been required to give more than one recognizance; but between 1485 and 1509 twenty-three nobles subscribed to two or more, while two peers entered into twelve and the hardpressed Mountjoy into twenty-three! According to the leading student of the subject:

> Thus there developed in the later years of Henry VII's reign an immensely tangled, complicated series of relationships in which a majority of the peerage were legally and financially in the King's power and at his mercy, so that in effect people were set under heavy penalties to guarantee the honesty and loyalty to their fellows. The system was so extensive that it must have created an atmosphere of chronic watchfulness, suspicion, and fear.[26]

That Henry was within his legal rights in using such methods is indisputable; but whether it was wise to take such action against so many powerful members of the political nation is an altogether different question. If continued over a long period, such a programme was likely to cause resentment of staggering proportions, which would cause Henry's efforts to pave the way for his son's peaceful accession to backfire. Although Polydore Vergil insisted that the royal policy of "financial terror" was eminently successful,[27] circumstantial evidence indicates that the king himself was aware of the hazards of his course. As early as August 1504 he invited subjects with grievances against the Crown to present their complaints to a special committee chaired by Bishop Fox and Sir John Fineux, Chief Justice of the King's Bench. And in the funeral sermon preached over his bier in 1509, Bishop Fisher revealed that Henry had come to regret many of his actions during the last few years of his life, a remarkable admission to be made in a eulogy.[28]

Although there was never any danger that the House of Tudor would be overthrown, there was little the king could do to shield his closest associates, Empson and Dudley, from the popular fury that mounted during this period. Empson, who has been called "a vigorous, competent, and ruthless administrator,"[29] had been a legal officer of the Duchy of Lancaster since 1485, and in 1491 he served as Speaker of the House of Commons as well. After being knighted in 1504, he was appointed

Steward of Cambridge University, and within another year he had been named to the Chancellorship of the Duchy. Dudley, who came from an older and more influential family than Empson, seems to have spent several years at Oxford before proceeding to Gray's Inn, where he was called to the bar and twice served as Reader. A member of every parliament since 1484 (with the possible exception of the one that convened in 1497), Dudley was the main legal adviser to the corporation of London between November 1496 and December 1502. After serving as Speaker of the House of Commons in 1504, he was appointed Lord President of the Council in July 1506.[30]

Empson and Dudley had long been political and business associates, and for a time they even occupied adjacent houses in St. Swithin's Lane. Together they dominated the Council Learned in the Law, a subcommittee of the Council that functioned as a kind of inner cabinet between 1500 and 1509. Most of the members of the Council Learned, of whom eleven have been identified, also belonged to the full Council, to which they were legally accountable. On several occasions the Council Learned tried cases comparable to those heard by the Court of Requests and the Council in Star Chamber, although the Council Learned was more concerned with government actions than with private suits. The principal responsibility of the Council Learned was to oversee the royal finances, in the supervision of which Henry VII was less active after Sir Reginald Bray's death in 1503. For the most part the Council Learned served as a debt-collecting agency for the Chamber of the Household, which was now auditing 90% of the king's ordinary revenue; and because it was quicker and considerably more efficient than the Exchequer, it frequently summoned debtors to pay up or explain why they should not be held for contempt.[31]

Although Empson and Dudley used the Council Learned to increase Henry's income, thereby winning his eternal gratitude and prompting him to include them among the executors of his will, they soon became identified with oppressive exactions, for which they were bitterly hated. Moreover, they exploited their official position to make large profits for themselves. Although both men were only moderately rich at the beginning of the reign, they had acquired great wealth by 1509. Indeed the Great Chronicle of London stresses the fact that on the eve of Henry VII's death, Dudley owned lands in thirteen counties and movable goods valued at more than £5000.[32] Furthermore, Dudley's house in London was a great showplace, perhaps the most ostentatious of the period, with "two galleries, one above the other looking into the garden. . . . The house had a further closed gallery next to the great chamber."[33] Less is known about Empson's acquisitions, but presumably they were on the same extravagant scale as those of his slightly younger associate. That both men exacted bribes in return for political favors and used their legal knowledge to enrich themselves helps to explain why, shortly after Henry VII died, the other members of the Council selected them to be the necessary scapegoats for the late king's unpopular policies. Arrested only a few days after Henry VIII mounted the throne, they were convicted of "constructive treason" during the summer of 1509. After being held captive in the Tower for more than a year, they were executed during the summer of 1510, to the enormous satisfaction of the general public.[34]

Although a great legal scholar holds that the darkest blot on Henry VII's record was "the abuse of the law, through the agency of Empson and Dudley,"[35] the king's disgraceful treatment of Catherine of Aragon during these years is just as deserving of condemnation. Henry considered his former daughter-in-law nothing more than a pawn in the game of European power politics; and when a bitter quarrel arose in 1504 between her father and her brother-in-law, the Archduke Philip, Henry's attitude towards her became considerably harsher than it would have been otherwise, to the great detriment of his subsequent reputation.

The quarrel between Ferdinand of Aragon and the Archduke Philip, which eventually led to hostilities that might be characterized as the War of the Castilian Succession, dominated the European scene for almost two years. Tension mounted immediately after the death of Isabella the Catholic in November 1504 and was resolved only by the unexpected death of the archduke in September 1506. During that period the latter waged a vigorous campaign to secure the Castilian inheritance of his wife Joanna, which was deliberately being withheld from her by her father. Ferdinand naturally hoped to preserve the fragile unity of the Spanish Crowns, which had been established only by his marriage of thirty-five years to Isabella. Should control of Castile, Leon, and Granada, along with the fabulous wealth of "the Indies," now pass to his incompetent daughter and her husband, that unity might be destroyed forever; and he, as ruler of little more than the small kingdom of Aragon, would lose his commanding position in the councils of Europe. Thus he had no option but to oppose his son-in-law with all the forces he could muster.

Henry VII's part in these unhappy proceedings was determined by what he conceived to be the national interests of his country as well as the dynastic well-being of his House, which were fortunately in agreement. During the last decade he had signed treaties with Ferdinand and the archduke, both of whom he wished to retain as friends. But if it came to a choice between them, as it now had done, it was inevitable that he would side with the archduke. England's trade with the Low Countries was far more profitable than her somewhat limited commercial intercourse with Spain. In addition, because he believed the Spanish rulers had sought to dupe him over the widowed Queen of Naples,[36] Henry was reluctant to feel much charity towards the Aragonese monarch. Moreover, most of the advantages in the contest seemed to rest with the archduke, a younger and more vigorous man than his elderly father-in-law, who was disliked by the proud nobles of Castile. And by throwing his support to Philip, Henry might at last gain custody of the Earl of Suffolk and thereby terminate the Yorkist threat to his throne once and for all. On the other hand, should he assist Ferdinand, he would alienate both the archduke and his father Maximilian, who might well retaliate by fomenting a new conspiracy against him.

Henry's first step to prepare for closer cooperation with the archduke was to abrogate the Anglo-Spanish marriage agreement of June 1503. Luckily he had a convenient pretext for doing this, since the balance of Catherine's dowry had still not been sent to England; and should Philip succeed in breaking his father-in-law's grip on Castile, it would prove a great embarrassment for Prince Henry to have married the daughter of such an insignificant ruler as the King of Aragon. Indeed Henry VII was now giving serious consideration to another proposal, first raised in 1500 during his meeting with the archduke, that the prince should be betrothed to Philip's daughter Eleanor. To preserve his freedom of action in this regard, the English ruler directed his son to appear before Bishop Fox and several other councillors in the Star Chamber on 27 June 1505. Under oath Prince Henry declared that his betrothal to Catherine had been arranged without his prior knowledge or approval. Consequently he would never consent to the marriage contract, which he insisted was null and void and ought to be recognized as such.[37] Prince Henry's appearance in the Star Chamber occurred in strictest secrecy, in order to keep from alerting the Spanish ambassador about Henry VII's new intentions; and with un- abashed duplicity the English monarch even warned Dr. Puebla that Catherine's marriage could not take place until the remainder of her dowry had arrived in London.

These maneuvers, which Professor Mattingly once characterized as "a piece of treachery,"[38] were the real beginning of Catherine's problems in England. In later years she maintained that, except for her mother's death in 1504, she would not have been subjected to the taunts and indignities that were her lot for the remainder of the reign. This is undeniably true, for the struggle for the Castilian throne, with the prospect of her father's defeat, caused her to appear quite suddenly an undesirable catch from Henry's vantage point. Furthermore, within a short time of Isabella's death, the Castilian Council of Regency revoked a new commercial agreement with England that Dr. Puebla had taken great care to negotiate. This treaty was considered too liberal by the parochial conservatives of Castile, who failed to see the logic of granting special trading rights to Englishmen in return for reciprocal advantages allowed to Spanish merchants in England. The commerce between the two countries fell off immediately; and in August 1505 several hundred English traders who had been living at Cadiz and Lisbon returned to London "all lost and ruined" by the reimposition of the old navigation laws. Furious at being outmaneuvered in this way, Henry summoned Dr. Puebla to an audience, " 'and the words that came from his mouth were vipers.' "[39] The king also retaliated by revoking the pension of £100 per month that had been Catherine's chief support for the past two years, since her father rarely sent her any money. This petty act, prompted by a vengefulness that was totally uncharacteristic of him, compelled the princess to give up her separate establishment at Durham House and move into rooms at court, which were invariably situated in the least desirable wing of the palace, above the servants' quarters or the stables. Such callous treatment of a weak and defenseless girl goes a long way to explain why Henry acquired a reputation for exceptional meanness during his last years. For her part, Catherine bore her sufferings with great courage and equanimity, thereby winning the respect of scores of admirers, whose sympathy would be a valuable solace when she faced even greater tribulations at the hands of Henry VIII.[40]

Dr. Puebla sent a stream of appeals to Ferdinand and did his best to solve the difficulties now developing between England and Spain. But the Aragonese king was in no position to challenge the action taken by the Council of Castile, whose support he must obtain if he was to have any chance of defeating his son-in-law. Nor was he able to send the remainder of Catherine's dowry to England, for he had just obligated himself to pay a million crowns to Louis XII of France. The ever-practical Ferdinand knew he must do his utmost to keep Philip from being assisted by the French government, so in October 1505 he concluded a far-reaching agreement designed to keep his two great enemies apart. Ferdinand agreed to recognize the French annexation of Milan and to pay Louis an indemnity of 1,000,000 crowns, in return for which France would not only remain neutral in the coming war over Castile but would also acknowledge the Spanish claim to Naples. Shortly afterwards the two monarchs sealed their cooperation by a marriage alliance between Ferdinand and Germaine de Foix, a beautiful niece of the French king's.[41]

Meanwhile the archduke was desperately seeking English aid against his father-in-law. In April 1505 Henry lent £108,000 to Philip, and five months later he advanced him another £30,000. During October a special ambassador arrived from the Low Countries with an invitation for Henry to join openly with the archduke and his father the emperor. This prompted the English ruler to send an emissary to Brussels to discuss the terms of a possible alliance. But the Anglo-Burgundian talks failed to culminate in a treaty, owing to the skillful maneuvers of Bishop Ayala, still a trusted member of Ferdinand's diplomatic service and a resident of the Low Countries for the last several years.[42]

Although Philip failed to secure an open pledge of English aid during the autumn of 1505, he raised an army of several thousand men and set sail for Spain on 10 January 1506. Only two days out of the Zeeland ports, the Burgundian ships were scattered by a sudden squall. Several transports sank with all hands aboard, while others took refuge wherever they could find it. The galleon carrying Philip and his wife almost capsized but ultimately anchored at Melcombe Regis, in Dorset. Once Henry learned of the presence of the archduke and the titular Queen of Castile in the West Country, he sent a delegation of courtiers to escort them to Windsor, where they were grandly entertained while the damage to their ships was being repaired. On 9 February the archduke was formally invested with the Garter, after which Prince Henry was inducted into the equivalent Burgundian order of the Golden Fleece.[43] For several weeks the two rulers engaged in confidential talks ranging over a variety of problems. Henry agreed to extend formal recognition to Philip and Joanna as joint sovereigns of Castile, and of greater significance he cancelled the loans of £138,000 that he had extended during the previous year for the coming attack on Ferdinand. In return for these two English concessions, Philip instructed several of his attendants to remain in London after his own departure in order to participate in new commercial talks with Henry. These quickly led to the conclusion of a treaty so favorable to England that Bacon dubbed it the *Intercursus Malus*. Indeed English merchants trading with the Low Countries received such extensive rights by the new agreement, which was initialed on 30 April, that Philip's subjects were deeply offended. As a result the treaty was never ratified by either side; and in 1507 another agreement, modelled on the *Intercursus Magnus* of 1496, was negotiated, and in that way the interests of both countries were safeguarded.[44]

At the same time Philip consented to the conclusion of a new Anglo-Burgundian commercial agreement, he made a concession even dearer to Henry's heart: he gave orders for the immediate surrender of the Earl of Suffolk, who had recently been transferred from Wageningen to the great fortress at Namur. On 16 March 1506 the unfortunate Yorkist was at last handed over by Burgundian agents to the English commander at Calais, who at once put him aboard a ship bound for London. Although Suffolk had been attainted by the parliament of 1504, Henry honored a promise he made to the archduke that he would not have the earl executed. Rather, after the latter had been paraded through the streets of the capital on 24 March, he was imprisoned in the Tower, where he remained until 1513, when he was at last beheaded on orders from Henry VIII.[45] As for Suffolk's brothers, Lord William recovered his freedom shortly after Henry VII died in 1509, whereas Lord Richard remained in exile on the continent, supporting himself as a soldier of fortune. He died in 1525 while fighting with the French army in northern Italy.

During his stay at Windsor the archduke raised the possibility of a series of marriage agreements between England and Burgundy. A union between Prince Henry and Philip's daughter Eleanor was considered, as was an alliance between the Princess Mary of England and the archduke's young son Charles of Ghent, the future Emperor Charles V. Yet at this juncture Henry VII was chiefly interested in a possible marriage alliance involving himself and the archduke's sister, Margaret of Savoy, who, although already twice widowed, was still considered a fine catch. On 20 March Philip and Joanna promised to do their best to promote the match, even persuading Maximilian to furnish a dowry of 300,000 crowns, or approximately £60,000. Nothing came of this plan, however, for the strong-willed Margaret had no intention of taking a third husband.[46]

In mid-April the archduke and his wife embarked for Spain for a second time, and on the 26th they landed at Corunna, where they received a tumultuous welcome. During their march into old Castile, they attracted more and more support, and by mid-summer 1506 they had taken control of the kingdom's government. Because Ferdinand had failed to procure any foreign assistance, he had no choice but to acquiesce in the victory of his daughter and her husband. By the treaty of Villafavila, he recognized Philip as regent for his wife and withdrew across the border into his own dominions. But the archduke's triumph was not to be an enduring one, for on 25 September he died. (Ferdinand's enemies immediately proclaimed that the had had his son-in-law poisoned, which may have been the case.) Philip's possessions in the Low Countries at once devolved on his six-year-old son Charles, for whom Margaret of Savoy served as regent. In Castile Juanna was acknowledged as the rightful monarch; but because she never recovered from the shock of her husband's death, she was incapable of governing. Consequently Ferdinand was able to reassert his control over the Castilian government; and with the aid of Cardinal Ximenes, he ruled with an iron hand until his own death a decade later.

This dramatic turn of events caused Henry to reassess his position, which was far weaker now than it had been the previous year. Indeed it appeared that he had backed the wrong man, whereas in actuality he had supported the stronger of the two rivals, whose untimely death alone he had not foreseen. During the autumn of 1506 Henry's chief aim was to recover Ferdinand's good will, and early the next year he suggested that he himself should marry the incapacitated Joanna. By almost all historians Henry has been condemned for this maneuver, which a respected German scholar once denounced as "an obnoxious proposal."[47] In truth, however, there was nothing unseemly about it, as most contemporaries recognized at the time. In 1507 no one knew that Joanna's malady was incurable, for her husband had died but a few months before and she was expected to recover from her depression momentarily. Little was known about mental illness during the sixteenth century, and it was not altogether fanciful for Henry to believe that the attentions of a considerate husband like himself, and of a loving sister like Catherine, would hasten Joanna's recovery. Besides, the English monarch had good reason to suspect that Ferdinand was exaggerating the seriousness of her illness, since it was in his self-interest to convince others that her condition was irreversible. When in February 1508 a new Spanish ambassador, Don Gutierre de Fuen-salida, arrived in London, Henry asked him pointed questions about Joanna's malady.

"Tell me, ambassador, is the Queen such as they say she is? If what they say is true, God forbid that I should marry her for three kingdoms such as hers, but there are those who say it is your King who keeps her shut up and spreads this rumor [of insanity] about her. Indeed I have had reports from Spain that she listens and replies rationally and seems quite normal. When I saw her two years ago [at Windsor] . . . I saw her speak and act rationally and with great grace and dignity. I thought her sane then, and I think her so now. On your honor, is she not such as her husband would desire?"[48]

Fuensalida was unable to find convincing answers to Henry's inquiry. That the ambassador had seldom seen Joanna at close hand since 1506 gave the king little satisfaction, particularly since he needlessly added that, despite the queen's emotional condition, Henry was surely too old to think of remarrying.[49]

For almost a year Henry persisted in believing that Ferdinand would ultimately agree to the match, since the removal of Joanna to England would eliminate an obvious embarrassment for him and ease his task of ruling Castile. But Ferdinand was angrier than Henry realized and had no desire for a reconciliation. When Henry eventually grasped this, he vented his frustration on the defenseless Catherine once again by withholding *all* financial support from her. Consequently she was compelled to pawn her jewels and plate in order to meet the demands of her most pressing creditors. Time and again she implored her father to send the remainder of her dowry to England, so that her marriage to Prince Henry could take place. But Ferdinand sent the chilling reply that her dowry was a charge on the Castilian treasury and would never be paid from Aragon.[50]

Because Henry soon realized that the old cooperation between England and Spain would not be reestablished during his lifetime, he had no choice but to direct his efforts elsewhere. Perhaps he might be able to isolate Ferdinand and construct a system of alliances against him. During the winter of 1507–8 he conferred on numerous occasions with Sigismund Frauenberg, the imperial ambassador to his court. Frauenberg and the emperor were anxious to secure English support for a campaign on behalf of Charles of Ghent, in order to break the Aragonese grip on Castile. To this end Frauenberg proposed three marriages: between Henry VII and Margaret of Savoy, between Henry's daughter Mary and the Archduke Charles, and between Prince Henry and Charles's sister Eleanor. Nothing came of the first and third proposals, since Margaret of Savoy was still adamantly against the idea of remarrying, while Henry VII now hoped to marry his heir to a niece of Louis XII, Margaret of Angoulême. But the second proposal was seriously discussed and led in December 1507 to the conclusion of a draft agreement, which called for an eventual union between Princess Mary of England and the young archduke. Several months later the Earl of Surrey and several other high English officials were sent to Antwerp to confer directly with the emperor. Another round of talks followed, and on 1 October 1508 Margaret of Savoy ratified the marriage treaty. Two months later Mary and the eight-year-old Charles were married by proxy at Richmond.[51]

Yet Henry's triumph was not even to last out the month. To his chagrin Maximilian was about to sign a new agreement with Ferdinand, whom Henry had labored so hard to isolate. Under the joint leadership of the Aragonese king and Pope Julius II, a congress of European rulers assembled at Cambrai in December 1508 and concluded an alliance against Venice, which was to be attacked the following year. Of all the prominent rulers of the age, only Henry VII was excluded from the deliberations at Cambrai, largely because he had always refused to intervene in Italian affairs in the past.[52] Thus all his diplomatic efforts appeared to have been in vain, since he rather than Ferdinand was isolated. However, the League of Cambrai was not directed against him, and, with the sole exception of the Spanish ruler, none of its members bore him any ill will. By the winter of 1508–9 the other monarchs of the age had long accepted him as a member-in-good-standing of their charmed circle. Because of his obvious wealth and undeniable grip on his throne, his friendship was prized everywhere but Spain, and possible matches with his children received the careful consideration they deserved. The adventurer of 1485 had clearly established himself in the eyes of the world, and few contemporaries were willing to waste their resources on frivolous plots against him.

These considerations must have been a solace during the winter of 1508–9, as his health became progressively weaker. For more than a year Henry had been far from well, his affliction being described by the royal physicians as "a quinsy," although it was probably from tuberculosis that he suffered. As early as March 1507 there had been serious fears for his life, and in February 1508 he was forced to keep to his bed once again by repeated attacks of the gout. Although his condition improved during subsequent months, he was still so weak in July that is was widely reported that he was *in extremis*.[53]

Yet he staged another rally during the autumn of 1508 and went on pilgrimages to Canterbury and Walsingham. He was now devoting long hours each day to religious matters and making repeated efforts to secure the canonization of his Lancastrian predecessor, Henry VI. Although the pope was willing for Henry VI's remains to be transported from Windsor to Westminster, he insisted that such an obviously mediocre king could not qualify for sainthood. During this period Henry VII was also giving increasing time to his charities; and because of a substantial royal donation, a large hospital for the poor was erected on the site of the old Savoy Palace in London.[54] In addition he was making plans for the eventual construction of an even larger hospital at Bath.

Before work on that project could be seriously discussed, Henry suffered a relapse, which his doctors were convinced would lead to his death. He constantly complained of sharp pains in his chest, while his breathing became labored and irregular. Because of continual discomfort, he was moody and irascible and often railed at his mother and children, his confessor and legal advisers. On the last day of March 1509, he completed his will, which directed that he should be buried alongside his wife in the great new chapel he had constructed at the Abbey, for the maintenance of which he bequeathed 500 marks. Within a month of his death, 10,000 masses were to be performed for the benefit of his soul, at twice the usual fee of 3d. each. Because of his interest in education and continuing admiration for Henry VI, he instructed that £5000 should be provided for the completion of the large new chapel at Cambridge that his Lancastrian predecessor had started half a century earlier. He also bequeathed 10,000 marks to the new hospital of St. John the Baptist in London and left large sums to the Observant monasteries at Greenwich, Sheen, and London. Likenesses of himself at prayer were to be erected near the shrines of Edward the Confessor, Thomas à Becket, and Our Lady of Walsingham; and every parish church in the kingdom was to be provided with a silver alter box, or pyx, worth at least 80s., which would serve as "a perpetual memory of us."[55]

Although Henry's will has been called "one of the last great extravaganzas of pre-Reformation piety,"[56] several of the king's bequests were of a secular and not a religious nature. For the construction of better roads and bridges between Windsor, Richmond, Southwark, and Canterbury, he earmarked £2000, while an equal amount was to be distributed for the aid of the poor immediately after his death. Henry also provided funds to defray the legal expenses of jailed individuals who had not yet been brought to trial, and he offered a general pardon to all criminals excepting thieves and murderers. In addition he cancelled all debts of less than 40s. owed to the Crown and gave detailed instructions as to how his executors should discharge his own debts after his death. Precise directions were also given to the Florentine sculptor, Pietro Torrigiano, who had been brought to England to construct a suitable memorial in the Abbey for himself and his wife. But the most important advice was reserved for Prince Henry, who was instructed to be prudent and avoid war and to marry Catherine of Aragon as soon as he could conveniently do so.[57]

Henry's will was sealed on the tenth day of April. Yet he continued to linger, and on the 14th he made his final confession and received the sacrament for the last time. In addition he issued a general pardon in which he excused a variety of petty offenses "committed before the tenth of April last past.".

Henry finally died in the royal bedchamber of his beloved Richmond on 21 April 1509. For twelve days thereafter his body lay in state in the Great Hall of the palace. Then an elaborate funeral procession set out for the capital. Several dozen clerics intoning prayers walked alongside the hearse, which was surmounted by an effigy holding both a sceptre and an orb, while 600 servants carrying lighted tapers followed along in silence behind. At Southwark the Lord Mayor and twenty-six Aldermen of London joined the mourners. After being transported across the bridge, Henry's coffin was censed and placed on a bier in St. Paul's Cathedral.

The next day the Bishop of London performed a requiem mass, after which the Bishop of Rochester delivered a eulogy that emphasized Henry's merits and achievements. Then the coffin was removed to Charing Cross, where it was censed again by three abbots, and thence to Westminster for a third censing by the two archbishops. Six noblemen carried the coffin into the Abbey, after which a brief memorial service took place. The next day—the 11th of May—three masses were performed before Henry's body was at last laid to rest alongside that of his wife. His sword, shield, helmet, and spurs were offered up, after which his principal ministers broke their staves of office and pitched them into the open grave.[58] Then the entire company retired to the Great Hall of Westminster Palace for a hearty dinner before resuming his work of bringing order and civility to England.

XII

Epilogue

Most historians are hardy individualists who scorn to accept anything on authority, least of all the conclusions of other scholars. Such is certainly the case in regard to judgments of Henry VII's contributions to English history. The great nineteenth-century constitutionalist William Stubbs refused to consider the first of the Tudors the equal of William I, Henry II, Edward I, or Henry VIII, whom he felt to have been the greatest rulers in English history. More recently, S. B. Chrimes has insisted that Henry VII's achievements were inferior to those of Edward IV, whose leading biographer, C. D. Ross, maintains however that Henry VII's accomplishments exceeded those of his Yorkist predecessor. Yet another respected specialist, R. L. Storey, feels that Henry VII was far from the greatest of the Tudor line, that place being reserved for his granddaughter Elizabeth I. But a recent biographer of the last Tudor monarch, Lacey Baldwin Smith, stresses her faults and the role sheer luck played in all her successes and considers the founder of the dynasty to have been a greater ruler by far. Wherein lies the truth, in view of such a welter of opinions?

Before attempting to answer this question, an effort should be made to explain the yardstick—or yardsticks—being applied. One obvious test of a monarch's effectiveness is a comparison between the situation at his accession and that at his death; whereas another relevant test is whether most of his subjects were better or worse off for his time on the throne. By these measures Henry VII does extremely well; indeed on these two scores he deserves to be ranked as one of the two or three most outstanding rulers in English history. The firm and steady rule he provided led to a resumption of conditions extremely conducive to economic and commercial growth; whereas his generally merciful nature led to a significant decline of the executions and atrocities that had typified the previous century. Consequently, when he died in 1509 the realm was far more unified and peaceable than it had been at his accession; and the problems resulting from the harsh financial policies of his last few years were easily solved by his successor.

By comparison, most other English rulers who have any claim to greatness either caused new hardships for a majority of their subjects or bequeathed more serious problems to their successors. William I's reign was extraordinarily disruptive of town life, which took more than half a century to recover from the harmful effects of the Norman Conquest, and it additionally saw the establishment of an alien aristocracy in England, with all the bitterness and acrimony that naturally resulted. Henry II's reign was a period of recurrent fighting, since the king was confronted not only by a succession of challenges within his own family circle but also by French attempts to disrupt the unity of his empire. Of greater significance, the reign of the first Plantaganet monarch is notable for a rapid escalation of those aristocratic tensions that were to culminate in Magna Carta during the reign of his son King John. After much hard fighting Edward I succeeded in conquering and annexing Wales; but during his last fifteen years on the throne, he continually meddled in Scottish affairs, with the result that there was a sharp increase of Anglo-Scottish tension. Out of fears for the future the Scots turned to France and concluded the Auld Alliance, which was to plague the English Crown for the next three centuries. Edward IV enjoyed extraordinary success during the last twelve years of his reign; but when he died in 1483 the latent hostility between his wife's circle and that of his brother Richard of Gloucester, which he had done nothing to control, burst into the open and led to the bitterest phase of the Wars of the Roses. The reign of Henry VIII, which opened with so much optimism and promise, ended in an agony of beheadings, war, and deliberate currency manipulation, which provoked a dangerous price spiral that cruelly affected the well-being of almost all his subjects. Between 1558 and 1588 Elizabeth I enjoyed an exceptional degree of success; but during her last fifteen years on the throne, almost everything about her government turned sour, with official corruption, political factionalism, and religious persecution mounting. Thus, by the two tests considered here, Henry VII emerges as one of the truly outstanding—if not the single most outstanding ruler—in English history.

However, there is a third and final yardstick to be applied if Henry

VII's reign is to be seen in true perspective. To what degree was his reign a truly important one? In what ways did it witness significant advances in regard to government, religion, culture, and similar matters? On this score the reign of the first Tudor pales by comparison with those of his son Henry VIII and his granddaughter Elizabeth I. The second Tudor monarch broke the ties that bound the English church to Rome, promoted the spread of Protestantism by dissolving the monasteries and allowing the Scriptures to be translated into English, laid the foundations of the modern British navy, and, with the aid of his great minister Thomas Cromwell, modernized the basic institutions of national government. For her part, Queen Elizabeth maintained religious peace between her Protestant and Catholic subjects, presided over the greatest cultural flowering in English history, and, by following a brilliant policy in regard to Scotland, severed the Auld Alliance and thereby made possible a total change in Anglo-Scottish affairs. If Henry VII's positive achievements fell far short of those of his two great successors, neither did they equal those of his most outstanding predecessors: the consolidation of feudalism by William I, the establishment of the common law by Henry II, the development (albeit along with the manipulation and exploitation) of parliament by Edward I, and the revitalization of the main institutions of national government by Edward IV. Thus, although Henry VII was in many ways a great and exceptionally successful ruler, his reign does not qualify as one of the four or five most important ones in English history. Only in the sense that he completed the work of Edward IV and greatly strengthened royal power, thereby enabling Henry VIII and Elizabeth I to make the contributions they did, did he play a truly significant role in English history. Many men could have done what he did, although it is questionable whether they would have done it as well.

Yet Henry VII's reign was a period of notable advance in numerous small ways. The naval administration was strengthened and the quality of the ships improved; the powers of the Justices of the Peace were increased, with the result that local government was more effective than ever by 1509; foreign scholars patronized by the king helped to establish humanism on solid foundations in England; explorers such as John and Sebastian Cabot greatly advanced English knowledge and awareness of the New World; the royal finances were placed on a sounder footing than at any other time; and by actively supporting the work of the common-law courts, the first Tudor made possible a revival of the jury system. Even more significant, perhaps, by the time Henry VII died he had brought a permanent end to the Wars of the Roses, greatly strengthened the ties between England and Ireland, and secured the marriage of his daughter Margaret to James IV of Scotland, without which the union of the English and Scottish Crowns could not have occurred in 1603. Thus, Henry VII's reign was far from devoid of accomplishment, and it deserves greater recognition than it usually receives. In fact in almost all areas other than government, which remained medieval in spirit until the 1530s, it marked the beginning of a long transition period during which England gradually emerged from the Middle Ages into the modern world. That this transition period was generally a calm and well-ordered one was due at least in part to his success in strengthening royal power and shackling the forces of disorder. He was the right man at the right time who instinctively knew what policies to pursue and responded in masterful fashion to the challenges of his time. Posterity can hardly bestow a more favorable judgment than that.

Abbreviations Used in the Notes

A. H. R.	*American Historical Review*
A. J. L. H.	*American Journal of Legal History*
B. I. H. R.	*Bulletin of the Institute of Historical Research*
B. J. R. L.	*Bulletin of the John Rylands Library*
Bacon, *Henry VII*	Sir Francis Bacon, *The History of the Reign of King Henry the Seventh*, ed. J. R. Lumby. Cambridge, 1885.
Bryan, *Life of Kildare*	Donough Bryan, *Gerald Fitzgerald, the Great Earl of Kildare (1456–1513)*. Dublin, 1933.
C. Q. R.	*Church Quarterly Review*
Cal. Carew MSS.	*Calendar of the Carew Manuscripts, preserved in the Archiepiscopal Library at Lambeth*, 6 vols., ed. J. S. Brewer and William Bullen. London, 1867–73.
Cal. Close Rolls	*Calendar of the Close Rolls, preserved in the Public Record Office, Henry VII*, 2 vols. London, 1955–63.
Cal. Inquisitions Post Mortem	*Calendar of Inquisitions Post Mortem and Other Analogous Documents*, 3 vols. London, 1898–1955.
Cal. Pat. Rolls	*Calendar of the Patent Rolls, preserved in the Public Record Office, Henry VII*, 2 vols. London, 1914–16.
Cal. S. P. Milan	*Calendar of State Papers and Manuscripts, relating to English Affairs, existing in the Archives and Collections of Milan, vol. I, 1385–1618*, ed. Allen B. Hinds. London, 1912.
Cal. S. P. Spain	*Calendar of Letters, Despatches, and State Papers, relating to the Negotiations between England and Spain, preserved in the Archives at Simancas and Elsewhere, vol. I: Henry VII, 1485–1509*, ed. G. A. Bergenroth. London, 1862.
Cal. S. P. Ven.	*Calendar of State Papers and Manuscripts, relating to English Affairs, existing in the Archives and Collections of Venice, and in Other Libraries of Northern Italy, vol. I, 1202–1509*, ed. Rawdon Brown. London, 1864.
Campbell, *Materials*	William Campbell, ed., *Materials for a History of the Reign of Henry VII*, 2 vols. Rolls Series, 1873–7.
Croyland Chronicle	*Ingulph's Chronicle of the Abbey of Croyland with the Continuations by Peter of Blois and Anonymous Writers*, ed. H. T. Riley. London, 1854.
D. U. J.	*Durham University Journal*
E. H. R.	*English Historical Review*
Ec. H. R.	*Economic History Review*
Eng. Hist. Doc.,	*English Historical Documents 1327–1485*, ed. A. R.

1327–1485	Myers. New York, 1969.
Eng. Hist. Doc., *1485–1558*	*English Historical Documents 1485–1558,* ed. C. H. Williams. New York, 1967.
Fisher, *Pol. Hist.*	H. A. L. Fisher, *The Political History of England, vol. V. From the Accession of Henry VII to the Death of Henry VIII,* 2nd ed. London, 1919.
G. J.	*Geographical Journal*
H. J.	*Historical Journal*
H. L. Q.	*Huntington Library Quarterly*
I. H. S.	*Irish Historical Studies*
J. B. S.	*Journal of British Studies*
J. E. H.	*Journal of Ecclesiastical History*
J. H. I.	*Journal of the History of Ideas*
L. & P.	James Gairdner, ed., *Letters and Papers illustrative of the reigns of Richard III and Henry VII,* 2 vols. Rolls Series, 1861–3.
McElroy, "Literary Patronage"	Mary M. D. McElroy, "Literary Patronage of Margaret Beaufort and Henry VII: A Study of Renaissance Propaganda (1483–1509)." Unpublished Ph.D. dissertation, University of Texas, 1964.
P. B. A.	*Proceedings of the British Academy*
Pollard, *Cont. Sources*	A. F. Pollard, ed., *The Reign of Henry VII from Contemporary Sources,* 3 vols. London, 1913.
Rot. Parl.	*Rotuli Parliamentorum; ut et petitiones et placita in parliamento,* 6 vols., ed. J. Strachey and others. London, 1767–77.
Rymer, *Foedera*	Thomas Rymer, ed., *Foedera, Conventiones, Literae, et cujuscunque generis acta publica, inter reges Angliae,* 3rd ed., 10 vols. The Hague, 1741.
S. H. R.	*Scottish Historical Review*
Somers Tracts	Sir Walter Scott, ed., *A Collection of Scarce and Valuable Tracts,* 2nd ed., 13 vols. London, 1809–15.
T. R. H. S.	*Transactions of the Royal Historical Society*
Tucker, *Life of Surrey*	Melvin Tucker, *The Life of Thomas Howard, Earl of Surrey and Second Duke of Norfolk, 1443–1524.* The Hague, 1964.
Tudor Proclamations	*Tudor Royal Proclamations, Volume I: The Early Tudors (1485–1558),* ed. Paul L. Hughes and James F. Larkin. New Haven, 1964.
Tudor Studies	*Tudor Studies, presented by the Board of Studies in History in the University of London to Albert Frederick Pollard,* ed. R. W. Seton-Watson. London, 1924.
U. B. H. J.	*University of Birmingham Historical Journal*
Vergil, *Anglica Historia*	Polydore Vergil, *The Anglica Historia of Polydora Vergil, A. D. 1485–1537,* ed. Denys Hay. Camden Society, 1950.
W. H. R.	*Welsh History Review*

Notes

PREFACE

1. N. L. Harvey, *Elizabeth of York: The Mother of Henry VIII* (New York, 1973). See also Hester Chapman's recent study of Henry VII's daughters, Margaret and Mary, which is entitled *The Thistle and the Rose: The Sisters of Henry VIII* (New York, 1972).

2. John Harley, *Music in Purcell's London* (London, 1968), p. 55.

CHAPTER I

1. Sir Thomas More, *History of Richard III*, ed. P. M. Kendall (New York, 1965), p. 32. Cf. *The Complete Works of St. Thomas More*, II, ed. R. S. Sylvester (Yale U. P., 1963), p. 4. See also *Croyland Chronicle*, pp. 481–2.

2. Dominic Mancini, *The Usurpation of Richard III*, ed. C. A. J. Armstrong, 2nd ed. (Oxford, 1969), p. 59.

3. The will of Edward IV is no longer extant, but there is a printed version of it in Samuel Bentley, ed., *Excerpta Historica*, 2nd ed. (London, 1833). For evidence that Edward IV added at least one codicil to his will before he died, see *Croyland Chronicle*, p. 484.

4. For the best contemporary description of Richard of Gloucester, see Mancini, *The Usurpation of Richard III*, pp. 137–8. In regard to the question of Richard's appearance, it is important to remember that most of the writers of the period delighted in portraying inner spirituality by means of physical appearance. Thus a man regarded as inherently evil would be pictured as stooped, crooked, or hunchbacked.

5. Before her marriage in 1464 to Edward IV, Elizabeth had been the wife of Sir John Grey of Groby, who died of battle wounds in 1461. By her first husband she had two sons: Thomas, who was created Marquess of Dorset in 1475, and Richard.

6. For a discussion of Richard's powers as Lord Protector, see J. S. Roskell, "The Office and Dignity of Protector of England, with Special Reference to its Origins," *E.H.R.*, LXVIII (1953), p. 227.

7. For Lord Hastings' role during the early stages of Richard's usurpation of the throne, see *Croyland Chronicle*, p. 566.

8. For a good account of Catesby's actions during this period, see J. S. Roskell, "William Catesby, Councillor to Richard III," *B.J.R.L.*, XLI (1959–60).

9. *Letters of the Kings of England*, 2 vols., ed. J. O. Halliwell-Phillips (London, 1848), I, 150–1.

10. Mancini, *The Usurpation of Richard III*, p. 91; *Croyland Chronicle*, p. 488; *The Great Chronicle of London*, ed. A. H. Thomas and I. D. Thornley (London, 1938), p. 231; *The Paston Letters*, 4 vols., ed. James Gairdner (Westminster, 1901), III, 305–6; *Three Books of Polydore Vergil's English History*, ed. Sir Henry Ellis (Camden Society, 1844), pp. 179–82. Alison Hanham has recently suggested that Hastings met his death not on the 13th but on the 20th of June. For this view, see Hanham, "Richard III, Lord Hastings and the historians," *E.H.R.*, LXXXVII (1972), pp. 233–48, and *Richard III and his early historians, 1483–1535* (Oxford, 1975), p. 11. See also the vigorous refutation of Miss Hanham's thesis by B. P. Wolffe, "When and why did Hastings lose his head?," *E.H.R.*, LXXXIX (1974), pp. 835–44, and by J. A. F. Thomson, "Richard III and Lord Hastings—A Problematical Case Reviewed," *B.I.H.R.*, XLVIII (1975), pp. 22–30.

11. More, *History of Richard III*, ed. Kendall, p. 58; *The Complete Works of St. Thomas More*, II, ed. Sylvester, p. 34; Mancini, *The Usurpation of Richard III*, p. 89; *Three Books of Polydore Vergil's English History*, p. 178.

12. Lady Eleanor Butler had died in 1468, whereas the two sons of Edward IV were not born until 1470 and 1473. For an analysis of the alleged pre-contract, see Mortimer Levine, "Richard III—Usurper or Lawful King?," *Speculum*, XXIV (1959), pp. 391–2.

13. *Ibid.*, p. 397; *Three Books of Polydore Vergil's English History*, p. 185.

14. *The Great Chronicle of London*, pp. 231–2; More, *History of Richard III*, p. 86; Mortimer Levine, *Tudor Dynastic Problems 1460–1571* (London, 1973), pp. 28–30.

15. Mancini, *The Usurpation of Richard III*, p. 97. For the petition delivered to Richard, see *Rot. Parl.*, VI, 240–2. See also E. F. Jacob, *The Fifteenth Century 1399–1485* (Oxford, 1961), p. 620; and J. S. Roskell, *The Commons and Their Speakers in English Parliaments 1376–1523* (Manchester, 1965), p. 301.

16. Most of the Mowbray lands in the West Country went to the Howards' cousin William, Lord Berkeley, who was subsequently created Earl of Nottingham. The Howards seem to have been satisfied with this division of the property.

17. Although it is generally held that Lord Rivers was beheaded along with the others on 25 June, there is evidence to suggest that he died five days earlier. See *Cal. Inquisitions Post Mortem*, I, 14.

18. For a contemporary account of the coronation, see Bentley, *Excerpta Historica*, pp. 380–4.

19. James Gairdner, *History of the Life and Reign of Richard the Third* (hereafter cited as *Richard III*), rev. ed. (Cambridge, 1898), p. 251. See also Wolffe, "When and why did Hastings lose his head?," p. 839.

20. Mancini, *The Usurpation of Richard III*, p. 93. See also Jacob, *The Fifteenth Century*, pp. 623–4.

21. B.M., Harleian MS. 433, as cited by P. M. Kendall, *Richard the Third* (New York, 1965), p. 441.

22. *L. & P.*, I, xxv; *Eng. Hist. Doc., 1327–1485*, p. 337; Mancini, *The Usurpation of Richard III*, pp. 21–3.

23. Hanham, *Richard III and his early historians*, p. 158 and passim. According to R. S. Sylvester, "What has not often enough been recognized is that a great many of the details which More embodied in his narrative had already been recorded by other historians of Richard's reign. [Bernard] André and [Pietro] Carmeliano had portrayed the defeated king as the blackest of monsters; [while John] Rous added a large number of physical details, including Richard's deformed shoulder, his small stature, and his toothed and hairy birth." See *The Complete Works of St. Thomas More*, II, lxxviii.

24. *Ibid.*, pp. 83–5; More, *History of Richard III*, ed. Kendall, pp. 103–6.

25. The confession made by Tyrell shortly before his execution in 1502 is regarded by most historians as spurious. See S. B. Chrimes, *Henry VII* (London, 1972), p. 93.

26. See the comments made by A. F. Pollard in "The Making of More's *Richard III*," in *Historical Essays in Honour of James Tait*, ed. J. G. Edwards (Manchester, 1933). See also the comments of R. S. Sylvester in *The Complete Works of St. Thomas More*, II, lxv; and A. R. Myers, "The Character of Richard III," *History Today*, IV (1954), p. 517.

27. Lawrence Tanner and William Wright, "Recent Investigations concerning the Fate of the Princes in the Tower," *Archaeologia*, LXXXIV (1934), pp. 19, 24–5.

28. For an informed discussion of who was responsible for the deed, see Kendall, *Richard the Third*, pp. 438–68.

29. Tucker, *Life of Surrey*, p. 39. See also Kendall, *Richard the Third*, p. 301.

30. In his discussion of who murdered the princes, Kendall contends that Buckingham was the chief instigator of the crime. According to this view, Buckingham hoped to discredit

Richard III by saddling him with responsibility for the crime, which would thereby enable the duke to assert his own claim to the throne. Yet there is not a shred of evidence, contemporary or otherwise, for such a thesis; nor is it at all clear that the rather woolly-headed Buckingham was capable of formulating such a machiavellian plan. Furthermore, Buckingham was not even in London at the time the murder probably occurred. He accompanied Richard on his post-coronation progress towards the West, remaining with the royal party until it reached Gloucester, where on 2 August he took his leave of the king and retired to his castle at Brecknock, in Wales.

31. Edmund Tudor was the eldest son of Owen Tudor, head of a prominent Welsh family that claimed descent from the legendary Princes of Cadwallader. Edmund's mother was Katherine of Valois, daughter of Charles VI of France and widow of Henry V of England, whose sole heir was their son Henry VI. Edmund had two younger brothers, Jasper, who was later to be created Earl of Pembroke as well as Duke of Bedford, and Owen, who for many years was a monk in Westminster Abbey.

32. The Tudors became the political heirs of the House of Lancaster in 1471, following the execution of Henry VI and the death in battle of Edward of Lancaster, the only child of Henry VI and Margaret of Anjou.

33. For an analysis of the problems connected with the Beaufort-Tudor claim, see Levine, *Tudor Dynastic Problems*, pp. 33–4.

34. For a detailed account of Henry's early life, see Chrimes, *Henry VII*, pp. 3–16.

35. Vergil, *Anglica Historia*, p. 145.

36. Some historians, and especially those of Welsh origin, hold that Henry fathered an illegitimate son, one Roland de Veleville, during his years in Brittany. For example, see David Williams, "The Family of Henry VII," *History Today*, IV (1954), p. 84. Professor Chrimes maintains, however, that there is no evidence "to justify the assertion that Veleville's father was Henry VII." See Chrimes, "Sir Roland Veleville," *W.H.R.*, III (1967), p. 288.

37. Gairdner, *Richard III*, p. 106. See also Robert Somerville, *History of the Duchy of Lancaster, 1265–1603* (London, 1953), p. 258.

38. *Letters of the Kings of England*, I, 155–6; Kendall, *Richard the Third*, p. 300.

39. Jacob, *The Fifteenth Century*, pp. 625–6; A. L. Rowse, *Tudor Cornwall: Portrait of a Society*, new ed. (New York, 1969), pp. 110–11.

40. T. B. Pugh, ed., *The Marcher Lordships of South Wales 1415–1536: Select Documents* (Cardiff, 1963), pp. 240–1; Chrimes, *Henry VII*, pp. 23–6.

41. D. M. Loades, *Politics and the Nation 1450–1660* (Brighton, 1974), p. 91; B. P. Wolffe, *The Royal Demesne in English History* (Athens [Ohio], 1971), p. 191; See also Charles Ross, *Edward IV* (Berkeley, 1974), p. 420; and Albert Makinson, "The Road to Bosworth Field, August 1485," *History Today*, XIII (1963), pp. 240–1.

42. H. G. Hanbury, "The Legislation of Richard III," *A.J.L.H.*, VI (1962), p. 105. See also Loades, *Politics and the Nation*, p. 91.

43. J. M. W. Bean, *The Decline of English Feudalism 1215–1540* (Manchester, 1968), pp. 239, 245.

44. J. R. Lander, "Attainder and Forfeiture, 1453 to 1509," *H.J.*, IV (1961), p. 122.

45. S. B. Chrimes, "The Fifteenth Century," *History*, new series, XLVIII (1963), p. 23.

46. J. R. Lander, *The Wars of the Roses* (New York, 1967), p. 252, note; S. B. Chrimes, ed., *Fifteenth-Century England 1399–1509: Studies in Politics and Society* (Manchester, 1972), p. 114.

47. Richard III was the first English monarch to receive a lifetime grant of tunnage and poundage from the first parliament to meet after his accession. Edward IV had received the duties from his *second* parliament.

48. J. S. Roskell, "William Catesby, Councillor to Richard III," *B.J.R.L.*, XLI (1959–60), p. 169.

49. *Croyland Chronicle*, pp. 499–500; *Eng. Hist. Doc.*, *1327–1485*, pp. 342–3; Gairdner, *Richard III*, pp. 205–7; Kendall, *Richard the Third*, p. 366; Jacob, *The Fifteenth Century*, pp. 636–7.

50. *Ibid.*, pp. 627–8.

51. R. L. Storey, *The Reign of Henry VII* (New York, 1968), p. 56.

52. *L. & P.*, I, 85–7; Jacob, *The Fifteenth Century*, pp. 640–1.

53. Gairdner, *Richard III*, pp. 196–8.

54. For a detailed account of Henry's march through Wales and his subsequent negotiations with the Stanleys, see Chrimes, *Henry VII*, pp. 40–4.

55. *Ibid.*, pp. 45–6.

56. For the periodic friction between Richard and Northumberland during the 1470s, which may also have influenced the earl's behavior on 22 August, see J. M. W. Bean, *The Estates of the Percy Family 1416–1537* (Oxford, 1958), p. 133.

57. *Letters of the Kings of England*, I, 163–4.

58. Edward Hall, *Hall's Chronicle; containing the History of England during the Reign of Henry the Fourth, and the Succeeding Monarchs, to the End of the Reign of Henry the Eighth* (London, 1809), p. 419; Chrimes, *Henry VII*, p. 49; Eric N. Simons, *Henry VII: The First Tudor King* (London, 1968), p. 57.

CHAPTER II

1. Charlotte A. Sneyd, ed., *A Relation, or rather a true Account of the Island of England* (Camden Society, 1847), pp. 28–9, 31; J. R. Lander, *Conflict and Stability in Fifteenth-Century England* (London, 1969), p. 47. At the close of the Middle Ages an agricultural labourer could grow enough to feed 1.5 persons; today such a labourer grows enough to feed himself and nineteen others.

2. C. V. Malfatti, ed., *Two Italian Accounts of Tudor England* (Barcelona, 1953), pp. 36–7; Pollard, *Cont. Sources*, II, 335; Sneyd, *A Relation, or rather a true account of the Island of England*, pp. vii, 42–3.

3. R. S. Schofield, "The Geographical Distribution of Wealth in England, 1334–1649," *Ec.H.R.*, 2nd series, XVIII (1965), pp. 483–510; E. H. Phelps-Brown, "Seven Centuries of the Prices of Consumables," in *Essays in Economic History*, ed. E. M. Carus-Wilson (London, 1962), II, 189. See also F. R. H. DuBoulay, *An Age of Ambition* (New York, 1970), pp. 41–3; A. R. Bridbury, *Economic Growth: England in the Later Middle Ages* (London, 1962), pp. 25, 27, 33, 52, 80–1, 104; Peter Ramsey, *Tudor Economic Problems* (London, 1968), pp. 48–9, 53, 55.

4. Conrad Russell, *The Crisis of Parliaments: English History 1509–1660* (Oxford, 1971), p. 6; Wilhelm Busch, *England under the Tudors*, trans. by A. M. Todd and A. H. Johnson (London, 1895), p. 254.

5. K. B. McFarlane, "The Wars of the Roses," *P.B.A.*, L (1964), p. 114.

6. For evidence of Henry's use of the patronage at his disposal between Bosworth and the coronation, see Campbell, *Materials*, I, 1–241 passim. For a good brief discussion of his actions at this time, see Loades, *Politics and the Nation*, pp. 22, 96, 117.

7. *Letters of the Kings of England*, I, 169; Pollard, *Cont. Sources*, I, 11; Chrimes, *Henry VII*, p. 51; Lander, *Conflict and Stability*, p. 163.

8. C. E. Mallet, *A History of the University of Oxford*, 3 vols. (London, 1924), I, 313. See also McFarlane, "The Wars of the Roses," p. 102.

9. Sydney Anglo, "The Foundation of the Tudor Dynasty: The Coronation and Marriage of Henry VII," *The Guildhall Miscellany*, II (London, 1960), p. 4; J. D. Mackie, *The Earlier Tudors 1485–1558* (Oxford, 1952), p. 54.

10. Anglo, "The Foundation of the Tudor Dynasty," p. 4.

11. Storey, *The End of the House of Lancaster*, p. 6. According to Professor Storey, "The

celebrated efficiency of Henry VII's administration was due to his employment of experienced 'Yorkist' officials."

12. For evidence of Henry's early administrative appointments, see *Cal. Pat. Rolls*, I, 11–84.

13. *Ibid.*, p. 11; C. G. Bayne and W. H. Dunham, eds., *Select Cases in the Council of Henry VII* (Selden Society, 1956), p. xvi; Wolffe, *The Royal Demesne in English History*, pp. 182–3; Roberto Weiss, *Humanism in England in the Fifteenth Century*, 2nd ed. (Oxford, 1957), pp. 124–6.

14. Chrimes, *Henry VII*, pp. 121–2; Bean, *The Decline of English Feudalism*, p. 245; C. S. Goldingham, "The Navy under Henry VII," *E.H.R..*, XXXIII (1918), p. 477.

15. Anthony Tuck, *Richard II and the English Nobility* (London, 1973), p. 187.

16. Busch, *England under the Tudors*, p. 23; Mackie, *The Earlier Tudors*, p. 58; Storey, *The Reign of Henry VII*, p. 59; G. R. Elton, *England under the Tudors* (London, 1955), p. 42; A. J. Slavin, *The Precarious Balance 1450–1640* (New York, 1973), p. 99; R. J. Hooker, "Notes on the Organization of the Tudor Military under Henry VII," *H.L.Q.*, XXIII (1959–60), p. 19.

17. In 1484, after Elizabeth Woodville left the Abbey and accepted an accommodation with Richard III, Dorset, had sought to return to England in order to come to terms with the king. This had naturally angered Henry, who retaliated by using him as a hostage the following year.

18. *Cal. Pat. Rolls*, I, 112; *Cal. Inquisitions Post Mortem*, I, 114–15; Kendall, *Richard the Third*, p. 463; Mackie, *The Earlier Tudors*, p. 76; MacGibbon, *Elizabeth Woodville*, pp. 188–90.

19. *Cal. Pat. Rolls*, I, 49; Mackie, *The Earlier Tudors*, p. 55; Sydney Anglo, *Spectacle, Pageantry, and Early Tudor Policy* (Oxford, 1969), p. 11; Anglo, "The Foundation of the Tudor Dynasty," p. 5.

20. W. A. Shaw, ed., *The Knights of England*, 2 vols. (London, 1906), I, 141–2.

21. Anglo, *Spectacle, Pageantry, and Early Tudor Policy*, p. 15; Anglo, "The Foundation of the Tudor Dynasty," pp. 6–9, 15–17; Simons, *Henry VII*, p. 71; Chrimes, *Henry VII*, pp. 59–60.

22. *Ibid.*, p. 160; Levine, *Tudor Dynastic Problems*, pp. 35–6; Elton, *England under the Tudors*, pp. 19–20; Fisher, *Pol. Hist.*, p. 8.

23. The declaration passed by parliament is available in *Statues of the Realm*, II, 499, and G. R. Elton, ed., *The Tudor Constitution* (Cambridge, 1960), p. 4.

24. Pugh, *The Marcher Lordships of South Wales*, pp. 241–2; Mackie, *The Earlier Tudors*, pp. 61–2.

25. *Ibid.*, p. 62; W. G. Benham, ed., *The Red Paper Book of Colchester* (Colchester, 1902), p. 64; Roskell, *The Commons and their Speakers*, pp. 300–1, 308; J. E. Powell and Keith Wallis, *The House of Lords in the Middle Ages* (London, 1968), p. 528; J. R. Lander, "Attainder and Forfeiture, 1453 to 1509," p. 133. According to Professor Lander, only nine peers were attainted during the entire reign, and of those nine six were ultimately reversed. See Lander, "Bonds, Coercion, and Fear: Henry VII and the Peerage," in *Florelegium Historiale*, ed. J. G. Rowe (Toronto, 1971), p. 333.

26. Chrimes, *Henry VII*, pp. 63, 205–6; Mackie, *The Earlier Tudors*, p. 63; Storey, *The Reign of Henry VII*, pp. 99–100.

27. *Ibid.*; *Rot. Parl.*, VI, 268; F. C. Dietz, *English Government Finance 1485–1558*, 2nd ed. (London, 1964), p. 20; N. S. B. Gras, *The Early English Customs System* (Cambridge, Mass., 1918), p. 84; Roger Lockyer, *Henry VII* (New York, 1968), p. 53.

28. Bayne and Dunham, ed., *Select Cases in the Council of Henry VII*, p. 50.

29. *Ibid.*

30. *The Red Paper Book of Colchester*, p. 64; *Statutes of the Realm*, II, 500–1; W. S. Holdsworth, *A History of English Law*, 3rd ed., 16 vols. (London, 1945), IV, 505; A. F. Pollard, "The Growth of the Court of Requests," *E.H.R.*, LVI (1941), p. 301.

31. *Rot. Parl.*, VI, 270; Fisher, *Pol. Hist.*, p. 10; Mackie, *The Earlier Tudors*, p. 65.
32. Chrimes, *Henry VII*, p. 65.
33. Storey, *The Reign of Henry VII*, p. 60.
34. Vergil, *Anglica Historia*, p. 7.
35. Perhaps it should be noted that a grandson of Elizabeth's sister Anne, the celebrated poet Henry Howard, Earl of Surrey, was executed for treason in January 1547, on the eve of Henry VIII's death. Henry VIII seems to have suspected that the Howards, led by Surrey and the third Duke of Norfolk, were planning to seize control of the government during the next reign, which meant a likely *coup d'état* against the young Edward VI. Thus Henry VIII was beset by many of the same fears that had plagued his father in 1485–86.
36. *Cal. S. P. Milan*, I, 322.
37. Pollard, *Cont. Sources*, I, 161–2.
38. James Gairdner, ed., *Three Fifteenth-Century Chronicles* (Camden Society, 1880), pp. 104–5; Bacon, *Henry VII*, p. 19; *Somers Tracts*, I, 25–6; John Leland, *Collectanea de Rebus Britannicis*, 2nd ed., 6 vols. (London, 1770), IV, 216; Anglo, *Spectacle, Pageantry, and Early Tudor Policy*, p. 53.
39. *Cal. Close Rolls*, I, 237; *Somers Tracts*, I, 25–6; *L. & P.*, I, 388–404.
40. Vergil, *Anglica Historia*, p. 146; Sneyd, *A Relation, or rather a true Account of the Island of England*, pp. 46–7.
41. Pollard, *Cont. Sources*, II, 226–7.
42. Bacon, *Henry VII*, p. 218; Busch, *England under the Tudors*, p. 307; Fisher, *Pol. Hist.*, p. 151; Somerville, *History of the Duchy of Lancaster*, p. 269; Chrimes, *Fifteenth-Century England*, p. 83; Storey, *The Reign of Henry VII*, p. 64.
43. John E. Stevens, *Music & Poetry in the Early Tudor Court* (London, 1961), p. 310.
44. Bruce Pattison, *Music and Poetry of the English Renaissance* (London, 1948), pp. 3, 50.
45. *Cal. S. P. Milan*, I, 341; *Cal. S. P. Ven.*, I, 267; Busch, *England under the Tudors*, pp. 308, 311–12; H. M. Smith, "The Will of Henry VII," *C. Q. R.*, CXVI (1933), pp. 247–8.
46. Bacon, *Henry VII*, p. 217. See also *Cal. S. P. Ven.*, I, 261.
47. *L. & P.*, II, xxvi.

CHAPTER III

1. Pollard, *Cont. Sources*, I, 17; Kendall, *Richard the Third*, pp. 423–4.
2. J. C. Meagher, "The First Progress of Henry VII," in *Renaissance Drama*, new series, I (1968), p. 46; Somerville, *History of the Duchy of Lancaster*, p. 258.
3. Anglo, *Spectacle, Pageantry, and Early Tudor Policy*, p. 21; C. H. Williams, "The Rebellion of Humphrey Stafford in 1486," *E. H. R.*, XLIII (1928), pp. 181–2.
4. *Ibid.*, p. 183; Mackie, *The Earlier Tudors*, p. 67; Fisher, *Pol. Hist.*, pp. 11–12.
5. Meagher, "The First Progress of Henry VII," p. 54.
6. Vergil, *Anglica Historia*, p. 63; Bacon, *Henry VII*, p. 66; Mackie, *The Earlier Tudors*, p. 68; Chrimes, *Henry VII*, p. 71.
7. Williams, "The Rebellion of Humphrey Stafford in 1486," pp. 185, 187; M. Hemmant, ed., *Select Cases in the Exchequer Chamber*, 2 vols. (Selden Society, 1933–48), I, 116–20; Elton, *England under the Tudors*, pp. 21–2; I. D. Thornley, "The Destruction of Sanctuary," in *Tudor Studies*, p. 199; H. M. Cam, "The Decline and Fall of English Feudalism," in *Liberties and Communities in Medieval England* (Cambridge, 1944), pp. 216–17.
8. Kenneth Pickthorn, *Early Tudor Government: Henry VII* (Cambridge, 1934), p. 179; David Knowles, *The Religious Orders in England. Volume III: The Tudor Age* (Cambridge, 1961), pp. 88–9; Fisher, *Pol. Hist.*, p. 21.
9. *Ibid.*, p. 96; Meagher, "The First Progress of Henry VII," pp. 67–73; Williams, "The

Rebellion of Humphrey Stafford in 1486," p. 188; Anglo, *Spectacle, Pageantry, and Early Tudor Policy*, pp. 31–5.

10. Richard Bagwell, *Ireland under the Tudors, with a succinct account of the earlier history*, 3 vols. (London, 1885–90), I, 90–1. Perhaps it should be noted that Warwick's father, the Duke of Clarence, had been born in Dublin in 1449 and was therefore regarded as a native Prince.

11. Bryan, *Life of Kildare*, pp. 1, 44–5, 56–7, 91, 186, 212–13. See also Edmund Curtis, *A History of Medieval Ireland* (London, 1923), pp. 285–6; James Lydon, *Ireland in the Later Middle Ages* (Dublin, 1973), pp. 156–7; Art Cosgrove, "The Gaelic Resurgence and the Geraldine Supremacy (c. 1400–1534)," in *The Course of Irish History*, ed. T. W. Moody (Cork, 1967), p. 167.

12. Bryan, *Life of Kildare*, pp. 101–2; Bagwell, *Ireland under the Tudors*, I, 104–5; Mackie, *The Earlier Tudors*, p. 72; Simons, *Henry VII*, p. 95.

13. For the King's later treatment of Dorset, see Chapter IV below. Perhaps it should be noted that in February 1490, Henry granted his mother-in-law an annuity of £400. See *Cal. Close Rolls*, I, 302.

14. *Ibid.*, p. 34; R. J. Knecht, "The Episcopate and the Wars of the Roses," *U. B. H. J.*, VI (1958), pp. 128–9. See also Mortimer Levine, "Richard III—Usurper or Lawful King?," p. 398; and Simons, *Henry VII*, p. 92.

15. Bryan, *Life of Kildare*, pp. 106–9; Curtis, *A History of Medieval Ireland*, pp. 394–5; Mary Hayden, "Lambert Simnel in Ireland," *I. H. S.*, IV (1915), pp. 628–9.

16. For a good account of the rebels' movements at this time, see Kendall, *Richard the Third*, pp. 419–20.

17. *Ibid.*, pp. 421–2; Storey, *The Reign of Henry VII*, p. 76; Chrimes, *Henry VII*, p. 77; Mackie, *The Earlier Tudors*, p. 74; A. H. Burne, "The Battle of Stoke," in *More Battlefields of England* (London, 1952), pp. 156–9.

18. Anglo, *Spectacle, Pageantry, and Early Tudor Policy*, p. 49.

19. Bryan, *Life of Kildare*, p. 116; Chrimes, *Henry VII*, p. 79. See also Bagwell, *Ireland under the Tudors*, I, 106; Loades, *Politics and the Nation*, p. 103; Hayden, "Lambert Simnel in Ireland," pp. 632–3.

20. *Ibid.*, pp. 634–7; Bryan, *Life of Kildare*, pp. 122–41; Curtis, *A History of Medieval Ireland*, pp. 396–7; A. J. Otway-Ruthven, *A History of Medieval Ireland* (London, 1968), pp. 404–6.

21. Shaw, ed., *The Knights of England*, II, 26; Anglo, *Spectacle, Pageantry, and Early Tudor Policy*, p. 49.

22. Mackie, *The Earlier Tudors*, p. 77.

23. Dietz, *English Government Finance*, p. 54; Pickthorn, *Early Tudor Government*, p. 20; Chrimes, *Henry VII*, p. 197; Storey, *The Reign of Henry VII*, p. 107.

24. Vergil, *Anglica Historia*, p. 147.

25. *Statutes of the Realm*, II, 509–10; Elton, *The Tudor Constitution*, pp. 163–4; I. S. Leadam, ed., *Select Cases before the King's Council in the Star Chamber*, 2 vols. (Selden Society, 1903–11) I, xlvii-xlviii; C. G. Bayne and W. H. Dunham, eds., *Select Cases in the Council of Henry VII* (Selden Society, 1958), pp. li-liii; Cora Scofield, *A Study of the Court of Star Chamber* (Chicago, 1900), pp. 40–2.

26. Richelieu's views are discussed in David Ogg, *Europe in the Seventeenth Century*, 8th ed., revised (London, 1961), pp. 201–2.

27. Bayne and Dunham, eds., *Select Cases in the Council of Henry VII*, p. xlii; G. R. Elton, *The Tudor Revolution in Government* (Cambridge, 1953), p. 34; Loades, *Politics and the Nation*, pp. 115–16.

28. Chrimes, *Fifteenth-Century England*, pp. 73–4.

29. Bayne and Dunham, eds., *Select Cases in the Council of Henry VII*, pp. xxix, xxi-xxii.

30. A. F. Pollard, *The Evolution of Parliament*, 2nd ed. (London, 1926), pp. 293–4.

31. J. R. Tanner, ed., *Tudor Constitutional Documents*, 2nd ed. (Cambridge, 1922), p. 216; A. L. Brown, "The King's Councillors in Fifteenth-Century England," *T. R. H. S.*, 5th series, XIX (1969), p. 114.

32. *Cal. S. P. Milan*, I, 335.

33. More, *The History of Richard III*, ed. Kendall, p. 109.

34. Storey, *The Reign of Henry VII*, p. 98. See also Chrimes, *Henry VII*, pp. 105–6, and McElroy, "Literary Patronage," p. 257.

35. Bayne and Dunham, eds., *Select Cases in the Council of Henry VII*, p. lxxv; Gladys Bradford, ed., *Proceedings in the Court of Star Chamber in the Reigns of Henry VII and Henry VII* (London, 1911), pp. 6–7; J. A. Guy, *The Cardinal's Court: The Impact of Thomas Wolsey in Star Chamber* (Totowa, N. J., 1977), pp. 5–6.

36. *Ibid.*, pp. 5, 15, 17, 19.

37. *Ibid.*, pp. 14–15, 19.

38. *Ibid.*, p. 16.

39. Bayne and Dunham, eds., *Select Cases in the Council of Henry VII*, pp. xlxx, clxxii; Bradford, ed., *Proceedings in the Court of Star Chamber*, pp. 6, 8, 18–19; Storey, *The Reign of Henry VII*, p. 127; E. W. Ives, "Ralph Egerton of Ridley," *B. J. R. L.*, LII (1970), pp. 348–9.

40. *The Red Paper Book of Colchester*, p. 64; A. F. Pollard, "The Growth of the Court of Requests," p. 301.

41. Pickthorn, *Early Tudor Government*, pp. 36–7.

42. A. F. Pollard, "Council, Star Chamber, and Privy Council under the Tudors," *E. H. R.*, XXXVII (1922), p. 352.

43. I. S. Leadam, ed., *Select Cases in the Court of Requests, A. D. 1497–1569* (Selden Society, 1869), pp. xii-xiii, li; Elton, *England under the Tudors*, pp. 62, 83.

44. Leadam, ed., *Select Cases in the Court of Requests*, p. lv.

45. This subject will be discussed in Chapter VII below.

46. Holdsworth, *History of English Law*, IV, 538; Mackie, *The Earlier Tudors*, p. 197; Loades, *Politics and the Nation*, p. 122.

CHAPTER IV

1. S. T. Bindoff, *Tudor England* (Harmondsworth, 1950), p. 65.

2. Loades, *Politics and the Nation*, p. 121.

3. Somerville, *History of the Duchy of Lancaster*, p. 264.

4. Dietz, *English Public Finance*, pp. 51–2.

5. *Ibid.*, p. 52. See also Pickthorn, *Early Tudor Government*, p. 20; and Chrimes, *Henry VII*, pp. 202–3, 217.

6. C. D. Ross, "The Reign of Edward IV," in Chrimes, ed., *Fifteenth-Century England*, p. 54.

7. Pollard, *Cont. Sources*, II, 4.

8. B. P. Wolffe, *The Crown Lands 1461 to 1536* (London, 1970), pp. 66–7; Storey, *The Reign of Henry VII*, pp. 101–2; B. P. Wolffe, "The Management of English Royal Estates under the Yorkist Kings," *E.H.R.*, LXXI (1956), pp. 24–5. For a different view, see G. R. Elton, "Henry VII: Rapacity and Remorse," *H.J.*, I (1958), p. 22.

9. B. P. Wolffe, *The Royal Demesne in English History* (London, 1971), pp. 211–12.

10. Storey, *The Reign of Henry VII*, p. 102.

11. See, for example, such works of B. P. Wolffe as *The Crown Lands 1461 to 1536* and "The Management of English Royal Estates under the Yorkist Kings." See also Chrimes, *Henry VII*, p. 212.

12. Wolffe, *The Royal Demesne in English History*, p. 220; Storey, *The Reign of Henry VII*, p. 101; W. C. Richardson, *Tudor Chamber Administration 1485–1547* (Baton Rouge, 1952), pp. 23–4; Dietz, *English Government Finance*, pp. 26–7.

13. *Cal. Inquisitions Post Mortem*, III, 510; Roskell, *The Commons and their Speakers*, p. 300; C. A. J. Skeel, *The Council in the Marches of Wales* (London, 1904), p. 37.

14. *Burke's Peerage*, 100th ed. (London, 1953), p. 191. See also Lawrence Stone, *Family and Fortune* (Oxford, 1973), p. 243.

15. *Cal. Inquisitions Post Mortem*, III, 392–3; Wolffe, *The Royal Demesne in English History*, pp. 220–1; Lander, *Conflict and Stability*, p. 111; C. D. Ross, *Edward IV* (Berkeley, 1974), pp. 376–7; Chrimes, *Henry VII*, pp. 206–7.

16. *Tudor Proclamations*, I, 10–11, 54–5, 59; Richardson, *Tudor Chamber Administration*, p. 13; Mackie, *The Earlier Tudors*, pp. 214–15.

17. Dietz, *English Government Finance*, pp. 27–8.

18. Elton, "Henry VII: Rapacity and Remorse," p. 23. See also H. E. Bell, *An Introduction to the History and Records of the Court of Wards and Liveries* (Cambridge, 1953), p. 4.

19. *Cal. Pat. Rolls, 1485–94*, p. 71; Elton, *The Tudor Revolution in Government*, pp. 28–9; Richardson, *Tudor Chamber Administration*, pp. 119–20; Elton, "Henry VII: Rapacity and Remorse," p. 23; Cam, "The Decline and Fall of English Feudalism," p. 215; D. M. Brodie, "Edmund Dudley, Minister of Henry VII," *T.R.H.S.*, 4th series, XV (1932), pp. 156–7.

20. Bell, *An Introduction to the History and Records of the Court of Wards and Liveries*, pp. 2–3; Joan Thirsk, ed., *The Agrarian History of England and Wales*, vol. IV (Cambridge, 1967), p. 259; Roger Lockyer, *Tudor and Stuart Britain* (New York, 1964), p. 27.

21. *Cal. Pat. Rolls, 1485–94*, pp. 48–9; *Cal. Pat. Rolls, 1494–1509*, p. 301; Richardson, *Tudor Chamber Administration*, pp. 108, 166.

22. Pickthorn, *Early Tudor Government*, pp. 17–18; Chrimes, *Henry VII*, p. 129; Stone, *The Crisis of the Aristocracy*, p. 600.

23. Bell, *An Introduction to the History and Records of the Court of Wards and Liveries*, p. 5; Richardson, *Tudor Chamber Administration*, p. 169.

24. For the early history of uses, see Holdsworth, *History of English Law*, 3rd ed., IV, 407–49; G. A. Holmes, *The Estates of the Higher Nobility in Fourteenth-Century England* (Cambridge, 1957), pp. 41–50; Joel Hurstfield, "The Revival of Fiscal Feudalism in Early Tudor England," *History*, XXXVII (1952), p. 139.

25. Bean, *The Decline of English Feudalism*, pp. 215, 233, 238–9; T. F. T. Plucknett, *A Concise History of the Common Law*, 5th ed. (London, 1956), pp. 579–80; Loades, *Politics and the Nation*, pp. 121–2.

26. *Statutes of the Realm*, II, 540–1; Bean, *The Decline of English Feudalism*, pp. 242–3; Holdsworth, *History of English Law*, IV, 448–9; Plucknett, *A Concise History of the Common Law*, pp. 580–7; E. W. Ives, "The Genesis of the Statute of Uses," *E.H.R.*, LXXII (1967), pp. 673–5.

27. Lander, *Conflict and Stability*, p. 104; Loades, *Politics and the Nation*, p. 120; Ross, *Edward IV*, p. 350; Chrimes, *Henry VII*, pp. 197, 201; Lockyer, *Henry VII*, p. 55, note.

28. *Rot. Parl.*, V, 372; Ross *Edward IV*, p. 342.

29. Perhaps it should be noted that Henry pressed for at least £90,000 in 1504 but was defeated by an opposition led by the young Thomas More. This will be discussed in Chapter X below.

30. Dietz, *English Government Finance*, p. 57; Lockyer, *Henry VII*, p. 55, note; Storey, *The Reign of Henry VII*, p. 108; G. L. Harris, "Aids, Loans, and Benevolences," *H.J.*, VI (1963), p. 12.

31. Pickthorn, *Early Tudor Government*, pp. 20–1, 23.

32. Lander, *Conflict and Stability*, pp. 112–13.

33. Dietz, *English Government Finance*, p. 31.

34. Christopher Hill, *Economic Problems of the Church*, rev. ed. (Oxford, 1968), pp. 14–15.

35. *Cal. Pat. Rolls, 1485–94*, pp. 454–5; *Cal. Pat. Rolls, 1494–1509*, pp. 185–6; Storey, *The*

Reign of Henry VII, p. 180; W. T. MacCaffrey, *Exeter, 1540–1640* (Cambridge, Mass., 1958), p. 175.

36. J. J. Scarisbrick, "Clerical Taxation in England, 1485 to 1547," *J.E.H.*, XI (1960), p. 50.

37. Chrimes, *Henry VII*, p. 201.

38. Bayne and Dunham, eds., *Select Cases in the Council of Henry VII*, pp. cxxiv, clxx, clxxii; Storey, *The Reign of Henry VII*, p. 127; Chrimes, *Henry VII*, p. 205; Elton, *England under the Tudors*, pp. 50–1; Bean, *The Estates of the Percy Family*, p. 143.

39. *Cal. Close Rolls, 1485–1500*, pp. 14, 61–2; *Cal. Pat. Rolls, 1485–94*, p. 238; Powell and Wallis, *The House of Lords in the Middle Ages*, p. 533; Lander, "Bonds, Coercion, and Fear," pp. 339–40.

40. *Ibid.*, p. 339; G. R. Elton, "Henry VII: A Restatement," *H.J.*, IV (1961), p. 13.

41. *Cal. Close Rolls, 1485–1500*, pp. 180–1; Storey, *The Reign of Henry VII*, p. 158; Lander, "Bonds, Coercion, and Fear," pp. 342–3. Professor Lander emphasizes the darker aspects of Henry's policy and criticizes his harshness towards Dorset. However, even after the arrangements of 1492 were made, the king made a sincere effort to treat the marquess considerately. In November 1494 Dorset had an honored place at Prince Henry's investiture as Duke of York, and during that ceremony Dorset's son was one of the thirty-three men knighted by the king. See *Cal. Close Rolls, 1485–1500*, p. 237.

42. Lander, "Bonds, Coercion, and Fear," pp. 339–40; Loades, *Politics and the Nation*, pp. 96–7, 119.

43. Wolffe, *The Royal Demesne in English History*, p. 219; Pickthorn, *Early Tudor Government*, p. 19.

44. Peter Ramsey, "Overseas Trade in the Reign of Henry VII: The Evidence of the Customs Accounts," *Ec.H.R.*, 2nd series, VI (1953), pp. 174–5.

45. For materials pertaining to Henry's coinage policies, which led him to mint England's first gold sovereigns (1490) and silver shillings (1504), thereby bringing "the actual coins used into relation with the denominations used in accountancy," see *Cal. Close Rolls, 1485–1500*, pp. 49–53; *Cal. Close Rolls, 1500–9*, pp. 213–16; *The Red Paper Book of Colchester*, p. 63; Mackie, *The Earlier Tudors*, p. 201; Chrimes, *Henry VII*, pp. 224–6; Brodie, "Edmund Dudley," p. 153; T. F. Reddaway, "The King's Mint and Exchange in London, 1343–1543," *E.H.R.*, LXXXII (1967), p. 18.

46. R. B. Wernham, *Before the Armada: The Emergence of the English Nation, 1485–1588* (New York, 1966), pp. 67–8.

47. Campbell, *Materials*, I, 192–3, 268; Mackie, *The Earlier Tudors*, pp. 81–2; Chrimes, *Henry VII*, pp. 279–80.

48. M. E. Mallet, "Anglo-Florentine Commercial Relations, 1465–1491," *Ec.H.R.*, 2nd series, XV (1962), pp. 251–3, 256–7, 260–1.

49. *Ibid.*, pp. 253, 260–1; Mackie, *The Earlier Tudors*, pp. 233–4.

50. Wernham, *Before the Armada*, p. 74.

51. *Ibid.*, pp. 71–4; Mackie, *The Earlier Tudors*, pp. 220–2; Fisher, *Pol. Hist.*, pp. 97–9; Lockyer, *Henry VII*, pp. 74–5.

52. James Gairdner, ed., *Memorials of King Henry the Seventh* (Rolls Series, 1858), pp. 328–34; Busch, *England under the Tudors*, pp. 52–3.

53. *Cal. S. P. Spain*, I, 21–4; Pollard, ed., *Cont. Sources*, III, 2–6.

54. *Cal. S. P. Spain*, I, 33–4; Wernham, *Before the Armada*, pp. 110–11.

CHAPTER V

1. Rymer, *Foedera*, XII, 362. By the treaty of Redon, Henry agreed to provide 6000 troops to fight at Brittany's expense only until 1 November 1489. As security for the payment of

these troops, the Breton government was to allow Morlaix and Concarneau to be garrisoned by English regiments.

2. Campbell, *Materials*, II, 378; *Cal. S. P. Milan*, I, 248; Pollard, *Cont. Sources*, I, 65.

3. Mackie, *The Earlier Tudors*, pp. 87–8; Wernham, *Before the Armada*, pp. 33–4.

4. *Ibid.*, p. 34.

5. *Rot. Parl.*, VI, 421 ff.; Dietz, *English Government Finance*, pp. 54–5; Pickthorn, *Early Tudor Government*, pp. 20–1; Mackie, *The Earlier Tudors*, p. 90; Storey, *The Reign of Henry VII*, pp. 107–8; Chrimes, *Henry VII*, pp. 198–9.

6. M. E. James, "The Murder at Cocklodge," *D.U.J.*, new series, XXVI (1965), p. 80.

7. *Ibid.*, pp. 81–5; Rachel Reid, *The King's Council in the North* (London, 1921), pp. 75–7. For contemporary reports of these happenings, see *Cal. S. P. Ven.*, I, 181, and Vergil, *Anglica Historia*, p. 39. The eulogies composed for Northumberland will be discussed in Chapter IX below.

8. James, "The Murder at Cocklodge," p. 86.

9. *Ibid.* p. 87; Loades, *Politics and the Nation*, pp. 105–6; Tucker, *Life of Surrey*, pp. 53–5, 73.

10. For the material in this and the succeeding paragraph, see Wernham, *Before the Armada*, p. 35, and Mackie, *The Earlier Tudors*, pp. 101–4.

11. *Ibid.*, pp. 104–5; Wernham, *Before the Armada*, p. 35.

12. Bacon, *Henry VII*, p. 147; Dietz, *English Government Finance*, p. 56; Chrimes, *Henry VII*, pp. 197, 203; Harris, "Aids, Loans, and Benevolences," pp. 9, 12.

13. Bryan, *Life of Kildare*, pp. 145–7, 153; Lydon, *Ireland in the Later Middle Ages*, pp. 169–70.

14. *The Great Chronicle of London*, pp. 284–5; James Gairdner, "The Story of Perkin Warbeck," in *History of the Life and Reign of Richard the Third*, rev. ed. (Cambridge, 1898), pp. 266–7.

15. Cecil Roth, "Perkin Warbeck and His Jewish Master," *Transactions of the Jewish Historical Society of England*, IX (1922), pp. 145–7, 149, 154–6.

16. *Ibid.*, p. 158.

17. Gairdner, "The Story of Perkin Warbeck," pp. 267–8; Storey, *The Reign of Henry VII*, pp. 81–2.

18. The plot in 1490 to release the Earl of Warwick from the Tower, which was organized by Edward Frank, head of a family that had been favored by Richard III, failed only because the conspirators did not know the exact cell in which the unfortunate earl was a prisoner. When they sought him along the wrong corridor, they were detected and apprehended. Frank was attainted early in 1490 and executed on Tower Hill shortly before Easter. His two principal accomplices, John Sant and Miles Saley, were pardoned, probably because both were Benedictine monks. For a brief discussion of this plot, see C. A. J. Armstrong, "An Italian Astrologer at the Court of Henry VII," in *Italian Renaissance Studies*, ed. E. F. Jacob (London, 1960), pp. 444, 446–7.

19. Wernham, *Before the Armada*, pp. 39–40; Simons, *Henry VII*, p. 153.

20. Bryan, *Life of Kildare*, p. 156; Curtis, *History of Medieval Ireland*, p. 397.

21. Bryan, *Life of Kildare*, pp. 158–9; Agnes Conway, *Henry VII's Relations with Scotland and Ireland, 1485–98* (Cambridge, 1932), pp. 49–50; Otway-Ruthven, *History of Medieval Ireland*, pp. 406–8.

22. Chrimes, *Henry VII*, pp. 82–3; Mackie, *The Earlier Tudors*, pp. 120–1.

23. Bryan, *Life of Kildare*, pp. 156, 163; G. O. Sayles, "The Vindication of the Earl of Kildare from Treason, 1496," *I.H.S.*, VII (1950), p. 41.

24. Conway, *Henry VII's Relations with Scotland and Ireland*, pp. 52–3. Cf. Lydon, *Ireland in the Later Middle Ages*, p. 170.

25. For a good account of Scotland's foreign policy at this time, see R. L. Mackie, *King James IV of Scotland* (Edinburgh, 1958), pp. 61–8.

26. Mackie, *The Earlier Tudors*, p. 107; J. R. Hooker, "Notes on the Organization of the Tudor Military under Henry VII," *H.L.Q.*, XXIII (1959–60), p. 31.

27. H.M.C., *Report on the Manuscripts of Lord Middleton, preserved at Wollaton Hall* (London, 1911), p. 267; *The Chronicle of Calais*, pp. 2–3; Pollard, *Cont. Sources*, I, 92; Fisher, *Pol. Hist.*, p. 45; Wernham, *Before the Armada*, pp. 36–7.

28. Mackie, *The Earlier Tudors*, pp. 108–9; Storey, *The Reign of Henry VII*, p. 80. At this time the exchange rate was 1 franc = 2s. In addition it should be noted that one gold crown was officially the equivalent of 1.75 francs.

29. Pollard, *Cont. Sources*, I, 93; Mackie, *The Earlier Tudors*, p. 109.

30. Dietz, *English Government Finance*, p. 57; Lockyer, *Henry VII*, p. 55, note.

CHAPTER VI

1. Vergil, *Anglica Historia*, p. 65; Bacon, *Henry VII*, p. 107.

2. Halliwell-Phillipps, ed., *Letters of the Kings of England*, I, 172–3.

3. *Hall's Chronicle*, p. 465.

4. Pollard, *Cont. Sources*, I, 98; Fisher, *Pol. Hist.*, p. 53.

5. Conway, *Henry VII's Relations with Scotland and Ireland*, p. 40.

6. Pollard, *Cont. Sources*, I, 95–6.

7. Gairdner, "The Story of Perkin Warbeck," pp. 280–3; Fisher, *Pol. Hist.*, p. 53.

8. Elton, *England under the Tudors*, p. 27.

9. For the trial and execution of Stanley, see Pollard, *Cont. Sources*, I, 100–3; C. L. Kingsford, *Chronicles of London* (Oxford, 1905), pp. 204–5; Ralph Flenley, ed., *Six Town Chronicles of England* (Oxford, 1911), pp. 164–6; Raphael Holinshed, *Chronicles of England, Scotland, and Ireland*, 6 vols., ed. Sir Henry Ellis (London, 1806), III, 509; Bacon, *Henry VII*, p. 126; W. A. J. Archbold, "Sir William Stanley and Perkin Warbeck," *E.H.R.*, XIV (1899), pp. 529–30.

10. *Cal. Carew MSS.*, V, 190; Pollard, *Cont. Sources*, III, 264–5; Busch, *England under the Tudors*, p. 97. For a good account of the squabbles in Ireland in 1492–3, see Bryan, *Life of Kildare*, pp. 165–70, and Lydon, *Ireland in the Later Middle Ages*, pp. 170–2.

11. Conway, *Henry VII's Relations with Scotland and Ireland*, p. 137. See also Otway-Ruthven, *History of Medieval Ireland*, p. 408; Curtis, *History of Medieval Ireland*, pp. 400–1; Lydon, *Ireland in the Later Middle Ages*, pp. 173–8.

12. Conway, *Henry VII's Relations with Scotland and Ireland*, pp. 118–43; Chrimes, *Henry VII*, pp. 264–8.

13. Gairdner, ed., *Memorials of King Henry VII*, pp. 393–9; Tucker, *Life of Surrey*, pp. 65–6.

14. Pollard, *Cont. Sources*, I, 103–7; Bacon, *Henry VII*, p. 130.

15. Pollard, *Cont. Sources*, III, 278–9; Bagwell, *Ireland under the Tudors*, I, 113; Curtis, *History of Medieval Ireland*, p. 404; Gairdner, "The Story of Perkin Warbeck," p. 298.

16. *Ibid.*, p. 301.

17. *Statutes of the Realm*, II, 568; Elton, *The Tudor Constitution*, pp. 2, 4–5; Pickthorn, *Early Tudor Government*, pp. 151-6; A. F. Pollard, "The 'de facto' act of Henry VII," *B.I.H.R.*, VII (1929–30), pp. 1–12.

18. Wernham, *Before the Armada*, p. 68.

19. Tucker, *Life of Surrey*, p. 66; Gairdner, "The Story of Perkin Warbeck," pp. 302–5.

20. *Ibid.*, p. 305; Pollard, *Cont. Sources*, I, 143, 150–5; Kingsford, *Chronicles of London*, p. 210; Sir Henry Ellis, ed., *Original Letters, illustrative of English History*, 3 series, 11 vols. (London, 1824–46), 1st series, I, 25–31.

21. Fisher, *Pol. Hist.*, pp. 68–9; Harris, "Aids, Loans, and Benevolences," p. 15.

22. *Statutes of the Realm*, II, 642–7; Pollard, *Cont. Sources*, II, 27–39; Dietz, *English Government Finance*, p. 58; Chrimes, *Henry VII*, p. 197.

23. Mackie, *The Earlier Tudors*, p. 141; Rowse, *Tudor Cornwall*, pp. 121–7.

24. Pollard, *Cont. Sources*, I, 149–50; Powell and Wallis, *The House of Lords in the Middle Ages*, p. 538.

25. Pollard, *Cont. Sources*, I, 178–9; *Tudor Proclamations*, i, 39–40; Ellis, ed., *Original Letters*, 1st series, I, 38–9; Shaw, ed., *The Knights of England*, II, 28–30; Fisher, *Pol. Hist.*, p. 75; Dietz, *English Government Finance*, p. 58.

26. See below, pp. 158–9.

27. Bagwell, *Ireland under the Tudors*, I, 115–16; Gairdner, "The Story of Perkin Warbeck," pp. 317–26.

28. Pollard, *Cont. Sources*, I, 169–71; Ellis, ed., *Original Letters*, 1st series, I, 34–5; Rowse, *Tudor Cornwall*, pp. 129–32.

29. Pollard, *Cont. Sources*, I, 176–7, 180–6; Gairdner, "The Story of Perkin Warbeck," p. 328.

30. Warbeck's ultimate fate will be discussed in Chapter X below.

31. Dietz, *English Government Finance*, pp. 58, 78–9; Pickthorn, *Early Tudor Government*, p. 23; Mackie, *The Earlier Tudors*, p. 217; Storey, *The Reign of Henry VII*, p. 109; Rowse, *Tudor Cornwall*, p. 317.

32. *Cal. S. P. Milan*, I, 324.

33. *Cal. S. P. Spain*, I, 210, 239.

34. *Cal. S. P. Milan*, I, 341.

35. *Cal. Carew MSS.*, V, 180; Lydon, *Ireland in the Later Middle Ages*, pp. 171, 174–5.

36. Bryan, *Life of Kildare*, pp. 10, 91, 183–4, 210, 216.

37. *Ibid.*, pp. 233–4; *Cal. Close Rolls, 1500–9*, p. 89. See also Lydon, *Ireland in the Later Middle Ages*, pp. 178–80.

38. In 1509 Henry VII left no more than seven ships to his son, who by 1512 had expanded the fleet to twenty-four vessels. For an analysis of the cost of Henry's Irish policy between 1491 and 1496, see Lydon, *Ireland in the Later Middle Ages*, pp. 176–7. It is interesting to note that historians who criticize Henry VII for not attempting a bolder course in Ireland invariabley follow Bacon in believing that he had sufficient resources for a more ambitious policy. Professor Elton, for example, contends that "Henry died possessed of a treasure worth between one and two millions" (*England under the Tudors*, p. 53; for his criticisms of Henry's Irish policy, *ibid.*, pp. 32–3), which, if correct, would suggest that the king ought to have attempted more fundamental reforms in Ireland. However, recent studies by B. P. Wolffe and others have convincingly shown that Henry left no more than £250,000 or £300,000 to his successor, which meant that he had no option but to pursue a moderate course in Ireland.

CHAPTER VII

1. At this time the principality of Wales consisted of the four shires of Caernarvon, Merioneth, Flint, and Anglesey in the north, along with the crown lands of Cardigan and Carmarthen in the south.

2. In January 1489 Henry merged the Earldom of March with the other lands of the royal demesne; and from 2 February all grants relating to the earldom's estates had to pass the Great Seal of England.

3. Chrimes, *Henry VII*, pp. 163, 248; T. B. Pugh, " 'The Indenture for the Marches' between Henry VII and Edward Stafford (1477–1521), Duke of Buckingham," *E. H. R.*, LXXI (1956), pp. 436, 438–9; C. A. J. Skeel, "Wales under Henry VII," in *Tudor Studies*, p. 3.

4. *Ibid.*, pp. 10–11; A. L. Rowse, *The Expansion of Elizabethan England* (London, 1962), pp. 48–9. For the career of David Cecil after 1485, see Rowse, "Alltyrynys and the Cecils," *E. H. R.*, LXXV (1960), pp. 58, 60–1.

5. Edward Foss, *The Judges of England, vol. V, 1485–1603* (London, 1857), pp. 5–6.

6. For an informed discussion of the Yorkist council, see C. A. J. Skeel, *The Council in the Marches of Wales* (London, 1904), pp. 19–28.

7. *Ibid.*, p. 29; *Eng. Hist. Doc., 1485–1558*, p. 552; Chrimes, ed., *Fifteenth-Century England*, p. 164.

8. R. Stewart-Brown, "The Cheshire Writs of Quo Warranto in 1499," *E. H. R.*, XLIX (1934), p. 678.

9. Pickthorn, *Early Tudor Government*, pp. 35–6. See also Skeel, *The Council in the Marches of Wales*, p. 31, and Storey, *The Reign of Henry VII*, p. 147.

10. *Eng. Hist. Doc., 1485–1558*, p. 553; Skeel, *The Council in the Marches of Wales*, p. 29; J. B. Smith, "Crown and Community in the Principality of North Wales in the Reign of Henry Tudor," *W. H. R.*, III (1966), pp. 167–8.

11. Elton, *The Tudor Constitution*, pp. 200–1; Reid, *The King's Council in the North* (London, 1921), pp. 504–5; Jacob, *The Fifteenth Century*, pp. 637–9; Loades, *Politics and the Nation*, p. 92.

12. Lockyer, *Henry VII*, p. 44.

13. Bindoff, *Tudor England*, p. 58.

14. *Ibid.*, p. 56.

15. For a good discussion of the 1487 act, see Holdsworth, *History of English Law*, IV, 527. The text of the act is available in *Statutes of the Realm*, II, 512, and in *Eng. Hist. Doc., 1485–1558*, p. 613.

16. *Statutes of the Realm*, II, 536–8; Elton, *The Tudor Constitution*, pp. 426–33; Pickthorn, *Early Tudor Government*, p. 63.

17. For the material related in this paragraph, see Bayne and Dunham, eds., *Select Cases in the Council of Henry VII*, p. cxxx; Bradford, *Proceedings in the Court of Star Chamber*, p. 24; Storey, *The Reign of Henry VII*, pp. 128, 136–7.

18. Pickthorn, *Early Tudor Government*, p. 66; Lockyer, *Henry VII*, pp. 60–1.

19. Chrimes, *Henry VII*, p. 171.

20. Elton, *England under the Tudors*, p. 60; Storey, *The Reign of Henry VII*, p. 139; Loades, *Politics and the Nation*, p. 123.

21. Sneyd, ed., *A Relation, or rather a true Account of the Island of England*, pp. 33–4.

22. Holdsworth, *History of English Law*, IV, 504. See also E. W. Ives, "Patronage at the Court of Henry VII: The Case of Sir Ralph Egerton of Ridley," *B. J. R. L.*, LII (1970), pp. 348–9.

23. For the act of 1495, which directed local officials to hold vagabonds and idlers in the public stocks for three days and three nights, see J. R. Tanner, *Tudor Constitutional Documents, A. D. 1485–1603*, 2nd ed. (Cambridge, 1922), pp. 473–4.

24. F. J. Fisher, "Commercial Trends and Policy in Sixteenth-Century England," *Ec.H.R.*, X (1940).

25. *Eng. Hist. Doc., 1485–1558*, p. 926; Fisher, *Pol. Hist.*, pp. 102–3; Chrimes, *Henry VII*, p. 223.

26. The 1468 act seemingly prohibited the use of all liveries and badges as well as the retention of all non-household servants by oath, promise, or indenture. However, because the act permitted a lord to employ advisers in a legal capacity or for "lawful service done or to be done," it had virtually no effect. At any rate, Edward IV tacitly accepted the continuation of the practice of retaining. On this, see Ross, *Edward IV*, p. 412, and Dunham, *Lord Hastings' Indentured Retainers*, pp. 73–7.

27. Reid, *The King's Council in the North*, p. 20; Hooker, "Notes on the Organization of the Tudor Military," pp. 22–3.

28. Russell, *The Crisis of Parliaments*, pp. 163–4; Hill, *Economic Problems of the Church*, p. 40.

29. By an act passed in 1487, private individuals were forbidden to retain any of the king's

tenants, while any such royal tenant who agreed to be retained would forfeit his tenement and any other emoluments. Two acts passed in 1495 declared that all Englishmen, regardless of social status, owed their allegiance primarily to the king, whom they were to assist in any way they could during wartime. Any man who failed to do so would lose any fees that he held. Furthermore the power of the J. P.s to enforce earlier statutes against retaining was strengthened. The fourth statute against retaining, which was enacted in 1504, will be discussed below.

30. Dunham, *Lord Hastings' Indentured Retainers*, pp. 84–6, 93, 105.

31. The text of the Statute of Liveries is available in *Statutes of the Realm*, II, 568–70; *Eng. Hist. Doc., 1485–1558*, p. 534; and Elton, *The Tudor Constitution*, pp. 34–7. For a discussion of the statute, see Dunham, *Lord Hastings' Indentured Retainers*, pp. 93–6; Elton, *England under the Tudors*, pp. 58–9; Chrimes, *Henry VII*, pp. 189–90; and Storey, *The Reign of Henry VII*, pp. 155–6.

32. For Henry's troubles with the Earl of Suffolk, see Chapter X below.

33. Storey, *The Reign of Henry VII*, p. 156; Dunham, *Lord Hastings' Indentured Retainers*, pp. 103, 105; Lander, "Bonds, Coercion, and Fear," p. 345.

34. Dunham, *Lord Hastings' Indentured Retainers*, pp. 100, 108.

35. Bacon, *Henry VII*, p. 69.

36. H. L. Gray, *The Influence of the Commons on Early Legislation* (Cambridge, Mass., 1932), p. 143.

37. Blackstone's opinion of Henry's legislation is discussed by William Stubbs in *Seventeen Lectures on the Study of Medieval and Modern History* (London, 1886), p. 365.

38. Storey, *The Reign of Henry VII*, pp. 131, 150–1.

39. Sneyd, ed., *A Relation, or rather a true Account of the Island of England*, p. 37.

40. On Henry's enforcement of the law, see the comments made by A. F. Pollard in *Cont. Sources*, I, xxxvii.

41. S. E. Lehmberg, *The Reformation Parliament 1529–36* (Cambridge, 1970), p. 243.

42. Gray, *The Influence of the Commons on Early Legislation*, p. 416. See also Pickthorn, *Early Tudor Government*, p. 124; G. O. Sayles, *The King's Parliament of England* (New York, 1974), p. 134; Helen Cam, "The Legislators of Medieval England," in *Historical Studies of the English Parliament*, vol. I (Cambridge, 1970), p. 183.

43. G. R. Elton, "State Planning in Early Tudor England," *Ec.H.R.*, 2nd series, XIII (1961), pp. 434, 436–7.

44. Although Professor Chrimes maintains that the seven parliaments of the reign sat for a total of seventy-two weeks, the view of R. L. Storey that they sat for only fifty-nine seems to be closer to the mark.

45. John Alcock, Bishop of Worcester, presided over the upper House in 1485–6, whereas Archbishop Morton officiated in 1487, 1489–90, 1491, 1495, and 1497. Henry Deane, who held the Great Seal in 1501–2, never had occasion to preside; while Deane's successor, Archbishop Warham, officiated only in 1504.

46. Edward IV's payments to his Speakers had actually varied between 200 marks and £200.

47. For a discussion of the talents and qualifications of Henry VII's Speakers, see J. S. Roskell, *The Commons and their Speakers in English Parliaments 1376–1523* (Manchester, 1965), pp. 298–307.

48. According to Professor Neale, Elizabeth I vetoed six bills in 1563, seven in 1576, one in 1581, nine in 1585, one in 1593, and twelve in 1597. See Neale, *The Elizabethan House of Commons* (London, 1949), pp. 410–11.

49. Mackie, *The Earlier Tudors*, p. 200. See also Pollard, *Cont. Sources*, I, xxxii–xxxiv; and S. B. Chrimes, *English Constitutional Ideas in the Fifteenth Century* (Cambridge, 1936), pp. 221–5.

50. Pickthorn, *Early Tudor Government*, pp. 92, 95.

51. May McKisack, *The Parliamentary Representation of the English Boroughs during the Middle Ages* (Oxford, 1932), pp. 64–5 and passim; Lehmberg, *The Reformation Parliament*, pp. 19, 25; Neale, *The Elizabethan House of Commons*, p. 290 and passim.

52. Josiah Wedgwood and A. D. Holt, *History of Parliament: Biographies of the Members of the Commons House 1439–1509*, 2 vols. (London, 1936–8), I, 285.

53. The parliamentary crisis of 1504 will be discussed in Chapter XI below.

CHAPTER VIII

1. Michael Oppenheim, ed., *Naval Accounts and Inventories of the Reign of Henry VII* (London, 1896), p. ix; C. F. Richmond, "English Naval Power in the Fifteenth Century," *History*, LII (1967), p. 11.

2. Michael Oppenheim, *A History of the Administration of the Royal Navy* (hereafter cited as *Administration of the Navy*) (London, 1896), p. 36; Oppenheim, ed., *Naval Accounts and Inventories*, pp. xxii, xxiv; C. S. Goldingham, "The Navy under Henry VII," *E.H.R.*, XXXIII (1918), pp. 474, 477.

3. Oppenheim, ed., *Naval Accounts and Inventories*, pp. xv-xvi.

4. *Ibid.*, pp. xvii-xviii; Goldingham, "The Navy under Henry VII," p. 478.

5. Oppenheim, ed., *Naval Accounts and Inventories*, pp. xxx-xxxii, xxxiv; Oppenheim, *Administration of the Navy*, p. 40.

6. *Ibid.*, pp. 39–40; Oppenheim, ed., *Naval Accounts and Inventories*, pp. xxxvi-xxxvii; Goldingham, "The Navy under Henry VII," pp. 480–1.

7. *Ibid.*, p. 487.

8. *Ibid.*, p. 474; Oppenheim, ed., *Naval Accounts and Inventories*, pp. xxvii, li.

9. Goldingham, "The Navy under Henry VII," p. 484.

10. Oppenheim, *Administration of the Navy*, p. 41.

11. Oppenheim, ed., *Naval Accounts and Inventories*, p. xxiv.

12. Goldingham, "The Navy under Henry VII," pp. 486, 488.

13. Michael Lewis, *The Navy of Britain* (London, 1949), pp. 37–8.

14. *Ibid.*, p. 38.

15. Scofield, *The Life and Reign of Edward IV*, II, 416; Ross, *Edward IV*, p. 352; Goldingham, "The Navy under Henry VII," p. 475.

16. Oppenheim, *Administration of the Navy*, p. 38.

17. Oppenheim, ed., *Naval Accounts and Inventories*, p. xxvii; Chrimes, *Henry VII*, p. 227; Goldingham, "The Navy under Henry VII," p. 475.

18. J. A. Williamson, *The Cabot Voyages and Bristol Discovery under Henry VII* (Cambridge, 1962), p. 7.

19. For the movements of Bartholomew Columbus, *ibid.*, p. 17; Pollard, *Cont. Sources*, II, 325–7; D. B. Quinn, *England and the Discovery of America, 1481–1620* (New York, 1974), pp. 75–7, 79–80.

20. Elton, *England under the Tudors*, p. 331.

21. Vergil, *Anglica Historia*, p. 117.

22. For the early life of John Cabot, see H. P. Biggar, ed., *The Precursors of Jacques Cartier, 1497–1534: A Collection of Documents* (Ottawa, 1911), p. vii; S. E. Morison, *The European Discovery of America: The Northern Voyages* (New York, 1971), pp. 158–60; Quinn, *England and the Discovery of America*, pp. 133–6; L. A. Vigneras, "The Cape Breton Landfall: 1494 or 1497," *C.H.R.*, XXXVIII (1957), pp. 219, 221, 225, 227.

23. For Cabot's geographical ideas, see Williamson, *The Cabot Voyages*, pp. 41–2, 47.

24. Rymer, *Foedera*, XII, 595; Pollard, *Cont. Sources*, II, 329–31; Biggar, ed., *Precursors of Cartier*, pp. 6–10; Morison, *The European Discovery of America*, p. xi.

25. Quoted in Williamson, *The Cabot Voyages*, p. 203. See also Gordon Connell-Smith, *Forerunners of Drake: A Study of English Trade with Spain in the Early Tudor Period* (London, 1954), p. 48.

26. According to a letter written shortly after this time, Cabot "went with one ship, his crew confused him, he was short of supplies and ran into bad weather, and he decided to turn back." See Vigneras, "The Cape Breton Landfall," p. 228.

27. Morison, *The European Discovery of America*, p. 167.

28. For the conflicting views of these three scholars as to the exact place Cabot sighted land, see Quinn, *England and the Discovery of America*, pp. 94–5, 100; Morison, *The European Discovery of America*, pp. 177–9; Williamson, *The Cabot Voyages*, pp. 63, 71–2, 83.

29. For detailed accounts of the voyage of 1497, see Morison, *The European Discovery of America*, pp. 167–72; Quinn, *England and the Discovery of America*, pp. 93–6; Williamson, *The Cabot Voyages*, pp. 55–65; J. T. Juricek, "John Cabot's First Voyage," *Smithsonian Journal of History*, II (1967–8), pp. 2–9.

30. Samuel Bentley, ed., *Excerpta Historica*, 2nd ed. (London, 1833), p. 113; Williamson, *The Cabot Voyages*, pp. 87–8; Morison, *The European Discovery of America*, p. 186.

31. Pollard, *Cont. Sources*, II, 333–6; Quinn, *England and the Discovery of America*, p. 137; Biggar, ed., *Precursors of Cartier*, p. 14.

32. *Ibid.*, pp. 14, 16.

33. *Ibid.*, pp. 22–4; Morison, *The European Discovery of America*, p. 190; Williamson, *The Cabot Voyages*, p. 91. According to Williamson, Cabot actually rented shipping for only 3d. a ton per month.

34. Morison, *The European Discovery of America*, p. 191.

35. *Ibid.*; Pollard, *Cont. Sources*, II, 345; Williamson, *The Cabot Voyages*, pp. 93–4; Boies Penrose, *Travel and Discovery in the Renaissance 1420–1620* (Cambridge, Mass., 1952), p. 146.

36. Pollard, *Cont. Sources*, II, 344–5.

37. Williamson, *The Cabot Voyages*, p. 107.

38. Biggar, ed., *Precursors of Cartier*, p. xiii; Penrose, *Travel and Discovery in the Renaissance*, p. 144.

39. Williamson, *The Cabot Voyages*, p. 109.

40. Vergil, *Anglica Historia*, p. 117.

41. Williamson, *The Cabot Voyages*, p. 116. In a papal bull of 1493, Alexander VI recognized the predominant interest of Spain and Portugal in trans-Atlantic exploration. This bull led to the treaty of Tordesillas of 7 June 1494, by which the two countries divided the Atlantic into two zones along a meridian 370 leagues west of the Cape Verde Islands. Portugal was to have an exclusive right to all lands discovered within the eastern zone, whereas Spain was to have ownership over all lands within the western one.

42. For a good account of João Fernandes's activities prior to 1501, see Morison, *The European Discovery of America*, pp. 211–13.

43. For the grant of 19 March 1501, see Biggar, ed., *Precursors of Cartier*, pp. 50–8.

44. Morison, *The European Discovery of America*, p. 218.

45. Pollard, *Cont. Sources*, II, 345; Quinn, *England and the Discovery of America*, p. 117.

46. *Ibid.*, pp. 117–18. See also Morison, *The European Discovery of America*, p. 218.

47. *Ibid.*, p. 219; Pollard, *Cont. Sources*, II, 345.

48. *Ibid.*, p. 347; Morison, *The European Discovery of America*, p. 219.

49. Pollard, *Cont. Sources*, II, 346–7; Biggar, ed., *Precursors of Cartier*, pp. 81–91; Williamson, *The Cabot Voyages*, pp. 132–3; Quinn, *England and the Discovery of America*, pp. 121–3.

50. Pollard, *Cont. Sources*, II, 345.

51. *Ibid.*, pp. 345–6; Quinn, *England and the Discovery of America*, pp. 123–6.

52. A. P. Newton, "An Early Grant to Sebastian Cabot," *E.H.R.*, XXXVII (1922), p. 565.

53. Williamson, *The Cabot Voyages*, p. 162. See also Pollard, *Cont. Sources*, II, 342, and Morison, *The European Discovery of America*, pp. 220–1. For a dissenting view, see Quinn, *England and the Discovery of America*, p. 129.

54. Pollard, *Cont. Sources*, II, 342; Morison, *The European Discovery of America*, p. 220.

55. Williamson, *The Cabot Voyages*, pp. 166, 170.

56. Pollard, *Cont. Sources*, II, 342; Penrose, *Travel and Discovery in the Renaissance*, p. 146; Quinn, *England and the Discovery of America*, p. 140.

57. *Ibid.*, p. 233; Williamson, *The Cabot Voyages*, p. 170.

58. *Ibid.*, pp. 146–7, 150; Quinn, *England and the Discovery of America*, pp. 144–50.

59. S. E. Morison, *The Oxford History of the American People* (New York, 1965), p. 42.

60. Quinn, *England and the Discovery of America*, p. 194.

CHAPTER IX

1. *Cal. S. P. Milan*, I, 323; A. L. Rowse, *The Elizabethan Renaissance* (London, 1971), p. 11.

2. Pollard, *Cont. Sources*, III, 156; Jacob, *Essays in Later Medieval History*, pp. 58–9; H. L. Gray, "Greek Visitors to England in 1455–1456," in *Anniversary Essays in Mediaeval History*, ed. C. H. Taylor (Boston, 1929), pp. 96, 98–9. For a detailed account of English contacts with Italy before 1485, see Weiss, *Humanism in England During the Fifteenth Century*, passim.

3. *Cal. Pat. Rolls, 1494–1509*, p. 154; Creighton, *Historical Essays and Reviews*, pp. 207–14; A. H. Thompson, *The English Clergy and Their Organization in the Later Middle Ages* (Oxford, 1947), p. 26; Lewis Einstein, *The Italian Renaissance in England* (New York, 1902), p. 183.

4. Hay, *Polydore Vergil*, pp. 2–3.

5. Mattingly, *Renaissance Diplomacy*, pp. 137–8.

6. *Cal. S. P. Spain*, I, 178.

7. William Nelson, *John Skelton, Laureate* (New York, 1964), p. 37.

8. *Ibid.*, pp. 12–13, 20–1; Campbell, *Materials*, I, 38; Weiss, *Humanism in England During the Fifteenth Century*, pp. 171–2; N. S. Aurner, *Caxton: Mirrour of Fifteenth-Century Letters* (New York, 1965), p. 43; Creighton, *Historical Essays and Reviews*, pp. 204–5; McElroy, "Literary Patronage," pp. 224–5.

9. Hay, *Polydore Vergil*, pp. 2–9, 81, 136, 138; Denys Hay, "The Historiographers Royal in England and Scotland," *S.H.R.*, XXX (1951), pp. 17–18; *Eng. Hist. Doc., 1485–1558*, pp. 88–9, 97; F. J. Levy, *Tudor Historical Thought* (San Marino, Cal., 1967), pp. 53–67; May McKisack, *Medieval History in the Tudor Age* (Oxford, 1971), pp. 98–103; A. B. Ferguson, "Circumstances and the Sense of History in Tudor England," in *Medieval and Renaissance Studies*, ed. J. M. Headley (Chapel Hill, N. C., 1968), pp. 177, 188.

10. Campbell, *Materials*, II, 305; Gairdner, ed., *Memorials of King Henry VII*, pp. ix-xiii; Rymer, *Foedera*, V, Part IV, 109; Nelson, *John Skelton*, p. 24; H. L. R. Edwards, *Skelton: The Life and Times of an Early Tudor Poet* (Freeport, N. Y., 1971), pp. 40–1; McElroy, "Literary Patronage," pp. 299, 304, 321.

11. *Ibid.*, pp. 304, 316–17; Nelson, *John Skelton*, pp. 28, 37.

12. Gairdner, ed., *Memorials of King Henry VII*, p. xi; McElroy, "Literary Patronage," pp. 228, 324.

13. C. S. Lewis, *Studies in Medieval and Renaissance Literature* (Cambridge, 1966), pp. 130–1.

14. C. S. Lewis, *English Literature in the Sixteenth Century, Excluding Drama* (Oxford, 1944), pp. 128–9.

15. *Ibid.*, p. 133.

16. Nan Cooke Carpenter, *John Skelton* (New York, 1967), pp. 16, 40–1; Nelson, *John Skelton*, pp. 44, 54.

17. Chambers, *English Literature at the Close of the Middle Ages*, p. 107. See also Lewis, *English Literature in the Sixteenth Century*, p. 134.

18. *Ibid.*, pp. 127, 133; Craig, *The Literature of the English Renaissance*, p. 27; Carpenter, *John Skelton*, p. 36.

19. *Ibid.*, p. 20.

20. *Ibid.*; Lewis, *English Literature in the Sixteenth Century*, p. 134; Albert C. Baugh, ed., *A Literary History of England*, 2nd ed. (New York, 1967), pp. 347–8.

21. Carpenter, *John Skelton*, pp. 22–3, 31, 35; Lewis, *English Literature in the Sixteenth Century*, p. 133, and note.

22. *Ibid.*, p. 135.

23. *Ibid.*, p. 138; John M. Berdan, *Early Tudor Poetry 1485–1547* (New York, 1920), pp. 314–15.

24. F. M. Nichols, ed., *The Epistles of Erasmus*, 3 vols. (New York, 1962), I, 389.

25. J. J. Scarisbrick, *Henry VIII* (Berkeley, 1968), p. 516.

26. *Ibid.* According to Professor Scarisbrick, Henry VIII "presided over a Court in many ways less open, less cosmopolitan and interesting than his father's."

27. Vergil, *Anglica Historia*, pp. 127, 129, 133, 143, 146–7.

28. *Cal. S. P. Milan*, I, 329; Pollard, *Cont. Sources*, I, 179, 203.

29. Garrett Mattingly, "The Reputation of Dr. Puebla," *E.H.R.*, LV (1940), p. 43.

30. Only a month after Henry VII's death, Lord Mountjoy wrote to inform Erasmus that, "The heavens laugh, the earth exults, all things are full of milk, of honey, of nectar! Avarice is expelled the country. Liberality scatters wealth with a bounteous hand. Our [new] King does not desire gold or precious metals, but virtue, glory, immortality." See Nichols, ed., *The Epistles of Erasmus*, I, 457. This letter is generally interpreted as an indictment of the last years of Henry VII, whereas it can just as easily be seen as evidence of the excessive generosity of his young successor. Furthermore, it should be remembered that between 1500 and 1509, Lord Mountjoy had had to sign more recognizances than any other English peer, which easily explains why he was so delighted by the death of a ruler who had forced him into such financial thralldom.

31. Bacon, *Henry VII*, pp. 20, 211.

32. Vergil, *Anglica Historia*, p. 7.

33. Pollard, *Cont. Sources*, I, 217–18.

34. McElroy, "Literary Patronage," pp. 99, 334–5, 339, 341, 343, 350.

35. *Cal. Pat. Rolls, 1494–1509*, p. 79; *Cambridge History of English Literature*, IV, 257; Kenneth Charlton, *Education in Renaissance England* (Toronto, 1965), pp. 141–2.

36. *Cal. Pat. Rolls, 1494–1509*, pp. 433, 519. For a license of 11 November 1507, by which Lady Margaret was allowed to settle additional lands on Christ's College, *ibid.*, p. 552. In addition, see McElroy, "Literary Patronage," p. 250, and J. B. Mullinger, *The University of Cambridge: From the Earliest Times to the Injunctions of 1535* (Cambridge, 1873), pp. 449–51. For the foundation of Jesus College, see John Steegman, *Cambridge* (New York, 1941), pp. 11–12, 62.

37. Mullinger, *The University of Cambridge*, p. 452; McElroy, "Literary Patronage," pp. 252–3.

38. *Ibid.*, p. 357; Antonia MacLean, *Humanism and the Rise of Science in Tudor England* (New York, 1972), p. 44.

39. H. S. Bennett, *English Books & Readers 1475 to 1557* (Cambridge, 1952), pp. 11–12; H. R. Plomer, *A Short History of English Printing, 1468–1898* (London, 1900), p. 7; E. G. Duff, *The Printers, Stationers and Bookbinders of Westminster and London from 1476 to 1535* (Cambridge, 1906), p. 6; Aurner, *Caxton*, pp. 54–6, 59–61; Markham, *Richard III*, pp. 161–2; MacGibbon, *Elizabeth Woodville*, pp. 207–8; Scofield, *The Life and Reign of Edward IV*, II, 456–7; Margaret Kekewich, "Edward IV, William Caxton, and Literary Patronage in Yorkist England," *Modern Language Review*, XLVI (1971), p. 487.

40. *Ibid.;* Baugh, ed., *A Literary History of England*, p. 184; Weiss, *Humanism in England During the Fifteenth Century*, p. 175; Neville Williams, *The Life and Times of Henry VII* (London, 1973), pp. 112; Blake, *Caxton and His World*, pp. 194–5; 212–14; Duff, *Printers, Stationers and Bookbinders*, p. 36.

41. *Ibid.*, pp. 11, 41; Plomer, *A Short History of English Printing*, pp. 23–6, 34; Bennett, *English Books & Readers*, p. 181; D. C. McMurtrie, *The Book: The Story of Printing and Bookmaking*, 3rd ed. (New York, 1943), p. 224; Mallet, *A History of the University of Oxford*, I, 328; Blake, *Caxton and His World*, pp. 211–12.

42. McElroy, "Literary Patronage," pp. 250, 342; *Cambridge History of English Literature*, IV, 259. Before the publication of Fisher's sermons in 1508, English preachers were expected to have their sermons memorized and rarely spoke from a text of any kind. Thus Lady Margaret Beaufort "helped to establish the custom of committing sermons to print." *Ibid.*

43. James Moran, *Wynkyn de Worde: Father of Fleet Street* (London, 1960), pp. 8, 17–18, 23, 32; Blake, *Caxton and His World*, p. 175; Plomer, *A Short History of English Printing*, pp. 21, 23, 35, 37; Bennett, *English Books & Readers*, pp. 188, 190.

44. *Ibid.*, pp. 82–3; Moran, *Wynkyn de Worde*, pp. 32, 41; McElroy, "Literary Patronage," pp. 294, 351.

45. F. S. Siebert, *Freedom of the Press in England, 1476–1776* (Urbana, Ill., 1952; repr. 1965), p. 32.

46. It is important to note that printing spread much more slowly in England during the second half of the fifteenth century than it did on the continent. Whereas there were only eight printshops in all of England—of which five were located in London—in 1500, Italy had seventy-three printing presses on that date, Germany had fifty-one, Spain twenty-four, the Low Countries fifteen, and Switzerland eight. English printers were also slower than their European counterparts in publishing truly scholarly works, and particularly critical editions of ancient Greek writings. Not until 1543 was an ancient Greek treatise published in England, whereas such works had been printed at Milan from 1476 and at Paris from 1507. See Myron P. Gilmore, *The World of Humanism* (New York, 1952), p. 188; MacLean, *Humanism and the Rise of Science*, p. 14; Joan Simon, *Education and Society in Tudor England* (Cambridge, 1967), p. 58.

47. Campbell, *Materials*, I, 211; McElroy, "Literary Patronage," pp. 290–2, 303; Siebert, *Freedom of the Press in England*, p. 32.

48. McElroy, "Literary Patronage," pp. 290–2, 303; H. R. Plomer, "Bibliographical Notes from the Privy Purse Expenses of King Henry the Seventh," *The Library*, 3rd series, IV (1913), p. 296.

49. *Ibid.*, pp. 297–9.

50. *Cambridge History of English Literature*, V, Part I, 103; Stevens, *Music & Poetry in the Early Tudor Court*, pp. 240, 270, 283, 299, 301, 314.

51. *Ibid.*, pp. 236, 239–40, 242, 244.

52. *Ibid.*, pp. 251, 297; Pattison, *Music and Poetry of the English Renaissance*, p. 50.

53. Pollard, *Cont. Sources*, II, 226–7; Stevens, *Music & Poetry in the Early Tudor Court*, pp. 246, 248.

54. Frederick S. Boas, *An Introduction to Tudor Drama* (Oxford, 1933), pp. 74–5.

CHAPTER X

1. For the material in this and the succeeding paragraph, see Wernham, *Before the Armada*, p. 69; Lockyer, *Henry VII*, p. 70; Mackie, *The Earlier Tudors*, pp. 149, 181–2.

2. *Ibid.*, p. 182; Pollard, *Cont. Sources*, I, 215; *The Chronicle of Calais*, pp. 3–4; Scarisbrick, *Henry VIII*, pp. 77–9.

3. *L. & P.*, I, xxxvii; *Rot. Parl.*, VI, 474–7; Powell and Wallis, *The House of Lords in the*

Middle Ages, p. 535; Busch, *England under the Tudors*, pp. 165–6; Fisher, *Pol. Hist.*, p. 88; Lander, "Bonds, Coercion, and Fear," p. 334.

4. *Cal. S. P. Spain*, I, 129–31, 143; Pollard, *Cont. Sources*, I, 206–8; Mackie, *The Earlier Tudors*, pp. 148–9; Fisher, *Pol. Hist.*, pp. 81–2.

5. *Cal. S. P. Spain*, I, 206; Pollard, *Cont. Sources*, I, 204–5; Bacon, *Henry VII*, p. 217; Plomer, "Bibliographical Notes from the Privy Purse Expenses of King Henry the Seventh," p. 301.

6. *Cal. S. P. Spain*, I, 213; Pollard, *Cont. Sources*, I, 211–13; Thomas Stapleton, ed., *Plumpton Correspondence* (Camden Society, 1839), pp. 141–3; C. L. Kingsford, *Chronicles of London* (Oxford, 1905), pp. 227–8; Powell and Wallis, *The House of Lords in the Middle Ages*, p. 539; Gairdner, "The Story of Perkin Warbeck," pp. 332–4.

7. Mackie, *The Earlier Tudors*, pp. 149, 172; Mattingly, *Catherine of Aragon*, p. 21.

8. *Ibid.*, pp. 22, 29–30; *L. & P.*, I, 126–8; M. A. E. Green, ed., *Letters of Royal and Illustrious Ladies of Great Britain*, 3 vols. (London, 1846), II, 123.

9. Mattingly, *Catherine of Aragon*, pp. 30, 33–5.

10. *Ibid.*, pp. 36–7.

11. *L. & P.*, I, 404–17; Thomas, ed., *The Great Chronicle of London*, pp. 296–310; Kingsford, *Chronicles of London*, pp. 234–5, 239. For a detailed account of the pageantry at the time of Catherine's entry into London, see Anglo, *Spectacle, Pageantry, and Early Tudor Policy*, pp. 59–97.

12. Elizabeth F. Rogers, ed., *The Correspondence of Sir Thomas More* (Princeton, N. J., 1947), p. 3.

13. Shaw, ed., *The Knights of England*, I, 145–7; Mattingly, *Catherine of Aragon*, pp. 39–42; John Leland, *Collectanea de Rebus Britannicis*, 6 vols., ed. Thomas Hearne (London, 1770), V, 356–73.

14. Stevens, *Music & Poetry in the Early Tudor Court*, p. 237.

15. Boas, *An Introduction to Tudor Drama*, pp. 62–3.

16. *Ibid.*, p. 62.

17. *Cal. S. P. Spain*, I, 269.

18. Leland, *Collectanea*, V, 373–4.

19. *Ibid.*, pp. 374–81; Mattingly, *Catherine of Aragon*, p. 52.

20. *Ibid.*; Pollard, *Cont. Sources*, III, 60.

21. Only in regard to the Hansa did Henry attempt to profit from the misfortunes of others. During the 1490s he quarreled periodically with the Hansards, whose privileged status under the Treaty of Utrecht of 1474 he was determined to destroy. During a conference at Bruges in 1498–9, English and Hanseatic representatives labored in vain to settle the difficulties that had arisen during previous years. Angered by what he considered an unreasonable attitude on the League's part, Henry was quick to seize an opportunity in 1499 to profit from Hanseatic weakness. When the government of Riga severed its connections with the League, he promptly suggested a reciprocal trade treaty with it, hoping thereby to extend English commerce into the eastern Baltic and Gulf of Finland. The merchants of Riga were given full trading rights in England in return for similar concessions to English traders within the city-state and its hinterland. Yet before much commerce could develop, the Rigan government came to terms with the League and petitioned for readmittance, whereupon England's treaty with the city fathers lapsed. For a fuller account of these happenings, see Wernham, *Before the Armada*, pp. 73–4, and Mackie, *The Earlier Tudors*, p. 222.

22. Pollard, *Cont. Sources*, I, 213–32; Bentley, ed., *Excerpta Historica*, pp. 128, 130; Chrimes, *Henry VII*, pp. 285, 304; Simons, *Henry VII*, pp. 241, 243.

23. Gairdner, ed., *Memorials of King Henry VII*, pp. 223–39; *Cal. S. P. Spain*, I, 359–61; Mackie, *The Earlier Tudors*, p. 175; Mattingly, *Catherine of Aragon*, p. 60. Although most

historians are critical of Henry for inquiring so closely into the appearance and disposition of the widowed Queen of Naples, this was in fact the normal practice of the age. In November 1489, for example, the Duke of Milan sent detailed instructions to Francisco Paganus, one of his most trusted agents, who was about to depart for England. Paganus was directed to learn everything he could about one of the younger sisters of Elizabeth of York, to whom the duke was thinking of proposing. In particular, Paganus was to discover whether she had any "personal defect" and whether she was "fitted for the match, with satisfaction to our taste." On this, see *Cal. S. P. Milan*, I, 251–2.

24. *Cal. S. P. Spain*, I, 306–8; Mattingly, *Catherine of Aragon*, pp. 55–6, 58–9.

25. *Ibid.*, p. 62.

26. Mackie, *The Earlier Tudors*, pp. 157–8; Tucker, *Life of Surrey*, p. 86; Mackie, *King James IV*, pp. 92–3.

27. *Ibid.*, pp. 93–4.

28. *Ibid.*; Mackie, *The Earlier Tudors*, p. 158; Tucker, *Life of Surrey*, p. 86.

29. *Ibid.*; Wernham, *Before the Armada*, pp. 47–8; Mackie, *King James IV*, pp. 98–9.

30. *Ibid.*, p. 97; Mackie, *The Earlier Tudors*, pp. 159–60.

31. Mackie, *King James IV*, p. 97; H. W. Chapman, *The Thistle and the Rose: The Sisters of Henry VIII* (New York, 1972), pp. 32, 39.

32. Tucker, *Life of Surrey*, pp. 86–7; Mackie, *King James IV*, pp. 105–6.

33. Ellis, ed., *Original Letters*, 1st series, I, 41–3; Tucker, *Life of Surrey*, pp. 87–8; Simons, *Henry VII*, pp. 240–1.

34. For a good account of Anglo-Scottish relations during these years, see Mackie, *The Earlier Tudors*, pp. 162–4.

CHAPTER XI

1. Vergil, *Anglica Historia*, p. 145; Chrimes, *Henry VII*, p. 299.

2. Mullinger, *The University of Cambridge*, pp. 451–2.

3. Vergil, *Anglica Historia*, p. 147.

4. *Ibid.*, pp. 145, 147.

5. For materials pertaining to court ceremonies during the latter part of the reign, see Gairdner, ed., *Memorials of King Henry VII*, pp. 282–303; Pollard, *Cont. Sources*, I, 276, 279; Shaw, ed., *The Knights of England*, I, 147; Bryan, *Life of Kildare*, pp. 233–4; Hay, *Polydore Vergil*, p. 5.

6. *Cal. S. P. Spain*, I, 238.

7. *Correspondencia de Gutierre Gomez de Fuensalida* (Madrid, 1907), p. 449; quoted in Scarisbrick, *Henry VIII*, pp. 6–7.

8. *L. & P.*, I, 233; Pollard, *Cont. Sources*, I, 245; Elton, ed., *The Tudor Constitution*, p. 5.

9. *Cal. S. P. Spain*, II, 9.

10. Pollard, *Cont. Sources*, I, 222; Simons, *Henry VII*, p. 249.

11. *Ibid.*, pp. 249–50; Mackie, *The Earlier Tudors*, pp. 170–1.

12. Lander, *Conflict and Stability*, p. 99.

13. Pollard, *Cont. Sources*, II, 272–3; *Statutes of the Realm*, II, 665; Wernham, *Before the Armada*, p. 73.

14. William Roper, "The Life of Sir Thomas More," in *Two Early Tudor Lives*, ed. R. S. Sylvester and D. P. Harding (New Haven, 1962), p. 199; *Eng. Hist Doc.*, *1485–1558*, p. 597; Tanner, ed., *Tudor Constitutional Documents*, 2nd ed., pp. 600–1; *Statutes of the Realm*, II, 675; R. W. Chambers, *Thomas More* (London, 1935), p. 87.

15. Vergil, *Anglica Historia*, p. 127. For Elton's defense of Henry's actions during these years, see "Henry VII: Rapacity and Remorse," *H. J.*, I (1958), and "Henry VII: A

Restatement," *ibid.*, IV (1961). For a refutation of Elton's view, see J. P. Cooper, "Henry VII's Last Years Reconsidered," *ibid.*, II (1959), and C. J. Harrison, "The Petition of Edmund Dudley," *E.H.R.*, LXXXVII, No. 342 (1972).

16. Although motivated primarily by financial considerations, Henry's cancellation of the legal restrictions imposed on Wales during the Lancastrian period was nevertheless beneficial to his Welsh subjects. For example, in August 1505 the inhabitants of Bromfield and Yale were granted permission to acquire freeholds in any of the English boroughs of Wales and also in England proper. Henceforth the descent of real property would be governed by the common law and not by gavelkind or any other form of Welsh tenure; and all Welshmen residing within the two lordships were declared fully capable of "holding the offices of sheriff, mayor, bailiff, constable [or] any other office therein . . . and of becoming burgesses in any English town of Wales." In 1506 similar liberties were extended to the inhabitants of Chirk and Denbigh and, in 1508, to Welshmen living within the lordship of Ruthin. In 1507 the charters granted half a century earlier to the people of Ceri and Cydewain by Richard of York were confirmed by Henry VII. For the latter's Welsh policy, see *Cal. Pat. Rolls, 1494–1509*, pp. 434, 464; Chrimes, *Henry VII*, pp. 252–3; J. B. Smith, "Crown and Community in the Principality of North Wales in the Reign of Henry Tudor," *W.H.R.*, III (1966), pp. 157–9, 169, 171.

17. *Rot. Parl.*, VI, 522–3, 532; Dietz, *English Public Finance*, pp. 31, 85; Gras, *The Early English Customs System*, pp. 123–5, 694–706; Lander, *Conflict and Stability*, pp. 104, 167; Powell and Wallis, *The House of Lords in the Middle Ages*, p. 540; Wernham, *Before the Armada*, pp. 72–3; Smith, "Crown and Community," pp. 158–9.

18. Dudley, *The Tree of the Commonwealth*, p. 6; Busch, *England under the Tudors*, p. 276; Simons, *Henry VII*, p. 300; Elton, "Henry VII: A Restatement," pp. 16, 23.

19. Lander, "Bonds, Coercion, and Fear," p. 334.

20. *Cal. Pat. Rolls, 1494–1509*, p. 388; Powell and Wallis, *The House of Lords in the Middle Ages*, pp. 549–50.

21. Bean, *The Estates of the Percy Family*, p. 143; Dunham, *Lord Hastings' Indentured Retainers*, pp. 102–3.

22. Bacon, *Henry VII*, pp. 192–3. See also Storey, *The Reign of Henry VII*, p. 156, and Simons, *Henry VII*, pp. 264–5.

23. *Cal. Close Rolls, 1500–9*, p. 311; Bayne and Dunham, eds., *Select Cases in the Council of Henry VII*, pp. cxx-cxxi; Kingsford, *Chronicles of London*, p. 261; Dunham, *Lord Hastings' Indentured Retainers*, p. 103; Lander, "Bonds, Coercion, and Fear," pp. 344–5.

24. Dunham, *Lord Hastings' Indentured Retainers*, pp. 84–5; Loades, *Politics and the Nation*, p. 119.

25. Lander, "Bonds, Coercion, and Fear," p. 341.

26. *Ibid.*, p. 347. According to Professor Lander, three-fourths of the peerage was entangled at one time or another during the reign in a bond or recognizance of some kind.

27. Vergil, *Anglica Historia*, pp. 127, 129.

28. Lander, "Bonds, Coercion, and Fear," p. 352. See also Chrimes, *Henry VII*, p. 315; Elton, "Henry VII: Rapacity and Remorse," pp. 36–7.

29. Somerville, *History of the Duchy of Lancaster*, I, 263–4, 267.

30. Dudley, *The Tree of the Commonwealth*, pp. vii-ix, 2–3; Wedgwood, *History of Parliament*, I, 285–6; Roskell, *The Commons and Their Speakers*, pp. 307–9; D. M. Brodie, "Edmund Dudley, Minister of Henry VII," *T.R.H.S.*, 4th series, XV (1932), pp. 134–6, 142, 148.

31. Bayne and Dunham, eds., *Select Cases in the Council of Henry VII*, pp. xv-xxviii; H. E. Bell, *An Introduction to the History and Records of the Court of Wards & Liveries* (Cambridge, 1953), pp. 4–5; G. R. Elton, *The Tudor Revolution in Government* (Cambridge, 1953), pp. 29–30; Chrimes *Henry VII*, pp. 150–2; Robert Somerville, "Henry VII's 'Council Learned in the Law'," *E.H.R.*, LIV (1939), pp. 428–39, passim.

32. *The Great Chronicle of London*, ed. Thomas, p. 348. Cf. Dudley, *The Tree of the Commonwealth*, p. 2, and Lander, *Conflict and Stability*, p. 113.

33. Mark Girouard, *Life in the English Country House* (New Haven, 1978), p. 100.

34. For evidence of the activities of Empson and Dudley between 1503 and 1509, see *Cal. Inquisitions Post Mortem, 1504–9*, p. 293; Bradford, ed., *Proceedings in the Court of Star Chamber*, pp. 18–19; Brodie, "Edmund Dudley," p. 145; Cooper, "Henry VII's Last Years Reconsidered," p. 119.

35. Holdsworth, *History of English Law*, IV, 26.

36. See Chapter X above.

37. Wernham, *Before the Armada*, pp. 54–5; Mackie, *The Earlier Tudors*, pp. 176, 179; Simons, *Henry VII*, pp. 265–6; Scarisbrick, *Henry VIII*, p. 9.

38. Mattingly, *Catherine of Aragon*, p. 68.

39. *Ibid.*, p. 67; Connell-Smith, *Forerunners of Drake*, pp. 52–5.

40. *Cal. S. P. Spain*, I, 422–3; Mackie, *The Earlier Tudors*, p. 180; Mattingly, *Catherine of Aragon*, pp. 66–7; Chrimes, *Henry VII*, p. 296.

41. *Ibid.*, p. 288; Wernham, *Before the Armada*, pp. 55, 59.

42. Mattingly, *Catherine of Aragon*, p. 71; Mackie, *The Earlier Tudors*, pp. 183–4.

43. *Ibid.*, pp. 184–5; Mattingly, *Catherine of Aragon*, pp. 78–81; Fisher, *Pol. Hist.*, p. 116; Wernham, *Before the Armada*, p. 56.

44. *Ibid.*, pp. 69–70; Pollard, *Cont. Sources*, II, 322–3; Mackie, *The Earlier Tudors*, p. 187; Fisher, *Pol. Hist.*, p. 118; Lockyer, *Henry VII*, p. 70.

45. *The Chronicle of Calais*, pp. 5–6; Busch, *England under the Tudors*, p. 192.

46. Fisher, *Pol. Hist.*, p. 118; Wernham, *Before the Armada*, p. 56.

47. Busch, *England under the Tudors*, p. 214.

48. Quoted in Mattingly, *Catherine of Aragon*, p. 101.

49. *Ibid.* See also Chrimes, *Henry VII*, pp. 291, 296–7.

50. Pollard, *Cont. Sources*, I, 317–18; Mackie, *The Earlier Tudors*, pp. 179–80; Mattingly, *Catherine of Aragon*, pp. 92–106, passim.

51. *Ibid.*, pp. 94–5, 104; *The Chronicle of Calais*, pp. 6–7; Fisher, *Pol. Hist.*, pp. 121–3; Tucker, *Life of Surrey*, p. 90.

52. Wernham, *Before the Armada*, pp. 59–60; Mackie, *The Earlier Tudors*, pp. 187–8.

53. Busch, *England under the Tudors*, pp. 307, 314; Chrimes, *Henry VII*, pp. 313–14; Simons, *Henry VII*, pp. 284, 297–8.

54. For the plan of Henry's great charitable foundation at the Savoy, see Colin Platt, *Medieval England: A Social History and Archaeology* (New York, 1978), p. 152.

55. Thomas Astle, ed., *The Will of Henry VII* (London, 1775), pp. 1, 4, 8–9, 11, 15–17, 28–9, 31–2; Mackie, *The Earlier Tudors*, p. 229; H. M. Smith, "The Will of Henry VII," *C.Q.R.*, CXVI (1933), pp. 249–51.

56. Lander, *Conflict and Stability*, p. 121.

57. Astle, ed., *The Will of Henry VII*, p. 11; Busch, *England under the Tudors*, p. 254; Simons, *Henry VII*, pp. 299–300.

58. Chrimes, *Henry VII*, p. 314; Astle, ed., *The Will of Henry VII*, p. 47; Smith, "The Will of Henry VII," pp. 246–7; Elton, "Henry VII: Rapacity and Remorse," pp. 37–8.

Bibliography

I. Primary Sources.

Allen, P. S. and H. M. Allen, eds. *Letters of Richard Fox, 1486–1527*. Oxford, 1929.

Arnold, Richard. *The Customs of London, otherwise called Arnold's Chronicle*, 2nd ed. London, 1811.

Astle, Thomas, ed. *The Will of King Henry VII*. London, 1775.

Baildon, William P., ed. *Select Cases in Chancery, A.D. 1364 to 1471* (Selden Society, vol. X). London, 1896.

Bayne, C. G. and W. H. Dunham, Jr., eds. *Select Cases in the Council of Henry VII* (Selden Society, vol. LXXV). London, 1956.

Benham, W. Gurney, ed. *The Red Paper Book of Colchester*. Colchester, 1902.

Bentley, Samuel, ed. *Excerpta Historica, or Illustrations of English History*, 2nd ed. London, 1833.

Bergenroth, G. A., ed. *Supplement to Volume I and Volume II of Letters, Despatches, and State Papers relating to the Negotiations between England and Spain, preserved in the Archives at Simancas and Elsewhere*. London, 1868.

Biggar, H. P., ed. *The Precursors of Jacques Cartier, 1497–1534: A Collection of Documents Relating to the Early History of the Dominion of Canada*. Ottawa, 1911.

Bradford, Gladys, ed. *Proceedings in the Court of the Star Chamber in the Reigns of Henry VII and Henry VIII*. London, 1911.

Calendar of Documents relating to Scotland, preserved in Her Majesty's Public Record Office, 4 vols., ed. Joseph Bain. Edinburgh, 1881–8.

Calender of Entries in the Papal Registers relating to Great Britain and Ireland: Papal Letters 1484–1492, London, 1960.

Calendar of Inquisitions Post Mortem and Other Analogous Documents preserved in the Public Record Office, 3 vols. London, 1898–1955.

Calendar of Letters, Despatches, and State Papers, relating to the Negotiations between England and Spain, preserved in the Archives at Simancas and Elsewhere, vol. I: Henry VII, 1485–1509, ed. G. A. Bergenroth. London, 1862.

Calendar of State Papers and Manuscripts, relating to English Affairs, existing in the Archives and Collections of Milan, vol. I, 1385–1618, ed. Allen B. Hinds. London, 1912.

Calendar of State Papers and Manuscripts, relating to English Affairs, existing in the Archives and Collections of Venice, and in other Libraries of Northern Italy, vol. I, 1202–1509, ed. Rawdon Brown. London, 1864.

Calendar of the Carew Manuscripts, preserved in the Archiepiscopal Library at Lambeth, 6 vols., ed. J. S. Brewer and William Bullen. London, 1867–73.

Calendar of the Charter Rolls, preserved in the Public Record Office, vol. VI. 5 Henry VI–8 Henry VIII. London, 1920.

Calendar of the Close Rolls, preserved in the Public Record Office, Henry VII, 2 vols. London, 1955–63.

Calendar of the Fine Rolls, preserved in the Public Record Office, Volume XXII: Henry VII, 1485–1509. London, 1962.

Calendar of the Patent Rolls, preserved in the Public Record Office, Henry VII, 2 vols. London, 1914–16.

Campbell, William, ed. *Materials for a History of the Reign of Henry VII*, 2 vols. (Rolls Series, No. 60). London, 1873–7.

Chrimes, Stanley B. and A. L. Brown, eds. *Select Documents of English Constitutional History 1307–1485*. London, 1961.

Constable, Robert. *Prerogativa Regis*, ed. S. E. Thorne. New Haven, 1949.

Dudley, Edmund. *The Tree of the Commonwealth*, ed. D. M. Brodie. Cambridge, 1948.

Ellis, Sir Henry, ed. *Original Letters, illustrative of English History*, 3 series, 11 vols. London, 1824–46.

————. *Three Books of Polydore Vergil's English History, Comprising the Reigns of Henry VI, Edward IV, and Richard III* (Camden Society, 1st series, Vol. XXIX). London, 1844.

Elton, Geoffrey R., ed. *The Tudor Constitution: Documents and Commentary*. Cambridge, 1960.

Fabyan, Robert. *The New Chronicles of England and France*, ed. Sir Henry Ellis. London, 1811.

Flenley, Ralph, ed. *Six Town Chronicles of England*. Oxford, 1911.

Gairdner, James, ed. *Historia Henrici Septimi, a Bernard Andrea* (Rolls Series, No. 10). London, 1858.

————. *Letters and Papers illustrative of the reigns of Richard III and Henry VII*, 2 vols. (Rolls Series, No. 24). London, 1861–3.

————. *Memorials of King Henry the Seventh* (Rolls Series, No. 10). London, 1858.

————. *The Paston Letters*, 4 vols. Westminster, 1901.

————. *Three Fifteenth-Century Chronicles with Historical Memoranda by John Stowe* (Camden Society, new series, vol. XXVII). London, 1880.

Gee, Henry and W. J. Hardy, eds. *Documents illustrative of English Church History*. London, 1910.

Green, Mary Anne Everett, ed. *Letters of Royal and Illustrious Ladies of Great Britain*, 3 vols. London, 1846.

Hall, Edward. *Hall's Chronicle; containing the History of England, during the Reign of Henry the Fourth, and the Succeeding Monarchs, to the End of the Reign of Henry the Eighth*. London, 1809.

Halliwell-Phillipps, James O., ed. *Letters of the Kings of England*, 2 vols. London, 1848.

Hay, Denys, ed. *The Anglica Historia of Polydore Vergil, A.D. 1485–1537* (Camden Society, 3rd series, vol. LXXIV). London, 1950.

Hemmant, Mary, ed. *Select Cases in the Exchequer Chamber before all the Justices of England*, 2 vols. (Selden Society, vols. LI and LXIV). London, 1933–48.

Hoffman, Bernard G., ed. *Cabot to Cartier: Sources for a Historical Ethnography of Northeastern North America 1497–1550*. Toronto, 1961.

Holinshed, Raphael. *Chronicles of England, Scotland, and Ireland*, 6 vols., ed. Sir Henry Ellis. London, 1806.

Hopper, Clarence, ed. *London Chronicles during the Reigns of Henry the Seventh and Henry the Eighth* (The Camden Miscellany, vol. IV). London, 1859.

Hughes, Paul L. and J. F. Larkin, eds. *Tudor Royal Proclamations, Volume I: The Early Tudors (1485–1553)*. New Haven, 1964.

Lander, J. R., ed. *The Wars of the Roses*. London, 1965.

Leadam, I. S., ed. *Select Cases before the King's Council in the Star Chamber, commonly called the Court of Star Chamber, A.D. 1477–1509*, 2 vols. (Selden Society, vols. XVI and XXV). London, 1903–11.

———. *Select Cases in the Court of Requests, A.D. 1497–1569* (Selden Society, vol. XII). London, 1898.

Leland, John. *Collectanea de Rebus Britannicis*, 6 vols., ed. Thomas Hearne. London, 1770.

Lodge, Eleanor C. and G. A. Thornton, eds. *English Constitutional Documents 1307–1485*. Cambridge, 1935.

Malfatti, C. V., ed. *Two Italian Accounts of Tudor England*. Barcelona, 1953.

Mancini, Dominic. *The Usurpation of Richard the Third*, 2nd ed., ed. C. A. J. Armstrong. Oxford, 1969.

More, Sir Thomas. *History of Richard III*, ed. Paul M. Kendall. New York, 1965.

Myers, A. R., ed. *English Historical Documents 1327–1485*. New York, 1969.

Nichols, Francis M., ed. *The Epistles of Erasmus*, 3 vols. New York, 1962.

Nichols, John G., ed. *The Chronicle of Calais, in the Reigns of Henry VII and Henry VIII to the Year 1540* (Camden Society, 1st series, vol. XXXV). London, 1846.

———. *Chronicle of the Grey Friars of London* (Camden Society, 1st series, vol. LIII). London, 1852.

———. *Grants, etc. from the Crown during the Reign of Edward the Fifth* (Camden Society, 1st series, vol. LX). London, 1854.

Nicolas, Nicholas H., ed. *Testamenta Vetusta: being illustrations from Wills, of Manners, Customs, &c. . . . from the Reign of Henry the Second to the Accession of Queen Elizabeth*, 2 vols. London, 1826.

Oppenheim, Michael, ed. *Naval Accounts and Inventories of the Reign of Henry VII, 1485–8 and 1495–7* (Navy Records Society, No. 8). London, 1896.

Pollard, Albert F., ed. *The Reign of Henry VII from Contemporary Sources*, 3 vols. London, 1913.

Pugh, T. B., ed. *The Marcher Lordships of South Wales 1415–1536: Select Documents*. Cardiff, 1963.

Ricart, Robert. *The Maire of Bristowe Is Kalendar*, ed. Lucy T. Smith (Camden Society, new series, vol. V). London, 1872.

Riley, Henry T., ed. *Ingulph's Chronicle of the Abbey of Croyland with the Continuations by Peter of Blois and Anonymous Writers*. London, 1854.

Rogers, Elizabeth F., ed. *The Correspondence of Sir Thomas More*. Princeton, N.J., 1947.

Rotuli Parliamentorum; ut et petitiones et placita in parliamento, 6 vols., ed. J. Strachey and others. London, 1767–77.

Rymer, Thomas, ed. *Foedera, Conventiones, Literae, et cumuscunque generis acta publica, inter reges Angliae*, 3rd ed., 10 vols. The Hague, 1741.

Scott, Sir Walter, ed. *A Collection of Scarce and Valuable Tracts*, 2nd ed., 13 vols. London, 1809–15.

Shaw, William A., ed. *The Knights of England*, 2 vols. London, 1906.

Sneyd, Charlotte A., ed. *A Relation, or rather a true Account of the Island of England; with sundry particulars of the customs of these people, and of the royal revenues under King Henry the Seventh, about the year 1500* (Camden Society, 1st series, vol. XXXVII). London, 1847.

Stapleton, Thomas, ed. *Plumpton Correspondence. A Series of Letters, Chiefly Domestick, written in the Reigns of Edward IV, Richard III, Henry VII, and Henry VIII* (Camden Society, 1st series, vol. IV). London, 1839.

Statutes of the Realm, 11 vols., ed. Alexander Luders and others. London, 1810–28.

Tanner, J. R., ed. *Tudor Constitutional Documents, A.D. 1485–1603, with an historical commentary*, 2nd ed. Cambridge, 1922.

Tawney, Richard H. and Eileen Power, eds. *Tudor Economic Documents*, 3 vols. London, 1924.

Thomas, A. H. and I. D. Thornley, eds. *The Great Chronicle of London*. London, 1938.

Williams, C. H., ed. *English Historical Documents 1485–1558*. New York, 1967.

Wriothesley, Charles. *A Chronicle of England during the Reigns of the Tudors, from A.D. 1485 to 1559*, 2 vols., ed. W. D. Hamilton (Camden Society, new series, vols. XI and XX). London, 1875-7.

II. Secondary Sources

Anglo, Sydney. *Spectacle, Pageantry, and Early Tudor Policy*. Oxford, 1969.

Aurner, Nellie S. *Caxton: Mirrour of Fifteenth-Century Letters*. New York, 1965.

Bacon, Sir Francis. *The History of the Reign of King Henry the Seventh*, ed. J. R. Lumby. Cambridge, 1885.

Bagwell, Richard. *Ireland under the Tudors, with a succinct account of the earlier history*, 3 vols. London, 1885-90.

Bainton, Roland H. *Erasmus of Christendom*. New York, 1969.

Baldwin, J. F. *The King's Council in England during the Middle Ages*. London, 1913.

Bean, J. M. W. *The Decline of English Feudalism 1215–1540*. Manchester, 1968.

———. *The Estates of the Percy Family 1416–1537*. Oxford, 1958.

Bell, H. E. *An Introduction to the History and Records of the Court of Wards and Liveries*. Cambridge, 1953.

Bennett, H. S. *English Books & Readers 1475 to 1557*. Cambridge, 1952.

Berdan, John M. *Early Tudor Poetry 1485–1547*. New York, 1920.

Bindoff, S. T. *Tudor England*. Harmondsworth, 1950.

Blades, William. *The Biography and Typography of William Caxton*, 2nd ed. New York, 1882.

Blake, N. F. *Caxton and His World*. London, 1969.

Boas, F. S. *An Introduction to Tudor Drama*. Oxford, 1933.

Bridbury, A. R. *Economic Growth: England in the Later Middle Ages*. London, 1962.

Bryan, Donough. *Gerald Fitzgerald, the Great Earl of Kildare*. Dublin, 1933.

Burwash, Dorothy. *English Merchant Shipping 1460–1540*. Toronto, 1947 (repr. 1969).

Busch, Wilhelm. *England under the Tudors*. London, 1895.

Carpenter, Nan Cooke. *John Skelton*. New York, 1967.

Caspari, Fritz. *Humanism and the Social Order in Tudor England*. Chicago, 1954.

Chambers, E. K. *English Literature at the Close of the Middle Ages*. Oxford, 1947.

Chambers, R. W. *Thomas More*. London, 1935.

Chapman, Hester W. *The Thistle and the Rose: The Sisters of Henry VIII*. New York, 1972.

Charlton, Kenneth. *Education in Renaissance England*. Toronto, 1965.

Chrimes, S. B. *English Constitutional Ideas in the Fifteenth Century*. Cambridge, 1936.

———. *Henry VII*. London and Berkeley, 1972.

———. *Lancastrians, Yorkists, and Henry VII*, 2nd ed. London, 1966.

———, C. D. Ross, and R. A. Griffiths, eds. *Fifteenth-Century England 1399–1509: Studies in Politics and Society*. Manchester, 1972.

Clarke, Maude V. *Medieval Representation and Consent*. New York, 1936 (repr. 1964).

Clive, Mary. *This Sun of York: A Biography of Edward IV*. London, 1973.

Coleman, C. D. *The British Paper Industry 1495–1860*. Oxford, 1958 (repr. 1975).

Connell-Smith, Gordon. *Forerunners of Drake: A Study of English Trade with Spain in the Early Tudor Period*. London, 1954.

Conway, Agnes. *Henry VII's Relations with Scotland and Ireland, 1485–98*. Cambridge, 1932.

Craig, Hardin. *The Literature of the English Renaissance*. Oxford, 1950 (repr. 1962).

Creighton, Mandell. *Historical Essays and Reviews*. London, 1903.

Crowson, Paul S. *Tudor Foreign Policy*. New York, 1973.

Curtis, Edmund. *A History of Medieval Ireland: From 1110 to 1513*. London, 1923.

Davies, C. S. L. *Peace, Print & Protestantism 1450–1558*. London, 1977.

Dietz, Frederick C. *English Government Finance 1485–1558*, 2nd ed. London, 1964.

DuBoulay, F. R. H. *An Age of Ambition: English Society in the Late Middle Ages*. New York, 1970.

Duff, E. Gordon. *The Printers, Stationers and Bookbinders of Westminster and London from 1476 to 1535*. Cambridge, 1906.

Dunham, William H. *Lord Hastings' Indentured Retainers 1461–1483* (Connecticut Academy of Arts and Sciences, vol. XXXIX). New Haven, 1955.

Edwards, H. L. R. *Skelton: The Life and Times of an Early Tudor Poet*. Freeport, N.Y., 1971.

Einstein, Lewis. *The Italian Renaissance in England*. New York, 1902.

Elton, Geoffrey R. *England under the Tudors*. London, 1955.

———. *The Tudor Revolution in Government*. Cambridge, 1953 (reprinted 1969).

Ferguson, Arthur B. *The Articulate Citizen and the English Renaissance*. Durham, N.C., 1965.

————. *The Indian Summer of English Chivalry: Studies in the Decline and Transforma-tion of Chivalric Idealism.* Durham, N. C., 1960.

Fisher, H. A. L. *The Political History of England, vol. V. From the Accession of Henry VII to the Death of Henry VIII,* 2nd ed. London, 1919.

Foss, Edward. *The Judges of England, vol. V, 1485–1603.* London, 1857.

Fowler, Elaine W. *English Sea Power in the Early Tudor Period* (Folger Booklets on Tudor and Stuart Civilization). Ithaca, N. Y., 1965.

Gairdner, James. *Henry the Seventh.* New York, 1889.

————. *History of the Life and Reign of Richard the Third. To Which is added the Story of Perkin Warbeck from Original Documents,* rev. ed. Cambridge, 1898.

Gilmore, Myron P. *The World of Humanism 1453–1517.* New York, 1952.

Gordon, Ian A. *John Skelton: Poet Laureate.* New York, 1970.

Gras, N. S. B. *The Early English Customs System.* Cambridge, Mass., 1918.

Gray, Howard L. *The Influence of the Commons on Early Legislation.* Cambridge, Mass., 1932.

Green, V. H. H. *The Later Plantaganets: A Survey of English History between 1307 and 1485.* London, 1955 (reprinted 1966).

Guy, John A. *The Cardinal's Court: The Impact of Thomas Wolsey in Star Chamber.* Totowa, N. J., 1977.

Hanham, Alison. *Richard III and His Early Historians 1483–1535.* Oxford, 1975.

Harbison, E. Harris. *The Christian Scholar in the Age of the Reformation.* New York, 1956.

Harvey, Nancy L. *Elizabeth of York.* New York, 1973.

Hastings, Margaret. *The Court of Common Pleas in Fifteenth-Century England.* Ithaca, N. Y., 1947.

Hays, Denys. *Polydore Vergil: Renaissance Historian and Man of Letters.* Oxford, 1952.

Hogrefe, Pearl. *The Sir Thomas More Circle.* Urbana, Ill., 1959.

Holdsworth, Sir William S. *A History of English Law,* 3rd ed., 16 vols. London, 1945.

Huizinga, Johan. *Erasmus and the Age of Reformation.* New York, 1957.

Jacob, E. F. *Essays in Later Medieval History.* Manchester, 1968.

————. *The Fifteenth Century 1399–1485.* Oxford, 1961.

————, ed. *Italian Renaissance Studies.* London, 1960.

Kendall, Paul M. *Richard the Third.* New York, 1956 (repr. 1965).

————. *The Yorkist Age: Daily Life during the Wars of the Roses.* New York, 1962.

Kingsford, Charles L. *Chronicles of London.* Oxford, 1905.

Knowles, David. *The Religious Orders in England. Volume III: The Tudor Age.* Cambridge, 1961.

Lander, J. R. *Conflict and Stability in Fifteenth-Century England.* London, 1969.

————. *Crown and Nobility 1450–1509.* Montreal, 1976.

Laslett, Peter. *The World We Have Lost,* 2nd ed. London, 1971.

Levine, Mortimer. *Tudor Dynastic Problems 1460–1571.* London, 1973.

Levy, Fritz J. *Tudor Historical Thought.* San Marino, Cal., 1967.

Lewis, Clive S. *English Literature in the Sixteenth Century, Excluding Drama.* Oxford, 1944.

Loades, D. M. *Politics and the Nation 1450–1660: Obedience, Resistance, and Public Order*. Brighton, 1974.

Lockyer, Roger. *Henry VII*. New York, 1968.

———. *Tudor and Stuart Britain 1471–1714*. New York, 1964.

Lupton, Joseph H. *A Life of John Colet, D. D.*, new ed. London, 1909.

Lydon, James. *Ireland in the Later Middle Ages*. Dublin, 1973.

MacGibbon, David. *Elizabeth Woodville (1437–1492): Her Life and Times*. London, 1938.

MacLean, Antonia. *Humanism and the Rise of Science in Tudor England*. New York, 1972.

McElroy, Mary M. D. "Literary Patronage of Margaret Beaufort and Henry VII: A Study of Renaissance Propaganda (1483—1509)" (unpublished Ph.D. dissertation, University of Texas). Austin, 1964.

McIlwain, Charles H. *The High Court of Parliament and Its Supremacy*. New Haven, 1910.

McKisack, May. *Medieval History in the Tudor Age*. Oxford, 1971.

———. *The Parliamentary Representation of the English Boroughs during the Middle Ages*. Oxford, 1932.

McMurtrie, Douglas C. *The Book: The Story of Printing & Bookmaking*, 3rd ed. New York, 1943.

Mackie, John D. *The Earlier Tudors 1485–1558*. Oxford, 1952 (reprinted 1962).

Mackie, Robert L. *King James IV of Scotland*. Edinburgh, 1958.

Mallet, Charles E. *A History of the University of Oxford*, 3 vols. London, 1924.

Markham, Sir Clements. *Richard III: His Life & Character*. London, 1906.

Marriott, J. A. R. *The Life of John Colet*. London, 1933.

Mattingly, Garrett. *Catherine of Aragon*. Boston, 1941.

———. *Renaissance Diplomacy*. Boston, 1955.

Mitchell, R. J. *John Tiptoft (1427–1470)*. London, 1938

Moran, James. *Wynkyn de Worde: Father of Fleet Street*. London, 1960.

Morison, Samuel E. *The European Discovery of America: The Northern Voyages A.D. 500–1600*. New York, 1971.

Mullinger, James B. *The University of Cambridge: From the Earliest Times to the Royal Injunctions of 1535*. Cambridge, 1873.

Myers, A. R. *The Household of Edward IV*. Manchester, 1959.

Nelson, William. *John Skelton, Laureate*. New York, 1964.

Oppenheim, Michael. *A History of the Administration of the Royal Navy*. London, 1896.

Otway-Ruthven, Annette J. *A History of Medieval Ireland*. London, 1968.

———. *The King's Secretary and the Signet Office in the XV Century*. Cambridge, 1939.

Parry, J. H. *The Age of Reconnaissance*. Cleveland, 1963.

Pasquet, D. *An Essay on the Origins of the House of Commons*, trans. by R. G. D. Laffon. Cambridge, 1925.

Paul, John E. *Catherine of Aragon and Her Friends*. New York, 1966.

Penrose, Boies. *Travel and Discovery in the Renaissance 1420–1620*. Cambridge, Mass., 1952.

Phillips, Margaret M. *Erasmus and the Northern Renaissance.* London, 1949.

Pickthorn, Kenneth. *Early Tudor Government: Henry VII.* Cambridge, 1934.

Plomer, Henry R. *A Short History of English Printing.* London, 1900.

Plucknett, Theodore F. T. *A Concise History of the Common Law,* 5th ed. London, 1956.

Pollard, Albert F. *The Evolution of Parliament,* 2nd ed. London, 1926.

Pollet, Maurice. *John Skelton: Poet of Tudor England,* trans. by John Warrington. Lewisburg, Penn., 1971.

Poole, A. L., ed. *Medieval England,* 2 vols., rev. ed. Oxford, 1958.

Powell, J. Enoch and Keith Wallis. *The House of Lords in the Middle Ages: A History of the English House of Lords to 1540.* London, 1968.

Power, Eileen and M. M. Postan, eds. *Studies in English Trade in the Fifteenth Century.* New York, 1966.

Quinn, David B. *England and the Discovery of America, 1481–1620.* New York, 1974.

Ramsay, G. D. *English Overseas Trade during the Centuries of Emergence.* London, 1957.

Ramsey, Peter. *Tudor Economic Problems.* London, 1968.

Reed, A. W. *Early Tudor Drama: Medwall, the Rastells, Heywood, and the More Circle.* London, 1926.

Reid, Rachel R. *The King's Council in the North.* London, 1921.

Reynolds, E. E. *Thomas More and Erasmus.* New York, 1965.

Richardson, Walter C. *Tudor Chamber Administration 1485–1547.* Baton Rouge, 1952.

Roper, William. "The Life of Sir Thomas More," in *Two Early Tudor Lives,* ed. Richard S. Sylvester and David P. Harding. New Haven, 1962.

Roskell, John S. *The Commons and their Speakers in English Parliaments 1376–1523.* Manchester, 1965.

Ross, Charles. *Edward IV.* Berkeley, Cal., 1974.

Rowse, Alfred L. *Tudor Cornwall: Portrait of a Society.* London, 1941.

Sayles, George O. *The King's Parliament of England.* New York, 1974.

Scarisbrick, J. J. *Henry VIII.* Berkeley, Cal., 1968.

Scofield, Cora L. *The Life and Reign of Edward IV,* 2 vols. London, 1923.

———. *A Study of the Court of Star Chamber.* Chicago, 1900.

Seebohm, Frederic. *The Oxford Reformers: John Colet, Erasmus, and Thomas More,* 3rd ed. London, 1913.

Senior, William. *Doctors' Commons and the Old Court of Admiralty.* London, 1922.

Seton-Watson, R. W., ed. *Tudor Studies, presented by the Board of Studies in History in the University of London to Albert Frederick Pollard.* London, 1924.

Simon, Joan. *Education and Society in Tudor England.* Cambridge, 1967.

Simons, Eric N. *Henry VII: The First Tudor King.* London, 1968.

———. *The Reign of Edward IV.* New York, 1966.

Skeel, Caroline A. J. *The Council in the Marches of Wales.* London, 1904.

Slavin, Arthur J. *The Precarious Balance 1450–1640: English Government and Society.* New York, 1973.

———, ed. *Tudor Men and Institutions: Studies in English Law and Government.* Baton Rouge, 1972.

Smith, Preserved. *Erasmus: A Study of His Life, Ideals, and Place in History.* New York, 1962.

Somerville, Robert. *History of the Duchy of Lancaster, Volume I, 1265–1603.* London, 1953.

Stevens, John E. *Music & Poetry in the Early Tudor Court.* London, 1961.

Storey, R. L. *The End of the House of Lancaster.* New York, 1967.

———. *The Reign of Henry VII.* New York, 1968.

Stubbs, William. *Seventeen Lectures on the Study of Medieval and Modern History.* London, 1886.

Tawney, Richard H. *The Agrarian Problem in the Sixteenth Century.* London, 1912.

Taylor, E. G. R. *Tudor Geography 1485–1583.* London, 1930.

Temperley, Gladys. *Henry VII.* London, 1917.

Thirsk, Joan, ed. *The Agrarian History of England and Wales. Volume IV: 1500–1640.* Cambridge, 1967.

Thompson, A. Hamilton. *The English Clergy and Their Organization in the Later Middle Ages.* Oxford, 1947.

Thrupp, Sylvia L. *The Merchant Class of Medieval London.* Ann Arbor, Mich., 1962.

Tucker, Melvin J. *The Life of Thomas Howard, Earl of Surrey and Second Duke of Norfolk, 1443–1524.* The Hague, 1964.

Wedgwood, Josiah and Anne D. Holt. *History of Parliament: Biographies of the Members of the Commons House 1439–1506,* 2 vols. London, 1936–8.

Weiss, Roberto. *Humanism in England During the Fifteenth Century,* 2nd ed. Oxford, 1957.

———. *The Spread of Italian Humanism.* London, 1964.

Wells, James. *William Caxton.* Chicago, 1960.

Wernham, Robert B. *Before the Armada: The Emergence of the English Nation, 1485–1588.* New York, 1966.

Wilkinson, Bertie. *Constitutional History of England in the Fifteenth Century.* New York, 1964.

Williams, C. H. *The Making of the Tudor Despotism,* 2nd ed. London, 1935.

Williams, Neville. *The Life and Times of Henry VII.* London, 1973.

Williamson, James A. *The Cabot Voyages and Bristol Discovery under Henry VII.* Cambridge, 1962.

———. *A Short History of British Expansion. Volume I: The Old Colonial Empire,* 3rd ed. London, 1961.

———. *The Tudor Age,* 3rd ed. New York, 1964.

Wolffe, B. P. *The Crown Lands 1461 to 1536: An Aspect of Yorkist and Early Tudor Government.* London, 1970.

———. *The Royal Demesne in English History: The Crown Estate in the Governance of the Realm from the Conquest to 1509.* London, 1971.

Wormald, Francis and Cyril E. Wright, eds. *The English Library before 1700.* London, 1958.

III. Articles.

Adamson, J. W. "The Extent of Literacy in England in the Fifteenth and Sixteenth Centuries," *The Library,* 4th series, X (September 1929).

Anglo, Sydney. "*The British History* in Early Tudor Propaganda," *Bulletin of the John Rylands Library*, XLIV (September 1961).

———. "The Foundation of the Tudor Dynasty: The Coronation and Marriage of Henry VII," *The Guildhall Miscellany*, II (1960).

Archbold, W. A. J. "Sir William Stanley and Perkin Warbeck," *E.H.R.*, XIV (July 1899).

Armstrong, C. A. J. "The Inauguration Festivities of the Yorkist Kings and their Title to the Throne," *T.R.H.S.*, 4th series, XXX (1948).

Bellamy, J. G. "Justice under the Yorkist Kings," *American Journal of Legal History*, IX (1965).

Brodie, D. M. "Edmund Dudley, Minister of Henry VII," *T.R.H.S.*, 4th series, XV (1932).

Brooks, Frederick W. "The Council of the North," Historical Association, General Series, No. 25 (1953).

Brown, A. L. "The King's Councillors in Fifteenth-Century England," *T.R.H.S.*, 5th series, XIX (1969).

———. "The Commons and the Council in the Reign of Henry IV," *E.H.R.*, LXXIX (January 1964).

Burne, Alfred H. "The Battle of Bosworth," in *The Battlefields of England*, 2nd ed. (London, 1951).

———. "The Battle of Stoke Field: 16 June 1487," in *More Battlefields of England* (London, 1952).

Cam, Helen M. "The Decline and Fall of English Feudalism," in *Liberties & Communities in Medieval England* (Cambridge, 1944).

———. "The Legislators of Medieval England," in *Historical Studies of the English Parliament*, vol. I (Cambridge, 1970).

———. "The Theory and Practice of Representation in Medieval England," in *Historical Studies of the English Parliament*, vol. I (Cambridge, 1970).

Cameron, A. "A Nottinghamshire Quarrel in the Reign of Henry VII," *B.I.H.R.*, XLV (May 1972).

Carus-Wilson, Eleanora M. "The Origins and Early Development of the Merchant Adventurers' Organization in London as shown in their own Medieval Records," *Ec.H.R.*, IV (April 1933).

Chrimes, S. B. "The Fifteenth Century," *History*, new series, XLVIII (1963).

———. " 'House of Lords' and 'House of Commons' in the Fifteenth Century," *E.H.R.*, XLIX (July 1934).

———. "Sir Roland de Veleville," *Welsh History Review*, III (June 1967).

Cooper, J. P. "Henry VII's Last Years Reconsidered," *Historical Journal*, II (1959).

Cornwall, Julian. "The Early Tudor Gentry," *Ec.H.R.*, 2nd series, XVII (1965).

Cosgrove, Art. "The Gaelic Resurgence and the Geraldine Supremacy (c. 1400–1534," in *The Course of Irish History*, ed. T. W. Moody and F. X. Martin (Cork, 1967).

Cussans, J. E. "Notes on the Perkin Warbeck Insurrection," *T.R.H.S.*, 1st series, I (1875).

Duhamel, P. Albert. "The Oxford Lectures of John Colet: An Essay in Defining the English Renaissance," *Journal of the History of Ideas*, XIV (1953).

Edwards, Sir John. "The Commons in Medieval English Parliaments," The Creighton Lecture in History for 1957 (London, 1958).

―――. "The Emergence of Majority Rule in English Parliamentary Elections," *T.R.H.S.*, 5th series, XIV (1964).

―――. "Historians and the Medieval English Parliament," The David Murray Lecture for 1955 (Glasgow, 1955).

―――. " 'Re-election' and the Medieval Parliament," *History*, XI (October 1926).

Edwards, R. Dudley and T. W. Moody. "The History of Poynings' Law: Part I, 1494–1615," *Irish Historical Studies*, II (June 1941).

Elton, G. R. "Henry VII: A Restatement," *Historical Journal*, IV (1961).

―――."Henry VII: Rapacity and Remorse," *Historical Journal*, I (1958).

―――. "The Problems and Significance of Administrative History in the Tudor Period," *Journal of British Studies*, IV (May 1965).

―――. "State Planning in Early Tudor England," *Ec.H.R.*, 2nd series, XIII (1961).

Ferguson, Arthur B. "Circumstances and the Sense of History in Tudor England: The Coming of the Historical Revolution," in *Medieval and Renaissance Studies*, ed. John M. Headley (Chapel Hill, N. C., 1968).

Fisher, F. J. "Commercial Trends and Policy in Sixteenth-Century England," *Ec.H.R.*, X (1940).

Fraser, Peter. "Public Petitioning and Parliament before 1832," *History*, XLVI (October 1961).

Gairdner, James. "A Supposed Conspiracy against Henry VII," *T.R.H.S.*, new series, XVIII (1904).

Gibson, Strickland. "Printed Books, The Book-Trade, and Libraries," in A. L. Poole, ed., *Medieval England*, 2 vols., new ed. (Oxford, 1958).

Goldingham, C. S. "The Navy under Henry VII," *E.H.R.*, XXXIII (October 1918).

Gray, Howard L. "Greek Visitors to England in 1455–1456," in *Anniversary Essays in Mediaeval History by Students of Charles Homer Haskins*, ed. C. H. Taylor (Boston, 1929).

Haines, Roy M. "The Associates and *Familia* of William Gray and his Use of Patronage while Bishop of Ely (1454–78)," *Journal of Ecclesiastical History*, XXV (July 1974).

Hanbury, H. G. "The Legislation of Richard III," *American Journal of Legal History*, VI (April 1962).

Hanham, Alison. "Richard III, Lord Hastings, and the Historians," *E.H.R.*, LXXXVII (April 1972).

Harris, G. L. "Aids, Loans, and Benevolences," *Historical Journal*, VI (1963).

Harrison, C. J. "The Petition of Edmund Dudley," *E.H.R.*, LXXXVII (January 1972).

Hay, Denys. "The Historiographers Royal in England and Scotland," *Scottish Historical Review*, XXX (April 1951).

―――. "History and Historians in France and England during the Fifteenth Century," *B.I.H.R.*, XXXV (November 1962).

Hayden, Mary. "Lambert Simnel in Ireland," *Irish Historical Studies*, IV (December 1915).

Hexter, J. H. "The Education of the Aristocracy in the Renaissance," in *Reapprais-als in History* (Evanston, Ill., 1961).

――――. "Thomas More: on the Margins of Modernity," *Journal of British Studies*, I (November 1961).

Hooker, James R. "Notes on the Organization of the Tudor Military under Henry VII," *H.L.Q.*, XXIII (1959).

――――. "Some Cautionary Notes on Henry VII's Household and Chamber 'System,' " *Speculum*, XXXIII (January 1958).

Houghton, K. N. "Theory and Practice in Borough Elections to Parliament during the later Fifteenth Century," *B.I.H.R.*, XXXIX (November 1966).

Hurstfield, Joel B. "The Revival of Feudalism in Early Tudor England," *History*, XXXVII (June 1952).

――――. "Was there a Tudor despotism after all?," in *Freedom, Corruption, and Government in Elizabethan England* (Cambridge, Mass., 1973).

Ives, E. W. "Andrew Dymmock and the Papers of Antony, Earl Rivers, 1482–3," *B.I.H.R.*, XLI (November 1968).

――――. "Patronage at the Court of Henry VIII: The Case of Sir Ralph Egerton of Ridley," *Bulletin of the John Rylands Library*, LII, No. 2 (1970).

――――. "The Genesis of the Statute of Uses," *E.H.R.*, LXXXII (October 1967).

Jackson, Melvin H. "The Labrador Landfall of John Cabot: The 1497 Voyage Reconsidered," *Canadian Historical Review*, XLIV (June 1963).

Jalland, Patricia. "The Influence of the Aristocracy on Shire Elections in the North of England, 1450–1470," *Speculum*, XLVI (July 1972).

James, M. E. "The Murder at Cocklodge," *Durham University Journal*, new series, XXVI (March 1965).

Jay, Winifred. "List of Members of the Fourth Parliament of Henry VII," *B.I.H.R.*, III (1925–6).

Juricek, John T. "John Cabot's First Voyage," *Smithsonian Journal of History*, II (1967–8).

Kekewich, Margaret. "Edward IV, William Caxton, and Literary Patronage in Yorkist England," *Modern Language Review*, LXVI (July 1971).

Kingsford, C. L. "Two London Chronicles, from the Collections of John Stow," in *The Camden Miscellany*. Camden Society, vol. XVIII (London, 1910).

Knecht, R. J. "The Episcopate and the Wars of the Roses," *University of Birming-ham Historical Journal*, VI, No. 2 (1958).

Lander, J. R. "Attainder and Forfeiture, 1453 to 1509," *Historical Journal*, IV (1961).

――――. "Bonds, Coercion, and Fear: Henry VII and the Peerage," in *Florilegium Historiale: Essays presented to Wallace K. Ferguson*, ed. J. G. Rowe and W. H. Stockdale (Toronto, 1971).

――――. "Council, Administration and Councillors, 1461 to 1485," *B.I.H.R.*, XXXII (November 1959).

――――. "Edward IV: The Modern Legend and a Revision," *History*, new series, XLI (1956).

――――. "Marriage and Politics in the Fifteenth Century: The Nevilles and the Wydevilles," *B.I.H.R.*, XXXVI (November 1963).

———. "The Yorkist Council and Administration, 1461 to 1485," *E.H.R.*, LXXIII (January 1958).

Lapsley, Gaillard T. "The Problem of the North: A Study in English Border History," *A.H.R.*, V (April 1900).

Leadam, I. S. "An Unknown Conspiracy against King Henry VII," *T.R.H.S.*, new series, XVI (1902).

Lehmberg, Stanford E. "Star Chamber, 1485–1509," *H.L.Q.*, XXIV (1960–1).

Levine, Mortimer. "Richard III—Usurper or Lawful King?," *Speculum*, XXXIV (1959).

McFarlane, K. B. "Parliament and 'Bastard Feudalism,' " *T.R.H.S.*, 4th series, XXVI (1944).

———. "The Wars of the Roses," *Proceedings of the British Academy*, L (1964).

Makinson, Albert. "The Road to Bosworth Field, August 1485," *History Today*, XIII (April 1963).

Mallet, M. E. "Anglo-Florentine Commercial Relations, 1465–1491," *Ec.H.R.*, 2nd series, XV (1962).

Mattingly, Garrett. "The Reputation of Doctor De Puebla," *E.H.R.*, LV (January 1940).

Meagher, John C. "The First Progress of Henry VII," *Renaissance Drama*, new series, I (1968).

Mitchell, R. J. "English Law Students at Bologna in the Fifteenth Century," *E.H.R.*, LI (April 1936).

———. "English Students at Ferrara in the XV Century," *Italian Studies*, I (1937).

Morison, J. L. "Sir Thomas More in his English Works," *Scottish Historical Review*, VI (1909).

Myers, A. R. "The Character of Richard III," *History Today*, IV (August 1954).

———. "Parliamentary Petitions in the Fifteenth Century," *E.H.R.*, LII, two parts (July–October 1937).

———. "Richard III and the Historical Tradition," in *The Historical Association Book of the Tudors*, ed. Joel Hurstfield (New York, 1973).

———. "Some Observations on the Procedure of the Commons in Dealing with Bills in the Lancastrian Period," *University of Toronto Law Journal*, III (1939–40).

Newton, Arthur P. "An Early Grant to Sebastian Cabot," *E.H.R.*, XXXVII (October 1922).

———. "The King's Chamber under the Early Tudors," *E.H.R.*, XXXII (July 1917).

Phelps-Brown, E. H. and Sheila Hopkins. "Seven Centuries of the Prices of Consumables Compared with Builder's Wage-rates," in *Essays in Economic History*, ed. E. M. Carus-Wilson, vol. II (London, 1962).

Plomer, Henry R. "Bibliographical Notes from the Privy Purse Expenses of King Henry the Seventh," *The Library*, 3rd series, IV (1913).

Plucknett, Theodore F. T. "The Place of the Council in the Fifteenth Century," *T.R.H.S.*, 4th series, I (1918).

Pollard, A. F. "Council, Star Chamber, and Privy Council under the Tudors," *E.H.R.*, XXXVII, two parts (July–October 1922).

———. "The Growth of the Court of Requests," *E.H.R.*, LVI (April 1941).

———. "The Making of Sir Thomas More's *Richard III*," in *Historical Essays in Honour of James Tait*, ed. J. G. Edwards (Manchester, 1933).

———. "Parliament in the Wars of the Roses" (Glasgow, 1936).

———. "Tudor Gleanings. I.—The 'de facto' act of Henry VII," *B.I.H.R.*, VII (1929–30).

Prall, Stuart E. "The Development of Equity in Tudor England," *American Journal of Legal History*, VIII (January 1964).

Pugh, Ralph B. "The Crown Estate: An Historical Essay" (London, 1960).

Pugh, T. B. " 'The Indenture for the Marches' between Henry VII and Edward Stafford (1477–1521), Duke of Buckingham," *E.H.R.*, LXXI (July 1956).

Quinn, David B. "The Argument for the English Discovery of America between 1480 and 1494," *Geographical Journal*, CXXVII (September 1961).

———. "The Early Interpretation of Poynings' Law, 1494–1534," *Irish Historical Studies*, II (March 1941).

———. "Henry VIII and Ireland, 1509–34," *Irish Historical Studies*, XII (September 1961).

———. "John Day and Columbus," *Geographical Journal*, CXXXIII (June 1967).

Ramsey, Peter. "Overseas Trade in the Reign of Henry VII: The Evidence of the Customs Accounts," *Ec.H.R.*, 2nd series, VI (1953).

Reddaway, T. F. "The King's Mint and Exchange in London, 1343–1543," *E.H.R.* (January 1967).

Rhodes, D. E. "The Princes in the Tower and Their Doctor," *E.H.R.*, LXXVII (April 1962).

Richardson, H. G. "The Commons and Medieval Politics," *T.R.H.S.*, 4th series, XXVIII (1946).

——— and G. O. Sayles. "Parliaments and Great Councils in Medieval England," *Law Quarterly Review*, LXXVII (April 1961).

Richardson, Walter C. "The Surveyor of the King's Prerogative," *E.H.R.*, LVI (January 1941).

Richmond, C. F. "English Naval Power in the Fifteenth Century," *History*, LII (February 1967).

Rosenthal, Joel T. "The Estates and Finances of Richard, Duke of York (1411–1460)," in *Studies in Medieval and Renaissance History*, vol. II, ed. William M. Bowsky (Lincoln, Neb., 1965).

Roskell, John S. "The Office and Dignity of Protector of England with Special Reference to its Origins," *E.H.R.*, LXVIII (April 1953).

———. "Perspectives in English Parliamentary History," *Bulletin of the John Rylands Library*, XLVI (March 1964).

———. "The Problem of the Attendance of the Lords in Medieval Parliaments," *B.I.H.R.*, XXIX (1956).

———. "The Social Composition of the Commons in a Fifteenth-Century Parliament," *B.I.H.R.*, XXIV (1951).

———. "William Catesby, Counsellor to Richard III," *Bulletin of the John Rylands Library*, XLII (1959–60).

Roth, Cecil. "Perkin Warbeck and His Jewish Master," *Transactions of the Jewish Historical Society of England*, IX (1922).

Rowse, Alfred Leslie. "Alltyrynys and the Cecils," *E.H.R.*, LXXV (January 1960).

———. "The Turbulent Career of Sir Henry de Bodrugan," *History*, New Series, XXIX (1944).

Ruddock, Alwyn A. "John Day of Bristol and the English Voyages across the Atlantic before 1497," *Geographical Journal*, CXXII (June 1966).

Sayles, G. O. "The Vindication of the Earl of Kildare from Treason, 1496," *Irish Historical Studies*, VII (March 1950).

Scammell, G. V. "English Merchant Shipping at the End of the Middle Ages: Some East Coast Evidence," *Ec.H.R.*, 2nd series, XIII (1961).

———. "Shipowning in England *circa* 1450–1550," *T.R.H.S.*, 5th series, XII (1962).

Scarisbrick, J. J. "Clerical Taxation in England, 1485 to 1547," *Journal of Ecclesiastical History*, XI (April 1960).

Schofield, R. S. "The Geographical Distribution of Wealth in England, 1334–1649," *Ec.H.R.*, 2nd series, XVIII (December 1965).

Sherborne, J. W. "The Port of Bristol in the Middle Ages." The Historical Association, No. 13 (Bristol, 1965).

Siegel, Paul N. "English Humanism and the New Tudor Aristocracy," *Journal of the History of Ideas*, XIII (1952).

Skeel, Caroline A. J. "Wales under Henry VII," in *Tudor Studies*, ed. R. W. Seton-Watson (New York, 1924).

Smith, H. Maynard. "The Will of Henry VII," *Church Quarterly Review*, CXVI (July 1933).

Smith, J. Beverley. "Crown and Community in the Principality of North Wales in the Reign of Henry Tudor," *Welsh History Review*, III (December 1966).

Somerville, Robert. "Henry VII's Council Learned in the Law,' " E.H.R., LIV (July 1939).

Steel, Anthony. "The Financial Background of the Wars of the Roses," *History*, new series, XL (1955).

Stewart-Brown, R. "The Cheshire Writs of Quo Warranto in 1499," *E.H.R.*, XLIX (October 1934).

Storey, R. L. "English Officers of State, 1399–1485," *B.I.H.R.*, XXXI (May 1958).

———. "The Wardens of the Marches of England towards Scotland, 1377–1489," *E.H.R.*, LXXII (October 1957).

Surtz, Edward L. " 'Oxford Reformers' and Scholasticism," *Studies in Philology*, XLVII (October 1950).

Tanner, Lawrence E. and William Wright. "Recent Investigations regarding the Fate of the Princes in the Tower," *Archaeologia*, LXXXIV (1934).

Taylor, E. G. R. "Imaginary Islands: A Problem Solved," *Geographical Journal*, CXXX (March 1964).

———. "Where did the Cabots go?," *Geographical Journal*, CXXIX (September 1963).

Thomson, J. A. F. "The Courtenay Family in the Yorkist Period," *B.I.H.R.*, XLV (November 1972).

————. "Richard III and Lord Hastings—a Problematical Case Reviewed," *B.I.H.R.*, XLVIII (May 1975)..

Vigneras, L. A. "The Cape Breton Landfall, 1494 or 1497: Note on a Letter from John Day," *Canadian Historical Review*, XXXVIII (September 1957).

Ward, Grace F. "The Early History of the Merchant Staplers," *E.H.R.*, XXXIII (July 1918).

Williams, C. H. "The Rebellion of Humphrey Stafford in 1486," *E.H.R.*, XLIII (April 1928).

Williams, David. "The Family of Henry VII," *History Today*, IV (February 1954).

Wolffe, B. P. "Acts of Resumption in the Lancastrian Parliaments," *E.H.R.*, LXXIII (October 1958).

————. "Henry VII's Land Revenues and Chamber Finance," *E.H.R.*, LXXIX (April 1964).

————. "The Management of English Royal Estates under the Yorkist Kings," *E.H.R.*, LXXI (January 1956).

————. "When and why did Hastings lose his head?," *E.H.R.*, LXXIX (October 1974).

Index

Newfoundland: 148-9
Nest, John: 141
Neville, Anne (wife of Richard III): 8, 11, 15, 23, 73
Neville, Cecily, Dowager Duchess of York: 10, 74, 166
Neville, Edward: 196
Neville, George, Lord Burgavenny: 134, 201
Neville, Ralph, Earl of Westmoreland: 81
Neville, Richard, Earl of Warwick ("The Kingmaker"): 3-4
Neville, Thomas: 133
New Battle Castle: 191
New College, Oxford: 159
Newark: 57
Newark, William: 173, 181
Newcastle: 60, 191
Newport: 26
Newton, John: 8
Norham: 118
Normandy: 3
North Parts: Yorkist feeling of, 49; defensive obligations of, 91-2; administration of, 1, 3, 44, 76-7, 127-8
Northcroft, George: 13-14
Northumberland, Earl of: see Percy, Henry
Norton, Sir Sampson: 196
Norwich: 30, 56
Nottingham: 26, 50, 56–7, 67
Nottingham, Earl of: see Berkeley, William, Lord

O'Connell of Offaly: 100
O'Donnell, Hugh (of Tyrconnell): 109, 112
Ormonde, Earl of: see Butler, Thomas
Ormonde, Sir James ("Black James Ormonde"): 99–100, 109–10, 119
Outer Banks, the: 150
Owen, Sir David: 125, 134
Oxford: 11, 34, 53, 55, 162, 165, 167, 170, 172, 203
Oxford, Earl of: see Vere, John de

Parliament: Speakers of, 137; social composition of, 138; royal management of, 136–8; revenue granted by, 60, 78–9, 91, 94, 96, 115; important acts passed by, 61, 65, 77–8, 128–30, 134–6; *of 1484*, 20–22, 25, 77; *of 1485*, 12, 36, 39–42, 50, 53, 128; *of 1487*, 60–1, 77, 128–9; *of 1489–90*, 91–2, 94, 129, 132; *of 1491*, 96; *of 1495*, 113, 129; *of 1497*, 115, 129; *of 1504*, 129, 198–9
Pasqualigo, Lorenzo: 148
Paston, Sir William: 101
Paromis, William: 179
Paulet, Amias: 119
Paul's Cross: 10, 177
Payne, John, Bishop of Meath: 47, 56–8, 121
Peachey, Sir John: 112
Pembroke Castle: 15
Percy, Henry, fourth Earl of Northumberland: present at Bosworth, 27; imprisoned after Bosworth, 32, 34; granted wide powers in the North, 35; aids Henry VII against the Staffords, 50; establishes a use for his son, 77; negotiates with Scottish commissioners, 84; killed in 1489 tax riot, 92; mentioned 57, 93, 127, 161–2
Percy, Henry, fifth Earl of Northumberland: 77, 81, 92, 132, 200
Peter's Pence: 157